Crypto Economy and International Law

The Hague Academy of International Law Monographs

VOLUME 12

The titles published in this series are listed at *brill.com/hamo*

Crypto Economy and International Law

Determining the Regulatory and Private Law Rules Governing the Blockchain

By

Matthias Lehmann

BRILL | NIJHOFF

LEIDEN | BOSTON

The Library of Congress Cataloging-in-Publication Data is available online at https://catalog.loc.gov
LC record available at https://lccn.loc.gov/2025018196

Typeface for the Latin, Greek, and Cyrillic scripts: "Brill". See and download: brill.com/brill-typeface.

ISBN 978-90-04-72513-3 (hardback)
ISBN 978-90-04-72514-0 (e-book)
DOI 10.1163/9789004725140

This book is printed on acid-free paper and produced in a sustainable manner.

Contents

Selected Publications (in English)

Cryptocurrencies in National Laws – A Global Survey (Brill 2025) (ed. with Tetsuo Morishita).

Digital Assets in Enforcement and Insolvency (Hart 2025) (ed. with Christian Koller).

"Digital Assets in the Conflict of Laws: A Comparative Search for the 'Ideal' Rule'", 1 (2024) Singapore Journal of Legal Studies 198.

Blockchain and Private International Law (Brill 2023) (ed. with Andrea Bonomi and Shaheeza Lalani).

Unfair Terms in Banking and Financial Contracts (Oxford University Press 2023) (ed. with Danny Busch).

"Multilateralizing Deference – A Proposal for Reforming Global Financial Law" (2023) 56 International Lawyer 191 (with Jonas Schürger).

"Conflicts of Jurisdiction" in Paul Beaumont and Jane Holiday (eds), *A Guide to Global Private International Law* (Bloomsbury and Hart 2022) (with Ardavan Arzandeh).

"CCP supervision after Brexit: from extraterritoriality to a model of shared control" (2022) Capital Markets Law Journal 5.

"Jurisdiction and Applicable Law in Investor Suits" in Arthur B Laby (ed), *The Cambridge Handbook of Investor Protection* (CUP 2022) 169.

"A new piece in the puzzle of locating financial loss: the ruling in VEB v BP on jurisdiction for collective actions based on deficient investor information" (2022) 18 Journal of Private International Law 1.

"Hacked crypto-accounts, the English tort of breach of confidence and localising financial loss under Rome II" (2021) Butterworths Journal of International Banking and Financial Law 708 (with Amy Held).

"National Blockchain Laws as a Threat to Financial Market Integration" (2021) Uniform Law Review 148.

"Who Owns Bitcoin? Private Law Facing the Blockchain" (2020) 21 Minnesota Journal of Law, Science, and Technology 93.

"Global Rules for a Global Market Place? The Regulation and Supervision of FinTech Providers" (2020) 38 Boston Journal of International Law 118.

"Conflict-of-law issues" in Matthias Haentjens and Bob Wessels (eds), *Research Handbook on Cross-Border Bank Resolution* (Edward Elgar 2019).

"New challenges of extraterritoriality: superposing laws" in Franco Ferrari and Diego P Fernández Arroyo (eds), *Private International Law* (Edward Elgar 2019).

European Financial Services Law – Article-by-Article Commentary (Beck, Hart and Nomos 2019) (ed. with Christoph Kumpan).

"Proportionality in the Single Rule Book" in Mario P Chiti and Vittorio Santoro (eds), *The Palgrave Handbook of European Banking Union Law* (Pelgrave Macmillian 2019) (with Bart Joosen).

"Securities Transfer and Applicable Law: Anything Goes?" (2018) Butterworths Journal of International Banking and Financial Law 622 (with Klaus Löber).

"Private International Law and Finance – Nothing Special?" (2018) Netherlands Journal of Private International Law 3.

"American vs. European Approaches to Extraterritoriality in Civil Litigation" in: Andrea Bonomi and Kristat Nadakavukaren Schefer (eds), *US Litigation Today: Still a Threat For European Businesses or Just an Paper Tiger?* (Schulthess 2018).

"Bonds", "Cheques", "Financial Instruments", "Guarantees", and "Loans" in Jürgen Basedow, Giesela Rühl, Franco Ferrari and Pedro De Miguel (eds), *Encyclopedia of Private International Law*, vol. 1 (Edward Elgar 2017).

"Legal Fragmentation, Extraterritoriality and Uncertainty in Global Financial Regulation" (2017) 37 Oxford Journal of Legal Studies 406.

"Bail-in and Private International Law: How to Make Bank Resolution Measures Effective Across Borders" (2017) 66 International and Comparative Law Quarterly 107.

"Prospectus Liability and Private International Law Assessing the Landscape After the CJEU's Kolassa Ruling (Case C-375/13)" (2016) 12 Journal of Private International Law 318.

"Civil Liability of Rating Agencies: An Insipid Sprout from Brussels" (2016) 11 Capital Markets Law Journal 60–83.

"Volcker rule, ring-fencing or separation of bank activities: Comparison of structural reform acts around the world" (2015) Journal of Banking Regulation.

"Commentary on Chapter 4, Art.7(1), (3), (5)-(7), Chapter 8, Chapter 11 (Art.31(1))" in Andrew Dickinson and Eva Lein (eds), *The Brussels I Regulation Recast* (OUP 2015).

"The Legal Measures Taken in Reply to the Crisis: Inventory, Presentation and Comments" (2013) European Banking and Financial Law Journal 373 (with Stefan Hoffmann).

"Exclusive Jurisdiction Under Art. 22(2) of the Brussels I Regulation: The ECJ Decision Berliner Verkehrsbetriebe v JPMorgan Chase Bank (C-144/10)" (2011) 13 Yearbook of Private International Law 507.

"Where Does Economic Loss Occur" (2011) 7 Journal of Private International Law 527.

"The Role and Prospects of International Law in Financial Regulation and Supervision" 13 Journal of International Economic Law 663 (with Christian Tietje), reprinted in Thomas Cottier, John H Jackson and Rosa M Lastra (eds), *International Law in Financial Regulation and Monetary Affairs* (OUP 2012) 133.

"Financial Instruments" in Franco Ferrari and Stefan Leible (eds), *Rome I Regulation: The Law Applicable to Contractual Obligations in Europe* (Walter de Gruyter 2009) 85.

Full list of publications available under https://eur-int-comp-law.univie.ac.at/team/lehmann-matthias/.

Preface

The book presented here is the English version of my course given at the Hague Academy of International Law in French (Collected Courses vol. 438 (2023)). It has been updated to reflect the state of the law in the summer of 2024.

The crypto economy is constantly evolving. I have strived to be as general as possible and focus on the most common features, without however ignoring the technological particularities. My hope is that this book will enrich the discussion between lawyers and the tech circles.

For valuable suggestions and comments to the English edition, I wish to thank Amy Held, Felix Krysa, Emeric Prévost and Darshini Waibel. Many thanks also to Julia Wachowicz, Lukas Petschning, Paul Eichmüller, Fabian Schinerl, Susanne Brück and Anna Oshafu for their help with the manuscript. A big thank you goes out to my students, who have raised many interesting questions that I have tried to answer as best as I can.

Introduction

Over recent years, digital technology has been evolving rapidly. Disruptive innovations have ensued with the power to transform existing professions or entire industries.[1] One notable example is Digital Ledger Technology (DLT). The most renowned type of DLT today is Blockchain technology. It has potential applications in various areas, notably the financial sector. The blockchain allows the creation of new types of digital assets that can be transferred directly from one person to another (a process known as "peer to peer").

The most prominent examples are cryptocurrencies like Bitcoin[2] or Ether. But DLT also allows the creation of other digital assets, such as Non-Fungible Tokens (NFT). In addition, it can be used to represent real-world assets, such as shares, bonds, rights in real estate or commodities. The blockchain can also record intellectual property rights, personal data or certificates of origin. Second-generation blockchains make more complex operations possible, such as performing obligations through "smart contracts" or organising collective decision-making through so-called "Decentralized Autonomous Organizations" (DAOs). More potential use cases of the technology are still to be expected.

One key question is which law governs the blockchain, more particularly the digital assets recorded on it, the manifold transactions concerning them, and the plethora of specialised intermediaries that have mushroomed around the blockchain in the last years, all of which can be summed up collectively as "the crypto economy". The issue of the law governing this economy concerns regulatory as well as private law aspects. They include, for example: which law regulates the custodian of crypto-assets, such as a wallet provider or a crypto exchange? Who should supervise the issuer of so-called stablecoins? Under what law are the rights of an investor in the insolvency of a crypto service provider to be determined? How can programmers of a decentralised finance application be held to account for any defects? The list goes on and on.

---

1 See Joseph L Bower and Clayton M Christensen, 'Disruptive Technologies: Catching the Wave' (1995) 73 Harvard Business Review 43; Erwin Danneels, 'Disruptive Technology Reconsidered: A Critique and Research Agenda' (2004) 21 Journal of Product Innovation Management 246; specifically on the impact for financial instruments see Chris Brummer, 'Disruptive Technology and Securities Regulation' (2015) 84 Fordham Law Review 977.

2 The term "Bitcoin" (with capital B) is used here when referring to the cryptocurrency as such or the network; "bitcoin" (with lower caps) is used to refer to a unit of the cryptocurrency ("one bitcoin").

 | DOI:10.1163/9789004725140_002

The question of the governing law needs to be answered before any legal problem can be solved. The answer is particularly thorny in the case of the blockchain, given its particular structure, which has been intentionally designed to avoid any connection to a specific country. This makes the determination of the governing law a genuine conundrum.

To fully grasp the extent of the problem, it is first necessary to study the technology, its functioning and origins, and the legal questions it raises. This will be done in Chapter 1, which describes the battle for supremacy between technology and the rule of law. Having concluded that state law is a necessary blockchain framework, Chapter 2 addresses the question of the applicable regulation. It will analyse which state is competent to apply its regulatory rules and extend the supervision by its authorities to actors, actions and events of the crypto economy and whether there is a need for more uniform rules on the global level. Following a brief interlude on the relationship between regulatory law and private international law, Chapter 3 will deal with the problem of the private law rules governing blockchain transactions, assets and entities. In particular, it will discuss the issues of determining the law applicable to property rights in crypto-assets, the law applicable to transactions such as sales or loans of cryptocurrencies, and the law governing smart contracts and DAOs. As Chapter 2, it will also include an analysis of the need and possibilities of more uniform rules. The study will then conclude with a proposal for a new balance between technology and law.

CHAPTER 1

Rule of Law or Rule of Code?

The blockchain is the first genuinely global mechanism for storing and transferring value. Despite many unrealistic hopes, it could revolutionise cross-border payments and investments and herald a new age of globalisation. At the same time, the blockchain raises numerous legal questions, particularly regarding cryptocurrencies and other digital assets recorded on it. These can be transferred without the help of intermediaries and are thus mainly impervious to control by state regulators, which is typically exercised through regulated and supervised intermediaries. They lend themselves to many types of criminal or otherwise illegal activity. They can serve as a conduit for tax evasion, money laundering or terrorist funding; they can represent high risks for private investors, who are in danger of falling victim to fraud, theft or extortion; and they also challenge the monopoly of central banks on issuing currency, which may potentially affect their ability to prevent and mitigate financial and economic crises.

This darker aspect of cryptocurrencies is no accident but was intended by their creators, who wanted them to be an alternative to traditional money issued by the state (so-called "fiat money"). Their goal was to create a medium of exchange that would not depend on financial institutions and not be subject to the control of state regulators and central banks. Cryptocurrency pioneers saw blockchain technology as a way to supersede all national institutions of democratic capitalism and to create a global "crypto anarchy" instead. They mostly expected and accepted the harm this would do to interests currently protected by the law.

Despite the somewhat far-fetched nature of a global crypto dystopia, it would be reckless for governments to ignore the severe dangers for public and private interests that may arise from the new world of digital assets. Nothwithstanding a significant wave of institutionalisation and a process of coming of age, many actors in the crypto space remain hostile to state law, which they see as an intrusion of their privacy and a danger to the proper functioning of the blockchain. It is common in the crypto economy to try to resist or circumvent any legislative intervention. The key question is who will gain the upper hand in this struggle – the technology or the law. This is not a foregone conclusion: The many attempts of regulators to tighten their grip on the market in the past years have failed to stop digital assets from burgeoning and the crypto actors from becoming ever more powerful.

 | DOI:10.1163/9789004725140_003

This chapter will begin by examining the technological workings of Bitcoin, the initial blockchain, before focusing on the second-generation blockchains, particularly Ethereum (1.1). Then, the anatomy of the crypto economy will be analysed (1.2). Next, the underlying philosophy will be studied, particularly the anarchist origins of the technology (1.3). After that, the legal problems raised by the crypto economy will be addressed (1.4), before a final discussion of alternative approaches to the application of national law (1.5).

1.1 Explaining the Technology

To gain a clearer understanding of the struggle between law and technology, it is necessary to have a basic understanding of the technological workings of the blockchain. In its essence, the blockchain is a digital database that serves to store and transmit information decentrally.[3] What makes it unique is its ability to protect data and data transfers against falsification without requiring the intervention of a central entity. For this reason, the blockchain is ideally suited to storing virtual assets and conducting cross-border transfers.

There are numerous types of blockchains. We will begin by examining the original blockchain used in the Bitcoin network (1.1.1). This will allow us to better understand the specific features of its successors (1.1.2).

1.1.1 *The First Generation Blockchains*

The blockchain first appeared in October 2008 with the publication of a whitepaper entitled "Bitcoin: A Peer-to-Peer Electronic Cash System".[4] The document, published on an internet discussion forum, was signed with the pseudonym *Satoshi Nakamoto*, who remains unidentified to this day.[5] It is impossible to establish whether this pseudonym refers to an individual author or a group. Throughout eight pages (plus a bibliography), the text describes Bitcoin's technology. This is essentially based on a combination of five innovations: 1. distributed storage, 2. encryption, 3. distributed consensus, 4. the proof-of-work mechanism, and 5. the permanent record.

3 On the technology in general see, e.g., Andreas M Antonopoulos, *Mastering Bitcoin* (2nd edn, O'Reilly 2017); Gautier Marin-Dagannaud, 'Le fonctionnement de la blockchain' (2017) 8(3) Réalités industrielles 42.

4 Satoshi Nakamoto, 'Bitcoin: A Peer-to-Peer Electronic Cash System' (2008) <https://bitcoin.org/bitcoin.pdf> accessed 15 April 2024.

5 In a legal dispute, one Craig Wright claimed to be *Satoshi Nakamoto*. The High Court of Justice for England and Wales left the point open because it did not matter for the case, see *Tulip Trading Limited v Wladimir Jasper van der Laan et al*, [2022] EWHC 667 (Ch) 17.

1.1.1.1 Distributed Storage

Information contained in the blockchain is distributed to a large number of computers. These computers, known as "nodes", form a network which covers the entire planet. Anyone can establish a Bitcoin "node", which is why the Bitcoin network is referred to as "open", "public" or "permissionless".[6] All that is required is to download software known as the Bitcoin protocol and the blockchain onto a computer. This then becomes a "server", which responds to user requests instead of simply issuing requests, as mere "clients" do. The number of possible nodes is potentially enormous considering the availability of computers among the general population. However, it should be noted that the blockchain has become so large that it would be difficult or impossible to store it on the hard drive of most personal computers.[7] Moreover, the calculations needed to validate transfers today require ultra-high-performance chips. This is why these functions are most commonly performed by powerful computers belonging to corporate or state actors.

On the Bitcoin network, there are different types of nodes. Those with the most comprehensive functionality are called "full nodes".[8] Full nodes each hold an identical copy of the database, which contains information on all previous transfers and is continually updated. In short, the blockchain is a ledger whose contents are spread across the entire planet, which explains the name "distributed ledger technology" (DLT). Distributed storage aims at making it very difficult to destroy or falsify information contained in the blockchain, as it continues to exist even if one or several nodes are damaged or corrupted. The operation of the blockchain is in many ways similar to that of the internet, which forms its basis. Yet it is essential to remember that, unlike the internet, the blockchain is not only a *communication* network but also a means of distributed *data storage*. This is crucial because only information that is stored in an unalterable way can be a unit of value. This enabled the blockchain to become the source of the world's first successful cryptocurrency.

1.1.1.2 Encryption

The second innovation relevant to understanding DLT is encryption. Data contained in the blockchain is encrypted. To transfer bitcoins, participants need

6 Andrew Miller, 'Permissioned and Permissionless Blockchains' in Sachin Shetty, Charles A Kamhoua and Laurent L Njilla (eds), *Blockchain for Distributed Systems Security* (Wiley 2020) 193 et seq.

7 At the mid of January 2024, the blockchain has grown to a size of 527 gigabytes, see Statista, 'Size of the Bitcoin blockchain from January 2009 to January 16, 2024' <https://www.statista.com/statistics/647523/worldwide-bitcoin-blockchain-size/>accessed 5 April 2024.

8 Antonopoulos (n 3) 172.

two types of information: the public key and the private key. These long strings of numbers and letters work together similarly to the username and PIN common in online banking.[9] The public key is available to any interested party; its shortened version is called "Bitcoin address".[10] On the other hand, the private key is secret and must not be communicated to an outside party, as it is used to sign Bitcoin transactions. Only the person holding the private key can unlock the amounts assigned to the public key.

The transaction must be authorised with the private key before being transferred to the nodes. The blockchain protocol produces an electronic signature proving which private key authorised the transaction. The private key is not transferred as such; if it were, any actor in the network would be able to access the funds. Instead, the electronic signature is encrypted or "hashed". The encryption is unidirectional, meaning it does not allow the nodes to see the private key but only to verify whether the correct key has been used. A comparable case in the real world is using a physical key to open a door, which allows an outside observer who does not know the shape of the key to nevertheless conclude that the person who manages to open the door with the key is authorised. This is why the encryption is also called "asymmetric encryption".[11]

Users rarely transfer whole bitcoins or the entire amount attached to a public key. Instead, they send subunits called "satoshi", with 100 million satoshis being equivalent to one bitcoin. The remaining balance is "credited back" to the sender's public key. Virtually any transfer on the network thus creates two "outputs", one on the recipient's public key and one on the sender's public key. The sum of all available and spendable bitcoins of one public key is known as "unspent transaction outputs" (UTXO).[12]

Crucially, once an amount associated with a public key has been transferred to another public key, the person holding the private key is prevented from "spending", i.e. transferring it a second time, as it is subsequently associated with a new public key. With the help of this mechanism, the blockchain prevents "double-spending" by the person holding the private key. This was one of

9 Blockchain France, 'La Blockchain décryptée' (2016) 4 <https://blockchainfrance.net/decouvrir-la-blockchain/la-blockchain-decryptee-les-clefs-dune-evolution/> accessed 11 March 2020; Sudeep Tanwar, *Blockchain Technology: From Theory to Practice* (Springer 2023); Antonopoulos (n 3) 61-109 (for a technical explanation of how private and public keys work and the underlying cryptographic mechanisms).

10 Antonopoulos (n 3) 168 (mentioning that a bitcoin address is in most cases generated from and corresponds to a public key, with some exceptions).

11 Matthieu Quiniou, *Blockchain: The Advent of Disintermediation* (Wiley 2020) 22–23.

12 Antonopoulos (n 3) 213.

the main goals outlined in Satoshi Nakamoto's whitepaper[13] and is undoubtedly a major innovation.

1.1.1.3 Distributed Consensus

On the network, data is first distributed (or "broadcast") to many computers. These must validate all new blocks containing information on the current state of the data in a process known as "distributed consensus".[14] This validation method distinguishes the blockchain from traditional ledgers maintained by a central authority. The Bitcoin network does not require such an authority, making it more resistant to attacks from inside and outside the network.

To incentivise the nodes to verify transactions, they receive bitcoins and transaction fees (also called "gas fees"[15]) as compensation. The bitcoins they receive are newly minted, which is why the performance of the validation work is also known as "mining", and the nodes that perform it as "miners".[15] The validity of the newly minted bitcoins is conditioned on the other participants' acceptance of the new block. This aims to align the miners' interests with those of the other network participants, which is to have a "true" – i.e., universally recognised – record of the transaction on the ledger.

1.1.1.4 Proof-of-Work (PoW) Mechanism

In a decentralised network, two nodes may validate blocks containing contradictory information. This possibility is reinforced by Bitcoin's openness, meaning anyone can establish a node by downloading the protocol onto their computer. Malicious actors may attempt to take advantage of such openness by adding many nodes to confirm specific blocks, for example a previously spent bitcoin.

To reduce this risk, nodes must solve a complex mathematical problem before they are permitted to create and add a new block to the chain. This method, known as "proof of work",[16] allows the system to randomly identify a node to create the next block. The mathematical problem is based on the cryptographic fingerprint of the block, generally referred to as the "hash"[17] as well as a random number. This makes it impossible to predict which node will

---

13 Nakamoto (n 4) 1.

14 Shetty, Kamhoua and Njilla (n 6) 5 et seq.

15 Antonopoulos (n 3) 524–525 (describing the purpose of mining as an incentive scheme).

16 William Magnuson, *Blockchain Democracy: Technology, Law and the Rule of the Crowd* (Cambridge University Press 2020) 55; Blockchain France (n 9) 5; Marin-Dagannaud (n 3) 44; Antonopoulos (n 3) 192–198.

17 Antonopoulos (n 3) 209–211; Arvind Narayanan and others, *Bitcoin and Cryptocurrency Technologies* (Princeton University Press 2016) 41; Gordon L Clark, Maryann P Feldman,

resolve the mathematical problem first. The "winning" node then transmits the new block with its solution to the other nodes. The other nodes can easily verify whether the solution is correct thanks to asymmetric cryptography, which is used here a second time.

This distributed consensus process makes falsifying the blockchain very hard because participants do not know which node will complete the proof of work task first. Still, a bad actor could try to take control of more than 50% of the network's computing power to secretly produce blocks at a much faster pace, eventually forcing a different version of the blockchain on the other miners. This is known as a 51% attack.[18] However, this strategy does not allow attackers to steal bitcoins; it merely enables them to approve double expenditure or deny service.[19] Therefore, the greater danger is not falsification but the degradation and eventual destruction of the blockchain.[20] The creators of Bitcoin believed that the participants in the network would have no interest in this, since they are paid in cryptocurrencies. Nevertheless, the perpetrators of these attacks may be motivated by various reasons, including the benefit from short sales of bitcoins they may have concluded previously.[21] For instance, a perpetrator could concentrate more than 50% of the computing power of a blockchain network with a plan to manipulate the exchange rate of the cryptocurrency to gain an economic advantage. This is known as a "Goldfinger" strategy.[22] The name is a reference to the Bond villain of the same name who sought to pollute the gold reserves in Fort Knox with nuclear radiation to increase the value of his own gold stocks.[23]

Meric S Gertler and Dariusz Wójcik, *The New Oxford Handbook of Economic Geography* (Oxford University Press 2018) 581.

18 Niaz Chowdhury, *Inside Blockchain, Bitcoin, and Cryptocurrencies* (Auerbach Publications 2019) 58 et seq.

19 Koshik Raj, *Foundations of blockchain: The pathway to cryptocurrencies and decentralized blockchain applications* (Packt Publishing 2019) 289.

20 David Canelis, 'China has the power to destroy Bitcoin ... and it's already manipulating the network' (2018) <https://thenextweb.com/hardfork/2018/10/08/china-means-intent-destroy-bitcoin/> accessed 15 April 2024.

21 Joseph Bonneau, 'Hostile Blockchain Takeovers (Short Paper)' in Aviv Zohar, Ittay Eyal, Vanessa Teague, Jeremy Clark, Andrea Bracciali, Federico Pintore and Massimiliano Sala (eds), *Financial Cryptography and Data Security: FC 2018 International Workshops, BITCOIN, VOTING, and WTSC Revised Selected Papers* (Springer 2019) 92, 93.

22 Joshua A Kroll, Ian C Davey, and E W Felten, 'The Economics of Bitcoin Mining, or Bitcoin in the Presence of Adversaries', in *The Twelfth Workshop on the Economics of Information Security (WEIS 2013)* (Georgetown University 2013) 2.

23 On the goldfinger strategy, see also Lawrence Trautman, 'Virtual Currencies: Bitcoin & What Now after Liberty Reserve, Silk Road, and Mt. Gox' (2013) 20(4) Richmond Journal of Law & Technology 1, 56; Jesus Fernández-Villaverde, 'Cryptocurrencies: A Crash Course in Digital Monetary Economics', (2018) 51(4) Australian Economic Review 514.

1.1.1.5 Permanent Record

On the blockchain, transfers are not processed one by one but as part of a block. A block contains the record of all blockchain transfers made within a certain period (about ten minutes). The collection of transactions that are broadcast over the network will be done by each node individually. The node must then carry out the proof of work for each new block it wants to suggest to the other nodes. Each block is timestamped, allowing the blocks to be assembled in chronological sequence.[24] Once the solution to the proof-of-work task has been shown to be correct, the block is added to the chain (hence the expression "blockchain"). If two nodes report the correct solution simultaneously, the protocol is programmed to prefer the longer blockchain. In other words, the chain with the largest number of approved transactions will prevail.[25]

Once a block has been added to the blockchain, it can no longer be changed. This is secured through another hash – called block hash – which will be altered in case of the slightest change of the information to the chain. The blockchain is therefore considered "unchangeable" or "irreversible". This is one of the most crucial aspects of blockchain technology.[26]

However, the famous immutability is not an absolute truth. Several times, the blockchain has already been split into two opposing versions. This phenomenon is known as a "hard fork".[27] In contrast to "soft forks", continuously created but overcome by the miners' preference for the longest chain, a hard fork leads to a persistent split of the blockchain into two. Hard forks may be caused intentionally or unintentionally.

A famous unintentional hard fork occured in March 2013.[28] A new version of the Bitcoin protocol had been introduced, which was not backward compatible with the older one. A certain number of nodes operating under the new version of the protocol had accepted a blockchain, which was rejected by the other nodes that had failed to download the new version of the protocol. For a short time, the same private key could be used twice for payments on two

---

24 Antonopoulos (n 3) 413 (underlining that timestamps are set by miners and describing the median-time-past measurement to avoid miners lying about the correct time); Marin-Dagannaud (n 3) 43.

25 Marin-Dagannaud (n 3) 44; Antonopoulos (n 3) 199 et seq.

26 Primavera De Filippi and Aaron Wright, *Blockchain and the Law: The Rule of Code* (Harvard University Press 2018) 89.

27 Primavera De Filippi and Benjamin Loveluck, 'The Invisible Politics of Bitcoin: Governance Crisis of a Decentralised Infrastructure' (2016) 5(3) Internet Policy Review 1, 7; Antonopoulos (n 3) 199 et seq.

28 See the description in Jack Parkin, 'The Senatorial Governance of Bitcoin: Making (de) Centralized Money' (2019) 48 Economy and Society 463, 473–475.

different networks. This situation was resolved by the nodes collectively downgrading to the previous version.

An intentional hard fork was caused in 2016 when a group of programmers suggested improving the scalability of the Bitcoin blockchain, i.e. the number of transactions the network can process simultaneously in a single block.[29] The proposal was not accepted by most nodes, which were concerned it might compromise the security and stability of the network. Frustrated, two coders published an alternative protocol called "Bitcoin XT", which raised the block size from one to eight Megabytes. Only a fraction of the Bitcoin community downloaded the new protocol, which led to a hard fork in January 2016.

Bitcoin XT was eventually abandoned because it failed to gain mass adoption. However, in 2017, a similar dispute over efficiency resulted in an altered version of Bitcoin called "Bitcoin Cash" (BCH).[30] The new cryptocurrency was distributed free of charge (through "airdrop") to those who held the original. Both versions continue alongside each other. Examples of such intentional hard forks exist for other cryptocurrencies as well.[31]

In practice, intentional hard forks remain rare exceptions. This is because they involve significant costs. Not only do they lead to duplication and, consequently, inflation of assets on competing blockchains, but they also undermine a core goal of the technology, which is to create user trust in the network. If users can no longer rely on the permanency of the blockchain and the values stored therein, they will turn their attention to other types of investment. Consequently, it is not economically rational to implement a hard fork to cancel a single transfer.

Overall, alterations to the blockchain appear unlikely. Putting aside certain exceptions, the attribute "irreversible" seems warranted. This is particularly true when comparing the blockchain with centralised ledgers, which their operators can change relatively easily and even retroactively.

In sum, the blockchain can be described as a cryptographic peer-to-peer transfer mechanism underpinned by a distributed and immutable ledger. What distinguishes the blockchain from the Internet and sets it apart is that it not only can transfer information but also store it safely so that it cannot be

29 De Filippi and Loveluck (n 27) 8–9.

30 For a study of this hard fork from a social science perspective, see Jeffery Atik and George Gerro, 'Hard Forks on the Bitcoin Blockchain: Reversible Exit, Continuing Voice Essays' (2018) 1 Stanford Journal of Blockchain Law & Policy 24.

31 See, e.g., the divide of the Ethereum and the Ethereum Classic network in the context of the first DAO *infra* 1.2.3.2.

unilaterally changed. This makes it an ideal register for value, such as private cryptocurrencies.

1.1.2 *The Second Generation Blockchains*

1.1.2.1 The Ethereum Network and DApps

Technological innovation continued after the development of Bitcoin. Since then, new types of database-networks have been developed, the best-known of which is Ethereum.[32] Ethereum is similar to Bitcoin in the sense that it contains its own (or "native") cryptocurrency called "Ether", which can be acquired and transferred. However, its objective is wider than that of a simple payment mechanism. Ethereum is designed to run algorithms (i.e. programmes) known as "Decentralized Applications" or "DApps". Like ordinary computer programmes, the potential applications of these algorithms are infinite; they are thus "Turing-complete".[33] Yet they also use the blockchain's strengths and, notably, the distributed consensus mechanism, which makes it impossible for a single node to alter, stop or modify a running programme.[34] In this way, DApps differ significantly from ordinary software.

1.1.2.2 Proof of Stake

"Proof of stake" is an alternative consensus mechanism. Unlike "proof of work", which is based on all the validating nodes competing against each other to validate a new block, "proof of stake" involves assigning the power to validate to one of the nodes according to the number of assets it holds and must pledge ("stake"). If the selected node fails to validate or irregularly validates a new block, the pledged assets will be forfeited. Depending on the particular protocol in question, the network may acquire and redistribute them among the other validating nodes, or simply delete them. On the other hand, if a new block is validated and successfully added to the chain, the validating node will receive a reward in the form of cryptocurrency allocated exclusively to it. Compared to proof of work, "proof of stake" therefore implements a consensus mechanism that admittedly favours those rich in assets but has the advantage of considerably reducing energy requirements and increasing the frequency

32 See, e.g., Andreas M Antonopoulos and Gavin Wood, *Mastering Ethereum* (O'Reilly 2018).

33 The notion "Turing-complete" derives from Alain Turing, one of the forethinkers of modern computer technology. Turing developed the idea of a machine that can perform any kind of action in his seminal paper 'On Computable Numbers, With an Application to the Entscheidungsproblem' (1936) s2–42 Proceedings of the London Mathematical Society 230.

34 Siraj Raval, *Decentralized Applications: Harnessing Bitcoin's Blockchain Technology* (O'Reilly 2016) 4.

with which new blocks are validated. "Proof of stake" also enables any participant in a blockchain network, directly or indirectly via an intermediary, to use their virtual assets to earn a return.[35]

1.1.2.3 Smart Contracts

The best-known DApps are so-called "smart contracts". They are algorithms that automatically execute a specific action on the blockchain when pre-defined conditions are met.[36] Their name is somewhat misleading because, according to an often-cited quote, "smart contracts are neither smart nor contracts".[37] This bon mot needs to be corrected because smart contracts may have relevance for the conclusion of the contract, for instance, when an automated offer is made or when a bargain by the parties is transcribed into computer code.[38] However, it remains true that most smart contracts are relevant only for the *performance* of contractual obligations rather than for their *conclusion*.

Smart contracts are created ("deployed") by sending the compiled code of the smart contract to a specific blockchain address.[39] The "Ethereum Virtual Machine" (EVM) then creates contract accounts, which are not associated with a private key and are therefore not susceptible to control by network users. They are different from the public addresses referred to as "Externally-owned Accounts" (EOAS), which allow users to initiate a transaction with their private key.[40] The smart contract self-executes when specific conditions are met. It can be activated by outside events, for example, when an index or share price reaches a certain level. This information is provided with the help of small programs known as "Oracles", in reference to the company that developed them.[41] Once activated, a smart contract cannot be stopped.

---

35 See *infra* 1.2.4.2.

36 See European Law Institute (ELI), 'Principles on Blockchain Technology, Smart Contracts and Consumer Protection' 23 <https://www.europeanlawinstitute.eu/fileadmin/user_upload/p_eli/Publications/ELI_Principles_on_Blockchain_Technology__Smart_Contracts_and_ Consumer_Protection.pdf> accessed 15 April 2024.

37 James Grimmelmann, 'All Smart Contracts Are Ambiguous' (2019) 2 Journal of Law & Innovation 1, 2; Veronica Carriero, 'Smart Contracts in the Blockchain Context: What Happens?' (2019) 1 European Journal of Privacy Law & Technologies 60, 63; see on this also exhaustively Farshad Ghodoosi, 'Contracting in the Age of Smart Contracts' (2021) 96(1) Washington Law Review 51, 64 et seq.

38 See ELI (n 36), 25, 28 et seq.

39 Antonopoulos and Wood (n 32) 112, 128.

40 See ethereum.org, 'Ethereum Accounts' <https://ethereum.org/en/developers/docs/accounts> accessed 22 May 2023.

41 See ethereum.org, 'Oracles' <https://ethereum.org/en/developers/docs/oracles/> accessed 6 April 2024.

What makes smart contracts interesting for lawyers is that they allow the automatic execution of obligations without any risk of interference by the debtor. The latter is prevented from opposing the transfer of an asset to the creditor, which improves contractual efficiency. Hence, it is hardly surprising that smart contracts have attracted great interest and are developing rapidly for a wide range of potential use cases.

An example from the financial sector is derivative contracts.[42] These contracts typically contain a mechanism for close-out netting, which enables the automatic set-off of respective amounts owed after certain pre-defined conditions have been met, such as the start of bankruptcy proceedings against one of the parties. This mechanism is particularly well-suited for automation. For this reason, the International Swaps and Derivatives Association (ISDA) has launched a joint project with a consortium known as R3. Based on R3's distributed ledger, called "Corda", this project could lead to the world's first automated swap.[43]

Smart contracts also underpin other innovations, such as NFTs and DAOs, which will be treated separately because of their unique characteristics.[44]

1.1.2.4 Decentralised Finance (DeFi)

Decentralised Finance ("DeFi") can be defined as the decentralised provision of financial services through a mix of infrastructure, markets, technology, methods and applications.[45] The ambition is to go beyond Bitcoin and mimic not only payment services but also to provide the entire gamut of products the financial industry offers through technological means on a fully decentralised basis, i.e. without any legal or natural persons involved. These range from exchange services to lending and derivatives transactions as well as asset management.[46]

---

42 Antony Welfare, *Commercializing Blockchain: Strategic Applications in the Real World* (Wiley 2020) 151.

43 EuromoneySeminars, 'Derivatives Body ISDA Part of "Smart Contract" Blockchain Group' <http://www.euromoneyseminars.com/articles/3570160/derivatives-body-isda-part-of-smart-contract-blockchain-group.html> accessed 15 April 2024.

44 See *infra* 1.2.1.4. and 1.2.3.2.

45 Dirk A Zetzsche, Douglas W Arner and Ross P Buckley, 'Decentralized Finance' (2020) 6 Journal of Financial Regulation 172, 173–174.

46 EU Blockchain Observatory and Forum, 'Decentralised Finance (DeFi)' (2022) 11 <https://digital-strategy.ec.europa.eu/en/library/eu-blockchain-observatory-and-forum-published-report-decentralized-finance-defi> accessed 15 April 2024; Sirio Aramonte, Wenqian Huang and Andreas Schrimpf, 'DeFi Risks and the Decentralisation Illusion' (2021) BIS Quarterly Review 21, 23.

DeFi is based on smart contracts. Yet to provide complex financial services on a fully automated basis, it is necessary to merge them with other innovations: artificial intelligence, cloud services, and big data.[47] Among the applications are, for instance, fully automated, decentralised crypto exchanges (also known as "Decentralised Exchanges" or "DEX").[48] DeFi has also opened the possibility of a whole range of new contracts, such as staking, crypto lending, and yield farming. These allow to generate income with crypto-assets, similar to securities and other financial instruments, which produce dividends and interest. Hence, the crypto economy has become self-referential and self-generating, increasing its importance and complexity.

1.1.2.5 Permissioned Networks

In recent years, blockchain technology has veered in a new direction. "Permissioned networks" – also known as "private" or "closed" networks – are increasingly appearing alongside the so-called "permissionless", "public" or open networks".[49] Permissioned networks have a central authority that can perform special functions depending on the respective protocol, in particular authorising new participants or those with the power to validate transfers.[50] Some of these systems even allow the central authority to cancel transactions previously approved by the nodes.

This represents a significant departure from the public and open ideals that marked the blockchain's early days. The first reason for this development is the increasing involvement of powerful corporate interests embracing DLT. One example is the multinational bank J.P. Morgan, which has created its own crypto protocol called "Quorum" to facilitate asset transfers between businesses in the financial sector.[51]

The second reason for the trend towards permissioned systems is the need to maintain confidentiality to prevent transactions from being published globally. This is hardly surprising considering the importance of confidentiality for

47 Zetzsche, Arner and Buckley (n 45) 172, 179 (characterising DeFi as a mix of AI, Big Data, Cloud, and DLT).

48 On DEX, see *infra* 1.2.2.3.

49 On the sometimes confusing terminology, see ENGIECSAI Lab and others, 'Permissioned vs. Permissionless Blockchain: How and Why There Is Only One Right Choice' (2021) Journal of Software 95.

50 Pranay Gupta, T. Mandy Tham, *Fintech* (Walter de Gruyter 2019) 112–116 (with regard to "private blockchains"); Michel Rauchs and others, 'Distributed Ledger Technology Systems: A Conceptual Framework' (August 2018), 58 (speaking of "closed DLT-systems") <https://www.jbs.cam.ac.uk/wp-content/uploads/2020/08/2018-10-26-conceptualising-dlt-systems.pdf> accessed 15 April 2024.

51 See J P Morgan, 'What is Quorum' <https://www.jpmorgan.com/country/UK/EN/Quorum> accessed 17 June 2020.

the financial sector in general. The blockchain, in contrast, is completely transparent and offers a comprehensive and indelible view of all historical transfers, which is not necessarily in the interests of the financial industry.

The third reason is the need for supervision by regulators. Regulators need someone they can regulate – i.e. an entity they can control. The beginnings of cryptocurrencies like Bitcoin left them somewhat perplexed, as no known issuer or developer could serve as a recipient for their regulatory measures. Regulators are much more at ease with permissioned systems, which have a central authority and a restricted group of participants which can be subjected to regulatory control. Although regulators cannot stop the emergence of Bitcoin and other fully decentralised systems, they can encourage and even force established actors like banks to avoid open, permissionless systems in favour of closed, permissioned systems.

For these reasons, financial crypto technology may evolve, in part, in the direction of private blockchains. The latter may allow incumbent financial institutions to transition into the "crypto future". At the same time, this does not mean that open or permissionless systems will disappear from the world. They continue to attract considerable investment, especially from those looking for an alternative store of value to those already in existence.

1.1.3 *Summary*

The blockchain allows users to store information in a secure, decentralised, and generally irreversible manner. As they do not depend on a central authority, participants are not required to place their trust in third parties. Parties to a transaction also do not need to know each other, as combining public and private keys limits the possibility of falsification or double-spending. Thus, the blockchain's key innovation is removing the need for trust in an intermediary or a central authority. It allows the peer-to-peer transfer of assets without requiring parties to establish contact and without the intervention of a trusted third party. For this reason, the technology is particularly well suited to globalisation, which involves exchanges between people who do not know each other and who live or are based in distant countries.

The main innovation of second-generation blockchains is the introduction of smart contracts, which automate the execution of contractual obligations. This avoids potential disputes and reinforces the blockchain's role as a "trust machine".[52] With the development of closed systems, we are seeing a certain centralisation of the technology, which is by nature decentralised. This apparent contradiction can be explained by the increasing interest in blockchain

---

52 See cover of "The Economist" from 31 October 2015.

technology by mainstream businesses and government regulators. Rather than postulating an inescapable trend towards an increasingly decentralised financial system with no intermediaries, it is more realistic to talk about opposing waves of decentralisation and centralisation, constantly reiterating at an ever-higher level.

1.2 The Crypto Economy

Since its humble beginnings, the blockchain has quickly become a global business phenomenon. Extensive applications have been developed for the technology, but we will concentrate on those critical for the financial sector (1.2.1). In addition, a whole range of service providers have sprung up around it (1.2.2). Collaborations among nodes and between users are increasingly common (1.2.3), and new types of transactions have been developed (1.2.4).

1.2.1 *Crypto-Assets*

1.2.1.1 Cryptocurrencies

The best-known use case of the blockchain is that of a payment mechanism. Bitcoin and Ether are "coins", i.e. digital currencies, which can be used to pay for goods and services. Their main innovation is enabling direct peer-to-peer payments without intermediaries and limitations by national borders. Cryptocurrencies that are largely inaccessible to regulators are particularly attractive for those seeking to avoid state restrictions like currency controls.

Another use for cryptocurrencies is investment. Because their exchange rates are highly volatile, cryptocurrencies have become a target for those who want to speculate. In the last few years, the purpose of speculation has become dominant. As the price of cryptocurrencies has been extremely volatile, spectacular gains could be made. New products have been invented to increase leverage, such as Contracts for Difference (CFDs) or other derivatives based on digital assets. Nevertheless, it would be wrong to consider investors in cryptocurrencies as mere speculators. One must bear in mind that for many people in developing countries, cryptocurrencies are the only way to access an asset that is not subject to government control and is easily convertible into other currencies.

1.2.1.2 Tokens Issued via Initial Coin Offerings (ICO)

Cryptocurrencies are not the only objects being transferred via the blockchain. Private entities regularly create other digital assets. Because these are offered to the public for the first time, one speaks in this context of an "Initial Coin

Offering" (ICO), similar to the Initial Public Offering (IPO) conducted for other financial instruments.

However, the terminology is somewhat confusing. The product of an ICO is not a "coin" but a so-called "token". The two terms are often used interchangeably but should be distinguished. The term "coin" designates cryptocurrencies, such as Bitcoin and Ether, which have their own protocol or specific network (therefore also referred to as "native" assets).[53] In contrast, tokens do not have a dedicated network. Instead, they rely on an existing network, such as Ethereum, and are based on a smart contract or other protocol deployed on that network (therefore, they are also called "protocol tokens").[54] ICOs are connected to the blockchain but do not represent a technological innovation; instead, they are a means for issuers to benefit from the new technology. ICOs pursue a different objective than cryptocurrencies. Their main purpose is to finance businesses – typically start-ups in the technology sector. Investors pay, often using cryptocurrency, and receive tokens in exchange.

The purpose of tokens varies. It is common to distinguish between three categories: payment tokens, investment tokens, and utility tokens.[55]

Payment tokens serve as a means of payment. In that, they are similar to cryptocurrencies like Bitcoin and Ether. Investment tokens, one the other hand, resemble financial instruments. They may represent a share in the issuer's business, a loan or a bond. Finally, utility tokens give access to products and services such as digital applications, cloud space, or goods and services in the real world. There are also hybrid tokens, which combine several functions,

53 Thomas Ankenbrand and others, 'Proposal for a Comprehensive (Crypto) Asset Taxonomy' (arXiv, 23 July 2020) 3–4 <http://arxiv.org/abs/2007.11877> accessed 22 February 2023 (speaking of a "token that is native to a specific blockchain").

54 ibid 4 (defining protocol token as "a token issued on an existing blockchain protocol").

55 See European Securities and Markets Authority (ESMA), 'Advice on Initial Coin Offerings and Crypto-Assets' (ESMA50-157-1391, 2019) 8 para 19 <https://www.esma.europa.eu/sites/default/files/library/esma50-157-1391_crypto_advice.pdf> accessed 15 April 2024; Philipp Hacker and Chris Thomale, 'Crypto-Securities Regulation: ICO s, Token Sales and Cryptocurrencies under EU Financial Law' (2018) 15(4) European Company and Financial Law Review 645; see also Iris Barsan, 'Legal Challenges of Initial Coin Offerings (ICO")' (2017) 3 Revue trimestrielle de droit financier 54 (distinguishing between currency like tokens and security like tokens). For a similar distinction between payment tokens, utility tokens and asset tokens including asset-backed tokens, see International Securities Services Association (ISSA), 'Infrastructure for Crypto-Assets: A Review by Infrastructure Providers' (October 2018) 10 <https://issanet.org/content/uploads/2016/ 02/2018-10_ISSA_report_Infrastructure_for_ Crypto-Assets.pdf> accessed 15 April 2024.

such as utility tokens that are bought as investments.[56] However, it is also possible that a token confers no rights against the issuer at all; this is even the most common case in practice.

Tokens can be dangerous for investors, especially since empirical studies show that ICOs often serve as vehicles for so-called Ponzi schemes which seek to defraud investors.[57] Most ICOs are not accompanied by a prospectus required by law for IPOs. Instead, they rely on a so-called "whitepaper", which contains very little information on their purpose and even fewer details concerning the issuer.[58] There is also no guarantee that the project described in a whitepaper is viable or will be fully implemented. And even when a project is successful, investors may still be short-changed because tokens do not always represent a legally enforceable right against the issuer.

1.2.1.3 Dark Net Coins

Alongside Bitcoin and Ether, several new networks have appeared. Some of them allow users to conceal their addresses. These networks are used for transactions in the so-called "dark net", a section of the internet where illegal products and services are traded. The first major website of this kind was "Silk Road", on which Bitcoin became the preferred payment method shortly after its launch. Although US authorities eventually shut it down, other platforms have since taken its place. New networks continue to emerge, allowing criminals to constantly change their names and addresses.

The advantage of the Bitcoin network from the point of view of law enforcement – and the downside from the point of view of criminals – is that it records every movement since the first transfer and inscribes it into an indelible ledger. This greatly facilitates the work of prosecutors, the police and other authorities. Once they have identified the person behind a specific public key, they can quite easily prove all of their past activity because it is safely stored in an independent and trusted register. For this reason, criminals increasingly resort to so-called "mixers", who break the transaction history, or "tumblers", who mix the cryptocurrencies they receive with those of other users.[59] Problematically, this approach requires trust in the person behind the mixer or tumbler. That is why new cryptocurrencies – so-called "dark net coins" – have been developed with

56 See ESMA (n 55) 8, para 19.

57 Dirk A Zetzsche and others, 'The ICO Gold Rush: It's a Scam, It's a Bubble, It's a Super Challenge for Regulators' (2019) 60 Harvard International Law Journal 267.

58 ibid 278.

59 Prastudy Fauzi and others, 'Quisquis: A New Design for Anonymous Cryptocurrencies' 1 <https://eprint.iacr.org/undefined/undefined> accessed 15 April 2024.

a built-in feature to protect the identity of the parties, such as Dash, Monero or Zcash. Their proponents euphemistically speak of "anonymity" and invoke the protection of "privacy".[60] Essentially, dark net coins allow users to pay without leaving a trail, a feature that makes them cherished above all by criminals. How this effect is achieved precisely depends on the particular network in question. It is important to note that dark net coins are "native assets" because they are based on their own dedicated network.

1.2.1.4 NFTS

One of the most hotly sought-after products of the crypto economy is the non-fungible token (NFT). As any other token, it is not a "native asset" because it does not have its own dedicated network. The particularity that sets it apart from other tokens is that an NFT is not considered interchangeable by the market with other tokens of the same type.[61] This is because NFTS are not issued *en masse* but are highly individualised. Their purpose precisely is the unique representation of some information or object. This could be, for instance, a digital picture, a piece of art that exists in the real world, like a statue, or even an event, such as a particular scene from a basketball match.

An important detail that purchasers often overlook is that most NFTS do not confer any right in the underlying asset or event, such as a copyright. Other users can thus continue to copy the digital picture or watch the event online in total legality. This leaves the neutral – and especially the older – observer wondering why NFTS are acquired in the first place. The best explanation is that owning an NFT confers a feeling of exclusivity and uniqueness in the digital space, similar to owning a tangible asset in real life. That this uniqueness does not transfer into the physical world no longer matters for younger generations who have grown up as digital natives.

Another point that may merit some clarification is the concept of fungibility. The attentive reader will have already remarked that two coins or two tokens are never identical, as they are all represented by a particular private key. Yet to be fungible with others, an item does not necessarily have to be identical to them. One egg, for instance, is never identical to another. What makes them nevertheless fungible is the fact that the general public treats them as identical by accepting one of them instead of the other. The same is true for bitcoins,

60 ibid.

61 See Usman W Chohan, 'Non-Fungible Tokens: Blockchains, Scarcity, and Value' (24 March 2021) 1 <https://papers.ssrn.com/abstract=3822743> accessed 15 April 2024 ("a non-fungible token can be seen as a unit of digital information (token) that is stored on a blockchain and is not inherently interchangeable with other digital assets (non-fungible)").

which, though they can be distinguished by their private keys and previous transfers, are generally considered to be interchangeable and thus fungible. The only exceptions are very special situations, such as stolen or "tainted" Bitcoins, which can be backtracked to addresses involved in illegal activities.[62] Assets linked to these addresses will certainly not be considered and accepted on the same footing as other assets of the same kind.

What makes NFTs different is thus their treatment by the public, particularly their commercial use. For instance, a typical NFT does not have an easily identifiable market price, is not available in large volumes and cannot be stored with any of the typical custodians, such as a wallet provider, but is typically held directly. Still, the craze for the new product has led to the emergence of "NFTs" that are issued and traded in large numbers, forming a series in which each unit represents only a fraction of the underlying asset. Each NFT would then be just one of the (fungible) units in a single series, the volume of which could be substantial. Given this peculiarity, they do not deserve to be called NFTs. That they carry this name is one of the many bizarreries of the crypto economy.

1.2.1.5 Stablecoins

Stablecoins are an attempt to remedy the high volatility of crypto-assets. They aim at a stable value by keeping a relation to another asset, index or benchmark over time. This can be done by backing the stablecoin up with real-world assets, such as currencies, commodities, or pieces of real estate. However, stablecoins must not necessarily be asset-backed – their "stability" can also be ensured via algorithms that balance offer and demand. In this case, they are known as "algorithmic" stablecoins.[63]

The term stablecoin is misleading in two respects. First, stablecoins are tokens, not coins. Second, they do not necessarily have a stable value in absolute terms: the degree of "stability" or risk depends on their design.[64] These two

62 Rolf van Wegberg, Jan-Jaap Oerlemans and Oskar van Deventer, 'Bitcoin Money Laundering: Mixed Results? An Explorative Study on Money Laundering of Cybercrime Proceeds Using Bitcoin' (2018) 25 Journal of Financial Crime 419.

63 See Aleksander Berentsen and Fabian Schär, 'Stablecoins: The quest for a low-volatility cryptocurrency' in Antonio Fatás (ed), *The Economics of FinTech and Digital Currencies* (CEPR Press 2019) 65, 66–67.

64 See, e.g., Swiss Financial Market Supervisory Authority (FINMA), 'Supplement to the guidelines for enquiries regarding the regulatory framework for Initial Coin Offerings ("ICOs")' (11 September 2019) <https://www.finma.ch/~/media/finma/dokumente/dokumentencenter/ myfinma/1bewilligung/fintech/wegleitung-stable-coins.pdf> accessed 15 April 2024.

points clearly show that the expression "stablecoin" is a marketing term coined by the industry, not a scientific description.

The best-known stablecoin project is Libra, promoted by a consortium of businesses and NGOs led by Facebook (now Meta). The consortium created a Swiss law foundation in 2019. "The Libra Foundation" aimed at issuing tokens on a blockchain. What made these planned tokens special was the possibility of spending them at all participating businesses and organisations. In addition, the tokens would be backed by a basket of state currencies, purporting to guarantee the tokens' value. This reserve would have consisted mainly of government bonds, and not cash, to avoid forgoing interest.

However, Libra never advanced beyond the planning stage. Faced with parliamentary scrutiny and pressure from regulators, the project was renamed "Diem", and its asset portfolio was limited to US dollars. Eventually, it was withdrawn.

Despite this setback, private stablecoins are clearly on the rise. There is an increasing number of different types. A dubious "claim to fame" lies with the TerraUSD protocol. TerraUSD was supposed to maintain a peg to the US dollar not through a currency reserve but rather by an algorithm – it was an algorithmic stablecoin. The underlying protocol relied on a two-token system, one being the Terra token and the other token being Luna. Investors could buy Luna and exchange them for Terra, or vice versa, but never directly buy Terra. The algorithm was supposed to stabilise Terra's offer and demand by contracting or expanding the Luna supply pool. Both collapsed, however, after a speculative attack.[65]

The Terra-Luna case offers a cautionary tale about the dangers of stablecoins, particularly algorithmic stablecoins. This asset class is still nascent. Whether it can be developed into something stable is still uncertain.

1.2.1.6 Central Bank Digital Currencies

Governments and central banks increasingly consider issuing official currency in digital form. These are referred to as central bank digital currencies (CBDCs),[66] by contrast to the private creations known as "cryptocurrencies."

---

65 For an in depth-analysis, see Antonio Briola and others, 'Anatomy of a Stablecoin's Failure: The Terra-Luna Case' (2023) 51 Finance Research Letters No 103358.

66 Bank of International Settlements (BIS), 'Central Bank Digital Currencies' <https://www.bis.org/cpmi/publ/d174.htm> accessed 15 April 2024; Raphael Auer and Rainer Boehme, 'The Technology of Retail Central Bank Digital Currency' <https://www.bis.org/publ/qtrpdf/r_qt2003j.htm> accessed 15 April 2024.

Many central banks are contemplating the issuance of CBDCs. Few of them, though, are planning to use blockchain technology for this purpose.

Sweden and Estonia were among the first countries to consider adopting a CBDC. The Venezuelan government has already introduced the blockchain-based Petro, a digital currency used to pay for crude oil supplies. China appears determined to expand the Renminbi by a digital version, the Digital Yuan, or "e-CNY".[67]

The European Central Bank has also announced plans for a "digital euro".[68] These developments mark a watershed. Governments and central banks recognise the potential of digital currencies and want to implement them for their benefit. This shows that the idea is not restricted to the private sector but can also be used for the public interest.

However, these projects pose many challenges, one of the main ones being to ensure convertibility between digital currencies issued by different states. Once the plans for different CBDCs have materialised, individuals, businesses, and central banks will be interested in exchanging them for each other. However, this will be difficult because digital currencies are based on a closed technological infrastructure that is likely to differ from one country to another. Moreover, central banks envision restrictions for using their CBDC, based e.g. on the holder's residence and the amount they can hold. Paradoxically, digitising money could introduce new divisions between national currencies that will be even greater than those existing today. This makes it vital to guarantee the interoperability of digital currencies, as is increasingly recognised by international institutions.[69]

It would be possible to avoid such difficulties, among others, by introducing a global currency. This proposal dates back to the end of World War II, when the English economist John Maynard Keynes suggested setting up a clearing union between different states by introducing a common currency under the name

---

67 Will Knight, 'China's Central Bank Has Begun Cautiously Testing a Digital Currency' (2017) 120(5) MIT Technology Review 22; J. Cheng, 'China Rolls Out Pilot Test of Digital Currency' (Wall Street Journal, 12 April 2020) <https://www.wsj.com/articles/china-rolls-out-pilot-test-of-digital-currency-11587385339> accessed 5 April 2024.

68 Fabio Panetta, 'Preparing for the euro's digital future' (ECB Blog, 14 July 2021) <https://www.ecb.europa.eu/press/blog/date/2021/html/ecb.blog210714~6bfc156386.en.html> accessed 15 April 2024.

69 See, e.g., Committee on Payments and Market Infrastructures, BIS Innovation Hub, IMF and World Bank, 'Options for Access to and Interoperability of CBDC s for Cross-border Payments – Joint Report to the G20' (11 July 2022).

of "*Bancor*".[70] In light of the new possibilities opened up by digital technology, Mark Carney, former Governor of the Bank of England, has renewed the debate by suggesting the creation of a "*Synthetic Hegemonic Currency*" (SHC) at the Jackson Hole Economic Policy Symposium in 2019.[71] This new global currency would take advantage of the potential of the new technologies and be backed by a basket of different national currencies. In this respect, the project has some similarities with *stablecoins* such as Libra, but unlike the latter, it would be managed by the public sector (i.e. central banks). For now, this proposal has not been taken up by other central banks. Still, it certainly deserves to be studied more closely by them and by international institutions such as the Bank for International Settlements (BIS) and the International Monetary Fund (IMF).

1.2.2 *Crypto Service Providers*

One of the drivers of blockchain technology was the idea that it would eliminate the need for intermediaries. The rise of crypto exchanges and wallet providers demonstrates that this is not the case. Instead, a whole ecosystem of intermediaries has developed around the new technology. This reality also offers certain advantages, as it provides the supervisory authorities with "points of contact" between the crypto economy and the real world, which allow for effective regulation and supervision of the sector.

1.2.2.1 Crypto Wallet Providers

As explained earlier, private keys are long strings of numbers and letters, which are essential for the operation of the blockchain and are used to authorise transfers.[72] The storage of the private key is a problematic issue. If the key has been lost, the crypto-asset is no longer accessible. Keeping it on a hard drive is risky because a computer may be hacked. Writing them on paper is not necessarily safer because the paper could be lost, destroyed, stolen or copied.

Service providers have developed different options for storing private keys. The first option is to use a wallet, a web-based service protected by a password. Because the wallet is online, it remains at risk to hackers, so it is referred to as

---

70 John Maynard Keynes, *The Collected Writings of John Maynard Keynes, XXV: Activities 1940–1944 Shaping the Post-War World – The Clearing Union*, (Palgrave Macmillan 1980).

71 Mark Carney, 'The Growing Challenges for Monetary Policy in the Current International Monetary and Financial System', Jackson Hole Symposium (2019) 15 <https://www.bankofengland.co.uk/-/media/boe/files/speech/2019/the-growing-challenges-for-monetary-policy-speech-by-mark-carney.pdf> accessed 15 April 2024.

72 See *supra* 1.1.1.2.

a "hot wallet". Specialised service providers and exchanges offer this type of service.

The second option involves saving the private key on a USB thumb drive. This can be removed from the computer, thereby increasing security. Companies propose specialised USB thumb drives, which offer added security even when attached to a computer. These are referred to as "cold wallets".

The storage of private keys is one of the greatest difficulties the new technology faces. An entirely satisfactory solution to this issue is yet to be found.[73] The importance of storing private keys on a tangible medium is paradoxical at a time when data is increasingly dematerialised and shifted to the cloud. The need to safeguard private keys on a tangible medium shows that we are stuck in a digital Middle Age.

1.2.2.2 Crypto Exchanges

The crypto economy would have difficulty functioning in autarky, i.e. in total disconnect from the outside world. There is a strong demand to acquire crypto-assets using official currencies. At the same time, certain investors feel the need to convert their crypto-assets back into traditional currency or other crypto-assets. These two needs are met by crypto exchanges. Unlike traditional exchanges, they do not use brokers but are online and fully automated. They also operate around the clock. Most of them double as wallet providers by allowing their customers to deposit their crypto-assets with them.

In most countries, crypto exchanges are not subject to regulatory oversight. Unsurprisingly, problems have occurred. The best known is the collapse of the exchange Mt. Gox. In 2013, Mt. Gox was the most important Bitcoin exchange, with an estimated market share of 80%.[74] One year later, allegations surfaced that Mt. Gox had lost 6% of the bitcoins it held.[75] Japanese authorities stepped in and closed the exchange. Many investors lost their holdings during the ensuing bankruptcy proceedings. A more recent example is the failure of FTX, which has spooked markets in 2022.[76] These cases illustrate the dangers faced by private investors dealing with these new service providers.

Crypto exchanges somewhat contradict the basic idea of DLT because they are new intermediaries. Although they work automatically, they are operated by a specific person, usually a company with a corporate seat and a board.

73 For an innovative approach using designed mobile devices see Welfare (n 42) 163.
74 Trautman (n 23) 101.
75 ibid.
76 On both cases, see *infra* 1.4.2.5.

This very much resembles the "old" world in which power was concentrated in the hands of intermediaries. This requires trust in individuals, which may be disappointed. A third party invariably opens the door to counterparty risk. Recent scandals and bankruptcies involving crypto exchanges, from Mt. Gox to FTX, illustrate the pitfalls for investors. Even more dangerous seem to be crypto derivative exchanges. They offer derivatives contracts, such as call options, on crypto-assets. The rewards but also the risks for investors are even higher than those of the crypto-assets themselves.

1.2.2.3 Decentralised Exchanges (DEX)

Alongside crypto exchanges operated by (legal or natural) persons, new operators have emerged that provide the same services but on a decentralised basis. These are *Decentralized Exchanges* (DEXs). They are platforms on which crypto-assets can be traded, invested or exchanged without the intervention of any intermediary.[77] Their work is based on a combination of numerous smart contracts. Once programmed, they operate entirely automatically, except for occasional updates or modifications of the protocol by a team of programmers.[78]

The best illustration of this is automated market makers (AMM), which replace traditional human market makers trading stock on conventional exchanges.[79] They provide the necessary liquidity in crypto-assets on the DEX when the market is flat. AMM are fully automated and fed by DeFi users, who provide liquidity in token pairs by operations such as yield farming. The AMM uses an algorithm calculating specific yields to balance the offer and demand for tokens.

DEX and DeFi generally promise a new financial system free from human errors. Yet, they may themselves have defects since they are programmed and updated by humans. This raises the question of possible remedies, which is particularly thorny because users interact exclusively with the decentralised programme. For example, there is no method of filing a complaint against a

---

77 See Raphael Auer and others, 'The Technology of Decentralized Finance (DeFi)' (2023) BIS Working Papers No 1066, 18–20; EU Blockchain Observatory and Forum (n 46) 27–29.

78 See EU Blockchain Observatory and Forum (n 46) 10–11 (mentioning the use of time-locked multi-signature administration keys used to update or modify the protocol in certain ways).

79 On AMM see EU Blockchain Observatory and Forum (n 46) 41–45; Aramonte, Huang and Schrimpf (n 46) 34.

DeFi platform or "project".[80] Also, enforcing liability claims against programmers, which are usually unknown, may present formidable challenges.[81]

1.2.3 *Collaborative Structures*

1.2.3.1 Mining Pools

The more validating nodes in a network, the less chance they stand to "win" the competition and obtain newly minted crypto-assets. That is why miners work together in so-called mining pools. These groups of miners share the effort and reward of mining a new block. They can be compared to the members of a lottery pool,[82] with the difference that mining a new block is not a game but an economic activity that generates profits.

Mining pools are prevalent and wield considerable power. In 2017, four dominated half of the Bitcoin network and only two dominated half of the Ethereum network.[83] In May 2023, two mining groups (Foundry USA and Antpool) monopolised more than half of the Bitcoin network.[84] Their position allows mining pools to control networks and shape their development.

1.2.3.2 Decentralized Autonomous Organizations (DAOs)

Second-generation blockchain applications improve the efficiency of contracts and can also be used to organise relationships within multilateral entities. The best-known example is the Decentralized Autonomous Organization (DAO).[85] A DAO is a "company" of sorts, with its articles of association programmed into an algorithm and protocol. Collective decisions by participants are taken with the help of tokens and then implemented using a range of smart contracts.[86] It is unnecessary to involve a board or managers and other central bodies. DAOs are thus new governance mechanisms that aspire to be decentralised, non-hierarchical, and directly democratic, with a flexible membership base. Most of them are, however, based on a financial commitment and with voters' rights depending on the capital they have invested.

---

80 EU Blockchain Observatory and Forum (n 46) 9.

81 See *infra* 2.4.2. and 2.4.3.

82 Antonopoulos (n 3) 102.

83 De Filippi and Wright (n 26) 40.

84 See the distribution of market shares measured in "exahashes" (quintillion hashes) per second (EH/s) at <https://btc.com/stats/pool> accessed 26 May 2023.

85 Laila Metjahic, 'Deconstructing the DAO: The Need for Legal Recognition and the Application of Securities Laws to Decentralized Organizations' (2017) 39(4) Cardozo Law Review 1533.

86 ibid 1542.

The notion "DAO" was first used in 2014 by Vitalik Buterin, the founder of the Ethereum network, in the Ethereum whitepaper. He described it as "long-term smart contracts that contain the assets and encode the bylaws of an entire organization".[87] An initial entity of this type was created under the name "*The DAO*" in 2016 by a group of programmers in Germany.[88] It served as the basis for a crowdfunding campaign to fund "projects" on which the investors would vote. Initially, "*The DAO*" was spectacularly successful, raising about US$150 million in cryptocurrency within 15 days.[89] Not long after, however, one-third of that capital had disappeared. Ethereum users then agreed to return "*The DAO*'s" funds to their initial state, leading to a hard fork on the Ethereum blockchain.[90] Yet this did not help "*The DAO*", which was forced to cease its activities shortly afterwards.

This false start does not diminish the technological potential of DAO s. Today, there exists a whole plethora of them serving a variety of different purposes, ranging from profitable to philanthropic activities. What unites them is that they allow decision-making between participants who do not know each other and automate the execution of the decisions taken via smart contracts. This makes cooperation between participants pseudonymous and more secure. More versions of the DAO idea are likely to thrive in the future.

1.2.4 *Crypto-Asset Transactions*

1.2.4.1 Derivative Transactions

Several types of operations are done with crypto-assets. These include derivative transactions, such as options or futures contracts. They allow trading in crypto-assets with leverage and betting against them via short selling. Derivatives transactions require less capital and promise higher returns, but they also involve more risks than trading directly in the underlying. Given the high

---

87 Vitalik Buterin, 'Ethereum – A Next Generation Smart Contract & Decentralized Application Platform' (Blockchain research network, November 2013) 1 <https://ethereum.org/669c9e2e2027310b6b3cdce6e1c52962/Ethereum_Whitepaper_Buterin_2014.pdf>accessed 15 April 2024 (calling DAO s the "logical extension" of smart contracts).

88 Paul Vigna, 'Fund Based on Digital Currency Ethereum to Wind Down After Alleged Hack' (Wall Street Journal, 18 June 2016) <https://www.wsj.com/articles/investment-fund-based-on-digital-currency-to-wind-down-after-alleged-hack-1466175033> accessed 15 April 2024.

89 See SEC, 'Report of Investigation Pursuant to Section 21(a) of the Securities Exchange Act of 1934: The DAO' (Release No. 81207, 25 July 2017) <https://www.sec. gov/litigation/investreport/34-81207.pdf> accessed 15 April 2024.

90 De Filippi and Wright (n 26) 141.

volatility of crypto-assets, one can surmise the even higher riskiness of their derivatives.

1.2.4.2 Staking, Yield Farming, Liquidity Mining and Crypto Lending

In the context of the proof-of-stake mechanism, a condition for the permission to validate transactions is to provide a certain amount of crypto-assets. Since nodes often do not dispose of sufficient crypto-assets themselves, they ask other users for the temporary transfer of such assets in return for a share of the profits generated, which correspond to the reward obtained following the validation of a new block on the chain (newly minted coins plus "gas fees"). The relevant transfer is done through smart contracts, possibly intermediated by a wallet provider. Such "staking" agreements offer investors a means to earn profits from their crypto-assets, which generally do not carry any interest or pay any dividend and are thus unremunerative.

Further operations can be done with crypto-assets. Yield farming is one such operation that allows DEX to provide its users with financial incentives to refrain from trading certain crypto-assets – usually the DEX's native token or cryptocurrency – to stabilise their value.[91] Another operation is liquidity mining, in which a liquidity token (Liquidity Provider token or LP token) is exchanged for a pair of crypto-assets, which are transferred to a pool that aims to provide liquidity to the crypto market.[92] Holders of crypto-assets thus have a choice between different types of complex operations to mobilise their crypto-assets and generate gains from them.

1.2.5 *Summary*

Although humble compared to traditional financial markets, the crypto economy is increasingly gaining ground. New applications and service providers are emerging, threatening incumbents and their business models. While it is still too early to tell, one cannot exclude that they will eventually replace them. Their very existence runs against the original design of the blockchain, which is entirely distributed and does not rely on any central authority.

Given this reality, the crypto economy is neither entirely distributed nor fully decentralised. Instead, many of its functions are highly concentrated in a handful of crypto exchanges and wallet service providers, which recreates the trust problem. The most significant difference between these new

---

91 Matthias Lehmann and others, 'Staking Your Crypto: What are the Stakes?' (2023) 19 Journal of Business & Technology Law 53, 64.

92 ibid 65.

intermediaries and the incumbents of the traditional financial system is that the first do not allow themselves to be defined by national borders. While they may be based in a state, their activity was never preconceived as limited to a specific territory, unlike banks and financial institutions that operate in the physical space. The crypto-asset service providers ignore state frontiers and do not rely on state institutions, such as a central bank as a provider of liquidity of last resort. They may thus be the nucleus of an emerging, truly global economy.

1.3 The Underlying Philosophy

To fully understand the nature of the crypto innovation, it does not suffice to be familiar with the functioning of the underlying technology. One must also grasp its history, purpose, and the general philosophical spirit that led to its emergence. These aspects throw light on the genesis of cryptocurrencies and explain why certain technical choices were made.

1.3.1 *Precursors of Bitcoin*

Providing an accurate overview of the historical development of digital currencies is very hard, given the lack of knowledge about the authorship of the Bitcoin whitepaper. Nevertheless, one thing is sure: The history of crypto technology started long before 2008, when the whitepaper was published.[93]

1.3.1.1 DigiCash

One year after 1984, in which George Orwell's eponymous novel is set, the computer scientist David Chaum described an electronic cash system, with the purpose – indicated by its title – "to make big brother obsolete".[94] This proposal aimed to create "untraceable electronic money" through digital signatures and cryptography. He built on the works on public-private-key cryptography done by Whitfield Diffie and Martin Hellman in the mid-1970s.[95] A few years later, Chaum also tried to address the double-spending problem in

93 For a short history of cryptocurrencies, see the overview in Indian Supreme Court, *Internet and Mobile Association of India v. Reserve Bank of India*, Written Petition (Civil) No. 373 (2018), judgment of 4 March 2020, 29–30.

94 David Chaum, 'Security Without Identification: Transaction Systems to Make Big Brother Obsolete' (1985) 28 Communications of the Association for Computer Machinery (ACM) 1030.

95 Whitfield Diffie and Martin E Hellman, 'Exhaustive Cryptoanalytics on the NBS Data Encryption Standard' (1977) 10(6) Computer 74. See also Steven Levy, 'Solving the Problem

a paper co-authored with two other scientists.[96] His insights formed the basis for the incorporation of his own company, "DigiCash", which he founded in 1990 and which used a number of cryptographic protocols.[97] The company went, however, bankrupt.

1.3.1.2 Hashcash

The development of cryptocurrencies saw further trailblazers. In 1997, Adam Back developed a mechanism to throttle systematic abuse of internet resources such as email by anonymous remailers. To this end, he employed a cryptographic hash-based proof-of-work algorithm, which required much work to compute but allowed to easily verify whether an email originated from a specific sender. The same technique was later used for the Bitcoin protocol. Back gave his invention the evocative name "hashcash".[98]

1.3.1.3 Bit Gold

Around the same time as Back was active, Nick Szabo started to develop "bit gold". This was a system in which computers mined for scarce digital commodities.[99] Before that, Szabo had published a historical analysis of the evolution of money, which strongly emphasised its private origins.[100]

Hal Finney continued on Szabo's and Back's path with the paper "Reusable Proofs of Work".[101] This was a significant stride in making the proof of work method more practical, lowering the cost for the token transfer. The major innovation, however, consisted of a security server designed to allow users

of Electronic Cash' in M. David Ermann, Mary B Williams and Michele S Shauf (eds), *Computers, Ethics, and Society* (2nd edn, Oxford University Press 1997) 99, 105.

96 David Chaum, Amos Fiat and Moni Naor, 'Untraceable Electronic Cash' in Shafi Goldwasser (ed), *Advances in Cryptology – CRYPTO '88* (Springer 1990) 319.

97 For a vivid portray of David Chaum, see Steven Levy, 'Solving the Problem of Electronic Cash' in M David Ermann, Mary B Williams and Michele S Shauf (eds), *Computers, Ethics, and Society* (2nd edn, Oxford University Press 1997) 99.

98 Adam Back, 'Hashcash – A Denial of Service Counter-Measure' <http://www.hashcash.org/ papers/hashcash.pdf> accessed 15 April 2024.

99 On Szabo, see, e.g., Finn Brunton, *Digital Cash: The Unknown History of the Anarchists, Utopians, and Technologists Who Created Cryptocurrency* (Princeton University Press 2019) 111; Lana Swartz, 'What Was Bitcoin, What Will It Be? The Techno-Economic Imaginaries of a New Money Technology' (2018) 32 Cultural Studies 623, 628.

100 Nick Szabo, 'Shelling Out: The Origins of Money' <https://nakamotoinstitute.org/shelling-out> accessed 15 April 2024.

101 Hal Finnley, 'Reusable Proofs of Work' <https://nakamotoinstitute.org/finney/rpow/index.html> accessed 15 April 2024.

worldwide to check the system's accuracy and integrity in real time. This innovation became instrumental for Bitcoin. Later, Finney would be the counterparty to Satoshi Nakamoto in the first Bitcoin transfer ever.[102]

1.3.1.4 Bmoney

Others also had a go at the creation of digital money. In 1998, computer engineer Wei Dai published a description of an anonymous and distributed cash system, which he called "bmoney".[103] It had many of the hallmarks of today's cryptocurrencies. For instance, senders and receivers were identified only by digital pseudonyms (i.e. public keys), and every message was to be signed by its sender and encrypted before being transferred to its receiver. However, the project was never put into practice.

1.3.1.5 From Then to the Genesis Block

These are just some illustrations of the efforts to create cryptocurrencies.[104] They demonstrate that Satoshi Nakamoto's whitepaper did not come out of thin air. On the contrary, when the paper was published in 2008, the essential ingredients of cryptocurrencies – namely distributed storage, encryption, and proof of work – were already present. Nakamoto's achievement was not to have invented them but to have put them together ingeniously.

After the whitepaper, the blockchain had to be coded. In doing so, Nakamoto connected – using his pseudonym – with several software specialists via messages posted on specialist blogs and an electronic mailing list.[105] At first, they worked in private; later, they uploaded the code to the online repository GitHub.[106] They used open source code, i.e., a human-readable programming language, as opposed to binary code, which merely consists of the numbers 0 and 1. Open source code allows other programmers to understand the software's design logic and add their code. This technique may have been chosen because of the intended non-commercial use of Bitcoin or to allow the involvement of more voluntary co-workers.

---

102 Steve Kaaru, '13 Years Ago, Satoshi Nakamoto Sent Hal Finney 10 Bitcoins in Bitcoin's First Transaction Ever' (*CoinGeek*, 12 January 2022) <https://coingeek.com/13-years-ago-satoshi-nakamoto-sent-hal-finney-10-bitcoins-in-bitcoins-first-transaction-ever> accessed 15 April 2024.

103 Wei Dai, 'B-money' <http://www.weidai.com/bmoney.txt> accessed 15 April 2024.

104 For a fuller and entertaining account see Finn Brunton (n 99).

105 Both can be found on <https://satoshi.nakamotoinstitute.org> accessed 15 April 2024.

106 Parkin (n 28) 467.

On 3 January 2009, the first Bitcoin block was validated. The first confirmations were done by Satoshi Nakamoto, who retained an enormous amount of bitcoin from this time. On 22 May 2010, Laszlo Hanyecz entered into a transaction with Jeremy Sturdivant over two pizzas, which were paid with 10,000 bitcoins (now worth around 400 million US dollars). From then on, others gradually joined the network, entered into transactions and confirmed transfers.

Even today, the development of the Bitcoin network is the result of a collective effort. On a specialised site, anyone can suggest an improvement to the protocol and invite others to code.[107] Once the new part of the code is ready, the community of Internet users will discuss its merits. However, only a restricted group of coders – known as 'developers' – have the passwords needed to make changes to the protocol. Any new version of the code must then be accepted by the majority of nodes to be implemented.

1.3.2 *Of Cypher Punks and Crypto-Anarchists*

As the identity of the person or persons behind the pseudonym Nakamoto is (still) unknown, one cannot be entirely sure about the motivations leading to the emergence of cryptocurrencies. However, certain clues can be followed, like in a scavenger hunt. The Bitcoin whitepaper shows an intimate familiarity with prior attempts at "making" digital money, and the Bitcoin mailing list included many people who were involved previously. This is a valuable indicator of the *milieu* in which Nakamato may have lived. At least it informs about the context in which cryptocurrencies have been developed and is therefore helpful in elucidating its background.

1.3.2.1 Eric Hughes and the "Cypherpunk's Manifesto"

The first group that played a conspicuous role in the emergence of Bitcoin are the "Cypherpunks".[108] The term, coined by Jude Mihon, is a combination of "cypher" and "punk".[109] The cypherpunks were a group of people that

107 <https://github.com/bitcoin/bitcoin> accessed 26 September 2024.

108 On cypherpunks and their culture, see Enrico Beltramini, 'Against Technocratic Authoritarianism. A Short Intellectual History of the Cypherpunk Movement' (2021) 5 Internet Histories 101; Craig Jarvis, 'Cypherpunk Ideology: Objectives, Profiles, and Influences (1992–1998)' (2021) 6 Internet Histories 1; Swartz (n 99) 625–626. For a portray of three cypherpunks, see Katie Hafner and John Markoff, *Cyberpunk* (Simon & Schuster 1991).

109 Rosie Cross, 'Modem Grrrl' <https://www.wired.com/1995/02/st-jude/> accessed 15 April 2024.

communicated in off- and online fora, most notably a mailing list.[110] They had strong concerns about threats to privacy by the rise of a "surveillance state" and wanted to preserve the identities and personal data of internet users through cryptography. Their motivations and aspirations are concisely summarised in "A Cypherpunk's Manifesto".[111] It was written by one of the co-founders of the Cypherpunks mailing list, Eric Hughes, in 1993 and provides an insight into their vision:

> "… privacy in an open society requires anonymous transaction systems. Until now, cash has been the primary such system. An anonymous transaction system is not a secret transaction system. An anonymous system empowers individuals to reveal their identity when desired and only when desired; this is the essence of privacy. …
>
> We cannot expect governments, corporations, or other large, faceless organizations to grant us privacy out of their beneficence …
>
> We must defend our own privacy if we expect to have any. We must come together and create systems which allow anonymous transactions to take place. …
>
> We the Cypherpunks are dedicated to building anonymous systems. We are defending our privacy with cryptography, with anonymous mail forwarding systems, with digital signatures, and with electronic money …"[112]

The Cypherpunk's Manifesto, whose title consciously alludes to the "Communist Manifesto", evidences strong scepticism towards governments and "other large, faceless organizations". One may imagine the latter to include, for instance, internet giants and multinational banks.

In the penultimate paragraph quoted, Hughes calls for creating systems that allow "anonymous transactions to take place", and the last paragraph explicitly references "electronic money". This strongly links electronic money and privacy, the Cypherpunks' main concern. This link becomes even more apparent when one realises that the blockchain is essentially a mechanism for the secret transfer and storage of *information* and not of *value*. This has resulted in

110 For an analysis of the cypherpunk mailing list, see Beltramini (n 108).

111 Eric Hughes, 'A Cypherpunk's Manifesto' (9 March 1993) <https://www.activism.net/cypherpunk/manifesto.html> accessed 15 April 2024.

112 ibid.

pseudonymity being one of the essential features and hallmarks of Bitcoin.[113] Pseudonymity is less than anonymity: All transactions on the network can be seen because they are broadcast to the nodes and recorded on the blockchain. Nevertheless, participants in the network do not need to reveal their identity to other users; they can hide behind their public addresses. This is enough to assuage the privacy concerns.

The Cypherpunk's Manifesto continues to describe the action taken to achieve these goals:

> "Cypherpunks write code. We know that someone has to write software to defend privacy, and since we can't get privacy unless we all do, we're going to write it. We publish our code so that our fellow Cypherpunks may practice and play with it. Our code is free for all to use, worldwide. We don't much care if you don't approve of the software we write. We know that software can't be destroyed and that a widely dispersed system can't be shut down."

This paragraph is reminiscent of the blockchain's open architecture and distributed nature. It puts software as a fact that cannot be destroyed or shut down, neither by governments nor "other large, faceless organizations". This idea is reflected in Bitcoin's design.

Finally, the Manifesto also addresses the relation with the law:

> "Cypherpunks deplore regulations on cryptography, for encryption is fundamentally a private act. The act of encryption, in fact, removes information from the public realm. Even laws against cryptography reach only so far as a nation's border and the arm of its violence. Cryptography will ineluctably spread over the whole globe, and with it the anonymous transactions systems that it makes possible."

The last quote demonstrates two things: First, Cypherpunks see regulation on cryptography as an intrusion into their private space. But second, they also think such an intrusion is bound to fail since laws are limited in space, whereas cryptography is borderless. This point is revealing and directly touches upon the subject of this book, the relation between technology and international law.

---

113 See De Filippi and Wright (n 26) 38–39; John Bacon and others, 'Blockchain Demystified: A Technical and Legal Introduction to Distributed and Centralised Ledgers' (2018) 25 Richmond Journal of Law & Technology 1, 103.

1.3.2.2 Timothy May and the "Crypto Anarchist Manifesto"

A second group that has played a crucial role in the evolution of Bitcoin's underlying philosophy is the Crypto anarchists. Although they are related to the Cypherpunks, the Crypto anarchists go one step further. Their aims are not limited to privacy but extend to protecting all human exchanges. Crypto anarchists see cryptography as a means to build a different society, one that is based on voluntarist, mutually beneficial contractual relationships in free markets without any organising or regulating central authority.[114]

The term "crypto anarchy" was coined by Timothy C May, one of the co-founders of the cypherpunk movement. In 1988, he published the "Crypto Anarchist Manifesto",[115] in an obvious nod to the "Cypherpunk's Manifesto" written by Eric Hughes in the previous year. May's text predicts that computer technology, especially "cryptologic methods", would "fundamentally alter the nature of corporations and of government interference in economic transactions" and be the basis of "social and economic revolution". Innovations such as "public-key encryption, zero-knowledge interactive proof systems, and various software protocols for interaction, authentication, and verification" would undermine the government's ability to tax and control economic interactions and to keep information secret.

Timothy C May predicts that the states would want to halt the spread of the technology since it may be used by drug dealers and tax evaders and for fears of "societal disintegration". He explicitly admits that many of these concerns are valid. Indeed, he foresees a market for the trading of national secrets as well as illicit and stolen material goods and even the emergence of "abhorrent markets for assassinations and extortion". Yet, much to the reader's surprise, he seems not overly worried by these dark prospects. Instead, he dryly observes that criminal uses will not halt the spread of "crypto anarchy".

At this point, some clarification is appropriate. The term "anarchy" is often connected to the political left, especially in Europe. It needs to be remembered, though, that an opposite version of anarchy exists, which hinges on libertarian views and is especially widespread in the United States. The prime exponent of this tendency is the philosopher Robert Nozick, who has argued for a minimalist state in his book "Anarchy, State, and Utopia".[116] As a consequence, it would be incorrect to think of all crypto anarchists as being socialist or even

114 Swartz (n 99) 626 et seq.

115 Timothy C May, 'The Crypto Anarchist Manifesto' <http://groups.csail.mit.edu/mac/classes/6.805/articles/crypto/cypherpunks/may-crypto-manifesto.html> accessed 15 April 2024.

116 Robert Nozick, *Anarchy, State, and Utopia* (Basic Books 2013).

communist. Many of them, including Timothy May, are attracted by the idea of abolishing the state and turning towards "anarcho-capitalism" or "libertarian capitalism".

Like the cypherpunks, the crypto anarchists have a tense relationship with the law. In another text, the "Cyphernomicon",[117] May explains that society would face a "great divide: privacy vs. compliance with laws". He weighs in for privacy, pronouncing himself in favour of free speech and privacy, "even if it means some criminals cannot be caught". Instead of the law and the police, individuals should rely on "self-protection", "as seen in the gun debate". In his view, this would also have profound implications for contractual exchanges. The conventional approach of enforcing transactions via the threat to use force would fail. In the crypto space, transactions can only be voluntary since the parties are "untraceable and can withdraw at any time".

1.3.2.3 Convergence and Divergence

The emphasis on voluntary exchanges, free markets and the reliance on self-defence distinguishes May, the self-professed "crypto anarchist", from the community of cypherpunks to which he belonged. May freely admits that his radical vision is not shared by all of them.[118] His statement belies an obvious contradiction that divides the tech community: everybody dreams of a better world, but they cannot agree on how it should look. Is it to stress solidarity or selfishness? Shall it be egalitarian or individualistic? These are just some of the questions plaguing the whole movement until today.

However, on other points, the cypherpunks and the crypto anarchists concur. For instance, both emphasise the importance of protecting privacy. Both also believe in May's vision of crypto as a "building material for a new age", characterised by "Transnationalism and Increased Degrees of Freedom".[119] In their eyes, and those of the cypherpunks as well, governments will be unable to control citizens' movements and communications, so borders would become transparent.[120] This anti-statist and anti-legalistic spirit unites both groups.

1.3.3 *The Privatisation of Money*

The previous section has shown a strong aversion to the state and its law, which is shared by opposite sides of the political spectrum, albeit for very different

117 Timothy May, 'The Cyphernomicon' <https://nakamotoinstitute.org/static/ docs/cyphernomicon.txt> accessed 15 April 2024.

118 ibid.

119 ibid.

120 ibid.

reasons. Bitcoin, the first cryptocurrency, does not diverge in this respect. It also has been motivated by a distrust of the state and one of its most potent symbols and major prerogatives: minting and issuing "fiat" money.

1.3.3.1 The Creation of Trust Outside the State

A clear sign of this distrust in state-issued money is found in the Bitcoin chain's first block, the so-called genesis block. Its metatext contained the following information: "The Times 03/Jan/2009 Chancellor on brink of second bailout for banks." This was the actual headline on the front page of *The* Times on the day Bitcoin started. Its use in the genesis block is often seen as a sly hint at the power of states to manipulate the traditional financial system.[121]

The Bitcoin whitepaper itself was not couched in political terms but remained mostly on a technical level. It was also not distributed via the cypherpunk mailing list but a different one.[122] However, Nakamoto became more explicit about his intentions in a separate post. He noted that the root problem with conventional currency is all the trust required to make it work: First, trust in the central bank not to debase the currency; second, trust in commercial banks to hold and transfer the money electronically; and third, trust in all of them to respect privacy.[123] Nakamoto had thus shifted the focus from privacy concerns to the problem of trust.

Bitcoin promised to create trust without the state and financial institutions. This chimes with the tradition of the cypherpunks, which were also suspicious of the government and "other large, faceless organizations". But Nakamoto's whitepaper went beyond that. It focused on how trust could be created outside the state and the financial system. His creature, Bitcoin, has therefore been correctly characterised as a "trust machine". It responds to the needs of an increasingly globalised society, in which parties to transactions do not know each other and do not confide in a particular state or government. Trust is the prerequisite and necessary condition for facilitating mutual exchanges, which the crypto anarchists cared about. Undoubtedly, Bitcoin also struck a chord with them.

Again, the idea of creating digital money resonated with both extremes of the political spectrum. The left thought cryptocurrency could reduce the

---

121 See, e.g., Eric D Chason, 'How Bitcoin Functions as Property Law' (2018) 49 Seton Hall Law Review 129, 132.

122 cryptography@metzdowd.com.

123 Satoshi Nakamoto, 'Bitcoin Open Source Implementation of P2P Currency' <https://satoshi.nakamotoinstitute.org/posts/p2pfoundation/threads/1> accessed 15 April 2024.

government's power and the banks' control over the economy.[124] They also hoped that greater social justice could be achieved by overcoming what they saw as oligopolistic and anti-democratic arrangements between "big capital" and the government.[125]

On the "right" end of the political spectrum, Bitcoin nurtured the hope that the state's monopoly in issuing money could finally be crushed. Theorists such as Friedrich August von Hayek blamed this monopoly for the excessive incurrence of public debt, the propagation of inflation and the destruction of prices as a signalling mechanism.[126] They believed that alternative forms of private or "competitive" money could end these irregularities and lead to a more stable currency worldwide.

Both views favoured cryptocurrencies, though for opposing reasons. Indeed, their development was to separate money from political divisions that were present even within the breeding ground in which Bitcoin was nested. Despite the political and ideological differences of communities such as cypherpunks and crypto anarchists, they all were united in the hope for a different society, which they thought cryptocurrencies could bring. The political project underlying Bitcoin can thus be described as "effectively getting rid of politics by relying on technology".[127]

Although visions such as these may seem idealistic and naive, one must not underestimate their importance for the evolution of the crypto economy. Projects like DAOs are often informed by altruistic goals such as improving society, for instance, by a more sustainable use of resources or a fairer distribution of wealth. Coins and tokens can play an instrumental role in such projects, but at the same time, they represent considerable promises of wealth and can lead to new inequalities. Bitcoin has thus not resolved the underlying tension between cypherpunks and crypto anarchists. This tension is still present in debates over the future of cryptocurrency, for instance, when it is discussed whether the Bitcoin protocol should emphasise certainty or scalability, which has already led to a hard fork in the network.[128]

---

124 Primavera De Filippi, 'Bitcoin: A Regulatory Nightmare to a Libertarian Dream' (2014) 3(2) Internet Policy Review 1.

125 De Filippi and Loveluck (n 27) 3.

126 Friedrich August Hayek, *Denationalisation of Money: The Argument Refined* (3rd edn, The Institute of Economic Affairs 1990) 100–107.

127 De Filippi and Loveluck (n 27) 3.

128 See *supra* 1.1.1.5.

1.3.3.2 As History Goes, or How the State Appropriates Itself of Private Currencies

The idea of creating a currency without and outside of the state may seem radical, but it was not new. On the contrary, money – defined by its three characteristics as a means of payment, a store of value and a unit of account – also existed in private forms. Private money preceded the "fiat money" issued by the state, as Nick Szabo and others had demonstrated.[129]

The first money to be used seems to have been shells and animal bones.[130] After that came metals like gold and silver. The state merely "improved" the money quality by giving it its official seal and ensuring its composition through "coinage". Later, notes were issued when it was impractical to carry and store coins. The first of them also came from private individuals: goldsmiths. They accepted deposits of coins and issued receipts in the form of bearer certificates.[131] Commercial banks did the same by issuing "banknotes" in exchange for coins deposited with them.[132] These notes or "banknotes" embodied the issuer's promise to pay the holder a certain amount of coins that had previously been deposited with the issuer. Only after that were central banks created, eventually monopolising the power to issue "banknotes".

This "private origins" of money shows a recurring pattern throughout history: At first, the "market", i.e. civil society, develops some form of unit as a medium of exchange, store of value or unit of account. Then, the state comes in, appropriates itself of the innovation, improves it by vesting it with additional credentials, and uses it for its purposes. For those who doubt the accuracy of this prediction for cryptocurrencies, there is specific evidence in Latin America, which we will now consider.

1.3.3.3 Turning Private Money into Legal Tender: The Case of El Salvador

As discussed, some states plan to replace private cryptocurrencies with central bank digital currency. This approach tends towards the opposite extreme: fully embracing digital currencies as currency. Once again, the state will seize an innovation from society – which it had previously denounced – for

129 See Szabo (n 100); Carl Menger, 'The Origins of Money' (1892) 2 The Economic Journal 239; Hayek (n 126); Ludwig von Mises, *The Theory of Money and Credit* (Yale University Press 1953); Shahzavar Karimzadi, *Money and Its Origins* (Routledge 2012). Karl Marx already developed the idea that money originated from a commodity to serve the exchange of (other) commodities, see Karl Marx, *Das Kapital*, vol. 1 (42nd edn, Dietz Verlag 2021).

130 Szabo (n 100).

131 Stephen Valdez, *An Introduction to Western Financial Markets* (Springer 2015) 10.

132 Vincent Lannoye, *The History of Money for Understanding Economics* (2nd edn, Vincent Lannoye 2015) 141.

its purposes. Typically, state authorities will issue this currency on their own infrastructure. However, there are even examples of a cryptocurrency being adopted outright as the national currency.

This ground-breaking transformation was made in El Salvador, which in 2021 adopted a special act to become the world's first country to consider Bitcoin as legal tender.[133] The Central African Republic followed suit but has since retracted Bitcoin as an official currency.[134]

Even in El Salvador, the US dollar continues to be used for accounting purposes.[135] However, the Salvadorian Bitcoin Act (*Ley Bitcoin*) explicitly requires every economic agent to accept payments in bitcoins for goods and services offered, with an exception only for those which notoriously and evidently do not have access to the necessary technology.[136] Remarkably, the Act also obliges the government to provide alternatives that allow the user to execute transactions in the private cryptocurrency and rely on automatic and instantaneous conversion into dollars if he so wishes.[137] To comply with this obligation, the government has introduced an e-wallet to store cryptocurrency, the *Chivo*.[138]

The preamble of the Act cites the reasons for the decision to make Bitcoin legal tender: the constitutional obligation of the government to stimulate and protect private initiatives to provide the necessary conditions for the increase of national wealth, benefitting the majority of the population; the lack of access to financial services by about 70% of the population; and the state's obligation to facilitate financial inclusion.[139] The legislator also does not fail to mention that Bitcoin is a digital currency whose value is determined "exclusively by free-market criteria", and expresses the hope that its adoption as legal tender will stimulate economic growth and national prosperity.[140]

The result of this decision is a strange beast: a private cryptocurrency that is simultaneously a country's official currency. Effectively, El Salvador's government cedes its monetary sovereignty – which it had so far entrusted to the United States Federal Reserve – partly to a new technology over which it has no control. The International Monetary Fund (IMF) has strongly criticised the decision, citing, among other things, the dangers to financial stability, the

133 Decreto n° 57 'Ley Bitcoin' 9 June 2021 (D.O. 110 vol. 431).

134 Loi n°22.004 du 22 avril 2022 régissant la cryptomonnaie en République Centrafricaine.

135 See Art. 6 Ley Bitcoin.

136 Art. 7 and 12 Ley Bitcoin.

137 Art. 8 Ley Bitcoin.

138 See <https://chivowallet.com> accessed 26 September 2024.

139 Recital I, III and IV Ley Bitcoin.

140 Recital V Ley Bitcoin.

possibility of money laundering and terrorism financing, and the risks to consumers and the public purse.[141] In addition, the IMF expects lower economic growth in the country due to the government's decision.[142] Yet, given the absence of any conclusive data, it still seems too early to judge the results of what is undoubtedly a bold experiment.

1.3.4 *Conclusion*

Money is neither private nor public but hybrid. History shows how it is constantly swinging back and forth between two poles: society on the one hand and the state on the other. Digital currencies may be about to take this next logical step. Today, we have reached a situation in which the use of physical cash in the form of coins and notes has become all but impracticable. Sooner or later, it will be replaced by electronic money. As usual, private society precedes public entities in developing the technology. But one can already see the state catching up, with central banks on the cusp of issuing their digital currencies. This development is furthered by the changing needs of society and the evolving technical knowledge. But it may also be seen as a response to the problems inherent to cryptocurrencies and other privately issued digital assets, which will be discussed in the following section.

1.4 Legal Problems Created by the Blockchain

Cypherpunks and crypto anarchists aimed for the new cryptocurrencies to operate outside any legal system. Their belief in technology and the private market underpins their conviction that DLT will make legal discussions unnecessary. Nevertheless, cryptocurrencies and other crypto-assets raise several legal issues.

141 International Monetary Fund (IMF), 'El Salvador: 2021 Article IV Consultation-Press Release; Staff Report; and Statement by the Executive Director for El Salvador' (2022) <https://www.imf.org/en/Publications/CR/Issues/2022/01/26/El-Salvador-2021-Article-IV-Consultation-Press-Release-Staff-Report-and-Statement-by-the-512245> accessed 15 April 2024.

142 International Monetary Fund (IMF), EL Salvador country team and IMF Western Hemisphere Department, 'El Salvador's Comeback Constrained by Increased Risks' (2022) <https://www.imf.org/en/News/Articles/2022/02/15/cf-el-salvadors-comeback-constrained-by-increased-risks> accessed 15 April 2024.

1.4.1 *A Stomping Ground for Criminals*

1.4.1.1 Money Laundering, Terrorism Financing, Evasion of Taxes and Sanctions

The blockchain's objective – to create a global peer-to-peer transfer mechanism – may seem innocuous. Still, the fact is that the technology has been quickly used and abused for criminal purposes. One example is money laundering. Due to its pseudonymous nature, cryptocurrency lends itself to this activity. Some have complained there would be little evidence of blockchain applications being directly linked to actual money laundering,[143] but it is in the nature of this crime that precise numbers are not available. There can be hardly any doubt that the magnitude is considerable. The Financial Action Task Force (FATF), an intergovernmental organisation to combat money laundering and the financing of terrorism, conducts an annual review of virtual assets and their providers. The 2021 review observed that

> "assets are sometimes laundered through services which aim to obfuscate ownership by taking in assets, co-mingling them, and then providing outputs of equal value to users, less a transaction fee, in a process known as "mixing". Criminals also sometimes move assets across multiple addresses, VASP s, types of virtual asset, or different blockchains."[144]

Another use to which cryptocurrencies lend themselves is financing terrorism. For this purpose, dark net coins are used since they are fitted with a mechanism that obfuscates data, making it considerably harder to trace transactions. Crypto-assets may also be used for tax evasion. Fiscal authorities find it hard to identify income made on the blockchain.

A further field of application for cryptocurrencies and other digital assets is the evasion of economic sanctions. The FATF's 2021 report has observed "sophisticated illicit activity by state actors using virtual assets for sanctions evasion".[145] This may have increased after the Russian invasion of Ukraine and

143 Malcolm Campbell-Verduyn and Marcel Goguen, 'The Mutual Constitution of Technology and Global Governance ' in Malcolm Campbell-Verduyn (ed), *Bitcoin and Beyond* (Routledge 2017) 69, 75.

144 Financial Action Task Force (FATF), 'Second 12-month Review Virtual Assets and VASP s' (2021) 22 para 70 <www.fatf-gafi.org/publications/fatfrecommendations/documents/second-12-month-review-virtual-assets-vasps.html> accessed 15 April 2024. 'VASP s' means 'Virtual Asset Service Providers'.

145 See ibid para 71.

included state actors and private individuals, from oligarchs seeking to preserve their riches to ordinary Russian citizens striving to avoid capital controls.

Cryptocurrencies can thus be (ab)used to undermine state power. This aligns with the intentions of the communities they sprang from, the cypherpunks and crypto anarchists.

1.4.1.2 Drugs, Arms, Exploitation of Children, Human Trafficking, and Blackmail

Financial crimes are by far not the only ones committed through the use of the blockchain. Indeed, there are many others. These include drug and arms dealing, child exploitation (especially pornography) and human trafficking.[146] An illustration is "Silk Road", a black-market website otherwise known as "Amazon for drugs", on which not only drugs but also illegal firearms were offered against payment in bitcoins.[147] According to estimates, the network had facilitated around US$1.2 billion worth of trades by the end of 2013.[148] The authorities had tried to shut it down but only succeeded after several attempts.[149]

Because of its pseudonymous character, DLT can also be abused for blackmailing. Cryptocurrencies have become the payment method of choice for criminals who engage in computer crimes.[150] The case *AA v Persons Unknown* brought before the High Court in London illustrates the typical strategy: first, the victim's server is infected with a virus, and then ransom payment is demanded, in Bitcoin or another cryptocurrency.[151] The pseudonymous nature of these currencies ensures that the perpetrators can enjoy the proceeds of their attack with minimal risk of being caught. This differs notably from bank payments since a bank account holder can be easily identified.

146 See ibid.

147 See Nikolei M Kaplanov, 'Nerdy Money: Bitcoin, the Private Digital Currency, and the Case Against its Regulation' (2012) 25 Loyola Consumer Law Review 111, 127; Trautman (n 23) 56 et seq.; John O McGinnis and Kyle Roche, 'Bitcoin: Order without Law in the Digital Age' (2019) 94 Indiana Law Journal 1497, 1536.

148 McGinnis and Roche (n 147) 1536.

149 Trautman (n 23) 12.

150 See Financial Action Task Force (FATF), 'Second 12-month Review of Revised FATF Standards – Virtual Assets and VASPs' (2021) 22 para 71 <https://www.fatf-gafi.org/en/publications/Fatfrecommendations/Second-12-month-review-virtual-assets-vasps.html> accessed 15 April 2024 (noting "a large increase in the value of virtual assets collected as ransomware payments" in the last year).

151 High Court of England and Wales, 13 December 2019, *AA v Persons Unknown & Ors, Re Bitcoin* [2019] EWHC 3556 (Comm).

1.4.1.3 Comparison with Fiat Currencies

The widespread use of crypto-assets, especially cryptocurrencies, for criminal purposes may well be shocking. Indeed, the reputation of blockchain technology has been tainted: many associate the name with secretive and illegal activities. The reality of these abuses cannot be denied. At the same time, it is worth recalling that other payment methods can also be abused. It suffices to consider that the means of payment preferred by criminals is still fiat currency, the US Dollar. This has to do with the features of cash: it is fungible, easy to carry, and universally accepted. Because cryptocurrencies imitate some of these features, they lend themselves to the same abuse. Yet this should not be used as an argument for their outright prohibition, as nobody would envisage banning the US dollar because it is used for crime.

In comparison to fiat currencies, most cryptocurrencies even facilitate law enforcement because they leave an indelible trail of all past transactions. Once the obstacle of pseudonymity is overcome and the person behind the public key is identified, the blockchain provides a confirmed and trusted protocol for all its activities. This can be used as evidence in criminal proceedings. Proving crime thus becomes very easy.

While it is important not to downplay the danger of abuse of digital assets for financial crime, it is equally vital to not fall into the other extreme and overstress the dangers. Certainly, pseudonymity is an issue beyond those posed by official currency. In contrast to physical money, digital money can be transferred without actually meeting in person or going through any intermediary, such as a bank. The answer to this problem, however, is not to stifle innovation that is useful to protect privacy but to increase the IT capabilities of the agencies tasked with law enforcement.

The overarching point is this: The fact that distributed ledger technology can be abused does not undermine the value of this innovation. Rather than trying to nip it in the bud, the goal should be to update the computer capabilities of law enforcement agencies to match those of criminals. In this way, the advantages of technology can be enjoyed by law-abiding citizens and society at large.

1.4.2 *Risks for Investor Protection*

The crypto economy is a source of risk not only for the general interest but also for individual investors. Some of these risks will be analysed in the following.

1.4.2.1 Asymmetric Information

Many tokens issued in an ICO resemble financial securities. They aim to fund start-ups, particularly in the technology sector.[152] However, unlike securities,

152 See *supra* 1.2.1.2.

most ICOs lack a prospectus, which traditionally provides investors with a range of detailed information about the company and the instrument, and which is usually required before securities can be offered to the public. Instead, they rely on a "whitepaper", which typically gives only a brief description of the project.[153] These whitepapers are also often coy about the rights that the investor receives. Worse still, they even fail to specify the issuing entity against which such a right could be claimed or exercised: A wide-ranging study of over 1,000 ICOs found that a mere 32% of them mentioned the issuing entity, its country of origin, and its address.[154] There is thus an extreme form of information asymmetry between the issuer and the investors: the first receives the latter's money but reveals very little about their intentions or themselves. Though not excluded in the real world, this is rather widespread in the virtual world.

1.4.2.2 Ponzi Schemes, Fraud and Gambling

In a significant number of cases, token issuers are criminals who simply want to defraud investors. From the beginning, they intend to deceive and illegally obtain money. Many ICO s are outright "Ponzi schemes" or snowball systems.[155] Investors are attracted by the prospect of high dividends or interest, which will initially be paid from the funds they have provided themselves. The issuer will part with the money when he thinks the moment is right. Some ICOs are also simple scams, where no dividend or interest is ever paid to investors.[156] The emergence of these fraudulent schemes is greatly facilitated by the distance between the issuer and the investors, a typical feature of the crypto economy. Tokens may also be used for gambling, which may be banned in some jurisdictions.[157]

1.4.2.3 Technological Defects

Loss in the crypto economy may not only be caused by criminal activity. It can also be the consequence of technological malfunctions. These are especially dangerous in DeFi, which provides complex financial products on a fully automated basis. Any computer glitch may have disastrous consequences.

Structural risks compound these technological risks. In effect, the technology is not as decentralised and automated as it may appear to the uninitiated. On the contrary, given the dominant influence of a small team of programmers, it concentrates enormous power in very few hands. This has been called

153 Zetzsche and others (n 57) 278.

154 ibid.

155 On the concept of the Ponzi scheme, see Mervyn K Lewis, *Understanding Ponzi Schemes* (Edward Elgar 2015).

156 SEC, 'In re Munchee Inc, Securities Act of 1933' (Release No 10445, 11 December 2017) <https://www.sec.gov/litigation/admin/2017/33-10445.pdf> accessed 15 April 2024.

157 See, e.g., on China *infra* 2.1.1.1.

the "DeFi illusion".[158] The centralisation of DeFi carries enormous risks for investors, e.g. in case of mistakes or fraud. This is compounded by the typical lack of knowledge about those responsible.

1.4.2.4 Theft

Crypto-assets represent considerable value, so it is little wonder that they are often stolen. Yet in the blockchain world, theft mainly works by hacking, either by gaining access to the private key or, more efficiently, by finding loopholes in the network protocol or in the code of smart contracts.

Such hacking cases are notorious and the source of many scandals.[159] The pseudonymous nature of the blockchain makes finding the perpetrators very difficult. However, sometimes their identity is revealed, and they are brought to justice. Where the amount taken is extremely large, introducing a hard fork can be a measure of last resort.[160]

One should not inflate the dangers of blockchain, though. It is worth recalling that cash can also be stolen. Without a doubt, cryptocurrencies and other crypto-assets present particular risks due to the global and pseudonymous nature of the crypto economy.

1.4.2.5 Insolvency

The increasing involvement of wallets and crypto exchanges in storing private keys creates another problem: the possibility that the intermediary may go bankrupt. This risk exists as well outside the blockchain, for instance, in the context of intermediated securities.[161] But the blockchain may add a layer of complexity. An illustration is provided by the insolvency of Mt. Gox, the once leading crypto exchange. After a considerable amount of bitcoins had been stolen, Mt. Gox filed for bankruptcy in March 2014 in the United States.[162] In the following month, insolvency proceedings were also opened in Japan.[163]

---

158 Aramonte, Huang and Schrimpf (n 46).

159 See, e.g., on the cases of stolen assets at the crypto-exchanges Mt. Gox and Bitfinex McGinnis and Roche (n 147) 1535.

160 See on the case of "*The DAO*" *supra* 1.2.3.2.

161 Eva Micheler, 'Custody Chains and Asset Values: Why Crypto-Securities Are Worth Contemplating' (2015) 74 The Cambridge Law Journal 505, 525; Luc Thevenoz, 'Intermediated Securities, Legal Risk, and the International Harmonization of Commercial Law' (2007) 13 Stanford Journal of Law, Business & Finance 384, 426.

162 McGinnis and Roche (n 147) 1535.

163 Kelvin F K Low and Wu Ying-Chieh, 'The Characterisation of Cryptocurrencies in East Asia' in David Fox and Sarah Green (eds), *Cryptocurrencies in Public and Private Law* (Oxford University Press 2019) 216.

A client sued the trustee in bankruptcy for the segregation of "his" bitcoins from the bankruptcy estate. The Tokyo District Court dismissed the action on the grounds that cryptocurrencies could not be the subject of property rights because they lacked the physical attributes of tangible objects.[164]

More recently, the demise of the crypto exchange FTX, run by the elusive Samuel Bankman-Fried, hit the headlines.[165] It has led to the parallel opening of bankruptcy proceedings in the US and the Bahamas. The hedge fund Alameda Research, which was set up by Samuel Bankman-Fried and run by his erstwhile partner, had withdrawn very significant amounts of crypto-assets from the accounts of FTX. When this news transpired to the market, FTX tokens were sold massively and customers tried to withdraw their funds. Prosecutors speak about "one of the biggest financial frauds in US history".[166] Samuel Bankman-Fried was eventually sentenced to 25 years in prison.[167] Still, the bankruptcy administrator found sufficient assets to satisfy all creditors' claims.[168]

These cases illustrate the particular risks flowing from the uncertain private law status of crypto-assets. This risk is especially strong in insolvency proceedings, but may show in many other contexts as well, for instance in cases of transfers induced by error, fraud or blackmail.[169] Up until this day, many jurisdictions have no clear rules on how to treat digital assets in these situations. Worse, it is even unclear how the private law governing crypto-assets is to be determined.[170]

164 Tokyo District Court, Civil Division 28, Judgment of 5 August 2015 (Year of Heisei 27), Heisei 26 (Year of 2014), *MtGox,* (Wa)33320, see ibid 216–217; a full translation of the judgment is provided by Louise Gullifer and others <https://www.law.ox.ac.uk/sites/files/oxlaw/mtgox_judgment_final.pdf> accessed 15 April 2024.

165 See, e.g., David Yaffe-Bellany, 'How Sam Bankman-Fried's Crypto Empire Collapsed' (New York Times, 14 November 2022) <https://www.nytimes.com/2022/11/14/technology/ftx-sam-bankman-fried-crypto-bankruptcy.html> accessed 15 April 2024.

166 Ken Sweet and Larry Neumeister, 'Fallen cryto mogul Sam Bankman-Fried sentenced to 25 years in prison' (Associated Press News, 29 March 2024) <https://apnews.com/article/sam-bankman-fried-ftx-cryptocurrency-sentencing-sbf-d7bb1a5e94b4c22039d74dfeab1a2ff1> accessed 15 April 2024.

167 MacKenzie Sigalos Mangan Dan, 'FTX Founder Sam Bankman-Fried Sentenced to 25 Years for Crypto Fraud, to Pay $11 Billion in Forfeiture' (*CNBC*, 28 March 2024) <https://www.cnbc.com/2024/03/28/live-updates-ftx-founder-sam-bankman-fried-sentencing.html> accessed 12 June 2024.

168 'FTX Creditors Will Get Paid In Full. They Just Want Crypto Back.' *Bloomberg.com* (15 May 2024) <https://www.bloomberg.com/news/articles/2024-05-15/ftx-bankruptcy-will-pay-customers-over-100-but-they-missed-crypto-rally> accessed 12 June 2024.

169 See *infra* 3.1.1.1.

170 See *infra* 3.2.-3-4.

1.4.2.6 Can the Law Afford to Ignore Crypto Investors?

It is tempting to consider all investments in cryptocurrencies and other crypto-assets as falling outside of the legal system altogether. Such a view may in particular be defended with the anti-state and anti-legal attitude that lies at the heart of the development of Bitcoin.[171] Indeed, it may be argued that crypto investors consciously renounce the protections of the law, so the law should not assist them when they call for help.

Such a view would however be cynical. Humans constantly create value that is not provided for in the law. For instance, they conceive inventions or enter into novel forms of agreements. The law should protect the value arising from these activities because otherwise, it would not incentivise innovation. Moreover, it can create a feeling of profound injustice if goods in which investments have been made are taken away. In addition, the sudden loss of these privately created riches could also lead to considerable social problems.

Any asset that is assigned value by the citizens and is used for trade and commerce in practice should therefore be protected by the law, whether tangible or intangible. Of course, this does not exclude the possibility of the state prohibiting certain assets from trading and commerce, such as arms, drugs or body parts. The point is rather that an asset should not be excluded from legal protection *merely because* it is issued in intangible form.

This results also from the protection of property under international, supranational and constitutional law. As the European Court of Human Rights (ECtHR) has emphasised, the notion of "possessions" under the First Protocol to the European Convention on Human Rights is not limited to ownership of physical goods but also covers intangible phenomena.[172] In the virtual world, these play a role equivalent to tangible goods in the real world. In particular, they share with them important characteristics such as exclusivity, rivalrousness and market value.[173] For these reasons, the state cannot stand idly by when investors are defrauded or blackmailed, or their crypto-assets are stolen or hacked. It must provide a remedy.

---

171 See *supra* 1.3.2.

172 See ECtHR, 18 September 2007, *Paeffgen GmbH v Germany* App nos 25379/04, 21688/05, 21722/05 and 21770/05 (for internet domain names).

173 Christian Rueckert, 'Cryptocurrencies and Fundamental Rights' (2019) Journal of Cybersecurity 1, 7.

1.4.3 *Macroeconomic Dangers*

1.4.3.1 Undermining Monetary Policy

In the traditional monetary system, the central bank controls the amount of currency. It has various tools, such as overnight deposit rates or open market transactions, allowing it to either throttle or increase the money supply to respond to the current economic situation. This is considered the best way to avoid deflation or inflation and to keep the monetary system stable.

In contrast, on a distributed network, the issuance of coins is determined by technology. For example, the only way to create new bitcoins is through mining. Moreover, the amount of bitcoins is predetermined: Overall, the supply is limited to an amount of about 21 million.[174] In addition, the software is programmed so that the reward for mining will halve approximately every four years until it runs out entirely in 2140.[175] Therefore, it is to be expected that the price of bitcoin will increase over time, which is equivalent to deflation.[176]

Which of the two systems is better, the traditional monetary system or the crypto economy? This is hard to say.

Aficionados of cryptocurrencies will point to the many financial crises that the traditional monetary system has experienced in the past. They will also highlight that many of these crises were caused rather than prevented by central banks.[177] They will further denounce that central banks are subject to political influence despite the assurances of their independence.[178]

Yet entrusting the money supply exclusively to technology seems like putting a plane on autopilot and throwing away the key to the pilot's cabin. There may always be contingencies that require human intervention. Nobody knows what kind of catastrophes the future holds. Therefore, it seems audacious to fix the money supply once and forever, regardless of what will happen.

At the same time, one must not forget that many people live in countries with double-digit or even higher annual inflation and without any access to foreign currency. For them, Bitcoin or other crypto-assets may present an attractive alternative.[179] Let us also remember that about two billion people worldwide

174 Swartz (n 99) 629; De Filippi and Wright (n 26) 26; Antonopoulos (n 3) 26.

175 Antonopoulos, ibid; De Filippi and Wright ibid.

176 Antonopoulos, ibid.

177 See, e.g., Hayek (n 126) 100–105.

178 McGinnis and Roche (n 147) 1507.

179 For example, the Turkish lira, with an inflation rate of about 40%, became the most traded currency against the coin Tether in the fourth quarter of 2021, see Caitlin Ostroff and Jared Malsin, 'Turks Pile Into Bitcoin and Tether to Escape Plunging Lira' (Wall Street Journal,

do not have access to a bank account.[180] In their eyes, a free cryptocurrency that can be accessed 24/7 from any point in the world and cannot be controlled by a corrupt government must seem like a blessing.[181]

The question which of these systems, the traditional or the new, is better cannot be finally answered here. There are reasonable arguments for and against cryptocurrencies from a monetary viewpoint. One must also not exaggerate the risks. Certainly, the *exclusive* use of a cryptocurrency on a worldwide level, replacing all national currencies, would be an experiment with high stakes and uncertain outcomes. Fortunately, this is not the choice the world is facing. For the time being, private and public currencies co-exist and compete with each other. It seems that this situation will continue for the foreseeable future.

1.4.3.2 Source of Financial Instability

Many investors use coins and tokens not as a means of payment, but for speculation. This seems appealing because of the extreme price volatility of crypto-assets. To illustrate, in November 2021, Bitcoin's price exceeded US$67,000, before falling below US$19,000 only eight months later.[182]

All speculation involves risks. Yet, investing in the crypto economy can convey the feeling of gambling. Depending on the scale of their adoption, a sudden loss in the value of cryptocurrencies and other digital assets could have significant repercussions for financial stability in general. It can, for instance, affect financial institutions such as banks and investment funds that hold large quantities of digital assets. If these assets lose significantly in value, this may wreak havoc on the balance sheet of such institutions, which would, in turn, undermine the market's confidence in them. A crypto market crash could also negatively impact retail investors, some of whom have dedicated a considerable part of their portfolio to crypto-assets. If they lose out in a major way, this diminishes their wealth and may have adverse effects on the economy as well as negative social consequences.[183]

---

12 January 2022) <https://www.wsj.com/articles/turks-pile-into-bitcoin-and-tether-to-escape-plunging-lira-11641982077> accessed 15 April 2024.

180 McGinnis and Roche (n 147) 1530.

181 On the role of cryptocurrencies for financial inclusion, see Daivi Rodima-Taylor and William W Grimes, 'Cryptocurrencies and Digital Payment Rails in Networked Global Governance' in Malcolm Campbell-Verduyn (ed), *Bitcoin and Beyond* (Routledge 2018), 109.

182 See <https://www.cointracker.io/price/bitcoin> accessed 26 September 2024.

183 See also FSB, 'Assessment of Risks to Financial Stability from Crypto-Assets' (2022) 8 <https://www.fsb.org/2022/02/assessment-of-risks-to-financial-stability-from-crypto-assets> accessed 15 April 2024.

A particular source of risk is stablecoins. While their suggestive name creates the impression of stability, in fact, many of them are highly volatile. The reasons are often inherent defects: the composition of their asset portfolio is frequently opaque, and the rights of the investor with regard to the assets are not clearly defined.[184] If investors become suspicious, they will want to exchange the tokens again, which can lead to a "redemption run". In order to satisfy their claims, issuers must carry out massive sales of the underlying assets. These fire sales depress the market value of the assets even further.[185] Special dangers could be created if a "global" stablecoin would emerge one day as the dominant means of payment across many countries. It is to be feared that a loss of confidence in such a global stablecoin may disrupt the financial system and spill over to the whole economy.[186]

At the moment, these risks are relatively modest, given that crypto-assets only represent a small portion of the overall financial market. For the time being, we are far from a world in which day-to-day transactions are paid in cryptocurrencies or tokens. However, risks may rapidly escalate if crypto-assets were more widely adopted.[187]

1.4.4 *Environmental Concerns*

The proof-of-work mechanism, an essential feature of many distributed networks, needs vast amounts of energy. Estimates of how much vary widely. One of the more serious indications can be found on a website run by the University of Cambridge.[188] It shows that the Bitcoin network demands 0.64% of the world's energy consumption, or 0.32% of the world's electricity consumption.[189] This figure compares to the energy needs of countries such as Egypt or Poland.[190] The number is all the more significant if one considers that there are other proof-of-work networks than Bitcoin. The energy is actually wasted since the proof of work does not result in any useful outcome but merely serves to protect the network against frivolous attacks.

In the context of the threats posed by climate change, such a large energy consumption with no apparent purpose has caused criticism. The Bank for International Settlements, in particular, has slammed Bitcoin as having "few

184 ibid 11 and 13.
185 ibid 11 and 13.
186 ibid 14.
187 ibid 1.
188 Cambridge Centre for Alternative Finance, 'Cambridge Bitcoin Electricity Consumption Index (CBECI)' <https://ccaf.io/cbeci/index> accessed 15 April 2024.
189 As of 15 April 2022.
190 As of 15 April 2022.

redeeming public interest attributes when also considering its wasteful energy footprint".[191] The Financial Stability Board has noted that the significant energy consumption of proof-of-work-based crypto-assets makes them highly vulnerable to changes in jurisdictions' climate policies and may place strains on local utility infrastructure.[192] Some countries have banned the mining of cryptocurrencies because of the risk they put to the goal of becoming carbon-neutral.[193]

Yet assessing the blockchain's environmental impact is actually more complex than one might think at first blush. Because Bitcoin mining can be performed anywhere on the planet, it is possible to do it with cheap and clean energy, for instance, hydroelectric power.[194] Moreover, many newer cryptocurrencies have replaced the proof-of-work with a proof-of-stake mechanism. In the latter, it is no longer necessary to solve a mathematical riddle in the validation process. Instead, nodes evidence their serious intentions by pledging crypto-assets they have in the network as collateral for the correct performance of their validation function.[195] On these blockchains, validating and adding a new block can be done with less than 1% of the energy required for proof of work.[196]

Future improvements may thus well hold the answer to the nagging environmental problems of the crypto economy. It would also be wrong to judge distributed ledger technology in general as being environmentally unsustainable. Quite to the contrary, the blockchain could be used to make more efficient use of natural resources, for instance, through smart contracts or DAOs, which aim to use and share the amount of available water more efficiently.[197] It is thus all too easy to dismiss the blockchain as wasteful of energy. A more nuanced approach is in order.

1.4.5 *Conclusion*

The dangers resulting from the blockchain are considerable. They concern public and private interests alike and range from criminal activities to risks for investors to environmental concerns. None of them should be taken lightly.

191 BIS, 'Annual Economic Report 2021' 67 <https://www.bis.org/publ/arpdf/ar2021e.pdf> accessed 15 April 2024.

192 FSB (n 183) 10.

193 Alun John, Samuel Shen and Tom Wilson, 'China's Top Regulators Ban Crypto Trading and Mining, Sending Bitcoin Tumbling' (Reuters, 24 September 2021) <https://www.reuters.com/world/china/china-central-bank-vows-crackdown-cryptocurrency-trading-2021-09-24> accessed 15 April 2024.

194 McGinnis and Roche (n 147) 1545–1546.

195 Antonopoulos and Wood (n 32) 321.

196 Peter Howson, 'Tackling Climate Change with Blockchain' (2019) 9 Nature Climate Change 644, 644.

197 Howson (n 196).

Particularly grave is the risk that not only the state but the whole society could lose the power to make monetary policy. A situation is looming in which machines might take the place of central banks, which would be a tremendous experiment whose outcome is entirely uncertain.

On the other hand, innovations rarely come without risks or negative consequences. These must be weighed against their benefits. On the positive side, there is the possibility of having an incorruptible means for the secure storage and global transfer of value. The existence and accessibility of this mechanism may push globalisation to a whole new level. That it works via algorithms and does not depend on direct human intervention is merely a reflection of the fact that there is no global state and no global central bank that could fulfil this function.

In the end, a discussion about the merits or dangers of the crypto economy may prove pointless. History demonstrates that innovations were rarely halted because of their downsides. They just went on. It seems that the blockchain is no different in this respect.

1.5 Non-State-Centered Approaches to the Blockchain

The previous section has forcefully demonstrated why the state cannot ignore the blockchain. The new technology raises many issues, from the facilitation of crimes to risks for financial stability and investor protection as well as environmental concerns. This explains the ongoing debate about the need to regulate the blockchain. However, such regulation clashes with the spirit and ambition of the technology, which aims to operate independently of state institutions and outside their control. The following section will study three approaches to the relationship between law and blockchain.

1.5.1 *Alegality: the Crypto Economy Outside of the Law?*

As we have seen, the driving motivation behind the creation of Bitcoin was a deep distrust of the state and its institutions.[198] The cryptocurrency was developed to operate beyond national frontiers and without the support of any state or other institution. Consonant with these early roots is the view that the blockchain would operate outside the legal system, or in other words, that it would be "alegal".[199] This view reflects the cypherpunks' and crypto anarchists belief that the law is dangerous and unnecessary because technology

198 See *supra* 1.3.2.

199 De Filippi and Wright (n 26) 44.

will provide better solutions.[200] They see judges and attorneys as part of the state and "other large, faceless organizations" that must be disempowered. It is emphasised that the technology works entirely autonomously from the law: Whoever holds a crypto-asset according to the blockchain or receives a token thanks to a smart contract application *is* the entitled owner. According to this crypto-centric view, there is no way or need to question this truth.

Yet the characterisation of the blockchain as "alegal" disregards the complex social environment blockchains operate in. The previous section has shown many instances in which merely accepting crypto-assets' distribution as recorded on the blockchain is irreconcilable with the requirements of public policy, justice and morals. For example, society cannot simply stand by when the blockchain benefits money launderers or terrorists. It would also be shocking that fraudsters or blackmailers can keep the cryptocurrencies they have obtained. The same applies to thieves who have stolen coins or tokens through hacking. In these cases, the law must intervene and correct socially, politically or ethically unacceptable results. For this reason, the blockchain cannot exist outside the legal sphere in an "alegal" vacuum.

1.5.2 *"Code is Law": Self-Sufficiency of the Blockchain*

A more sophisticated approach is not to pretend that technology would work without a legal system but instead to suggest that the technology functions like legal rules. [201] This view is epitomised by the slogan "Code is law."

Lawrence Lessig has coined the expression in the context of the internet, i.e. in a much more general sphere than blockchain. Lessig emphasised that how certain websites, social media platforms, or applications are programmed limits the users' abilities in the same manner that legal rules do in the physical realm.[201] The "architecture" of the internet – composed of the hardware, the code and specific structures – would be able to constrain the behaviour of users. However, Lessig's conclusion was not, as is often thought, a plea for regulatory abstention or a legal free space. Quite to the contrary, he was advocating the need for stricter internet regulation. He warned that without state regulation, the internet would risk becoming a tool of control.[202] Therefore, governmental intervention would be needed urgently.

Those using the slogan "Code is law" often purposefully overlook this pro-regulatory intention. Instead, they use it to argue that the technology itself

200 See *supra* 1.3.2.

201 Lawrence Lessig, *Code And Other Laws of Cyberspace* (2nd edn, Basic Books 2006) 38–60.

202 ibid 1–8.

would be best positioned to sort out all problems arising from it.[203] They consider the blockchain as "self-contained": it would all be able – thanks to contractual mechanisms – to perform what currently only the law does.[204] There would be no room, no place for the law in the sense that there would be no entry gap where default rules made by the state could step in.[205]

This belief in code as a substitute for the law is as misguided as the idea that the blockchain would be "alegal". There are many legal problems for which technology does not provide an acceptable solution. These problems need a legal answer if the crypto economy is to evolve into a stable, rule-based business environment. For instance, it cannot be left to code whether a transfer was fraudulent because this question is outside of its perimeter. The Bitcoin protocol merely avoids the problem of double-spending but provides no solution to misrepresentations to the counterparty. Indeed, a solution for this problem seems very hard to put into code. In the same vein, the algorithm does not make any provision for the case of theft. By definition, theft occurs on the blockchain by *breaking* the code, so it would be overly optimistic to expect the code to solve this problem. Nor can the code resolve other questions, such as what happens in case of insolvency or the death of a crypto-asset holder.

While it is important to recognise the code as ruling behaviour similar to law, it would be a grave misunderstanding to take it *as* law. The law is more than a mere collection of rules; it has at least the appearance of being legitimate. This legitimacy is based on the conviction that the rules are just, i.e. the conformity with the *opinio iuris*, or that they have been produced in a legitimate way, i.e. that their adoption complies with the procedural rules laid down for legislation. Such a belief in the legitimacy of either the content or the creation procedure does not exist in the case of code. The latter is defined by a group of programmers whose identity is often unknown and whose values and attitudes are not necessarily shared by the users. Apart from rare exceptions,

---

203 See, e.g., ChangeHero, 'Ethereum Classic: Code Is Law' (Medium, 7 February 2020) <https://medium.com/coinmonks/ethereum-classic-code-is-law-f07f183d5f42> accessed 15 April 2024 (hailing Ethereum Classic as being true to the philosophical stance 'code is law'); CryptoIQ, 'Coding for Better Regulatory Outcomes in The Internet Age of Bitcoin and Blockchains' (Medium, 8 May 2016) <https://medium.com/@CryptoIQ.ca/coding-for-better-regulatory-outcomes-in-the-internet-age-of-bitcoin-and-blockchains-2ddad303fbd1> accessed 15 April 2024 (hoping that a younger generation will step up and oblige governments and regulatory bodies to "do no harm" by programming a better future for everyone and all).

204 Usha R Rodrigues, 'Law and the Blockchain' (2018) 104 Iowa Law Review 679 (examining the DAO and its relation to state-made law).

205 ibid 682.

there is no public discussion of the value of the code and no possibility to vote on it. Users are instead facing the binary choice of either accepting the code by downloading it to their computer or rejecting it. To compare such a system with the legal system of a democratic state is quite fanciful. Code even pales in comparison to many forms of dictatorship, where at least the dictator's personality is known and may be admired for his charismatic features in the Weberian sense. A code not reigned in or subject to the law evokes an Orwellian technocratic nightmare because it is both dictatorial and intransparent.

1.5.3 *Lex Cryptographia: the Blockchain as a Legal System*

The theory of the *lex cryptographia* goes one step further than the adherents of the (misunderstood) expression "Code is law". It does not allege that algorithms could be self-sufficient by setting their own rules. Instead, it claims that code could create a legal system. The authors of this theory, Aaron Wright and Primavera De Filippi, make a conscious comparison to the *lex mercatoria*, or *law merchant*, which was said to exist in medieval times and which some believe to govern transnational commercial relations today.[206] They predict that from the already existing *lex informatica* as an "alternative legal system", a new form of law would emerge, the *lex cryptographia*.[207]

What this exactly means is quite nebulous because the theory is used to support very different claims. These need to be unpicked and separately evaluated.

A first claim made by De Filippi and Wright is that code would create autonomous systems that the law would no longer govern.[208] In the authors' view, the need for centralised authorities – such as the state – could be lessened with the rise of the blockchain.[209] The digital representation of information in an encrypted and decentralised form would allow for direct, instantaneous and pseudonymous communication, thus promising a "more flexible and fairer space of interaction".[210] While the authors seem to think these changes could be helpful, they also warn that the new systems could be designed "to undermine and erode existing social structures".[211] They stress that the code could

206 Aaron Wright and Primavera De Filippi, 'Decentralized Blockchain Technology and the Rise of Lex Cryptographia' (Social Science Research Network 2015) 39; see also De Filippi and Wright (n 26) 5 et seq.

207 De Filippi and Wright (n 26) 5 et seq.

208 ibid 5.

209 Wright and De Filippi (n 206) 19.

210 ibid.

211 ibid 51.

circumvent and complement the law, depending on the developers' desired outcome.[212]

There is nothing new about these claims. De Filippi and Wright have just taken a leaf out of the playbook of the Cypherpunks and Cyber anarchists and put it into legal terms. What is worrying, though, is the ambiguity of the authors about their position regarding this development. For instance, they write that as blockchain-based autonomous systems become increasingly used to provide internet services, governments will "need to adopt new techniques and approaches to shape or regulate those services".[213] At the same time, they predict that the current framework of the rule of law would eventually be replaced by "a system of algorithmic governance, operated exclusively by the rule of code".[214] This constant flipping between the call for tighter government regulation and the prediction that these spaces cannot be regulated characterises the ambiguity of the theory developed, which in this sense is not without reminiscence to the dim predictions of the crypto anarchists.

Second, De Filippi and Wright claim that the state could use blockchain technology to apply its rules more automatically and efficiently.[215] They stress the government's ability to put its laws and regulations into code, which could help resolve the uncertainty surrounding the interpretation of many rules and make their implementation more consistent and predictable.[216] These rules could be highly customised and more easily "fine-tuned" to specific individuals.[217] Moreover, thanks to the automated nature of applications such as smart contracts, governments could ensure compliance with the law, while at the same time facilitating accountability.[218]

These claims are, by and large, correct. Essentially, there is no reason why the government should not use blockchain technology where this is useful to implement the law. The possibilities for applications have already been discussed in the literature under the term "RegTech".[219] Especially promising are those areas of the law that are very technical and whose rules follow an "if-then" logic, such as tax or social welfare law. As a side note, the technology

212 De Filippi and Wright (n 26) 52.
213 ibid.
214 ibid 204.
215 ibid 193.
216 ibid 195.
217 ibid 196.
218 ibid 197.
219 See, e.g., Douglas W Arner, Janos Barberis and Ross P Buckley, 'FinTech, RegTech, and the Reconceptualization of Financial Regulation' (2017) 37 Northwestern Journal of International Law & Business 371.

used in this case does not need to be based on distributed ledgers; it can also be centrally run because there is no need to involve the citizens of the whole world in the implementation of the laws of a particular state.

Where the authors go wrong, however, is to call such a system of automated law enforcement a "*lex cryptographia*". A human-made law remains the same regardless of how it is enforced. De Filippi and Wright do not properly distinguish between the legislative and the executive parts of the state. While it is not problematic and worrisome, but on the contrary valuable and welcome that the executive become less bureaucratic and more reliant on technology, the same is not true for the legislative function. In a democracy, laws are made through public debate and votes, not by anonymous coders. The fact that programmers put such laws into code does not change the fact that these laws are the product of collective decision-making. This simple fact becomes evident when the code diverges from the law: in this case, it must be corrected through administrative acts or the courts.

In a third and most problematic final step, De Filippi and Wright combine their two propositions and, at the same time, exceed them by claiming that the blockchain, as code, could eventually overcome the law. They predict that national laws will "get pushed to the edges",[220] and foretell an "algocracy" in which algorithms increasingly shape social interactions.[221] No longer would centralised institutions such as the state bureaucracy define the possible actions individuals may or may not take. Instead, programmers deploying a code would dictate informal and often "invisible" rules, thus turning the "rule of law" into the "rule of code".[222] De Filippi and Wright do not only see downsides in this but also find comfort in the idea that it may enable "individuals to self-govern and deviate from long-standing rules of law".[223] While they warn that "autonomous code" may restrain individual behaviour in new and unforeseen ways, they also find that algocratic systems in which computers and their programmers dictate deterministic rules "could improve society in demonstrable ways".[224]

This prediction is outrightly frightening. A society ruled not by law but by code is a very dim dystopia. The biggest danger of this society is that it hides the underlying values of the rules in force. The rules of code may function like

220 De Filippi and Wright (n 26) 52.
221 ibid 55.
222 ibid.
223 ibid 56.
224 ibid 207.

law, and even more efficiently so as they are self-executing, but they lack the legitimacy of laws that a legislator has adopted.[225] Whoever complains about the government has to ask itself whether a dictatorship of programmers would be any better.

But Wright and De Filippi offer a more optimistic view. In another paper, they predict that governments being replaced by DAOs will allow people to band together and set rules for their governance, collect taxes and distribute wealth "in ways the group believes is fair".[226] In their view, such communities could "form into nations, unbounded by geographical boundaries, and governed through a set of algorithmic rules that can be both established and enforced through voting mechanisms and smart contracts", which could lead to "techno-democratic systems, allowing for a diaspora to be governed and organized into a self-governing state".[227] People would not be bound by the laws of a particular state but would be "free to choose among a particular set of provisions that better reflect their underlying preferences or needs", with the possibility to participate in "two or more regulatory frameworks, arbitrarily switching between one or the other".[228]

This blatant utopia has nothing to do with life as we know it. The authors ignore that the state is and remains the central power, with the task to protect citizens and the monopoly to apply force in the real world. Instead, they want to take us to a virtual world where communities can be formed independently of location, nationality or other traditional criteria. This would allow all forms of legal arbitrage or "law shopping": for instance, the rich could band with other wealthy persons in a community with little or no taxes, or the young with other youngsters and decide not to pay any pensions. Even more worryingly, racists could enter a space with other like-minded in which racial slurs are explicitly allowed, or child pornographers may create a community where it is perfectly legal to share their collections of photos. Who will protect one of the members of these virtual communities against aggressions from another, or those outsiders that are not members of any of them?

It is safe to predict that such a system could not. Even those who believe in the existence of autonomous virtual spaces will have to recognise the need for a default community which fixes the rules on the ground and holds the monopoly to enforce them in the real world. At this point, this default community is

225 See *supra* 1.5.3.
226 Wright and De Filippi (n 206) 39.
227 De Filippi and Wright (n 26) 39.
228 ibid 41.

the state. Whether one likes it or not, there is no viable alternative in sight, at least not for the years and decades to come. An algocracy with a *lex cryptographia* certainly cannot replace democratically elected parliament and the rule of law.

Conclusion of Chapter 1

The blockchain is a disruptive technology that has had a transformative impact on the legal sphere. Specifically, it has allowed the creation of private cryptocurrencies, which vie with fiat currencies as means of payment and stores of value. It has also led to the emergence of other crypto-assets, such as digital securities, utility tokens and NFTs, and a surrounding ecosystem of novel digital service providers. By providing a secure, distributed ledger that can be used to safely store information and reliably authenticate the author, the technology has the potential to upend other areas as well. In the future, it may be used for many other applications, such as notarial certification, health data communication or keeping land registers. It may also be used by law enforcement, for instance, to collect taxes or distribute social welfare benefits.

However, it would go too far to think that the blockchain can replace the law. The rule of law and the principle of equality do not allow for the existence of an autonomous, alegal space. Undeniably, there are difficulties in enforcing legal rules against open networks such as Bitcoin, but that does not mean these networks would not be subject to the law. Since the law is a normative system, the fact that it can be broken must not be confused with a situation in which the law ceases to apply. A legal rule requires compliance regardless of whether it can be practically enforced or not. In time, the states may find ways to identify those who commit crimes on the blockchain accountable, such as they did about those committing crimes on the internet. It is be crucial to uphold the universal rule of law in all real or virtual spaces.

The short answer to the question posed in the title of this Chapter 1 is that the law and not the technology rules. This may be unsurprising for lawyers, but it is still strongly contested by the crypto community. Unabashedly, they claim a regulatory-free space for inventions and new communities, for instance, the participants of a DAO. These claims must be rejected.

Nevertheless, it is also true that the law should refrain from exploiting its dominance and being overly restrictive about technology. For instance, cryptocurrencies should not be prohibited merely because they can be abused for illegal purposes. Instead, one should develop the law further to make the technology function efficiently and comply with legal requirements. For this, the digital capabilities of the public administration, courts and the police need to be improved urgently. However, there are also theoretical questions that need to be solved. One of the most important is the law that governs blockchain. This is a challenging problem, given the nature and global reach of the blockchain. It will be addressed in the following two chapters, firstly from a public law perspective, and secondly from a private law perspective.

CHAPTER 2

The International Regulation of the Crypto Economy

Regulation has the objective of maintaining public interests. Financial regulation, more specifically, aims to safeguard financial markets' functioning, ensure financial stability, and protect investors.[229] Chapter 1 described how the emergence of cryptocurrencies and other digital assets threatens these aims. Over the last few years, financial regulators and supervisors worldwide have been very busy trying to avoid or at least reduce them. In doing so, they have faced particular challenges, to which they have responded by developing various approaches. These and their interaction on the global level will be discussed in this Chapter.

2.1 The Confusion over Policy

2.1.1 *To Prohibit, to Tolerate, or to Favour*

The many risks posed by cryptocurrencies and tokens have prompted various reactions from regulators worldwide. They range from a total ban on crypto products and services to special regulatory regimes favouring them. In between lies a whole spectrum of different approaches.

2.1.1.1 Prohibiting Crypto

Several countries have prohibited crypto products and services. China is the most prominent example, but such bans have also been adopted, for instance, by Algeria, Bolivia, Egypt, Kazakhstan, Morocco, Nepal, Pakistan, Turkey, and Vietnam, among others.[230]

These bans come in different shapes and forms. They can be limited to certain products, such as cryptocurrencies, while leaving tokens untouched. Alternatively, they may focus on a particular activity, such as crypto mining

229 See, e.g., John Armour and others, *Principles of Financial Law* (Oxford University Press 2016) 61–71 (discussing also the prevention of financial crime and other goals).

230 See John Riley, 'The Current Status of Cryptocurrency Regulation in China and Its Effect around the World' (2021) 7 China and WTO Review 135, 139; Matthias Lehmann and Tetsuo Morishita, 'General Report' in Matthias Lehmann and Tetsuo Morishita (eds), *Cryptocurrencies in National Laws – A Global Survey* (forthcoming Brill).

 | DOI:10.1163/9789004725140_004

or exchanging crypto-assets against fiat money. The bans may be addressed to companies and private individuals, or merely to intermediaries, such as financial institutions, which may be prohibited from accepting, transferring or storing cryptocurrencies. They may be laid down by law or issued by a regulator, such as the central bank or the authority charged with anti-money laundering.

The gamut of solutions is illustrated by the case of China, which shall be studied here in more detail. In the span of a few years, the People's Republic has gradually hardened its stance on cryptocurrencies and other crypto-assets. This was done not by formal legislation but through different notices jointly adopted by several supervisory authorities.

The first of these notices, issued in 2013, prohibited financial institutions from participating in Bitcoin-related business and submitted crypto exchanges to anti-money laundering rules.[231] It was signed by the central bank (the People's Bank of China), the Ministry of Industry and Information Technology, the Banking Regulatory Commission, the Securities Regulatory Commission, and the Insurance Regulatory Commission.

In 2017, the same authorities, together with the Office for Cyberspace Affairs and the State Administration for Industry and Commerce, issued a second notice to deepen and confirm the previous one.[232] This notice prohibited ICOs, i.e. the issuance of tokens. It was not restricted to China and required crypto exchanges to block Chinese residents from participating in such issuances overseas. At the same time, the notice also addressed cryptocurrencies by prohibiting their exchange against fiat money.

The last and, for the moment, final stage was reached by a notice of 2021.[233] The authors of this notice also include the Supreme People's Court, the Supreme People's Protectorate, and the Chinese police department, underscoring the seriousness of the will for enforcement. The notice outlaws crypto derivatives transactions. It also introduces various restrictions on crypto mining in China,

231 People's Bank of China and others, 'Five Ministries Issue Circular on Preventing Risks of Bitcoin' (人民银行等五部委发布关于防范比特币风险的通知), circular dated 3 December 2013 <http://www.gov.cn/gzdt/2013-12/05/content_2542751.htm> accessed 15 April 2024.

232 People's Bank of China and others, 'Public Notice on Preventing Risks of Fundraising through Coin Offering' (人民银行等七部门关于防范代币发行融资风险的公), 4 September 2017 <http://www.gov.cn/xinwen/2017-09/04/content_5222657.htm> accessed 15 April 2024. A non-official translation can be found under <https://blog.qtum.org/china-regulatory-update-fe6c8037c008> accessed 15 April 2024.

233 People's Bank of China and others, 'Notice on Further Preventing and Resolving the Risks of Virtual Currency Trading and Speculation' (关于进一步防范和处置虚拟货币交易炒作风险的通知), 15 September 2021 <http://www.pbc.gov.cn/en/3688253/3689012/4353814/index.html> accessed 15 April 2024.

the global centre for this activity at the time. Furthermore, the notice supplements the previous one by prohibiting crypto exchanges outside the People's Republic from providing services to Chinese residents. In practice, this extra-territorial aspect of the crypto ban is secured through the "Great Firewall", which allows the government to block access to certain internet websites from Chinese territory.

The story shows how China, which was once the epicentre of the crypto economy, has become increasingly sceptical and restrictive towards the new technology.[234] As motives, the regulatory authorities mention rampant speculation, fraudulent schemes, and illegal fundraising, which have led to social problems. However, this does not mean that the People's Republic would be hostile to blockchain technology. Quite to the contrary, it is very keen to support its development. Testimony to this is the adoption of a "Cryptography Law" in 2020, which aims explicitly at promoting "cryptographic work".[235] It is also worth remembering that the People's Bank of China intends to launch its national central bank digital currency (the e-CNY).[236] Perhaps the crack-down on private cryptocurrencies may have partially been motivated by the desire to exclude a rival to the governmentally issued digital currency.

2.1.1.2 Tolerating Crypto

Many countries take a neutral stance. They neither prohibit nor favour crypto products and services but tolerate them. This liberal approach rests on the notion that the dangers associated with the technology may be contained through regulation and do not justify a full-blown ban. The neutral attitude implies the application of general rules and regulations on the crypto economy.

A typical example of this approach is the United States of America. The country's legal system does not contain any prohibition of Bitcoin & Co., nor does it have a particularly favourable regime. At the same time, the US administrative authorities unremittingly apply the existing regulations to the new phenomena. This can be witnessed, for instance, in the application of anti-money laundering or securities law, which will be discussed in more detail below.[237]

The European Union follows a similar approach. It applies the rules on anti-money laundering and counter-finance of terrorism to crypto offerings.[238] The

234 See the overview by Riley (n 230) 140–145.
235 ibid 145.
236 See *supra* 1.2.1.6.
237 See *infra* 2.2.1.1.
238 ibid.

European Commission is currently exploring the extent to which the rules of financial markets law also apply to them.[239] However, the EU has recently adopted a specific regime, the Markets in Crypto-Assets Regulation (MiCAR), which aims at the remaining crypto-assets that do not fall into the category of financial instruments, and in particular stablecoins.[240] This regulation deviates somewhat from the tolerant approach by establishing restrictions tailored to the crypto economy.[241] But far from prohibiting the issuance or offering of crypto-assets, the EU seeks to provide a stable legal framework for the crypto economy.

This generally tolerant attitude of the US and the EU is followed by other countries of the Western world, such as Canada, Japan, and New Zealand, as well as by the vast majority of countries that do not have any special legislation on crypto-assets.

Sometimes, courts need to impose this tolerance. An example is India, where the central bank – the Reserve Bank of India – had prohibited supervised financial institutions from dealing in virtual currencies and providing services to individuals or business entities. The Indian Supreme Court overturned these prohibitions based on the constitutional freedom to practise a profession and conduct a trade or business.[242] After carefully considering the regulations in several other countries and the EU, the Court judged the prohibitions to be disproportional. In particular, it bemoaned that the Reserve Bank of India had not shown "at least some semblance of any damage suffered" by the regulated entities through virtual currencies.[243]

The Indian example may be exceptional. However, it showcases that states should consider less intrusive measures than a comprehensive prohibition to contain the risks that result from the crypto economy. In particular, applying existing regulations may serve the same purposes without infringing constitutionally protected liberties. Of course, this view is subject to the future development of the crypto sector, which cannot be predicted. At least now, sufficient evidence to justify a complete ban seems lacking.

---

239 *Infra* 2.2.1.2.

240 See *infra* 2.2.2.3.

241 See the discussion ibid.

242 Indian Supreme Court, judgment of 4 March 2020, *Internet and Mobile Association of India v. Reserve Bank of India*, Written Petition (Civil) No. 373 (2018), 178–180; on this judgment, see, e.g., Nakul Dewan and Rohan Andrew Naik, 'Let's Trade Crypto: Indian Supreme Court Quashes Prohibition' (OBLB, 19 March 2020) <https://www.law.ox.ac.uk/business-law-blog/blog/2020/03/lets-trade-crypto-indian-supreme-court-quashes-prohibition> accessed 15 April 2024.

243 ibid 177.

2.1.1.3 Favouring Crypto

A third approach is providing special rules favouring crypto products and service providers. Numerous countries foresee a lighter regulation for them than for others. Examples include typical financial centres, such as Abu Dhabi, Hong Kong, Liechtenstein, Singapore, Switzerland, and the United Kingdom.[244] The motive behind this favourable attitude is to pave the way for the further development of the technology and to attract service providers to the national territory, which promises highly skilled jobs and burgeoning tax revenues.

A particular tool to achieve this aim are so-called "sandboxes", which are safe harbours exempting service providers from specific regulations. These special regulatory frameworks allow providers to experiment with new services without having to incur heavy administrative overheads or risk violating existing laws. The first of these sandboxes was introduced in 2016 by the United Kingdom.[245] Many other countries have followed suit and introduced similar rules, such as Australia, Abu Dhabi, Canada, Hong Kong, Malaysia, Mauritius, the Netherlands, Singapore, and Thailand.[246] Particularly interesting is the example of Switzerland, which aims to become the global "crypto valley". Its law will now be considered more closely.

The Swiss sandbox permits companies to accept deposits of up to CHF 1 million without applying for a banking licence.[247] These deposits can be made in any currency, not just cryptocurrency. The service provider is, however, barred from remunerating such deposits with interest and must inform depositors that it is not supervised by the Swiss financial authorities and not covered by a deposit guarantee. The provision was adopted to foster the nascent Financial Technology (FinTech) sector and is not limited to crypto service providers.

Another pillar of the Swiss strategy is the "FinTech" license, a kind of banking license "light" specifically targeting the crypto-asset sector. It was introduced in 2019 and allows companies to accept crypto-asset deposits valued at up to CHF 100 million.[248] The company will be supervised by the Swiss Financial Markets

---

244 For an overview see Dirk A Zetzsche and others, 'Regulating a Revolution: From Regulatory Sandboxes to Smart Regulation' (2017) 23 Fordham Journal of Corporate & Financial Law 31, 64–66.

245 UK Financial Conduct Authority (FCA), 'Financial Conduct Authority's Regulatory Sandbox Opens to Applications' (9 May 2016) <https://www.fca.org.uk/news/press-releases/financial-conduct-authority%E2%80%99s-regulatory-sandbox-opens-applications> accessed 15 April 2024.

246 For an overview Zetzsche and others (n 244) 64–66.

247 See Art. 6(2) Swiss Banking Ordinance (*Bankenverordnung*).

248 See Art. 1b Swiss Federal Act on Banks and Savings Banks (*Bundesgesetz über die Banken und Sparkassen*).

Authority (FINMA), but is subject to less extensive audit and reporting requirements than ordinary banks. As in the case of the sandbox, the remuneration of deposits with interest is excluded, and the firm must inform the depositors that it is not covered by a deposit guarantee. Yet one cannot fail to see that the FinTech license has a considerably wider breadth than the sandbox by allowing 100 times more value of crypto deposits than of ordinary deposits.

One problem that haunts these and similar frameworks is what happens once the cap has been reached. In virtually all countries concerned, the business must then apply for a regular licence. This limits the space for experimentation and is thought to secure the interests of the public, investors and competitors. Regardless, the existence of a "sandbox" serves as a signal that a particular country is open to technological innovation in the financial sector. This signal may be enough to attract additional financial firms to its soil. Once installed there, they are likely to stay even if they cross the regulatory threshold, in which case they must apply for a regular licence.

2.1.2 *Technological Neutrality vs. Technological Specificity*

The different approaches may seem to be a matter of pure policy choices. However, in the background lurks a more fundamental problem: Is it justified to introduce special rules for a specific sector based on the technology it uses? Or should regulation be technologically neutral, i.e. the same for all products and services regardless of their technology? The debate predates the crypto economy and is not confined to it.[249] But without a doubt, it is of utmost significance to the regulation of the sector.

According to the principle of technological or "tech" neutrality, all types of technology that fulfil the same or similar functions should be treated equally. Underlying this principle is the fundamental idea that the market and not the regulator should decide whether a specific technology is worth adopting. The prime advantage of technological neutrality is that it does not favour an innovative product or service over competing offerings but maintains a level playing field between them. Another advantage is that it makes regulations future-proof and spares them from frequent changes depending on technological development.

The principle of technological neutrality has several consequences. It requires the state to accept the use of innovative services when dealing with public administration, for instance, transferring documents via the blockchain

249 See Brad A Greenberg, 'Rethinking Technology Neutrality' (2015) 100 Minnesota Law Review 1495, 1495–1496 (tracing the principle back to the US Copyright Act of 1976).

or paying taxes in cryptocurrency.[250] Furthermore, it calls for the strict enforcement of the same rules that apply to other products and services, such as the rules on anti-money laundering or tax law.[251] In the latter sense, technological neutrality is favoured by those states that regulate crypto service providers in the same or a similar way as traditional financial service providers.

In contrast, the technologically specific approach implies the introduction of special regimes for certain products or services depending on the technological solutions on which they are based. An illustration is the proposal made in the literature to adapt the regulation to the specific architecture of the underlying market infrastructures.[252] As the previous discussion has demonstrated, this may lead to either unfavourable or favourable regulatory treatment of an innovative technology. Hence, two versions of technological specificity must be distinguished. The first is to prohibit crypto products and services; the second is, on the contrary to favour them by applying lighter regulatory rules. None of these approaches can be discarded per se. The argument for the first approach is the specific dangers that follow from the technology, such as the possibilities for money laundering or tax evasion that the blockchain offers. In contrast, the argument for the second approach is the potential of the technology, which should not be killed in its infancy by overwhelming regulatory requirements. Which of the two approaches will be followed is not only a matter of whether one takes a pessimistic or an optimistic view of the technology but also depends on the specific circumstances of a given country, for instance, whether it has a well-informed investor base or can withstand financial shocks.

In sum, tech neutrality is not necessarily better than tech specificity. Even though it has certain advantages, such as its time-proofness, introducing more specific rules may be appropriate under certain circumstances. Everything depends on the circumstances and the goals of the legislator or regulator.

---

250 The partial payment of taxes in cryptocurrency is for instance allowed in Ohio, see Kari Paul, 'Some Americans Already Pay Their Taxes in Bitcoin' (MarketWatch) <https://www.marketwatch.com/story/believe-it-or-not-some-americans-already-pay-their-bitcoin-in-taxes-2019-01-07> accessed 15 April 2024.

251 On these two aspects of tech neutrality, see Matthias Lehmann, 'Global Rules for a Global Market Place? – The Regulation and Supervision of Fintech Providers' (2020) 38 Boston University International Law Journal 118, 133–134.

252 Syrene Johnstone, *Rethinking the Regulation of Cryptoassets* (Edward Elgar 2021) 261–265 (suggesting a 'Determined-by-Architecture' taxonomy as the basis for regulating crypto technology).

2.1.3 *What Makes the Crypto Economy Special?*

The starting point for designing specific rules starts with a basic question: What features set blockchain technology apart from others and may call for a different treatment? In other words, why do we discuss here legal rules for the "crypto economy" and not for another domain, e.g. the "tech sector" or the "digital services sector"? Is it justified to use "crypto" instead of another notion to draw legal boundaries?

Several features can be identified that may serve as grounds for a more special treatment of the crypto economy compared to other industries, such as the technology or the digital services sector.

One of these characteristic features is pseudonymity, which is very specific to the crypto economy because it relies on cryptography. Pseudonymity offers vast opportunities for hiding a person's identity, which may justify introducing special rules. These rules may be prohibitive because of the dangers of pseudonymity, such as the possibility of abuse or crime. However, they may also be liberal because pseudonymity protects personal data and privacy.

Another feature of the blockchain that may justify a different regulatory treatment is the possibility of storing information in a way that protects it from change. Immutability is one of blockchain's hallmarks, distinguishing it from internet websites' ever-changing content. Immutability allows the permanent storage of information, which makes the blockchain more than a communication medium but a store of value. This feature also calls for special rules, be they restrictive – such as a prohibition of non-governmentally issued "money" – or permissive – such as excluding the need to store information about securities with a central depository.[253]

A third particularity of the crypto economy is its vulnerability to cyberattacks and software errors, i.e., its high operational risk.[254] The absence of human control and reliance on technology invite criminals to exploit security gaps to obtain crypto-assets, whose value can be considerable. Even without criminal activity, the software itself may fail due to bugs. Such defects and shortcomings also plague traditional financial firms, which increasingly

253 An example is the exclusion of certain rules of European Union financial law by the Pilot Regime (Regulation (EU) 2022/858 of the European Parliament and of the Council of 30 May 2022 on a pilot scheme for market infrastructures based on distributed ledger technology, [2022] OJ L 151, p. 1), see especially Art. 5.

254 Dirk A Zetzsche, Ross P Buckley and Douglas W Arner, 'The Distributed Liability of Distributed Ledgers: Legal Risks of Blockchain' (2018) University of Illinois Law Review 1361, 1377–1382 (citing inter alia tampering with data, cheats, brute-force and denial-of-service attacks); Philipp Paech, 'The Governance of Blockchain Financial Networks' (2017) 80 Modern Law Review 1073, 1085–1086 (discussing software loopholes in smart contracts).

optimise their processes through the broad-scale use of digital technology. Yet the crypto economy is special because it is built exclusively on algorithms and automated processes such as smart contracts, which can hardly be stopped. This may call for specific rules to protect against dangers for public and private interests.[255]

In sum, the blockchain presents specific characteristics that make it special. Whether these particularities justify the departure from the principle of technological neutrality is, in the end, for every legislator or regulator to decide. In doing so, it must respect the framework of its constitution and of international law, for instance, the freedom to exercise business or the principle of non-discrimination. Still, that leaves some margin of discretion, which may be exercised differently. The need to introduce a separate regime also depends very much on the structure and content of the existing rules, which will differ from country to country. It may thus not be said in the abstract whether the particularities of the crypto economy justify the introduction of special rules. One can, however, give the following advice to legislators and regulators: You should strive to achieve your objectives while maintaining a level playing field between different providers and not foreclose the rise of a particular technology based on limited knowledge about its potential.

2.2 The Confusion over Legal Categories

In most legal systems, the crypto economy is subject to regulation, whether it is more restrictive, identical or more favourable than that of other product and service providers. This makes it necessary to submit crypto-assets to a certain legal category, either an existing one (2.2.1) or a new one (2.2.2).

2.2.1 *Searching an Existing Category for Crypto-Assets*

Typically, the law contains distinct rules for specific categories of products, services and actors. For example, bank deposits are usually subject to one set of rules, securities to another, and insurances yet to another. The emergence of blockchain has confronted financial and legal authorities with a conundrum. What is a Bitcoin? Is it money? Or a security? Or something else?

Similar questions have been raised by other disruptive technologies before. For example, courts had to decide whether online taxi services, such as Uber,

255 An example is the the European Union's DORA Regulation (Regulation (EU) 2022/2554 of the European Parliament and of the Council of 14 December 2022 on the digital operational resilience of the financial sector, [2022] OJ L 333, p. 1).

are to be regarded as employers of the drivers or not.[256] Officials of various municipalities have been scratching their heads over whether online rental platforms, such as Airbnb, are to be considered as landlords, real estate agents, or merely as fora on which interested parties meet.[257] This is not to mention the numerous questions arising from artificial intelligence.[258]

Cryptocurrencies and tokens similarly upend state practice by defying any legal categorisation. In the words of the Indian Supreme Court, they

> "elude an exact and precise definition, making it impossible to identify them as belonging either to the category of legal tender or to the category of commodity/good or stock solely".[259]

George Friedman, the founder of Geopolitical Futures LLC, puts it even more bluntly:

> "Bitcoin is neither fish nor fowl ... The problem with bitcoin is not that it is not issued by the government, nor that it is unregulated. The problem is that it is hard to see what bitcoin really is."[260]

Against this background, it is appropriate to present the existing legal categories, starting with (1) money, then (2) securities, and ending with (3) goods, to understand to what extent cryptocurrencies might correspond to one of them.

---

256 CJEU, Case C-434/15 *Asociación Profesional Elite Taxi v. Uber Systems Spain SL* [2017] ECLI:EU:C:2017:981; Court of Appeal of England and Wales, 19 December 2018, *Uber BV and others v Aslam and others* [2018] EWCA Civ 2748, on appeal UK Supreme Court, 19 February 2021, [2021] UKSC 5.

257 CJEU, Case C-390/18 *Airbnb Ireland UC, Association pour un hébergement et un tourisme professionnels (AHTOP) et al [2019]* ECLI:EU:C:2019:1112 (asserting that the AirBnB platform is not a real estate agent but rather a provider of information society services); see also Cour d'appel de Paris, Pôle 4, Chambre 4, 30 janvier 2023, n° 20/08067 (upholding a first instance judgment that considered AirBnB as a content "*éditeur*" (publisher) and not simply an internet "hébergeur" (host), and therefore ordered the platform to pay damages for unlawful rental).

258 From the already considerable body of literature on the subject of AI, see, e.g., Bart Custers and Eduard Fosch-Villaronga (eds), *Law and Artificial Intelligence* (Springer 2022); Charles Kerrigan, *Artificial Intelligence: Law and Regulation* (Edward Elgar 2022); Thomas Wischmeyer and Timo Rademacher (eds), *Regulationg Artificial Intelligence* (Springer 2019).

259 Indian Supreme Court (n 242) 28.

260 George Friedman, 'Opinion: Why It Matters If Bitcoin Is a Currency or a Commodity – MarketWatch' <https://www.marketwatch.com/story/why-it-matters-if-bitcoin-is-a-currency-or-a-commodity-2017-12-13> accessed 15 April 2024.

2.2.1.1 Money

A first characterisation that comes immediately to mind when characterising Bitcoin is "money". This category seems especially appropriate for cryptocurrencies since they were designed to replace traditional or "fiat" currencies. Thus, it appears sound to take their inventors at their word and regulate cryptocurrencies as money.

Implementing this view is not as easy as it may seem, though, because the term "money" is not without ambiguity. "Money", in the sense of "fiat money" or "currency", is the official means of payment issued by a state, consisting primarily of banknotes and coins.[261] Besides fiat money, private, dematerialised money is also created by commercial banks. This so-called "scriptural money" or "book money" comes into being when a bank opens a loan for a customer, which she can then spend.[262]

Contrary to common belief, fiat and book money are not the same. Only fiat money has legal tender status, which means that any creditor must accept it for the settlement of debt.[263] The creditor has no duty to accept book money, i.e. the transfer of a sum to its account for the same purpose, but is free to do so. Even more importantly, only fiat money, i.e. notes and coins, can be the subject of property rights, whereas book money is legally speaking nothing more than a debt the bank owes to its customer. For this reason, economists also call it "account money".[264] One author has gone so far as to declare book money as "something which legally does not exist".[265] This is, however, wrong: book money is often considered money, especially by regulatory rules, such as those by the central bank on monetary policy or those fighting money laundering and the financing of terrorism. Book money can be money, also in the legal sense of the term.[266]

Cryptocurrency does not fall under either fiat or book money category: neither is it state-backed nor does a bank owe it to its clients. Hence, it is hard to characterise cryptocurrency as "money".

---

261 Wouter Bossu and others, 'Legal Aspects of Central Bank Digital Currency: Central Bank and Monetary Law Considerations' (2021) IMF Working Paper No. 20/254 8 <https://papers.ssrn.com/abstract=3758088> accessed 15 April 2024; Krispis calls this the 'money-res', Elias Krispis, 'Money in Private International Law' (1967) 120 Collected Courses of the Hague Academy of International Law 191, 201–203.

262 Bossu and others (n 261) 8.

263 See Charles Proctor, *Mann on The Legal Aspect of Money* (7th edn, Oxford University Press 2012) 74 para 2.25 ("legal tender is such money in the legal sense as the legislator has so defined in the statutes which organize the legal system").

264 Krispis (n 261) 203 footnote 24.

265 ibid 203.

266 See Proctor (n 263) 27 para 1.34 (explaining that claims against commercial banks are money according to the institutional theory).

In some jurisdictions, a third category is "electronic money" or "e-money".[267] This is a digital representation of a sum of official money previously deposited with an intermediary, such as a bank or a payment service provider.[268] Cryptocurrency does not fall into this category either because it does not necessarily result from the deposit of fiat money. While stablecoins backed up by official money may come very close to e-money, this is not true for other cryptocurrencies with no such backing.

In sum, cryptocurrency is very different from traditional money. This is also true from an economic perspective. At least for the time being, they do not serve, to the same extent as fiat money, the triple functions of 1. means of payment, 2. store of value, and 3. unit of account. The current usage of most cryptocurrencies focuses on the second function, less on the first, and almost never on the third. This does not exclude the possibility that they might one day fulfil all three economic functions of money. That day will come when they are accepted by many shops, restaurants and other businesses, displaying their prices in bitcoins, for example. However, some countries already regard cryptocurrencies as money in the legal sense of the term. Sometimes, this has been done by amending legislation or a simple judicial interpretation. The consequences have been vastly different.

The first and most radical consequence of the characterisation of cryptocurrencies as money is that they are considered incompatible with the state's monopoly to issue money and, as such, illegal. Countries that prohibit crypto products or services have often used this reasoning.[269] Frequently, they point out that virtual currencies do not have legal tender status and should not circulate in the market like currency.[270]

This legal reasoning is not immune to criticism: if cryptocurrencies are not legal tender, then they cannot usurp the function of the official currency, and are, therefore, unable to subvert the sovereign monopoly to coin money. This applies even more strongly to tokens, many of which do not have a payment function and thus do not even purport to compete with an official currency. But such a critique cannot deny that there are other powerful reasons to justify a prohibition of cryptocurrencies and tokens, such as their speculative nature

267 See, e.g., the EU's E-Money Directive (Directive 2009/110/EC of the European Parliament and of the Council of 16 September 2009 on the taking up, pursuit and prudential supervision of the business of electronic money institutions [2009] OJ L267/94).

268 See Proctor (n 263) 50 para 1.80.

269 See *supra* 2.1.1.1.

270 For an example, see the Chinese 'Notice on Further Preventing and Resolving the Risks of Virtual Currency Trading and Speculation' (n 233).

and the fact that they provide a hotbed to many illegal activities, like gambling, fraud, pyramid schemes, or money laundering.[271]

A different approach is fully embracing cryptocurrencies and giving them legal tender status. This decision has so far been adopted only by very few countries.[272] In any case, it requires specific legislation.[273]

Most countries have not fallen for either of these extremes but adopt a middle position: They neither prohibit cryptocurrencies nor accept them as legal tender. Instead, they regulate them as money.

Such regulation has emerged first in anti-money laundering and the fight against terrorism financing. The authorities charged with these tasks quickly established a legal parallel between cryptocurrency and money. As early as March 2013, hardly more than four years after the first bitcoin transfer, the Financial Crime Enforcement Network (FinCEN), a sub-unit of the US Treasury, issued a "guidance" on applying its regulations to cryptocurrencies.[274] These regulations were marked by a very traditional notion of currency, referring to the coin and paper money of the US "or any other country".[275] This would have excluded Bitcoin, which is not issued by any state. Yet the regulations also cover "other value that substitutes for currency".[276] The FinCEN believed cryptocurrencies fall under the latter category because they can be exchanged against fiat currencies. For this type, the agency used the notion of "convertible virtual currency", which should be treated like "real" currency. Therefore, those dealing with cryptocurrencies were qualified as "money transmitters", making them subject to the federal anti-money laundering and counter-terrorism financing rules. Incidentally, they also need a license in each state in which they are active.[277]

This approach trailed a blaze that others were happy to follow. Among the first was the French Authority of Prudential Control and Resolution (*Autorité de contrôle prudentiel et de résolution* – *ACPR*), which published a position paper on Bitcoin operations in France in January 2014.[278] Similar to its American

271 See *supra* 1.4.

272 See *supra* 1.3.3.3.

273 ibid.

274 FinCEN, 'Application of FinCEN's Regulations to Persons Administering, Exchanging, or Using Virtual Currencies' (18 March 2013, FIN-2013-G001). See also the later update FinCEN, 'Application of FinCEN's Regulations to Certain Business Models Involving Convertible Virtual Currencies' (9 May 2019, FIN-2019-G001).

275 31 CFR § 1010.100(m).

276 31 CFR § 1010.100(z)(ff)(5)(i)(A).

277 Carol R Goforth, 'The Case for Preempting State Money Transmission Laws for Crypto-Based Businesses' (2020) 73 Arkansas Law Review 301, 303.

278 Autorité de Contrôle Prudentiel et de Résolution (ACPR), 'Position de l'ACPR relative aux opérations sur Bitcoins en France' (Position 2014–P-01, 2014) <https://acpr.banque

counterpart, it focused on exchanging the new cryptocurrency against fiat money and classified this type of service as a payment service.

Similarly, Japan amended its Payment Services Act in 2016 and included a new chapter on cryptocurrencies.[279] The Japanese legislator used the term "virtual currencies", which confused markets over the legal tender status of Bitcoin and other crypto-assets included in the definition.[280] In 2019, the legislator changed the terminology to "crypto-assets" and imposed stringent rules for service providers, such as brokers, exchanges and custodians. Since then, the provision of crypto-exchange services requires prior registration with the Prime Minister.[281]

The European Union took more years to follow up. In 2018, it introduced in its anti-money laundering and counter-terrorism financing regime a new category of "virtual currency", to which the same rules as to currency apply.[282] This rule is not restricted to convertible virtual currency but goes way beyond. It covers every digital representation of value that "does not possess a legal status of currency or money, but is accepted by natural or legal persons as a means of exchange and which can be transferred, stored and traded electronically".[283] This definition relies on the general public's practical acceptance of virtual money.

The approach that becomes visible here could be called "sociological". Cryptocurrencies are not characterised as fiat money, but legal consequences are derived from the similar function they play in practice. Anyone brokering relationships or transactions involving cryptocurrencies (or virtual currencies) is subjected to the same duties as those brokering monetary transactions denominated in foreign currency. For example, they must subject their clients to a so-called "know-your-customer" (KYC) procedure, which requires, among other things, identification. In addition, they are also subject to the so-called "travel rule" under the Transfer of Funds Regulation, which requires them to collect

-france.fr/contenu-de-tableau/position-de-lacpr-relative-aux-operations-sur-bitcoins-en-france> accessed 9 June 2023

279 See Lehmann and Morishita (n 230).

280 See, e.g., Sam Nemazie, 'Is Bitcoin Legal Tender In Japan?' (Seeking Alpha, 24 December 2017) <https://seekingalpha.com/article/4133681-is-bitcoin-legal-tender-in-japan> accessed 15 April 2024.

281 ibid.

282 See Art. 3 No. 18 Directive (EU) 2015/849 of the European Parliament and of the Council of 20 May 2015 on the prevention of the use of the financial system for the purposes of money laundering or terrorist financing [2015] OJ 2015 L141/73, introduced by Art. 1(2)(d) Directive (EU) 2018/843 of the European Parliament and of the Council of 30 May 2018 [2018] OJ L156/43.

283 ibid.

and hold information about the parties of each transfer, such as the name, account number, address, official personal document number, customer identification number, date and place of birth of the payer, as well as the name and payment account number of the payee.[284]

Another area in which cryptocurrency and money have been equated is tax law. In 2015, the Court of Justice of the EU held in its now famous "Hedqvist" decision that Bitcoin should be treated as currency for the purposes of the Union's Directive on Value Added Tax (VAT).[285] Similarly to anti-money laundering, the Court of Justice referred to the use of cryptocurrency as a means of payment, making it more similar to a traditional currency than to a good or service. The Court of Justice also excluded treating Bitcoin like cheques, other negotiable instruments, or a current or deposit account.[286] It called Bitcoin and its progeny "non-traditional currencies", which have no purpose other than being a means of payment and being accepted by certain operators.[287] On that ground, it could only compare with "traditional currencies", i.e. banknotes and coins used as legal tender. As a result, the exchange of bitcoins against fiat money was considered exempt from VAT under the EU Directive. It must be noted that this case only dealt with tax law and has hardly any bearing on other issues, such as financial regulation.

While the sociological approach may appear as an elegant solution, it can simultaneously be the source of confusion. On the one hand, cryptocurrencies are denied the legal status of money; on the other hand, they are treated legally as money. As a result, cryptocurrencies are in a legal twilight zone: they are not official currencies but are regulated similarly. The approach reminds that of *Humpty Dumpty* in Lewis Carroll's famous novel:

> "When I use a word ... it means just what I choose it to mean – neither more nor less."

Alice replies:

> "The question is ... whether you can make words mean so many different things."

---

284 See, e.g., Art. 4(1) and (2) Regulation (EU) No 2023/1113 of the European Parliament and of the Council of 31 May 2023 on information accompanying transfers of funds and certain crypto-assets (recast) [2023] OJ L150/1. On the travel rule, see also *infra* 2.6.2.1.

285 CJEU Case C-264/14 *Skatteverket v. David Hedqvist* [2015] ECLI:EU:C:2015:718, para 57.

286 ibid paras 37–53.

287 ibid paras 49 and 52.

To which *Humpty Dumpty* retorts:

> "The question is ... which is to be master—that's all."[288]

Indeed, the state, as the ultimate master, can label whatever it wants as currency. It can even invent new words, such as "virtual currency", and put it on an equal footing with state currencies for the purposes of anti-money laundering and countering the financing of terrorism while refusing to recognise it as legal tender. This approach is unlikely to satisfy those who prefer clear doctrinal categories, yet it has the virtue of being pragmatic. It is an attempt to avoid grave dangers resulting from the emergence of new forms of payment without nipping the innovative power of blockchain technology in the bud.

One can hardly blame the regulators for the ambivalence of their legal characterisation of Bitcoin & Co. It merely reflects the ambiguous design of these crypto-assets, which oscillate between the categories of fiat money and private book money, or "fish and fowl". Thus, the founders of DLT have created themselves the legal problems which their technology is now facing.

2.2.1.2 Securities

Apart from "money", crypto-assets can also be assimilated to "securities" or financial instruments, such as shares or bonds. This characterisation seems particularly apt for investment tokens, many of which embody shareholdings in companies or bondholder rights. Yet it does not sit equally well with utility tokens, which merely offer possibilities to use a specific service, or with payment tokens, whose function is similar to that of currencies. This suggests drawing the categories along the lines of token types, as explained earlier.[289] Things are more complicated, however, because there are many hybrid crypto-assets, which mix the functions of investment, utility and payment token, while others do not embody any rights at all and often lack a known issuer.

One approach is to ignore such subtleties and apply securities law to virtually all crypto-assets. This method is followed by the US Securities and Exchange Commission (SEC). Its report on the famous case "*The DAO*" is a good illustration.[290] It is worth reviewing this report as it offers some general lessons.

As mentioned, "*The DAO*" issued tokens providing voting rights on projects submitted to its members.[291] In the SEC's opinion, however, these tokens were

288 Lewis Caroll, *Through the Looking Glass* (Henry Altemus Company 1897) 123.
289 See *supra* 1.2.1.2.
290 SEC (n 89).
291 See *supra* 1.2.3.2.

securities, the distribution of which to investors domiciled in the US required a previous registration statement by the issuer and an accompanying prospectus to enable potential buyers to make an informed investment decision. The agency reached this conclusion by applying the famous "Howey Test", named after a 1946 decision by the US Supreme Court, which, up until this day, defines the notion of an "investment contract", the fall-back category for the notion of "securities" under US law.[292] Under the Howey Test, an "investment contract" requires the cumulative presence of four elements: 1. an investment of money, 2. in a common enterprise, 3. with a reasonable expectation of profits from 4. the entrepreneurial or managerial efforts of others.[293]

The SEC did not spend much time with the first condition: Though the members of "*The DAO*" had provided Ether and not fiat money, the agency thought that this constituted "value" and hence could be characterised as an "investment of money".[294] The second element was relatively obvious: Although the parties did not know each other, they were engaged in a "common enterprise", much so like the investors in a public company.

The third element was somewhat problematic. Many members had joined "*The DAO*" to be part of a first-of-its-kind technological experiment, and it was also very unsure whether the organisation would ever make any revenue. Yet the SEC underscores that the investors stood to share any profits made on the projects voted on and that "a reasonable investor" would have been motivated, "at least partly", by the prospect of profits that could be generated by an increase in the token value.[295]

The final and most problematic issue was whether the expected profits were derived from the entrepreneurial or managerial efforts of others. The very concept of "*The DAO*", which was to make management decisions in a decentralised manner, seemed to speak against the presence of this criterion. But not in the opinion of the SEC: It highlights first that the founders of "*The DAO*" had put significant efforts into developing the algorithm for the decentralised organisation and into the making of proposals while holding themselves out to investors as Ethereum and blockchain experts; and second, that a group of individuals called the "Curators" had the power to suggest new projects and review any proposals made by the others.[296] In the eyes of the SEC, these were the persons on whose efforts the investors substantially depended and relied. In contrast,

292 US Supreme Court, 27 May 1946, *SEC v. W.J. Howey Co.*, 328 U.S. 293 (1946).

293 ibid 301.

294 Note that the US CFTC characterises Ether as a commodity, see *infra* 2.2.1.3.

295 SEC (n 290) 12, 15.

296 ibid.

their voting rights would not give them meaningful control because they could mostly only accept or reject proposals made by the founders or the Curators.

The SEC's approach is particularly rigid. While it is true that tokens can be used for investment purposes, the agency wilfully ignores the many other motivations investors in DAOs may have more than merely monetary aims, such as contributing to technological innovation or furthering projects in the public interest. As a result, virtually any crypto-asset will qualify as a security and thus fall under the US securities laws. This leads not only to the requirement of a registration statement and an accompanying prospectus but also to the applicability of other rules, such as the anti-fraud provisions and the prohibition of insider trading.[297] The SEC actively controls their observance. In the last years, it has brought many enforcement actions against a wide range of offerings, making it the most active crypto supervisor in the world.[298]

In comparison, the EU approach is less pro-active. Until today, it has not been finally decided whether crypto-assets may be characterised as "financial instruments" (essentially securites in the US sense) and thus trigger the application of regulatory texts such as the Prospectus Regulation or the Markets in Financial Instruments Directive (MiFID) II. The European Commission has published a consultation on this issue to make up its mind.[299] Among the

297 Sec. 10b Securities and Exchange Act and Rule 10b-5 promulgated thereunder.

298 See, e.g., the actions brought against Poloniex LLC, SEC, *SEC v. Poloniex, LLC*, 9 August 2021, Proc. File No. 3–20455, <https://www.sec.gov/news/press-release/2021-147> accessed 15 April 2024; SEC, *SEC v. Rivetz Corp, Rivetz International SEZC, and Steven K Sprague*, Litigation Release No. 25198, 8 September 2021, Proc. File No. 3:21-cv-30092 (D Mass Sept 8, 2021), <https://www.sec.gov/litigation/litreleases/lr-25198> accessed 15 April 2024; SEC, 'SEC Files Subpoena Enforcement Action Against Terraform Labs and Its CEO' (Litigation Release No. 25262, 12 November 2021) <https://www.sec.gov/litigation/litreleases/lr-25262> accessed 15 April 2024; US District Court for the Southern District of New York, *Securities and Exchange Commission v. Terraform Labs PTE, Ltd and Do Kwon*, No. 21-mc-810 (S.D.N.Y, SEC complaint lodged 12 November 2021) <https://www.sec.gov/litigation/litreleases/2021/lr25262.htm> accessed 9 June 2023; US District Court for the Southern District of New York, *SEC v. Telegram Group Inc and TON Issuer Inc*, 448 F. Supp. 3d 352 (S.D.N.Y. 2020) (decision of 24 March and 1 April 2020); US District Court for the Northern District of California, 30 March 2022, *In re Tezos Securities Litigation*, 17-cv-06779 (N.D. Cal. 2022), order by judge Richard Seeborg <https://www.courtlistener.com/docket/6230817/in-re-tezos-securities-litigation> accessed 13 November 2023; SEC, 'SEC Charges Ripple and Two Executives with Conducting $1.3 Billion Unregistered Securities Offering' (2020–338, 22 December 2020) <https://www.sec.gov/news/press-release/2020-338> accessed 15 April 2024; SEC, 'BlockFi Agrees to Pay $100 Million in Penalties and Pursue Registration of its Crypto Lending Product' (2022–26, 14 February 2022) <https://www.sec.gov/news/press-release/2022-26> accessed 15 April 2024.

299 European Commission, 'Consultation Document on a EU-Framework for Crypto-Assets' <https://ec.europa.eu/info/law/better-regulation/have-your-say/initiatives/12089

various types of financial instruments listed in MiFID II, the only one seemingly fitting for crypto-assets is that of "transferable securities". However, EU law is missing a substantive definition of the term, and the CJEU has yet to decide on its interpretation. Without clarity at Union level, Member States are free to conduct their own assessments.[300] What already seems clear, however, is that the EU is unlikely to equate nearly as many crypto-assets with securities as the US. The very existence of MiCAR, which regulates crypto-assets that do not qualify as financial instruments, bears witness to a contrary approach.

2.2.1.3 Commodities

Even in the US, not all crypto-assets are considered to be securities. An exception is made for the two most important cryptocurrencies, Bitcoin and Ether. The Commodity Futures Trading Commission (CFTC), which enforces the Commodity Exchange Act, categorises them as "commodities".[301]

To understand how the CFTC came to this position, it is necessary to delve into some details of the agency. Historically, the CFTC started as the supervisor over the market for agricultural products. However, many trades over such products are not to be fulfilled on the spot, but at some later point in the future. They are derivatives, such as "options", "forwards", or "futures".[302] In addition to the physical commodity markets, the CFTC supervises the commodity derivatives markets. This raises the question of what "commodities" actually are. The Commodity Exchange Act contains a precise list of mainly agricultural products, but at the end provides a catch-all clause that includes "all services, rights, and interests in which contracts for future delivery are presently or in the future dealt in".[303]

The first time the CFTC applied this definition to Bitcoin was in the case *CoinFlip*.[304] The defendants had created and operated a platform where Bitcoin options – "calls" and "puts" – could be traded without having previously registered with the agency. The CFTC ruled that

-Directive-regulation-establishing-a-European-framework-for-markets-in-crypto-assets /public-consultation_en> accessed 9 June 2023.

300 See, e.g., Corte di cassazione, decision of 17 September 2020, No. 26807.

301 See the case law *infra*.

302 On these different instruments, see Alastair Hudson, *The Law on Financial Derivatives* (6th edn, Sweet & Maxwell 2017).

303 Sec. 1a(9) CEA (7 U.S.C. § 1a(9)).

304 Commodity Futures Trading Commission (CFTC), 'In re Coinflip, Inc., d/b/a Derivabit, and Francisco Riordan' (CFTC Docket No. 15–29).

> "The definition of a "commodity" [by the Commodities Exchange Act] is broad [...] Bitcoin and other virtual currencies are encompassed in the definition and properly defined as commodities."[305]

Consequently, the CFTC considered the platform a "swap execution facility", which must be registered with the agency. Since the platform operator had failed to apply for such registration, the CFTC issued a cease-and-desist order.

Later, the CFTC extended its control from the oversight of derivatives markets to the underlying spot markets on which Bitcoin is traded, insofar as fraud or manipulation is involved.[306] For instance, it applied the antifraud provisions of the Commodity Exchange Act to a Bitcoin Ponzi scheme that did not involve future contracts.[307] It also claimed jurisdiction over a virtual currency trader who allegedly had misappropriated investors' funds.[308]

US courts have accepted the CFTC's view that Bitcoin is a commodity.[309] There is some tension with the SEC, which also claims jurisdiction over crypto-assets. However, a director of the SEC has signalled a possibility of compromise by stating that Bitcoin and Ether were *not* securities because of their decentralised nature, which would lead to the absence of any managerial or entrepreneurial efforts on the part of others.[310] This does not extend to crypto-currencies that have a central operator. In the eyes of the SEC, that is the case with Ripple's XRP, which the SEC claims to be a security.[311] The first instance ruled that Ripple is a security insofar as it is sold to institutional investors but not when sold to retail investors, on the theory that only the first would have nurtured a reasonable expectation of profits.[312] The SEC's appeal to this – quite

305 ibid 3.

306 Commodity Futures Trading Commission (CFTC), 'A CFTC Primer on Virtual Currencies' (LabCFTC, 2017) slide 11 <https://www.cftc.gov/sites/default/files/idc/groups/public/documents/file/labcftc_primercurrencies100417.pdf> accessed 15 April 2024 (finding the CFTC has jurisdiction "if there is fraud or manipulation involving a virtual currency traded in interstate commerce").

307 *CFTC v. Gelfman Blueprint, Inc.*, Case No. 17–7181 (S.D.N.Y. filed Sept. 21, 2017).

308 See *CFTC v. McDonell*, 287 F. Supp. 3d 213, 228 (E.D.N.Y. March 6, 2018).

309 *CFTC v. McDonell*, 287 F. Supp. 3d 213, 228 (E.D.N.Y. March 6, 2018), reconsideration denied, 321 F. Supp. 3d 366 (E.D.N.Y. 2018); *CFTC v. My Big Coin Pay, Inc.*, 334 F. Supp. 3d 492, 495–98 (D. Mass. 2018); *CFTC v. Reynolds*, (S.D.N.Y. March 2, 2021) Comm. Fut. L. Rep. P 34,935 para 25.

310 William Hinman, 'Digital Asset Transactions: When Howey Met Gary (Plastic)' <https://www.sec.gov/news/speech/speech-hinman-061418> accessed 15 April 2024.

311 See the complaint in *Sec. & Exch. Comm'n v. Labs, Inc.*, 20-cv-10832 (S.D.N.Y. December 22, 2020).

312 *SEC v. Ripple Labs, Inc.*, 682 F.Supp. 3d 308 (S.D.N.Y. July 13, 2023).

unusual – judgment is currently pending in the courts. Thus, there remains room for interagency conflict over who is competent to rule on crypto-assets, especially if other agencies like FinCEN also claim a stake in this area.

The debate retraced here is due to the particular supervisory landscape in the US, which features several different agencies with often overlapping jurisdiction. Internationally, the characterisation of cryptocurrencies as a commodity is rather exceptional. Nevertheless, the discussion perfectly illustrates the uncertainties and challenges crypto-assets create for very established legal systems. These uncertainties and challenges also have a flipside because they create risks for the crypto economy itself.[313] In particular, it remains unsure which legal rules it has to obey.

2.2.2 *Introducing a New Regulatory Category*

Given the difficulties of incorporating crypto-assets into the received nomenclature, some legislatures have embarked on a different path and introduced novel categories to capture the new phenomena. The following analysis provides some examples; it is by no means exhaustive.

2.2.2.1 Virtual Currency

Several legal systems have devised a new notion of so-called "virtual currencies". In the EU, this category is merely a sub-category of currency and leads to the application of anti-money laundering and counter-terrorism finance rules.[314] However, the notion takes on an independent role in other parts of the world.

This is the case for the State of New York, which in 2015 introduced a "BitLicense" as a prerequisite for conducting any "Virtual Currency Business Activity".[315] The term "Virtual Currency" covers not only cryptocurrencies but "any type of digital unit that is used as a medium of exchange or a form of digitally stored value".[316] The legislator has added that the notion should be "broadly construed to include digital units of exchange" regardless of whether they are centralised or decentralised and whether they "may be created or obtained by computing or manufacturing effort".[317] Remarkably, the category "Virtual Currency" is not restricted to assets recorded on a blockchain or another distributed ledger. However, the New York legislator has excepted

313 Syrene Johnstone (n 252) 208.

314 See *supra* 1.4.1.1.

315 N.Y. Comp. Codes R & Regs. Tit. 23 § 200 (2019).

316 ibid § 200.2(p).

317 ibid.

from the definition digital units used solely within online gaming platforms, have no market or application outside of those gaming platforms, and cannot be converted into or redeemed for fiat money or virtual currency. Examples of such a digital unit are the V-bucks used in the online game "Fortnite" or the gold in "World of Warcraft".[318] "Virtual Currency Business Activity" is equally given a broad meaning and includes, for instance, receiving, transmitting, storing, holding, maintaining custody or control of, buying, selling, controlling, administrating, or issuing Virtual Currency in the sense of the law.[319]

To obtain a BitLicense, the applicant must provide a variety of information, including its business structure, financial situation, and profit model. The license holder must comply with various obligations regarding its capital, the custody and protection of customer assets, risk and anti-money laundering assessment, and cyber security.[320] It must also inform the supervisory authority of any material change to its business, maintain books and records, file reports and financial disclosures, permit and assist examinations of itself and its affiliates, prepare a written business continuity and disaster recovery ("BCDR") plan, and keep advertising and market material for at least seven years.

At first blush, New York's BitLicense is a model for rational regulation and can prevent or at least reduce the dangers resulting from the new crypto economy. It is worth highlighting, however, that the new law has not been copied by other states in the US or the world. The result was an exodus of crypto firms from New York State.[321] The mayor of New York City even urged the State to abandon the law because it would stifle innovation and economic growth.[322]

This story shows the difficulties of imposing regulatory requirements that are out of sync with those of other countries. When trying to avert the problems of the crypto economy, a state cannot go it alone; it needs to coordinate and cooperate with others.

---

318 On these and similar items, see, e.g., Chris Stalmans, 'More than Just Games: Virtual Property Rights in Massively Multiplayer Online Games', 12 Asper Rev. Int'l Bus. & Trade L. 203 (2012).

319 N.Y. Comp. Codes R & Regs. Tit. 23 § 200.2(q) (2019).

320 N.Y. Comp. Codes R & Regs. Tit. 23 §§ 200.8–9,15–16 (2019).

321 Usman W Chohan, 'Oversight and Regulation of Cryptocurrencies: BitLicense' in Stéphane Goutte, Khaled Gesmi and Samir Saadi (eds), *Cryptofinance* (World Scientific 2021).

322 Jesse Coghlan, 'New York Mayor Urges State to Abandon "Stifling" BitLicense Scheme' (Cointelegraph, 28 April 2022) <https://cointelegraph.com/news/new-york-mayor-urges-state-to-abandon-stifling-bitlicense-scheme> accessed 17 May 2023.

2.2.2.2 Digital Asset

France has taken another approach by introducing a special regime for those that provide services relating to "digital assets" (*actifs numériques*). Under this notion, the French legislator regroups 1. utility tokens (*jetons d'usage*) and 2. virtual currencies, as defined by the European anti-money laundering regime.[323] Expressly excluded from the notion "digital assets" are assets that – even though they are based on a distributed ledger – qualify as financial instruments; these are submitted to the rules of securities law. The French legislator has also introduced a new category of intermediaries, that of the "Providers of Services Relating to Digital Asset" (*prestataire de services sur actifs numériques*, or "PSAN"). The relevant services are defined in a very broad manner and include, inter alia, the custody over digital assets, the purchase and sale of such assets against fiat money, the exchange of digital assets against other digital assets, the operation of a platform on which digital assets are traded, the reception and transmission of orders and the portfolio management relating to such assets, the advice relating to them, and various forms of placement of such assets.[324]

Those that render such services are subject to several regulatory requirements. They must be of good repute, have the necessary competencies to perform their duties, and be capable of complying with anti-money laundering and countering terrorism finance rules; in the case of legal persons, these requirements also apply to those that hold more than 25% of the capital of the digital asset service provider.[325] They must also have professional liability insurance or sufficient capital, adequate security and internal controls, a resilient and secure information technology (IT) system, and a system for managing conflicts of interest.[326] French law also imposes rules of conduct, such as the obligation to provide clear, accurate and non-misleading information, warn the customer of the risks associated with digital assets, and segregate the client's digital assets from their own.[327]

Remarkably, these rules do not cover the issuance of digital assets. This can be explained by the fact that such issuance is not a "service". Nevertheless, the French legislator has introduced a special license for token issuers (*émetteurs de jetons*).[328] The token (*jeton*) is defined in the following way:

323 Art. L54-10-1 French Monetary and Financial Code (*Code monétaire et financier*).
324 Art. L54-10-2 French Monetary and Financial Code.
325 Art. L54-10-3 French Monetary and Financial Code.
326 Art. L54-10-5 French Monetary and Financial Code.
327 Art. L54-10-5 French Monetary and Financial Code.
328 Art. L552-1 – L552-7 French Monetary and Financial Code.

> "a token is any intangible asset representing, in digital form, one or more rights that can be issued, recorded, stored or transferred by means of a shared electronic recording device that allows the owner of the asset to be identified, directly or indirectly."[329]

The obtainment of the license is purely voluntary and comes with relatively few obligations, in particular the provision of clear, accurate and non-misleading information to the public.[330] It is offered only to issuers incorporated or headquartered in France.[331] The French license for token issuers is thus better understood as a brand of quality than a mandatory requirement.

The French notion has, however fallen victim to subsequent developments. In particular, it has been displaced by the EU's MiCAR, which will be discussed now.

2.2.2.3 Crypto-Asset

On 31 May 2023, the European Union adopted the Markets in Crypto-Assets Regulation ("MiCAR").[332] This text provides a fundamental legal framework for the crypto economy. It fully applies from 31 December 2024 throughout the 27 EU Member States. At the same time, the Regulation has very significant extraterritorial effects because it covers every offer of crypto-assets and related services towards residents in the EU. Because of the size of the Union's market, it is to be expected that MiCAR will become a cornerstone of the global crypto economy's legal framework.

MiCAR contains many rules that resemble mini-versions of existing regulations for financial services. For instance, it contains disclosure rules for the whitepaper that are similar to, but less extensive than those governing the prospectus required for the issuance of financial instruments under the Prospectus Regulation;[333] it also provides rules for "investment service providers" that are reminiscent of those governing market operators and investment firms (MiFID II/MiFIR[334]);[335] it furthermore features capital requirements which are

329 Art. L552-2 French Monetary and Financial Code (translation by the author).

330 Art. L552-4 French Monetary and Financial Code.

331 Art. L552-5 French Monetary and Financial Code.

332 Regulation (EU) 2023/1114 of the European Parliament and of the Council of 31 May 2023 on markets in crypto-assets [2023] OJ L150/40.

333 Art. 6, 19, 51 MiCAR.

334 Directive 2013/36/EU of the European Parliament and of the Council of 26 June 2013 relating to the taking up and pursuit of the business of credit institutions and to the prudential supervision of credit institutions and investment firms [2013] OJ L 176/338; Regulation (EU) No 575/2013 of the European Parliament and of the Council of 26 June 2013 on prudential requirements for credit institutions and investment firms, [2013] OJ L 176/1.

335 Art. 59 et seq. MiCAR.

similar to those that apply to banks and securities firms;[336] and it even includes rules on on-going disclosure, insider trading and market manipulation that are modelled on those reigning on traditional capital markets (MAD/MAR[337]).[338]

The scope of MiCAR covers a wide range of activities and services, including the issuance, exchange for funds or other crypto-assets, custody, or operation of a trading platform for such assets.[339] It thus addresses virtually all crypto economy actors, from issuers to crypto exchanges and wallet providers.

The fulcrum of MiCAR is the notion "crypto-asset", defined as "a digital representation of a value or a right which may be transferred and stored electronically, using distributed ledger technology or similar technology".[340] It must be borne in mind that the Regulation does not apply to financial instruments, which remain regulated by other texts, such as MiFID II/MiFIR and MAD/MAR. Thus, most investment tokens are outside of the new Regulation's scope. Its focus is on cryptocurrencies, payment tokens, utility tokens, and stablecoins.

MiCAR's rules are tiered according to different types of crypto-assets, with an escalating level of regulation. The least strict rules are foreseen for cryptocurrencies and utility tokens. They require the issuer to publish a whitepaper with a mandatory minimum content and in a particular form.[341] They also regulate marketing communications by the issuer.[342]

A second tier is reserved for "asset-referenced tokens", which are regulated more strictly. The key element of an asset-referenced token is that it "purports to maintain a stable value by referencing to any other value or right or a combination thereof, including one or more official currencies".[343] This definition covers both stablecoins backed by reserve assets and synthetic stablecoins, which purport to maintain their value by referencing an index or other external parameters.[344] On an equal footing with asset-referenced tokens, the EU legislator has put "e-money tokens", which refer to a single official currency.[345] E-Money tokens have been explicitly submitted to the EU's rules on electronic

336 Annex IV, Art. 67 MiCAR.

337 Market Abuse Directive (Directive 2014/57/EU of the European Parliament and of the Council of 16 April 2014 on criminal sanctions for market abuse, [2014] OJ L 173/179); Market Abuse Regulation (Regulation (EU) No 596/2014 of the European Parliament and of the Council of 16 April 2014 on market abuse, [2014] OJ L 173/1).

338 Art. 86–92 MiCAR.

339 Art. 2(1), 3(1) No 18.

340 Art. 3(1) No 5 MiCAR.

341 Art. 6 MiCAR.

342 Art. 7 MiCAR.

343 Art. 3(1) No 6 MiCAR.

344 See Recital 41 MiCAR.

345 Art. 3(1) No 7 MiCAR.

money.[346] Asset-referenced and e-money tokens are treated the same for most other purposes. In particular, the issuer of both must be based in the EU and needs authorisation by the national supervisory authority – unless it is a credit institution, which is supervised anyway.[347] The granting of such authorisation depends on several conditions being met, which resemble those required for credit institutions and investment fund managers. Inter alia, MiCAR requires robust government arrangement and that the managers of the issuer "are of sufficiently good repute and possess appropriate knowledge, skills and experience to manage the applicant issuer".[348] Moreover, issuers of asset-referenced and e-money tokens are subject to capital requirements that are not as strict as those for banks or investment firms but may still be challenging to meet, especially for start-ups.[349] MiCAR also provides miniature versions of the rules for acquiring qualified holdings in banks and for recovery plans to be drawn up by them.[350] The required content of the whitepaper is more detailed than for other crypto-assets; in particular, it must include information about the referenced assets and an easy-to-understand summary with key information, as well as data about the consensus mechanism's impact on the climate and other environmental risks.[351] In addition, MiCAR sets standards for marketing communications and ongoing information, procedures for handling complaints, and conflicts of interest.[352] For instance, the issuer of asset-referenced tokens must publish ongoing information to holders about the number of tokens in circulation and the value and composition of the reserve assets, which must be updated at least every month.[353] Crucially, the Regulation also contains specific requirements regarding the segregation of the reserve assets from those of the issuer, as well as their custody and investment.[354] Furthermore, it grants investors redemption rights similar to those of investors in mutual funds.[355]

The third tier concerns "significant" asset-referenced or e-money tokens. These are defined by certain thresholds, such as the number of holders, the

346 Art. 48(2) MiCAR.

347 Art. 16 et seq., 48 MiCAR.

348 Art. 18(2)(i) MiCAR.

349 Art. 35 MiCAR (requiring own funds in the amount of EUR350,000 or 2% of the reserve assets or a quarter of the fixed overhead of the previous year, whichever is the highest). More complex requirements apply to the own funds of e-money-token issuers, see Art. 5 E-Money Directive.

350 Art. 41 et seq. MiCAR.

351 Art. 19 MiCAR.

352 Art. 29–32 MiCAR.

353 Art. 30 MiCAR.

354 Art. 36–38 MiCAR.

355 Art. 39 MiCAR.

value of the reserve assets or the volume of daily transactions worldwide.[356] Issuers of asset-referenced tokens must obey additional duties, e.g. concerning remuneration policy, the custody of the reserve assets, liquidity management and stress testing.[357]

The pinnacle is reached with those asset-referenced or e-money tokens widely used as a means of exchange. They may be called "super-significant tokens", although this term is not used by the EU legislator. These are tokens in which more than 1 million transactions with a volume of EUR100 million (or equivalent) are carried out daily within a single currency zone of the EU (e.g. the Euro Area). When there cumulative criteria are reached, the issuer must stop issuing the tokens and present a plan to the authorities on how to reduce their usage so that it is kept below the threshold.[358] In other words, stablecoins can never become a significant means of payment in the Euro Area.

Regarding the provision of crypto services, such as the custody of crypto-assets, their exchange for cash or other crypto-assets, or the operation of a trading platform, MiCAR provides a fairly strict regime. This includes the requirement for the service provider to obtain authorisation from the national authorities, which implies meeting several conditions.[359] Among other things, the applicant must prove that it meets specific prudential requirements, describe its governance arrangements, and demonstrate that the members of its management body have a sufficiently good reputation and possess the appropriate knowledge, skills, and experience to fulfil management functions. The service provider must also have its registered office and effective administrative headquarters in the EU, and at least one of its directors must reside in the EU.[360]

The rules of MiCAR demonstrate an intense preoccupation with the dangers of stablecoins. In particular, the EU legislator frets that these could become significant and widely used in the Union, thus competing with the official currencies such as the Euro. However, it has not addressed the dangers of other crypto-assets, in particular cryptocurrencies and payment tokens, which could become strong competitors to fiat money without being referenced to a reserve asset, for instance where they are issued by a commercial giant dominating large parts of the internet. Moreover, MiCAR adopts a rather classic type of regulation, imposing prudential requirements and conduct of business rules

356 See Art. 43 MiCAR.
357 Art. 45 MiCAR.
358 Art. 23(1) MiCAR.
359 Art. 62 MiCAR.
360 Art. 59(2) MiCAR.

on intermediaries, thereby wholly ignoring the increasing role of DeFi platforms and projects, which lack addressees for regulation and supervision.[361] Particularly, the requirement of a seat in the EU may prove an obstacle for platforms and projects that are active worldwide and have no firm establishment in any particular country, such as Aave, Lido or SushiSwap. Finally, MiCAR imposes heavy bureaucratic burdens that token issuers, such as start-ups, will struggle to fulfil. This poses no small danger to the development of the crypto economy. The EU may either become a safe haven for crypto investors or a "fortress Europe" that lags behind the technological development in other parts of the world. Only the future can tell which of these two options will materialise.

2.2.3 *Conclusion*

The above examples are not exhaustive but illustrate the plethora of categories into which legislators and regulators try to shoehorn crypto-assets. Given their ambiguous nature, the proper characterisation lends itself to theoretical discussions, leading to a dead end. Instead, one should focus on the consequences that one or the other characterisations may have. Money, securities and commodities are subject to very different rules. To illustrate, a money transmitter must follow distinct rules compared to a securities broker. While for the first, it is generally sufficient to determine the customer's identity, the second must also enquire about the customer's investment goals and risk tolerance. The discussion should focus on these consequences rather than on the abstract nature of crypto-assets.

A simple solution is to impose new, tailor-made rules for the crypto world. For instance, the novel regulatory categories of virtual businesses or crypto-asset service providers lead to further obligations, e.g. regarding IT security. These may be well justified. On the other hand, fashioning new rules for the crypto economy may clash with the principle of technological neutrality.

While the different characterisations may already be confusing on the national level, they lead to utter chaos at the international level, as the next section will show.

2.3 The Confusion over Jurisdiction

By design, blockchains transcend state frontiers. Several states may therefore stake a claim to regulate the crypto economy. This adds a further layer of

361 On DeFi, see *supra* 1.1.2.4.

complexity, as the problem of substantive law characterisation is compounded by that of determining the competent national authority.

2.3.1 *The Permissive Standard of Public International Law*

2.3.1.1 Extraterritoriality of Legislation and Adjudication

Public International Law is very permissive regarding jurisdictional claims over the crypto economy. This is true independently of whether one follows the more liberal or the more restrictive approach to jurisdiction.[362]

The more liberal approach starts from the *Lotus* case decided by the Permanent Court of International Justice in 1927.[363] As is well known, the Court held that restrictions upon jurisdiction imposed by international law were not to be presumed. Consequently, states were allowed to exercise jurisdiction in their territory concerning acts which have taken place abroad, but not to use force in the territory of another state.[364] This decision gave rise to the distinction between "jurisdiction to enforce" on the one hand, and "jurisdiction to prescribe" and "jurisdiction to adjudicate" on the other, which has survived until this day.[365] Some authors maintain the continuing relevance of the decision and suggest that only the first type of jurisdiction is territorially limited. At the same time, the second and third have only very few limits, such as the intervention in another state's affairs.[366]

---

362 On these two approaches, see Cedric Ryngaert, *Jurisdiction in International Law* (2nd edn, Oxford University Press 2015) 29.

363 Permanent Court of International Justice, *ss Lotus* (*France v. Turkey*), judgment of 7 September 1927, Series A, No. 10, 18.

364 ibid.

365 See Ryngaert (n 362) 83; James Crawford and Ian Brownlie, *Brownlie's Principles of Public International Law* (8th edn, Oxford University Press 2012) 447. See also American Law Institute, *Restatement of the Law Fourth, The Foreign Relations Law of the United States* (American Law Institute Publishers, 2018) § 401:
"The foreign relations law of the United States divides jurisdiction into three categories:
(a) jurisdiction to prescribe, i.e., the authority of a state to make law applicable to persons, property, or conduct;
(b) jurisdiction to adjudicate, i.e., the authority of a state to apply law to persons or things, in particular through the processes of its courts or administrative tribunals; and
(c) jurisdiction to enforce, i.e., the authority of a state to exercise its power to compel compliance with law."

366 See, e.g., Karl M Meessen, 'Antitrust Jurisdiction Under Customary International Law' (1984) 78 American Journal of International Law 783; Pierre-Marie Dupuy and Yann Kerbrat, *Droit international public* (16th edn, Dalloz 2022) 112–113, para 105.

The proponents of the more restrictive approach criticise the *Lotus* decision as being "retrograde",[367] "grossly overrated",[368] or "highly problematic right from the beginning".[369] They point to subsequent developments, especially the *Nottebohm* decision by the International Court of Justice, which requires a "genuine connection" between the state and the situation in question to exercise any jurisdiction.[370] The Lotus judgment itself had foreseen a further evolution by considering that its solution was valid only "in the present state of international law". In this respect, several treaties have overruled the *Lotus* decision precisely in the area it concerned, i.e. the law of the High Sea.[371]

Yet even the restrictive approach imposes few practical limits on exercising jurisdiction over the crypto economy. The first reason is that according to its proponents, the "genuine connection" does not necessarily have to exist with the territory of a state but may also relate to the persons involved, especially its nationals.[372] More importantly, even the proponents of the restrictive approach accept the "effects doctrine", according to which the genuine connection may consist in effects on the state's territory or, more generally, on its interests.[373]

This last point significantly limits the restrictions international law poses on jurisdiction today. In a globalising world, virtually any act or event may have effects in other countries. Whether it concerns the protection of the environment, data security or the stability of financial markets, the consequences of actions in one part of the world increasingly reverberate across the planet. Therefore, it is not surprising that states constantly strive to extend the realm

367 Francis A Mann, 'The Doctrine of Jurisdiction in International Law' (1964) 111 Collected Courses of the Hague Academy of International Law 1, 35.

368 Rosalyn Higgins, *Problems and Process: International Law and How we Use it* (Oxford University Press 1994) 77.

369 Armin von Bogdandy and Markus Rau, 'Lotus, The' in *Max Planck Encyclopedia of Public International Law* (June 2006) para 16.

370 ICJ, 6 April 1955, *Nottebohm case* (*Liechtenstein v. Guatemala*), second phase, I.C.J. Reports 1955, p. 4, 23.

371 See Art. 5 United Nations Convention on the High Seas, done in Geneva on 29 April 1958; Art. 91 United Nations Convention on the Law of the Sea, done in Montego Bay on 10 December 1982.

372 Mann (n 367) 79; Crawford and Brownlie (n 365) 433–444.

373 See American Law Institute, *Restatement of the Law Fourth, The Foreign Relations of the United States*' (American Law Institute Publishers 2018); American Law Institute, 'Restatement Fourth, Foreign Relations Law of the United States – Jurisdiction, Tentative Draft No 3' (approved 2016) § 213 ("International law recognizes a state's jurisdiction to prescribe law with respect to conduct that has a substantial effect within its territory."); Ryngaert (n 362) 83; Crawford and Brownlie (n 365) 447.

of their laws to events and actions outside of their borders.[374] Extraterritoriality, thus, no longer deserves to be a term for bad behaviour but should be considered the "new normal".[375] The reasons are ground-breaking technological, economic and ecological changes, which diminish the practical importance of the limits international law poses to the exercise of extraterritorial jurisdiction.[376]

2.3.1.2 Omniterritoriality of the Blockchain

The blockchain perfectly illustrates the reduced importance of the territorial limits of the law. It is the world's first truly global system for permanently recording and safely transferring information and value. As such, it has connections to virtually any country. Its nodes are intentionally distributed worldwide, and its information can be accessed from any point on the planet.

Elsewhere, I have called the ubiquity of the blockchain its "omniterritoriality".[377] Omniterritoriality means that the blockchain operates simultaneously in all states of the world, whether through nodes or the possibility of access. Note the difference in emphasis to the theory of alegality, which claims blockchain would not be subject to any legal system.[378] This theory is based on the claim that the network is "anational" because it would be connected to the territory of any state. From a regulatory perspective, it is the other way around: since the blockchain operates in and is accessible from all states of the world, it affects all of their interests. Hence, it is not anational, but omniterritorial.

Omniterritoriality has practical consequences. Since the blockchain has connections with all countries, a state that regulates crypto-assets and offerings

---

374 See, e.g., for information privacy and data protection Julia Hörnle, *Internet Jurisdiction* (Oxford University Press 2021) 31.

375 Matthias Lehmann, 'New Challenges of Extraterritoriality: Superposing Laws', in Franco Ferrari and Diego P Fernández Arroyo (eds), *Private International Law – Contemporary Challenges and Continuing Relevance* (Edward Elgar 2019) 258, 259 (noting that far from being a suspicious exception, extraterritoriality has become ubiquitous and is often legitimate).

376 Gary B Born, 'A Reappraisal of the Extraterritorial Reach of U.S. Law' (1992) 24 Law and Policy in International Business 1 '("This century's profound international political, economic, technological, and legal transformations have significantly undermined the strict territoriality presumption that prevailed in nineteenth century conceptions of public international law.").

377 Matthias Lehmann, 'Extraterritoriality in Financial Law', in Austen Parrish and Cedric Ryngaert (eds), *Cambridge Handbook on Extraterritoriality in International Law* (Cambridge University Press 2023), pp. 412, 427.

378 See *supra* 1.5.1.

can hardly be reproached for applying its laws extraterritorially. Quite to the contrary, it applies its laws to facts that happen (also) on its territory. In other words, in blockchain cases, the existence of a "genuine connection" allowing the exercise of jurisdiction can be presumed.

One view in the literature objects that a state could not claim to regulate the blockchain as a whole but only the behaviour of individual participants, i.e. natural or legal persons present on its territory or having its nationality.[379] The only exception would be cryptocurrencies likely to affect the state's monetary sovereignty. Yet currently, the effects of the new assets would (still) be "too insignificant" to justify the exercise of jurisdiction over the whole network.[380]

This view is correct insofar as dangers to the state's monetary sovereignty justify the exercise of sweeping state powers. However, it is too restrictive as it limits the states' power to persons on its territory or having its nationality. This view creates confusion between jurisdiction to enforce on the one hand and jurisdiction to prescribe and adjudicate on the other: While the state may find it difficult to use force against persons abroad, Public International Law allows the regulation of the behaviour of such persons even if they are located outside of its territory. Otherwise, jurisdiction would be too much curtailed. To illustrate, a state could not regulate fraudulent offerings or tax evasion schemes that are suggested to its residents by foreign persons over the internet. On the other hand, Public International Law prohibits a state from exercising its *enforcement power* on the territory of another state.

One could at least condition a state's jurisdiction upon evidence that one of its citizens, companies or residents is implicated in a blockchain transfer. Yet, such a view would still restrict the exercise of state power too much. Given the pseudonymity characteristic of the blockchain, it is challenging, if not impossible, to reveal the parties' identity and location. This should not lead to the conclusion that the state lacks jurisdiction because this would effectively exclude its regulatory power over a network where everybody hides their identity. Instead, a state must be allowed to extend its legislation and adjudication to the whole network, save for exceptional cases in which no genuine connection to the state exists.[381]

In addition, we could limit the state's legislative power to network activities that take place on its territory. In particular, it is conceivable to accept the

379 Andreas Kerkemeyer, 'Blockchain-Transaktionen im Internationalen Recht' (2020) 184 Zeitschrift für das gesamte Handels- und Wirtschaftsrecht 793, 811.

380 ibid 810.

381 See on the exception of permissioned blockchains limited to one state *infra* at the end of this section.

state's legislative jurisdiction only for transfers confirmed by a node on its territory. However, such a view can hardly be defended because of the technological particularities of the network. The blockchain works such that it is impossible to predict in advance which node may validate a transfer. The proof-of-work or proof-of-stake mechanism determines the selection of the node. The aleatory nature of this process makes the confirmation by a specific node fortuitous, which allows any state where nodes are established to claim jurisdiction over the whole network.

Moreover, the confirmation is not the work of a single node. To be permanently inscribed on the blockchain, the other nodes must also accept a new, confirmed block. This is because the nodes can still prefer a different version of the blockchain at a later stage.[382] Since final confirmation requires consensus by most nodes, claims of jurisdiction by states where nodes are located cannot be rejected outright.

Above all, however, the location of the nodes is not necessarily decisive since other reasons justify the application of a national law. In particular, crypto-transfers are usually preceded by marketing efforts directed to residents of a specific state, e.g. on a website. This connection usually suffices to justify the application of the state's law.[383]

Moreover, even those countries to which no marketing efforts are directed and in which no nodes are operated do not, for these reasons, lack jurisdiction. This is because the blockchain can still be accessed from most of these countries; its citizens may have stored assets on it and use it for transfers. They may abuse this access for illegal activity, which will interest the state in question. The blockchain can also affect the country's interests in other ways, such as its monetary or financial stability. These factors create a genuine connection. There is thus no shortage of arguments to justify the exercise of jurisdiction by the national legislature or judiciary, at least when it comes to permissionless networks.

Permissioned networks, in which a central authority plays a key role, would have to be viewed differently. Here, only the state in which validators or participants are situated can be presumed to have legislative and judicial authority.[384] On the other hand, even these networks may affect the interests of a state, for instance, when they are used to plan terrorist activity on its soil or avoid its taxes. In this regard, the burden of proof should lie with the state alleging such effects from a network with no nodes or participants on its soil.

382 See *supra* 1.1.1.3.

383 See the arguments made in the decision in the *Tezos* case *infra* 2.3.2.3.

384 Kerkemeyer (n 379) 812.

2.3.1.3 Compounded by the Uncertain Characterisation

As if the blockchain's many connections would not suffice, the debate about its nature widens the scope for legislation and adjudication even further. A state's interest in regulation depends very much on how crypto-assets are characterised, e.g., as money or as securities. As a result, what constitutes the "genuine connection" varies.

It is relatively easy, for instance, to show that the crypto economy affects monetary sovereignty. Cryptocurrencies such as Bitcoin are designed as means of payment. They can be transferred from any point in the world to any other and are increasingly accepted as forms of payment, thereby challenging the state's monopoly to coin money. Thus, a state can regulate or restrict its use in the name of monetary sovereignty.

The characterisation of crypto-assets as securities can equally be used to justify jurisdiction. Based on its investor protection purpose, securities law can be said to apply as soon as crypto-assets are bought by or sold to persons domiciled in a particular state. The offer of such transactions on the internet thus suffices to trigger the application of a state's securities law unless there are mechanisms to exclude residents of this state. In practice, whoever offers such assets on the internet bears the burden of proof that she did not deliver them to a particular state.

Monetary and securities law jurisdiction is thus very wide, yet their combination renders any limits of jurisdiction illusory. Given the chameleon-like nature of crypto-assets such as Bitcoin, a legislator or a court may choose to invoke either their use as means of payment in cross-border commerce to apply its monetary law or the fact that the offering targeted investors residing in its territory to justify the extraterritorial application of its securities law. In practice, this leads to the concurrent jurisdiction of all states over the same offering or transfer.

2.3.2 *The "Presumption Against Extraterritoriality" Does Not Bite*

Theoretically, one may have expected US law to take a more restrictive view of jurisdiction. That is because it had explicitly adopted a presumption against extraterritoriality as part of its federal law.

2.3.2.1 The Presumption Explained

In 2010, the US Supreme Court rendered its seminal judgment in *Morrison v. Australia National Bank*, which underscored the role played by the "presumption against extraterritoriality" in construing the reach of federal law.[385] The

385 *Morrison et al. v. National Australia Bank Ltd. et al.*, 561 U.S. 247, 248, 255–261 (2010).

presumption had been mentioned before in the case law,[386] but the Court vowed to apply it from now on with much more vigour. The content of the presumption is that Congress should not be presumed to have legislated for events or activities outside of US territory. This was particularly true in securities law, the scope of which was the subject of the *Morrison* decision. The case concerned financial legislation, particularly the scope of the anti-fraud provisions of the Securities Exchange Act. In the view of the Court, the Securities Exchange Act should only be applied to 1) "transactions in securities listed on domestic exchanges" and 2) "domestic transactions in other securities".[387]

The presumption against extraterritoriality is one of the most hotly disputed judicial constructs of US law.[388] It is important to note that the presumption is nothing more than a canon of construction, which applies only in case of doubt. Congress was expressly left free to rebut it by stating a contrary intention.[389]

2.3.2.2 Conduct and Effects Test

It took the federal legislator only a few days to reverse the presumption precisely in securities law, for which it was established. The same week the *Morrison* decision was published, Congress adopted the Dodd-Frank Act, which includes a provision to amend the *Securities Act of 1933* and the *Securities Exchange Act of 1934*.[390] This reinstated the old "conduct and effects test", which

386 *EEOC V. Arabian American Oil Co*, 499 U.S. 244, 248 (1991).

387 *Morrison et al. v. National Australia Bank Ltd. et al.*, 561 U.S. 247, 267.

388 See, e.g., Hannah L Buxbaum, 'Morrison v. National Australia Bank: Defining the Domestic Interest in International Securities Litigation' (2011) 105 American Society of International Law Proceedings 402 (concluding that the Morrison decision is troubling in that it encourages disengagement from the debate over private versus public enforcement in the name of a falsely parochial national interest); Hannah L Buxbaum, 'Public Regulation and Private Enforcement in a Global Economy: Strategies for Managing Conflict' (2019) 399 Collected Courses of the Hague Academy of International Law 269, 321–326 (noting that "one consequence of the new articulation of the presumption is that it may result in unnecessary retreat from the project of transnational regulation"); William S Dodge, 'The Presumption Against Extraterritoriality after Morrison' (2011) 105 American Society of International Law Proceedings 396, 397 (interpreting the decision as shifting the presumption to focus on effects, which would be a positive development); Austen Parrish, 'Morrison, The Effects Test, and the Presumption Against Extraterritoriality: A Reply to Professor Dodge' (2011) 105 American Society of International Law Proceedings 399, 401 (defending the Morrison decision on the ground that extraterritorial laws are problematic for international law and pose a threat to effective global governance).

389 *Morrison et al. v. National Australia Bank Ltd. et al.*, 561 U.S. 247, 255.

390 § 929P(b) Dodd-Frank Wall Street Reform and Consumer Protection Act, Pub. L. 111–203, 124 Stat. 1376–2223 (2010).

had been applied pre-*Morrison* and under which either conduct or effects on the US soil sufficed as a basis of jurisdiction for US courts.[391] Whether the reform achieved this aim was not beyond doubt and remains debatable because the legislator had extended court jurisdiction for enforcement actions by the SEC and the Department of Justice, but not the scope of the applicable law.[392] However, US courts later accepted that the scope of the federal securities laws had been extended insofar as one of the agencies decides to bring an action in this area.[393]

This far-reaching power has been used in many cases by the SEC to justify the applicability of US law. To illustrate, in the case *Terraform and Do Kwon* the SEC went after a Singapore company and its South Korean co-founder and Chief Executive Officer with a subpoena.[394] The latter rejected the agency's jurisdiction. Yet the agency's position prevailed in court, and the defendants were ordered to comply with the SEC's subpoena.[395] There was not much discussion of the extraterritorial applicability of US law. In other cases, the SEC refrained from even arguing this point and just started from the assumption that US law applies.[396]

2.3.2.3 Domestic Transactions Test

The reopening of the scope of federal law and the concomitant jurisdictional authority by the Dodd-Frank Act is limited to the antifraud provisions of US securities law. It does not cover other types of action, particularly for failure to register securities with the SEC or false or misleading registration statements.

391 See, e.g., US Court of Appeals 2nd Circuit, 29 May 1968, *Schoenbaum v. Firstbrook*, 1968, 405 F. 2d 200; US Court of Appeals 2nd Circuit, 28 April 1975, *Bersch v. Drexel Firestone, Incorporated*, 1975, 519 F. 2d 974; US Court of Appeals 2nd Circuit, 28 April 1975, *IIT v. Vencap Ltd.*, 1975, 519 F. 2d 1001.

392 See, e.g., Richard Painter, Douglas Dunham and Ellen Quackenbos, 'When Courts and Congress Don't Say What They Mean: Initial Reactions to Morrison v. National Australia Bank and to the Extraterritorial Jurisdiction Provisions of the Dodd-Frank Act' (2011) 20 Minnesota Journal of International Law 1.

393 *SEC v. Scoville*, 913 F.3d 1204, 1218 (10th Cir. 2019), cert. denied, 140 S. Ct. 483 (2019).

394 SEC, '*SEC Files Subpoena Enforcement Action Against Terraform Labs and Its CEO*' (Litigation Release No. 25262, November 21, 2021) <https://www.sec.gov/litigation/litreleases/lr-25262> accessed 15 April 2024.

395 *United States Securities and Exchange Commission v. Terraform Labs PTE Ltd. and Do Kwon*, 21-MC-810 (JPO) (S.D.N.Y. Mar. 1, 2022).

396 See, e.g., SEC, '*SEC v Poloniex, LLC*' (Proc File No 3–20455, 9 August 2021) <https://www.sec.gov/news/press-release/2021-147> accessed 15 April 2024; SEC, '*SEC v. Rivetz Corp., Rivetz International SEZC, and Steven K Sprague*' (Litigation Release No 25198, Proc. File No. 3:21-cv- 30092, D. Mass. filed Sept. 8, 2021) <https://www.sec.gov/litigation/litreleases/lr-25198> accessed 15 April 2024.

For these, the general criteria on the scope set out by the Supreme Court in *Morrison* continue to apply. Therefore, these actions can only be brought where they concern 1) transactions in securities listed on domestic exchanges and 2) domestic transactions in other securities.[397]

Yet US courts have encountered little difficulty using both criteria against non-registered crypto offerings. For instance, they have applied the US securities laws against the founders of the Tezos blockchain project even though it was overseen by a non-profit foundation in Switzerland and investors had to pay in Ether.[398] The court justified the applicability of US law in this case with the following grounds: First, the lead plaintiff had used an interactive website that was hosted on a server in Arizona and ran primarily by a Californian resident; second, he had presumably learned about the Tezos ICO and participated in response to marketing activity that almost exclusively targeted US residents; and finally, the lead plaintiff's contribution of Ether to the ICO became irrevocable only after it was validated by a network of global "nodes" which, according to the court, was clustered more densely in the US than in any other country.[399] While the court remarked that "no single one of these factors is dispositive to the analysis", it was adamant that, taken together, they would "support an inference" that the securities purchase occurred inside the US.[400] Indeed, from the perspective of international law, each of these factors alone would have sufficed to justify the application of US law.

Another rationale to support the applicability of US law, despite the presumption against extraterritoriality, was followed in *SEC v. Ripple Labs* et al.[401] Despite the protests by the defendants to the contrary, the District Court concluded that the offer and sale of Ripple XRP took place in the US and were, therefore, "domestic transactions" for the purposes of the *Morrison* test. The court argued that the platforms on which these offerings and sales had been made were not only incorporated, but also "based" in the US, with one of them having its principal place of business in California. Accepting an analysis suggested by the SEC, the court held the platform's location relevant because the XRP tokens were allocated to the investors' accounts in the platform's records. The court concluded:

> "Taken together, these allegations plausibly allege (sic!) that the Individual Defendants' sale of XRP on Platforms A and B occurred in the United States."[402]

---

397 *Morrison et al. v. National Australia Bank Ltd. et al.*, 561 U.S. 247, 267.

398 *In re Tezos Sec. Litig.*, No. 17-CV-06779-RS, 2018 WL 4293341 (N.D. Cal. Aug. 7, 2018).

399 ibid.

400 ibid.

401 *SEC v. Ripple Labs Inc. et al.*, 2020 Civ. 10832 (AT) (SN) (S.D.N.Y. 2022).

402 ibid 27.

The court also followed the SEC by holding that the defendants executed offers and sales through accounts "based in the United States". It concluded that irrevocable liability "may" attach when digital assets enter and leave these accounts, and that the transaction was therefore "domestic" in the sense of *Morrison*.[403] The court weighed the defendant's pleading for making an exception when the offer and sale are "predominantly foreign" but ruled that this was not the case here.[404]

Whether based on "the conduct and effects test" or the "domestic transaction test", US courts thus have found various ways to justify the application of US law to token offerings on global blockchain networks. At least in the context of the crypto economy, the "presumption against extraterritoriality" therefore does not limit the application of US law. This is because any crypto-asset offer is "territorial" for the US unless its residents are expressly excluded. In other words, US law applies because the transaction is domestic.

2.3.3 *The Plethora of Connecting Factors Used in State Practice*

States have used the permissive framework provided by international law for their purposes. They refer to various factors as connecting points to justify the applicability of their legislative and regulatory rules.

2.3.3.1 Location of Traditional Financial Service Provider

One recurring practice is indirectly regulating crypto products and services by imposing special prohibitions or other rules on traditional service providers. An example of this technique is the 2013 Chinese ban, addressed to banks and other intermediaries.[405] Another example is the imposition of rules on anti-money laundering and countering the financing of terrorism, which is followed in the US, the EU and other parts of the world.[406] In this case, the connecting factor is the establishment of the financial service provider or any other person handling the money on the state's soil. This factor has the advantage of being relatively undisputed and leading to orders that are easy to enforce.

It is straightforward to prohibit financial intermediaries established on the state's territory from offering crypto services, such as their custody or the exchange against fiat money. An early example of this is the Chinese notice dating back to 2013.[407] Although its wording is not limited to financial institutions

---

403 ibid.

404 ibid 28–29.

405 See *supra* 2.1.1.1.

406 See *supra* 2.2.1.1.

407 See *supra* 2.1.1.1.

established on the People's Republic's soil, it is mainly addressed to them. This becomes clear when reading the order's last paragraph, according to which the Shanghai Headquarters of the People's Bank of China, all branches, business management departments, and central sub-branches in provincial capital cities are requested to forward the notice to all local financial institutions and payment institutions within their jurisdiction.[408] Similar directions addressed to all financial institutions in a state's territory exist in other countries.[409] They show states are willing to enforce their extraterritorial laws and regulations via orders addressed to the traditional financial intermediaries established in their jurisdiction.

There can be hardly any doubt that this practice conforms to Public International Law. A state′s power to regulate the behaviour of financial institutions on its soil is unquestionable. This results in an important lever that allows regulators to impose discipline on blockchain networks despite their omniterritorial nature.

2.3.3.2 Location of Crypto Issuer or Service Provider

A state has the power to regulate the new players of the crypto economy that have a seat or an office in its territory. This may concern issuers of crypto-assets or crypto service providers, such as crypto exchanges or wallet providers. China has taken this step by prohibiting all kinds of fundraising activities, such as token issuances or exchanging crypto-assets against fiat money, in its second notice of 2017. Although it was not clear at the time whether this ban was limited to issuers located in the territory of the People's Republic, this was clarified later in the third notice dating from 2021, which explicitly extended the ban extraterritorially to foreign service providers. For this extension to make any sense, it must be assumed that the original ban was limited to Chinese territory. The legality of the extension under Public International Law will be discussed next.

2.3.3.3 Residence of the Investor

Another possible criterion to use is the residence of crypto investors. Although this criterion may, at first glance, seem territorially related, it may justify the assertion of extraterritorial jurisdiction. Thanks to it, legislators, regulators and courts may control activities directed at their residents even though they are carried out by providers established outside the state's territory.

---

408 ibid.

409 See for instance on New York's BitLicense *supra* 2.2.2.1.

This was the criterion that the SEC used in the case "*The DAO*" to claim jurisdiction over the offering of tokens to the public. Besides the DAO itself, the addressees of the SEC's action were a German corporation and its cofounders, two non-US individuals. Despite the lack of US connections, the SEC thought it had jurisdiction because *The DAO*'s website was publicly accessible, including to individuals in the United States.[410] Similarly strong assertions have been made in other cases.[411]

China has made a similar argument. Its third crypto notice, dating from 2021, expressly states that

> "Provision of services by overseas virtual currency exchanges to residents in China via the internet is also considered to be an illegal financial activity."[412]

Consequently, in addition to the "domestic" staff of such exchanges, all legal persons, unincorporated organisations and natural persons who knew of these activities may be held accountable in accordance with the law.[413]

The implicit argument here is one of investor protection. It has never been questioned that states have jurisdiction to regulate offerings to investors on their soil. This is one of the most important consequences of the "effects doctrine", according to which a state may protect its citizens or residents against dangers from abroad. The limit is reached when the latter go voluntarily abroad or enter a system that is not directed to them. This situation is known as "reverse solicitation".[414] In such a case, applying the investor's home-state law is no longer justified.

---

410 See SEC (n 89) 16.

411 See, e.g., the cases *SEC v. Rivetz Corp, Rivetz International SEZC, and Steven K Sprague*, Proc. File No. 3:21-cv-30092 (D Mass Sept 8, 2021); US District Court for the Southern District of New York, *Securities and Exchange Commission v. Terraform Labs PTE, Ltd and Do Kwon*, No. 21-mc-810 (S.D.N.Y, SEC complaint lodged 12 November 2021); see also US District Court for the Southern District of New York, *SEC v. Telegram Group Inc and TON Issuer Inc* 448 F. Supp. 3d 352 (S.D.N.Y. 2020), specifically the decisions of 24 March and 1 April 2020.

412 See People's Bank of China and others (n 233) section I(3).

413 ibid.

414 Niamh Moloney, 'Capital Markets Union, Third Countries, and Equivalence', in Danny Busch, Emilios Avgouleas and Guido Ferrarini (eds), *Capital Markets in Europe* (Oxford University Press 2018) 109 para 6.23 (stating that the reverse solicitation route is available for EU clients demanding financial services from British companies after Brexit).

2.3.3.4 Trading on a Crypto Exchange

In some cases, regulators also invoke the place of a crypto exchange, not to regulate the exchange itself but to establish jurisdiction over offerings and transactions made on it. The argument is, however, typically made only in situations where it leads to the state's jurisdiction. An example is the ruling of the SEC in the case *The Ripple Labs et al.*, in which the agency based its jurisdiction, among others, on the fact that offerings and sales of crypto-assets issued by the defendant *Ripple Labs* had been made on a US platform. The District Court uncritically followed this analysis in highlighting that the platforms were not only incorporated but were also "based" in the US, with one of them having, in addition, its principal place of business in California.[415] While the court did not exclusively rely on this criterion, it is dangerous because it cuts both ways. In case an offer to US persons had been executed on a foreign platform, this could have been used as an argument to deny the applicability of US law, undermining investor protection.

2.3.3.5 Place of Nodes

An equally dangerous because unpredictable and fortuitous criterion is that of the place of the majority of the nodes of a particular network. It was used by a US District Court in the case *In re Tezos* as an additional argument for the applicability of US law.[416] In particular, the court held that the contribution of Ether by the plaintiffs to the ICO became irrevocable only after it was validated by a global network of nodes – i.e. the Ethereum network –, which is "clustered more densely in the US than in any other country".[417] This may be factually true, but the argument is specious. If applied *e contrario*, it seems to deny other countries the right to apply their laws to a network clustered in the US. Moreover, it is unlikely that courts would refuse, in the opposite hypothesis (i.e. when the network is more densely grouped in another country), the applicability of their national law to offerings targeting US residents. In reality, an analysis of the concentration of nodes is unnecessary. The presence of a small part of the network and even its mere accessibility could suffice to justify its jurisdiction over assets and transactions carried out on the network.[418]

---

415 *SEC v. Ripple Labs Inc. et al.*, 2020 Civ. 10832 (AT) (SN) (S.D.N.Y. 2022).

416 *In re Tezos Sec. Litig., No.* 17-cv-06779, 2018 WL 4293341, Order on the Defendant's Motion to Dismiss (N.D. Cal. Aug. 7, 2018).

417 ibid 14 (mentioning that no single of the factors mentioned is dispositive to the analysis).

418 See *supra* 2.3.3.3.

2.3.3.6 Other, or No, Factors

All of the mentioned connecting factors are compatible with the very permissive standards of Public International Law. Countless other criteria can be used to justify jurisdiction over blockchain offerings, purchases, sales, and transfers.

Often, the state does not provide any limitation on its ban. Examples of this practice abound.[419] The fact that the legislator or regulator does not think about the scope of its ban is unsurprising, given that it is mainly focused on domestic issues. Its omission may be even more forgiven in the context of the blockchain, which by its very nature is not connected to a specific state and, therefore, can be rightfully considered as domestic by all of them. In this case, the relevant restrictions are identical to those concerning enforcement.[420]

2.3.4 *Conclusion*

This section has shown that virtually every state of the world can claim its laws apply to the blockchain because of the effects doctrine. This has nothing to do with extraterritoriality. As the blockchain is omniterritorial, every country is affected by it; applying one's rules is thus a domestic affair. Hence, even the US presumption against extraterritoriality of federal laws does not stand in the way of applying laws to crypto offerings.

This susceptibility to regulation by multiple or all legal systems creates problems. However, the founders of the blockchain bear some responsibility for these difficulties. By choosing a technology that operates worldwide, they have made themselves subject to the jurisdiction of all states worldwide.

2.4 Problems in Service and Enforcement

Blockchain creates a new global and virtual reality. Because of these characteristics, authorities have difficulty enforcing their national law even in cases where the latter applies. These problems are often neglected in the legal literature but play a crucial role in practice. Thus, they shall be discussed here.

Insofar one must distinguish between several different problems for law enforcement. First, the veil of pseudonymity it difficult to identify persons acting on the blockchain (2.4.1). One can try to hold those who programme the protocols accountable. Still, they typically work in transnational teams, which creates a second problem because such teams often operate in more than one country (2.4.2). The task of supervisors is further complicated by

419 See, e.g., the People's Bank of China and others (n 233) and accompanying text.

420 See *infra* 2.4.

the high mobility of crypto actors and crypto-assets, which is a third obstacle (2.4.3). Sometimes, even a person seems lacking, especially in the DeFi context, making law enforcement elusive (2.4.4). But suppose one tries to draw the technology users into the circle of liability, the opposite problem arises of an overabundance of possible addressees of regulatory measures (2.4.5). If all these obstacles can be overcome, the problem of the immutability of the blockchain remains (2.4.6).

2.4.1 *The Difficulty in Identifying the Responsible Persons*

The blockchain is like an open book that can be read from A to Z. It contains a meticulous account of every activity that has ever occurred, from the very first transfer to the most recent. In addition, this account is verified by independent third parties and is tamper-proof. Theoretically, this makes the blockchain an ideal tool for regulatory purposes; supervisors could use it to check which assets are held by a specific person. The blockchain also lends itself as evidence in criminal proceedings, because it provides full proof of any transfer from one public address to another.

Yet pseudonymity, characteristic of DLT, puts a spanner in the works for any such effort. Pseudonymity makes it nearly impossible to know the identity of the holder of a crypto-asset or the parties to a specific transfer. For this reason, cryptocurrencies are popular with criminals, for instance, as a means of payment for arms or drug deals, blackmail, or ransomware attacks.[421] While Bitcoin still plays a dominant role in this context, criminals increasingly use mixers, tumblers and dark net coins to hide their traces.[422] This high level of secrecy is difficult to overcome because it is in the blockchain's DNA. After all, the latter was programmed by cypherpunks or crypto anarchists to make their identification impossible. Thus, it is little wonder that problems in law enforcement persist to this day.

2.4.2 *The Collaborative Approach across Border vs the National Approach to Supervision*

One possibility for law enforcement would be to go after the programmers. Yet virtually all blockchains are not created and maintained by a single individual

421 See, e.g., Financial Action Task Force (FATF), 'Targeted Update on Implementation of FATF's Standards on VAs and VASPs' (2022) 21 para 42 <https://www.fatf-gafi.org/en/publications/Fatfrecommendations/Targeted-update-virtual-assets-vasps.html> accessed 15 April 2024(highlighting the ongoing and growing threat of criminal misuse of virtual assets for the receipt and laundering of illegal proceeds from ransomware attacks).

422 ibid.

but by a team of programmers. In the brave new crypto world, these individuals typically reside in different countries and have different nationalities; they often hardly know each other, as they work together mainly over the internet.[423] This collaborative, transnational approach starkly contrasts with the nature of executive power, which is still nationally based and limited to a specific territory.

Supervisory authorities, therefore, frequently need to reach beyond their borders and hold foreign nationals accountable. This is illustrated by the practice of the SEC. In the case "*The DAO*", for instance, it pursued two programmers based in Germany, one of German and the other of British nationality.[424] In the *Terraform* case, the target was a Singaporean company and its South Korean co-founder and Chief Executive Officer.[425]

Any type of cross-border enforcement is fraught with practical difficulties. Already service in another country is not easy, let alone arresting an individual. The exercise of sovereign powers, for instance by issuing subpoenas against foreign nationals residing abroad, may create tensions with other states, who protect their nationals and jealously guard their monopoly to use force in their territory. As shown above, the territorial limitation on the use of force is a cornerstone of Public International Law.[426]

To be fully effective, cross-border enforcement requires the cooperation of foreign supervisory agencies. Yet these cannot always assist because they lack the necessary capabilities, resources or time. And even if they have all of these, they may lack the proper incentives to lend a helping hand to their foreign counterparts. This is because some states are less affected than others by blockchain offerings and because their political stance towards the crypto economy differs widely. As a result, the promise of a *quid pro quo* for cross-border collaboration does not always work. Mutual assistance and exchanges of goodwill are far from assured, and their lack can be exploited by technologists.

2.4.3 *The High Mobility of the Crypto Economy*

Every administrative and criminal sanction in countries following the rule of law presupposes strict compliance with a determined procedure. It typically starts with the service of a document and ends with adopting a measure or

423 See Paech (n 254) 1085 (noting that the person or persons controlling the software in case of Bitcoin and other cryptocurrencies are typically informally associated individuals that may be scattered around different jurisdictions).

424 On the DAO case, see *supra* 2.1.1.2.

425 On the *Terraform* case, see *supra* 2.3.3.2.

426 See *supra* section VIII(A)(1).

sanction. This gives the addressee time to move to another country. This is not a trivial matter: one must remember that most players working in the crypto economy are highly mobile and switch their residences frequently.[427] Before any measure against them can be adopted, they may have already gone abroad.

Even more challenging is the seizure of a crypto-asset. Assuming a supervisor has traced such an asset and identified the person holding it, the latter can transfer the asset in a matter of seconds to another address, possibly under the control of a person in a different country. The supervisor thus needs to request the cooperation of the other country's authorities. But before long, the asset risks being transferred again out of the latter's jurisdiction.

The situation resembles an international cat-and-mouse game in which private actors are always one step ahead. To escape law enforcement, they consciously make use of state borders. This poses no small challenge for the authorities seeking to enforce the rule of law in the crypto economy.

2.4.4 *The Lack of an Addressee for Enforcement Measures*

Traditionally, legal rules, regulations and administrative orders are addressed to persons, whether natural or legal. On a distributed ledger, such persons are hard to find. For instance, on a peer-to-peer network, there is no intermediary to whom specific regulatory rules could be applied.[428]

Fortunately for regulators, the blockchain is not as decentralised as it may seem. Protocols are programmed by human beings. They are maintained and updated by a group of select individuals, the so-called "core developers".[429] This may change with the advent of artificial intelligence, but it has yet to acquire the necessary capabilities to programme and update a DeFi application. Even if it were to obtain them, the AI would be the product of some human whose administrative or criminal responsibility could be engaged. Moreover, the nodes are not as scattered as they may seem at first sight. For example, the Bitcoin network is not fully decentralised but rather characterised by an oligopolistic market structure, with a handful of mining pools exercising the validation function.[430]

---

427 See, e.g., Laura Shin, *The Cryptopians* (PublicAffairs 2021) (describing the multinational group of coders that built the Ethereum network).

428 Paech (n 254) (noting that there is no one on hand to perform the functions that lie at the core of anti-money-laundering and related regimes).

429 De Filippi and Loveluck, (n 27) 18 (noting that only a small number of individuals (the core developers) have the power to decide which changes shall be incorporated into the main branch of the software).

430 See *supra* 1.2.3.1.

Even more challenges arise from DeFi. In this case, a person to which one could address an order or sanction seems to be utterly lacking. Instead of centralised exchanges run by an operator, they are entirely decentralised and operate autonomously by means of an algorithm. The market makers in DeFi are also fully automated. Even the issuance of a DeFi token is initiated by an algorithm rather than by a person. A completely decentralised financial system thus appears to be run entirely by machines, with no human being that could be held to account. This is the ultimate nightmare for regulators.

Again, one must not exaggerate the problems. The smart contracts underlying DeFi are programmed by some individuals, and even in DeFi some persons may intervene when the code is not working properly. This was exemplified by the Terra-Luna debacle, in which validators stopped the activity of the network and halted the blockchain to prevent a further meltdown of token prices.[431] This incident vividly illustrated that DeFi is not immune to human intervention.

Still, it may be difficult for law enforcement agencies to get hold of the core developers of blockchains or DeFi applications. Often they will be abroad, highly mobile and able to flee to other jurisdictions. The same may be said of the validators and mining pools: Despite their considerable infrastructure, they have shown in the past the ability to migrate to other countries if necessary.[432] The problem with decentralisation is thus not so much that a human being to which orders could be addressed would be lacking. It is rather the distribution of the relevant individuals and knowledge all over the globe.

2.4.5 *Too Many Addressees*

DAOs raise a different problem: not too few, but too many individuals are involved. This makes it difficult for regulators to decide whom to address: The DAO? Or the individual token-holders, and which? This is a real puzzle. According to some, it calls for a rethink of legal categories, which would have to move away from an author- and entity-based approach to one more adapted to the

431 Jacquelyn Melinek, 'Terra Halts Its Blockchain to Prevent Hacks amid UST Crash' (TechCrunch, 12 May 2022) <https://web.archive.org/web/20220512175406/https://techcrunch.com/2022/05/12/terra-halts-its-blockchain-to-prevent-hacks-ust/amp> accessed 15 April 2024.

432 ElminMedia, 'Bitcoin's "Halving" Sparks Migration of US Mining Computers Overseas' (*TokenPost*) <https://tokenpost.com/Bitcoins-Halving-Sparks-Migration-of-US-Mining-Computers-Overseas-11456> accessed 30 April 2024.

aggregated, open-ended and evolving fragments of a decentralised, peer-to-peer environment.[433]

The problem is illustrated by the case of the *Ooki DAO*. In 2022, the CFTC brought a complaint against this DAO in the Federal District Court for Northern California for alleged violations of the Commodities Exchange Act.[434] The Commission first tried several traditional means of service, without success. It then filed a motion for "alternative service". The court effectively allowed the CFTC to serve the complaint by posting a message on the help chat box on *Ooki*'s website and a contemporaneous notice in a discussion forum linked through this website.[435] This was a primer for serving an action, but it was met with feverish protestations from the blockchain community.[436] The CFTC responded with equal zeal.[437]

At the heart of the discussion lies a point much more critical than the formalities of service. The Commission's underlying thesis was that the DAO is an unincorporated partnership, which explains why the Commission deemed the DAO's members to be duly notified once the complaint was posted on its website.[438] The blockchain community tried to combat this view so fiercely because of its broader implications: If the DAO was indeed an unincorporated partnership, it could be sued, and all its members would be liable for its debt.[439]

433 Melanie Dulong de Rosnay, 'Peer-to-Peer as a Design Principle for Law: Distribute the Law' (2015) Journal of Peer Production 1, 4 (noting that distributed architectures fragment data and actions, thus challenging the localised rights model where each object or right can be assigned to one actor).

434 Commodity Futures Trading Commission (CFTC), 'Plaintiff's Consolidated Opposition to Amicus Curiae Motions for Reconsideration of Order Granting Plaintiff's Motion for Alternative Service' (14 November 2022) 8.

435 US District Court for the Northern District of California, *CFTC v. Ooki DAO*, Order Granting Plaintiff's Motion for Alternative Service, 3 October 2022.

436 See the various *amicus curiae* briefs filed with the aim to make the District Court reconsider its order for alternative service, e.g. Brief Amicus Curiae Brief of LexPunk Regarding Plaintiff's Motion for Alternative Service, 17 October 2022; Amicus curiae brief of Andreessen Horowitz regarding Plaintiff's Motion for Alternative Service, 7 December 2022; Reply Brief of Amicus Curiae DeFi Education Fund Regarding Plaintiff's Motion for Alternative Service, 7 December 2022.

437 CFTC, 'Plaintiff's Consolidated Opposition to Amicus Curiae Motions for Reconsideration of Order Granting Plaintiff's Motion for Alternative Service' (14 November 2022).

438 See, e.g., Amicus curiae brief of Andreessen Horowitz (n 436) 1 (stressing that "under the CFTC's theory, even if a token holder's only vote is the 'perfectly lawful' release of treasury funds, he or she nonetheless can be jointly and severally liable for all of the association's purportedly unlawful acts").

439 ibid.

The Federal District Court did not mention this debate in its very brief order. Still, for all intents and purposes, it has accepted the DAO as a legal entity with the capacity to be served and have standing in court.

The theory that a DAO can be an unincorporated association with liability of its members for any debt had already been developed well before this case by Dirk Zetzsche, Douglas Arner and Ross Buckley.[440] The authors were, however, careful to also consider other theories of liability.[441] Which of these ultimately applies depends on the governing private law. Here lies the catch: Neither the CFTC nor the Federal District Court for the Northern District of California explained why the Ooki DAO should be subject to the partnership law of *California* rather than that of another state. They simply assumed Californian law to apply. Yet the determination of the private law governing a DAO is one of the greatest mysteries of Private International Law, as will be shown in Chapter 3.[442] The failure of the CFTC and the court even to address this point makes the reasoning legally deficient.

2.4.6 *The Immutability of the Blockchain*

The factors considered so far are compounded by the immutability of the blockchain. Even if the supervisors manage to identify the responsible persons, serve them with an order or complaint, perhaps in a cooperative effort with foreign authorities, and make them comply with their orders, they cannot amend the blockchain because it cannot be retroactively changed.[443] Thus, it is likely that the ill-gotten gains from a crypto hack, ransomware attack or money laundering will stay with the same address. In sum, the results of criminal activities cannot be reversed.

This immutability of the blockchain is not definitive. The authorities or courts may order the criminal to engage in a reverse transfer, and if she does not comply, they may use coercive means, such as fines or imprisonment. However, it will not be possible for them to change the blockchain itself. Should the criminal remain unidentified, at large, or resistant to force, it is, therefore, challenging to bring the state of the blockchain in compliance with the law.

---

440 Zetzsche, Buckley and Arner (n 254) 1399–1400 (analysing liabilities of nodes in a blockchain and investors in a DAO).

441 ibid 1392–1398, 1400–1401 (examining liability under contract, tort and competition law).

442 See *infra* 3.2–3.4.

443 See Paech (n 254) 1097 (noting that any kind of ex post review is limited to the possibility of claiming damages in court, which is potentially unsatisfying).

One way would be to order the core developers to change the blockchain through a software patch. This possibility has been weighed in a civil action in the Royal Courts for England and Wales.[444] However, if courts or administrative authorities were allowed to order a correction of the distributed ledger, its main features would become obsolete. The ledger would no longer be run in a decentralised manner, but centrally through a court or authority. It would no longer function without trust, but depend on the trust of the users in the judicial or executive branch of a given country. Courts and authorities in other countries could then be expected to follow suit. As a result, it would no longer be a permanent, anational store of value, but a provisional register that stands to be corrected by state authorities at any time. Consequentially, it would be deprived of most of the features that set it apart from other types of registers, and risk becoming useless besides them.

2.4.7 *Conclusion*

Practically, it is very complicated to identify actors of the crypto economy, serve claims to them, seize crypto-assets and restore them to their rightful holder. While not entirely impossible, these actions require strong cooperation between national authorities. Yet such cooperation is challenging to obtain given their different capabilities, attitudes and incentives. Moreover, criminals can easily play out one state against the other by frequently changing the country, thus thwarting any effort to hold them accountable.

2.5 Worldwide Jurisdictional Chaos

2.5.1 *Overlapping Jurisdiction of Several Regulators*

As an effect of the blockchain's connections with different countries around the world and the uncertainty over its legal nature, states vie for control over the crypto economy. They use various legal characterisations and connecting factors to justify the application of their law to the blockchain. They also use different mechanisms to enforce their rules or orders to the participants and actors. As a result, any transfer on the blockchain may be simultaneously subject to a plethora of possibly contradicting rules and measures.

In theory, a different analysis could apply to permissioned networks, i.e., those that feature a central authority. It has been suggested that a state should allow access to such networks only where the participants choose a specific

444 High Court for England and Wales, *Tulip Trading Limited v Wladimir van der Laan et al.*, per Falk J, [2022] EWHC 667 (Ch); Court of Appeals, [2023] EWCA Civ 83.

law (viz: its own law).[445] Yet such a view grossly overstates the importance of choice of law, which does not change the applicable regulatory regime. A state will apply its rules on anti-money laundering, tax evasion or market manipulation regardless of the law the participants have selected. Also with respect to permissioned networks, different legal regimes will therefore continue to overlap and cannot be avoided by a choice-of-law clause.

It is true, though, that foreign supervisors are typically less interested in networks whose participants are exclusively based in another state. Their interest increases with the number of connections to their citizens or residents. At the same time, the varying characterisations make it challenging to foresee the basis on which the application of national law may be justified. This makes any prognosis of the laws that will actually be applied highly uncertain.

2.5.2 *Uneven Enforcement*

Despite the difficulties described above, for some states, ensuring respect for their law is quite easy. They do not have to use force abroad but can instead use their power of coercion over persons and assets on their own territory. Suppose a foreign resident does not comply with an administrative order issued by the authority of a certain state. In that case, the authority may, for instance, target its enforcement measures against the foreign resident's assets on the soil of its state. It may also take *ad personam* measures against the domestic shareholders of a foreign company. Even orders against foreign directors of such a company are not excluded: once they enter the state's territory, they will be subject to enforcement measures, such as a fine or even imprisonment.

Of course, this possibility exists only for states that are powerful economic and/or financial centres and attractive locations for foreign capital or visitors. The US, the Member States of the EU, and China are some cases in point. Given their economic and political weight, the chances of ensuring their law is applied are comparatively high. Other states, particularly small ones, may have fewer chances and need to act together with others or with the benefit of surprise. Consequently, there is not only a wide range of different applicable laws, but also a significant divergence in their implementation.

2.5.3 *Challenges for the Crypto Economy*

The variety of potentially applicable and actually applied laws presents a real conundrum for crypto service providers. They would have to know the rules of

445 Kerkemeyer (n 379) 812; Andreas Kerkemeyer, ‚Herausforderungen des Blockchain-Netzwerks für das Gesellschaftsrecht' (2020) Zeitschrift für Unternehmens- und Gesellschaftsrecht 654, 679.

all states in order to shield themselves from any liability. For instance, a crypto issuer can foresee some of the connecting criteria used, such as its place of establishment or the location of the crypto exchange on which its assets are traded, but not others, such as the location of the crypto investors. The same goes for crypto service providers, such as exchanges and wallet providers. As a result, it is hard to predict which law will apply to a particular offering or service. In light of this uncertainty, players in the crypto economy should start from the principle of the potential applicability of *all* the world's laws.

Nobody can know all these laws, but that does not exempt providers from the need to respect them. All countries follow in one or the other form the maxim: "*nul n'est censé d'ignorer la loi*", i.e. everybody is presumed to know the law. Against this background, there is no excuse for not respecting the law, whatever country it comes from. But this will often be impossible because laws may have contradictory requirements. And if one is to follow the strictest law on the crypto economy, one would be prohibited from making any offering at all.

Therefore, each actor of the crypto economy, e.g. a crypto issuer or service provider, faces the unenviable alternative of either strictly controlling its investor base or risking sanctions by a foreign state. Nobody can claim to have an overview of the crypto regulation of all states of the world, and buying legal advice on all of them would be prohibitively costly.

An alternative could be to focus on the major systems with the most relevant enforcement power. However, this approach still leaves considerable risks on the table. Even those actors that comply scrupulously with the regulations known to them cannot exclude running afoul of restrictions in some countries.

It has been argued above that being subject to all laws of the world is the price crypto issuers and service providers pay for the global nature of their business.[446] While this is true, it would be wrong to blame them for the mess of different regulations. Ultimately, it results from dividing the world into sovereign states, the effects of which the blockchain seeks to overcome.

2.5.4 *Opportunities through Regulatory Competition and Arbitrage*

But this is not the end; the chaos is even greater than one might assume based on the account made so far. Besides those states that prohibit or tightly regulate crypto activities, there are others that treat them especially favourably.[447] These states have created sandboxes and other "light" regulatory frameworks and vie to become the world's future crypto hub. In other words, they engage in

446 See *supra* 2.3.4.

447 See *supra* 2.1.1.3.

"regulatory competition"[448]: Each is trying to offer the most enticing legislative and regulatory package to attract service providers to its soil. This competition leads to possibilities of "regulatory arbitrage"[449]: Each economic actor is able to select the country with the lightest rules as its establishment. It can then offer its products and services from there to clients worldwide. While the countries adopting a more restrictive approach have introduced bans and try to enforce them on actors sitting abroad, these measures are not always effective. At any rate, it is, in principle, better for an issuer or service provider to sit in a low-regulation country than in a high-regulation country.

The story of regulatory competition and arbitrage is familiar and has been told many times before.[450] What makes the case of the crypto economy exceptional, though, is that some countries try to attract crypto activity while others try to completely ban it. States thus do not simply compete with each other to offer the best regulatory "deal"; instead, they contradict each other as to whether the crypto activity should be allowed at all. This makes regulatory arbitrage turn from a tactic to a necessity. The actors of the crypto economy must be constantly on the lookout for a safe haven from which they can operate. From this secure base, they deploy their activities to all countries except those with stringent rules and enforcement, such as the US.

2.5.5 *Consequences for the World Economy*

From a bird's eye view, the picture of global regulation thus looks particularly patchy. At one end of the spectrum, one finds countries where crypto-assets are strictly prohibited, at the other end, safe havens with a strong fervour for the crypto economy. This situation is anything but normal; it is testimony to the deep rift that the emergence of crypto has created between the states of the world. The possibilities offered by regulatory competition and arbitrage,

---

448 On regulatory competition see Larry E Ribstein and Bruce H Kobayashi, 'An Economic Analysis of Uniform State Laws' (1996) 25 The Journal of Legal Studies 131, 138–140; Anthony Ogus, 'Competition Between National Legal Systems: A Contribution of Economic Analysis To Comparative Law' (1999) 48 The International & Comparative Law Quarterly 405; Roberta Romano, 'The Need for Competition in International Securities Regulation' (2001) 2 Theoretical Inquiries into the Law 387.

449 On regulatory arbitrage see Hilton McCann, *Offshore Finance* (Cambridge University Press 2006) 173; Wolf-Georg Ringe, 'Regulatory Competition in Global Financial Markets' (2016) 1 Annals of Corporate Governance 175, 176 et seq.; Dirk A Zetzsche, 'Competitiveness of Financial Centers in Light of Financial and Tax Law Equivalence Requirements' in Ross P Buckley, Emilio Avgouleas and Douglas W Arner (eds), *Reconceptualising Global Finance and Its Regulation* (Cambridge University Press 2016) 390, 394, 398.

450 See authors in the two preceding footnotes.

and the difficulties of securing extraterritorial enforcement, heighten the political differences even more.

Whatever its attitude towards the crypto economy, no state can be content with this situation. Restrictive countries cannot because their bans are porous and ineffective. As long as there are safe havens that allow the crypto economy or even support its development, prohibitions enacted by certain states will be easy to circumvent. But the safe havens can also not be satisfied with the current situation. The bans in other countries have external effects and undermine the value of their industry. The overlapping and contradicting regulation thus hurts the interests of all states.

2.6 A Global Regulation for a Global Phenomenon

2.6.1 *The Need for Global Rules*

The interconnected and interdependent nature of the worldwide financial system makes strong coordination and cooperation between states indispensable. Concerning the blockchain, one needs a set of globally uniform rules. The reason for this is the global nature of the blockchain. It operates all over the planet and is accessible around the world. Each state can claim to regulate it, but will inevitably encounter difficulties in practically enforcing its rules.

Moreover, submitting DLT to divergent national rules undermines its benefits. The technology harnesses enormous potential for the development of the economy. As the world's first universally accessible and incorruptible store of value, the blockchain incentivises wealth creation across the globe. If properly and uniformly regulated, DLT might even trigger a new industrial revolution. However, as long as crypto service providers struggle with different national regulations, states will not benefit from the full range of possibilities offered by this technology.

Hence, there is an obvious case for uniform regulatory rules. Even laymen will immediately understand that the blockchain can be effectively regulated only by rules that apply worldwide. Common sense suggests that a global phenomenon calls for global rules.

Yet, in the current legal context, this possibility is very improbable. National regulation is dominant, and global rules are the rare exception. The cause of this is, of course, the absence of a global financial regulator. There are good reasons for its non-existence. Among them are the pervasive political differences in financial matters between states, the importance to keep some governmental "policy space" in the area of finance, including the possibility for experimentation, the need to adapt to local circumstances, and the planetary risks that an error by a single regulator would have.[451]

While these concerns are, in principle, sound, they have the disadvantage of leading to the adoption of very different regulatory rules. The blockchain shows the limits of the fragmented regulatory approach to a global phenomenon. The previous chapters have described the chaotic crisscross of contradictory regulations and the difficulties of their enforcement. As long as this continues, states will not achieve their regulatory purposes. At the same time, the operators of the crypto economy will suffer from the burden of multiple and often contradictory regulations.

2.6.2 *Global Standards for the Crypto Economy*

The fact that there is no global regulator does not mean that there would be no global institution in charge of financial markets. On the contrary, there are several organisations and fora where financial regulation is discussed and proposals for harmonisation are developed. They have issued reports and suggestions that amount to a partially global regulation of the crypto economy.

2.6.2.1 Fighting Money Laundering, the Financing of Terrorism, and Weapons of Mass Destruction

The first area in which states have become active and collaborated is anti-money laundering ("AML"). At the global forefront in this area is the Financial Action Task Force (FATF), a body created at the behest of the G7 in 1989.[452] Since the attacks of September 11, 2001, the FATF has broadened its mandate to countering the financing of terrorism ("CFT"). Recently, it has also added the fight against the proliferation of weapons of mass destruction to its agenda.[453]

451 On this debate, see, e.g., Tajinder Singh and Chris Brummer, 'Does Today's World Need a Global Financial Regulator' (2014) 33 International Financial Law Review 18; Roberta Romano, 'The Need for Competition in International Securities Regulation' (2001) 2 Theoretical Inquiries in Law 387; Roberta Romano, 'For Diversity in the International Regulation of Financial Institutions: Critiquing and Recalibrating the Basel Architecture' (2014) 31 Yale Journal on Regulation 1; Christian Tietje and Matthias Lehmann, 'The Role and Prospects of International Law in Financial Regulation and Supervision' (2010) 13 Journal of International Economic Law 663.

452 James K Jackson, 'The Financial Action Task Force: An Overview' (2017) <https://crsreports.congress.gov/product/details?prodcode=RS21904> accessed 15 April 2024.

453 FATF, 'International Standards on Combating Money Laundering and the Financing of Terrorism & Proliferation' (2012–2023) <https://www.fatf-gafi.org/en/publications/Fatfrecommendations/Fatf-recommendations.html> accessed 15 April 2024; see also James K Jackson, 'The Financial Action Task Force: An Overview' (2017) 4.

The FATF was the first global body to respond to the rise of the crypto economy. This can hardly be a surprise given that Bitcoin was an attempt to create a global currency beyond the control of states, which as such, provided vast opportunities for money laundering and the financing of crime. As a reaction, the FATF published a report on virtual currencies' potential AML/CFT risks as early as 2014.[454] The report provides key definitions, underlines legitimate uses, but also highlights dangers. It discusses, inter alia, the case of *Silk Road*, which had become a global marketplace for arms and drug dealing.[455]

Since this initial report, the FATF has adopted an abundance of other texts about virtual currencies. In 2015, it issued "Guidance on Virtual Currencies" and suggested national authorities adopt a "risk-based approach";[456] in 2018, it updated its "Recommendation on New Technologies" and included in its "Glossary" definitions for the new terms "virtual asset" and "virtual asset service provider";[457] in 2019, it issued an interpretative note on this Recommendation to clarify further how the regulatory requirements should apply to virtual assets and the related service providers;[458] since 2020, it has performed an annual review of its revised standards;[459] in 2020, it published for the first time "Red Flag Indicators" for virtual assets;[460] in 2021, it provided a "targeted update" regarding the implementation of its standards on virtual assets and virtual asset service providers.[461]

---

454 FATF, 'Virtual Currencies – Key Definitions and Potential AML/CFT Risks' (2014) <http://www.fatf-gafi.org/media/fatf/documents/reports/Virtual-currency-key-definitions-and-potential-aml-cft-risks.pdf> accessed 15 April 2024.

455 See *supra* 1.4.1.2.

456 FATF, 'Guidance for a Risk-Based Approach to Virtual Currencies' (2015) <https://www.fatf-gafi.org/en/publications/Fatfgeneral/Guidance-rba-virtual-currencies.html> accessed 15 April 2024.

457 FATF, 'Opportunities and Challenges of New Technologies for AML/CFT' (last updated 2021) <https://www.fatf-gafi.org/en/publications/Digitaltransformation/Opportunities-challenges-new-technologies-for-aml-cft.html> accessed 15 April 2024.

458 FATF, 'Guidance for a Risk-Based Approach to Virtual Assets and Virtual Asset Service Providers' (2019) <http://www.fatf-gafi.org/publications/fatfrecommendations/documents / Guidance-RBA-virtual-assets.html> accessed 15 April 2024.

459 The publications to date may be accessed at <https ://www.fatf-gafi.org/en/publications/Virtualassets/Virtual-assets.html> accessed 15 April 2024; the following have been published so far: FATF, '12 Month Review of Revised FATF Standards – Virtual Assets and VASPs' (2020); FATF, 'Second 12 Month Review of Revised FATF Standards – Virtual Assets and VASPs' (2021).

460 FATF, 'Money Laundering and Terrorist Financing Red Flag Indicators Associated with Virtual Assets' (2020) <https://www.fatf-gafi.org/en/publications/Methodsandtrends/Virtual-assets-red-flag-indicators.htm> accessed 15 April 2024.

461 FATF, 'Targeted Update on Implementation of FATF's Standards on VAs and VASPs' (2021) <https://www.fatf-gafi.org/en/publications/Fatfrecommendations/Targeted-update-virtual-assets-vasps.html> accessed 15 April 2024.

When evaluating the importance of these texts, it is crucial to remember that the FATF has no formal legislative or executive powers but can merely issue recommendations, i.e. "*soft law*". Nevertheless, these have significantly affected the global regulation of the crypto economy. All industrialised countries today follow the procedures and rules suggested by the FATF.[462]

As the geographical scope of the recommendations issued by the group expanded, their material scope has, in tandem, widened considerably. In the beginning, the recommendations focused on convertible virtual currencies and the duties of those involved in the conversion from and into fiat money.[463] Since then, their scope has been extended to other areas, such as exchanging virtual currencies against others.[464] Today, almost any activity related to virtual assets falls under their purview. The FATF Report 2021 urges countries also to consider peer-to-peer transactions, although they function without the intervention of any intermediary.[465] This is justified because peer-to-peer transactions may be the most dangerous, given they happen away from the public gaze.

While the main focus of the FATF has been on anti-money laundering and countering terrorism financing, over the last years, it has turned to other risks as well. Its 2021 report mentions, for instance, fraud, market abuse and manipulation, sanctions evasion, ransomware payments and "other nefarious purposes".[466] This awareness of the broader context is necessary and has to be welcomed. Unfortunately, the mandate of the FATF does not cover them so far.

Particularly influential has been the FATF Interpretative Note to Recommendation No. 15 on New Technologies.[467] In this note, the body suggested that member countries should consider virtual currencies as "property",

---

462 For a comparative overview, see Matthias Lehmann and Tetsuo Morishita, 'General Report' in Matthias Lehmann and Tetsuo Morishita (eds), *Cryptocurrencies in National Laws – A Global Survey* (forthcoming Brill).

463 See FATF (n 456).

464 See FATF (n 458).

465 FATF, 'Updated Guidance for a Risk-Based Approach to Virtual Assets and Virtual Asset Service Providers' (2021) paras 37–41 <https://www.fatf-gafi.org/publications/fatfrecommendations/documents/guidance-rba-virtual-assets-2021.html> accessed 15 April 2024.

466 ibid paras 4 and 19.

467 FATF, Interpretative Note to Recommendation No. 15 on New Technologies (INR. 15), reprinted in Nadine Schwarz, Ke Chen, Kristel Poh, Grace Jackson, Kathleen Kao, Francisca Fernando, Maksym Markevych, 'Virtual Assets and Anti-Money Laundering and Combating the Financing of Terrorism (1): Some Legal and Practical Considerations' Annex 1 <https://www.imf.org/en/Publications/fintech-notes/Issues/2021/10/14/Virtual-Assets-and-Anti-Money-Laundering-and-Combating-the-Financing-of-Terrorism-1-463654> accessed 15 April 2024.

"proceeds", "funds", "funds or other values", or "other corresponding value" within the meaning of its recommendations in general. This has opened the door to applying the whole gamut of AML/CFT requirements to virtual currencies.

Of particular significance in this context is the Customer Due Diligence (CDD) Recommendation, which calls for the identification of the customer at the initiation of any business relation and a special control when certain thresholds are exceeded or when a client engages in suspicious activity.[468] The extension of this recommendation to virtual asset service providers led to crypto exchanges and wallet providers now having to identify and control their customers.

Very influential has also been the "travel rule", which requires financial institutions to obtain and hold certain information about the originators and beneficiaries of any transfer and make it available to the appropriate authorities on request.[469] This recommendation has been extended to virtual asset service providers.[470] As a result, crypto exchanges and wallet providers must keep and share data about their clients and their transfers and make the data available to the supervisor if asked.

With its definitions and recommendations, the FATF has shaped the regulatory landscape worldwide. Despite their non-binding nature, these texts have had significant repercussions on national law.[471] They are the main reason AML/CFT requirements across many countries are broadly similar. It is to be welcomed that the global industry is subject to a uniform set of rules on money laundering and counter-terrorism financing. This makes illegal activities more difficult. Regrettably, the substantive domain of the global rules is relatively limited. Though the FATF rules tackle some of the gravest dangers of the new technology, these are far from the only ones.

2.6.2.2 Tax Evasion

Another danger is that the blockchain may be abused to avoid paying taxes. This concerns the hiding of income by transforming it into virtual crypto-assets and the non-declaration of income derived from these assets, for

468 ibid, Recommendation 10.

469 ibid, Recommendation 16.

470 FATF (n 465) Annex A para 9 (calling on countries to ensure that originating VASPs obtain and hold required and accurate originator information and required beneficiary information on virtual asset transfers, submit this information to the beneficiary VASP or financial institution (if any) immediately and securely, and make it available on request to appropriate authorities).

471 See on the effects in the United States, France and the EU *supra 2.2.1.1*.

instance from staking, crypto lending or yield farming.[472] The issue is not so much about capturing these types of earnings – fiscal law is quite nimble and has few problems in putting them into categories such as personal earnings. Challenges arise from new assets received without consideration through a hard fork or an airdrop, but through the enactment of special rules, even these assets can be subjected to taxation.[473]

The biggest practical problem, however, is to get the relevant data about the crypto-asset holdings. The pseudonymity of the blockchain and the worldwide distribution of nodes provide ideal conditions for those who want to hide their wealth. National fiscal authorities worldwide have just started grappling with this issue. To be successful, they will need to get information from other countries. What is required, again, is global coordination and cooperation. On this front, things move only slowly. The Organization for Economic Co-operation and Development (OECD) has published a consultation on this issue.[474] In the interests of safeguarding public finances and the principle of equality before the law, it is hoped that this initiative will soon lead to concrete outcomes.

2.6.2.3 Financial Stability

The crypto economy also creates macroeconomic dangers, in particular the risk of financial instability and crises.[475] These risks are closely monitored by global institutions.

A leading role is taken by the Financial Stability Board (FSB), a body created by the G7 and the successor of the former "Financial Stability Forum".[476] It cooperates on the crypto economy with other global regulatory bodies, in particular the Committee on Payments and Market Infrastructures (CPMI), the International Organization of Securities Commissions (IOSCO) and the Basel Committee on Banking Supervision (BCBS). Since 2018, they have been

---

472 See *supra* 1.2.4.2.

473 See, e.g., Eric D Chason, 'Cryptocurrency Hard Forks and Revenue Ruling 2019–24' (2019) 39 Virginia Tax Review 279; William Elman, 'New Coins on the Block: How Should Cryptocurrency Hard Forks Be Taxed?' (2021) 74 Federal Communications Law Journal 55.

474 OECD, 'Crypto-Asset Reporting Framework and Amendments to the Common Reporting Standard' (2022) <https://www.oecd.org/tax/exchange-of-tax-information/crypto-asset-reporting-framework-and-amendments-to-the-common-reporting-standard.pdf> accessed 15 April 2024.

475 See *supra* 1.4.3.

476 On the origins, development, membership and functions of the FSB, see Tony Porter, 'Financial Stability Board' in Christian Tietje and Alan Brouder (eds), *Handbook of Transnational Economic Governance Regimes* (Martinus Nijhoff 2009) 345–353.

working together on the topic of crypto-assets.[477] Their efforts are supported by national authorities, such as the US Federal Reserve or the European Central Bank (ECB).

The financial authorities are particularly worried about the transmission of risks from the crypto economy to the rest of the financial sector. They have identified various "transmission channels" through which such risks could spill over to the whole financial system.[478] Among these channels are financial institutions, which increasingly have crypto-assets in their portfolios and, therefore, might be negatively affected by their loss in value.[479] Furthermore, the FSB frets about "wealth effects", i.e. the risk that a downturn in the crypto market could lead to a substantial reduction in the value of investors' portfolios, and "confidence effects", i.e. the potential consequences of the crypto economy's demise to investors' trust in the financial system as a whole.[480] The FSB also sees risks for payments and settlement as well as for the environment.[481] Yet so far, it has not proposed any specific regulation to address these risks.

Presently, stablecoins are in the crosshairs of financial authorities.[482] They complain about the intransparency of the reserve assets backing the coins, issuers' inconsistent disclosure practices, and the market's high concentration.[483] Special concerns are triggered by stablecoins that are backed up by fiat currencies. In particular, it is feared that large-scale redemptions by investors could lead to a fire sale of those currencies, disrupting markets.[484]

The biggest concerns, however, are caused by so-called "*global stablecoins*". These are defined as those having "a potential reach and use across multiple

---

477 See FSB, 'Crypto-Assets: Report to the G20 on the Work of the FSB and Standard-Setting Bodies' (2018) <https://www.fsb.org/2018/07/crypto-assets-report-to-the-g20-on-the-work-of-the-fsb-and-standard-setting-bodies/> accessed 15 April 2024.

478 FSB (n 183) 4–10.

479 ibid 4–5.

480 ibid 6–8.

481 ibid 8–10.

482 See, e.g., FSB (n 183); FSB (n 477); ECB Crypto-Assets Task Force, 'Stablecoins: Implications for Monetary Policy, Financial Stability, Market Infrastructure and Payments, and Banking Supervision in the Euro Area' (2020) ECB Occasional Paper Series No. 247 <https://www.ecb.europa.eu/pub/pdf/scpops/ecb.op247~fe3df92991.en.pdf> accessed 15 April 2024; President's Working Group on Financial Markets, the Federal Deposit Insurance Cooperation, and the Office of the Comptroller of the Currency, 'Report on Stablecoins' (2021) <https://home.treasury.gov/system/files/136/StableCoinReport_Nov1_508.pdf> accessed 15 April 2024; Committee on Payments and Market Infrastructures (CPMI) and Board of the International Organization of Securities Commissions, 'Application of the Principles for Financial Market Infrastructures to Stablecoin Arrangements' (2021) <https://www.bis.org/cpmi/publ/d198.pdf> accessed 15 April 2024.

483 FSB (n 183) 11.

484 ibid.

jurisdictions and which could become systemically important in and across one or many jurisdictions, including as a means of payment".[485] The paradigm is Facebook's Libra/Diem project, which would have fulfilled these criteria had it not been abandoned. Another operator with a worldwide customer base might nevertheless decide to follow in Facebook's footsteps and create a similar token. The FSB fears a disorderly run on such a global stablecoin could lead to disruptions in the real economy and spillovers into the broader financial system.[486]

These worries are not unfounded, yet they seem premature at this stage. Currently, no stablecoin is in sight that could replace one of the major fiat currencies. It is to be expected that any token which could take this place will be carefully scrutinised by depositors and the media for its soundness. More than by the danger of financial instability, the frenzy of regulators about stablecoins may be motivated by the fear of losing control over monetary policy. This should not cloud their judgement about the potential of stablecoins and hastily kill this technology in the bud.

2.6.2.4 Cyber Security

There have been some efforts on the global level to strengthen national legal frameworks against cyber risks. The G7, for instance, has published Guidelines on cyber security in the financial sector.[487] The FSB has also been active on this topic. It has delivered a stocktake to the G20 and drawn some conclusions.[488] It has also dealt with the practically very relevant reporting of cyber incidents, making recommendations on it could be harmonised.[489] Other organisations have been active in this field as well.[490]

These activities are not limited to the crypto economy but also cover other areas in which technology plays a crucial role. They are, however, of special

485 ibid 25.

486 ibid 14.

487 HM Treasury, 'G7 Fundamental Elements for Effective Assessment of Cybersecurity in the Financial Sector' (3 February 2023) <https://www.gov.uk/government/publications/g7-fundamental-elements-for-effective-assessment-of-cybersecurity-in-the-financial-sector> accessed 15 April 2024.

488 FSB, 'Summary Report on Financial Sector Cybersecurity Regulations, Guidance and Supervisory Practices' <https://www.fsb.org/2017/10/summary-report-on-financial-sector-cybersecurity-regulations-guidance-and-supervisory-practices/> accessed 15 April 2024 (presenting conclusions from the FSB's cybersecurity stocktake delivered to the G20).

489 FSB, 'Recommendations to Achieve Greater Convergence in Cyber Incident Reporting: Final Report' <https://www.fsb.org/2023/04/recommendations-to-achieve-greater-convergence-in-cyber-incident-reporting-final-report/> accessed 15 April 2024 (setting out recommendations that aim to promote convergence among cyber incident reporting frameworks and encourage better practices).

490 See for an overview Iain Sheridan, *Financial Regulation and Technology: A Legal and Compliance Guide* (Edward Elgar 2022) 65–84.

relevance for the blockchain because it harbours enormous values, making it an especially interesting target for cyber criminals. It is thus hoped that these guidelines, reports and recommendations will increase the awareness of cyber risks and lead to a heightened level of security around the globe.

2.6.2.5 The Remaining Differences

The global regulation of blockchain remains full of gaps. Only very few questions raised by the new technology have been addressed by international authorities. These concern primarily global "bads" – money laundering and financial instability – and common concerns – the ability to tax and cyber security. But they often ignore possible global "goods", such as the ability of DLT to facilitate global trade,[491] enhance cross-border payments[492] and further financial inclusion.[493] These advantages of the technology have yet to be fully used. But to do so, international standardisation and closer cooperation between the competent authorities are needed.

Besides money laundering, financial instability and tax evasion, many other matters remain in the realm of national regulators. The latter determine, for instance, the standards to be met by issuers of security tokens or stablecoins. They define differently what these assets are and which prudential and conduct requirements, if any, apply to them. There is even no agreement on whether such assets can be offered and traded at all.

From this emerges a fragmented regulatory landscape. The conditions crypto offerings must comply with vary widely from one state to another. The contrast to the blockchain's global nature and the worldwide aspiration of its creators could not be starker. Whereas DLT was intended to become a global mechanism of payment and storage of value, it is today governed by a patchwork of different national regulations. Arguably, these differences are even greater than in the case of classic securities and payment instruments, which are offered, managed and traded through traditional intermediaries, such as

491 On this topic, see, e.g., Deepesh Patel and Emmanuelle Ganne, 'Blockchain & DLT in Trade: Where do we Stand?' (Trade Finance Global and World Trade Organization, November 2020) <https://www.wto.org/english/res_e/booksp_e/blockchainanddlt_e.pdf> accessed 15 April 2024 (examining the use of DLT in trade documentation, digitalisation of trade processes, and the exchange of trade data).

492 On this topic, see, e.g., Dirk A Zetzsche and others, 'DLT-Based Enhancement of Cross-Border Payment Efficiency – a Legal and Regulatory Perspective' (2022) BIS Working Paper Series No 1015 (suggesting *inter alia* to use DLT for a network of central banks or as an AML/KYC utility).

493 See World Bank Group, 'Distributed Ledger Technology (DLT) and Blockchain' (2017) FinTech Note No 1, 23 (noting the benefits of DLT for cross-border remittances).

banks or brokers. Every state pursues its own, idiosyncratic policy towards the new phenomenon. As a result, there is not one global crypto economy, but different behemoths that are more often than not based in "crypto havens", whose activities are considered to be illegal in other countries where crypto is banned. This situation seems hardly tenable in the long term.

2.6.3 *No Mitigation of Regulatory Conflicts through Deference*

The classic means of reducing regulatory conflicts is deference. States defer to foreign regulatory and supervisory regimes to the extent they judge them to achieve basically similar outcomes as their own.[494] There are different names, concepts and rules for this; national variations include the expressions "substituted compliance" and "equivalence".[495] These mechanisms are critical to integrating global markets as they allow providers and products to avoid double regulation and supervision by more than one country.

However, in the area of crypto-assets and their providers, deference is – at least to this day – as rare as the proverbial hen's teeth. The US, for example, does not recognise the submission of a crypto intermediary to any foreign state's regulation or supervision as a substitute for compliance with its own rules. This has been explained by pointing out that no other jurisdiction would have sufficiently well-established regulations to justify substituted compliance.[496] The EU legislator has merely tasked the Commission to assess whether an equivalence regime should be established for third-country providers and token issuers, without providing such a regime itself.[497] The fact that the EU

494 See, e.g., Matthias Lehmann, 'Legal Fragmentation, Extraterritoriality and Uncertainty in Global Financial Regulation' (2017) 37 Oxford Journal of Legal Studies 406, 429 et seq.; Niamh Moloney, 'Reflections on the EU Third Country Regime for Capital Markets in the Shadow of Brexit' (2020) 17 European Company and Financial Law Review 35, 39; Pierre-Hugues Verdier, 'Mutual Recognition in International Finance' (2011) 52 Harvard International Law Journal 55, 71 et seq.

495 From the voluminous literature on these subjects, see Ethiopis Tafara and Robert J Peterson, 'A Blueprint for Cross-Border Access to U.S. Investors: A New International Framework' (2007) 48 Harvard International Law Journal 31; Howell E Jackson, 'Substituted Compliance: The Emergence, Challenges, and Evolution of a New Regulatory Paradigm' (2015) 1 Journal of Financial Regulation 169; Matthias Lehmann and Jonas Schürger, 'Multilateralizing Deference – A Proposal for Reforming Global Financial Law' (2023) 56 International Lawyer 191; Jonas Schürger, *Equivalence and Substituted Compliance in International Financial Markets Law* (Oxford University Press 2023); Eddy Wymeersch, 'Third-Country Equivalence and Access to the EU Financial Markets Including in Case of Brexit' (2018) 4 Journal of Financial Regulation 209, 215.

496 Freya (Fangheng) Zhao, 'Initial Coin Offerings and Extraterritorial Application of U.S. Securities Laws' (2022) 39 The Banking Law Journal 174, 203.

497 Art. 140(2)(v) MiCAR.

contains over 40 different equivalence regimes in other pieces of legislation shows how unusual this state of affairs is.[498]

The degree of regulatory coordination regarding the crypto economy is thus well behind that of other areas, such as securities law or the regulation of payment services. This is regrettable but a direct consequence of the diverse rules states apply to crypto-assets and their providers.

2.6.4 *The Coordination and Cooperation Deficit*

The fragmentation of legal regimes around the world further complicates their enforcement. Because states have very distinct approaches to the crypto economy, they find cooperating in supervision and enforcement difficult. This is not just a question of the different rules but also of different attitudes. Host countries, i.e. those to which crypto offerings are targeted, try to regulate foreign providers because their activity is illegal or criminal under local law. Meanwhile, home countries, i.e. those from which crypto products and services are exported, often shield them as national unicorns and pioneers heralding a new era of finance. Because of these diverging attitudes, host countries have difficulty finding a helping hand when investigating foreign providers, while home countries see obstacles and market barriers for their tech champions everywhere.

At the same time, regulatory and supervisory cooperation is urgent in the crypto space. The networks span the globe, the nodes are spread over an array of countries, and the teams of programmers are mostly multinational and highly mobile. Therefore, effective enforcement is possible only when states and their authorities cooperate.[499] To take the most egregious example, the crypto bans many countries have adopted can be easily circumvented as long as other states do not help their enforcement. Given the global distribution and accessibility of blockchain networks, it is very hard to shut them down. The government can prohibit intermediaries from offering crypto-assets or miners from engaging in mining, yet blocking citizens from storing and accessing crypto-assets on an existing blockchain is challenging. While they may not be able to spend them in the countries where they are banned, they can use them in other countries or in cyberspace.

This clearly shows the particular need for global rules on the regulation and supervision of blockchain. As long as there are at least a few countries

---

498 See the overview in Schürger (n 495) 28–57.

499 See also Syrene Johnstone, *Rethinking the Regulation of Cryptoassets* (Edward Elgar 2021) 280–281 (calling for a G20 initiative similar to those on OTC derivatives and rating agencies).

in which mining is allowed, the crypto economy will not vanish from the face of the Earth. At the same time, those countries that favour the technology will hardly have their way if others insist on maintaining their bans. For exports of crypto-assets and related services to surge, importing countries are needed.

Every state would thus benefit from more regulatory coordination and supervisory cooperation in the realm of the crypto economy. But for such coordination and cooperation to occur, the regulatory goals and supervisory instruments must converge at least to a minimal extent. One could think, for example, of uniform rules regarding transparency, reliability and capital requirements that issuers of tokens would have to meet, as well as rules on the custody of the asset pool of stablecoins. Regulating marketing communications, governance issues, and conflicts of interest would be advisable as well. The introduction of such a uniform regime by a number of states could facilitate liberalisation in other states that have adopted a rather reserved stance towards the crypto economy until now.

It is true that such global uniform rules would be completely new. However, we must not lose sight of the fact that blockchain technology is also new. Only if states agree on some basic principles will they stand a chance of regulating and supervising the crypto economy efficiently. Otherwise, the crypto economy will always remain an outcast of world finance, with few benefits for investors and citizens but the potential to hide illegal activities and create financial stability risks.

Conclusion of Chapter 2

The regulation of the crypto economy is extremely fragmented. State legislation and practice exhibit various approaches, ranging from a total prohibition of crypto-assets and services to favourable rules of "sandboxes" that aim to reduce the regulatory burden for the crypto economy. The differences are exacerbated by the fact that the diverging rules are often intended to be applied extraterritorially to reach providers, activities or events outside the legislating state. This results in a multitude of different rules that crypto providers have to obey.

This chaos of overlapping and contradicting rules is incomparable to the regulation of any other financial sector. It is particularly deplorable because it contradicts the global nature of the blockchain. The technology runs the same way worldwide, yet it is subject to divergent regulatory rules and standards. As a consequence, the providers are sitting in a regulatory halfway house, being permitted and even incentivised to operate in some countries while being considered criminals in others.

That is why global standards are urgently needed. They must go beyond the few select areas where international regulators have been active so far. In the future, they should govern the whole breadth of the crypto economy. Admittedly, it will take much work to find political agreement on such principles, given national legislators and regulators' varying attitudes and policies. However, adopting common and uniform principles at the international level is indispensable, whether one wants to develop the blockchain or prohibit it. The blockchain is a global phenomenon, and the answer to the problems it raises must also be global.

Interlude: Conflicts of Regulation and Conflicts of Private Law – Differences and Interconnections

Many regulatory problems analysed in Chapter 2 strongly resemble the conflict-of-laws issues to be discussed in Chapter 3. For instance, some regulatory categories – e.g. money or intermediated securities – have a sibling in Private International Law. Also, several factors used to determine the scope of regulatory acts – e.g. the location of the issuer or the place of establishment of the crypto exchange – may also be relevant for determining the applicable private law. Furthermore, there are interconnections between the two fields, for instance when it comes to the legal personality of a DAO, which is determinative for both regulatory and private law.[500]

Nevertheless, one must not confound Private International Law with international regulatory law. Both deal with different issues. One concerns the determination of the law governing private relations, the other the relation between the state and the individual; one deals with the international application of private law rules, whereas the other deals with the international application of public law rules. The distinction between both is not due to a historical coincidence but the result of the different perspectives and purposes of private and public law.[501] The old saying by *Ulpian* still rings true: Public law is concerned with the relation between the individual and a particular state

---

500 See *supra* 2.4.5.

501 See on the enduring relevance of this distinction Burkhard Hess, 'The Private-Public Law Divide in International Dispute Resolution' (2018) 388 Collected Courses of the Hague Academy of International Law 49.

and aims at protecting the general interest, whereas private law focuses on the relation between individuals and the balancing of their mutual interests.[502]

The different perspectives and purposes of regulatory law and private law also have repercussions on the level of conflict of laws. Regulatory rules, which have been discussed in Chapter 2, apply unilaterally, ignoring the rules of other countries. In contrast, conflict rules for private law, which will be the subject of Chapter 3, are typically multilateral, i.e. they determine the applicability of the rules of the forum and those of other countries. As a result, the same cross-border activity will frequently be governed by a plurality of different regulatory laws, while this state of affairs is – fortunately – not the norm in private relations. Quite to the contrary, the ideal and goal of Private International Law is for all legal systems to submit the same private relationship to a single substantive law.

One must not overstress the difference between both fields, though. On the one hand, regulation often also protects individual interests, including those of investors. Moreover, the one-sided nature of regulation also reverberates into Private International Law, e.g. through public policy or overriding mandatory rules. To illustrate, where national legislation prohibits dealings in cryptocurrencies or other crypto-assets, this will have repercussions on the validity of private transactions. On the other hand, private law may serve as a means to implement public interest goals. An example is the liability of crypto issuers or service providers, which helps the enforcement of regulation through a private cause of action. Also, regulators should strive to use connecting factors likely to reduce conflicts with other nations as much as possible. In particular, they should avoid imposing diverging organisational requirements on the same operator.

Still, the basic principles, the conceptual apparatus and the nomenclature of regulatory law and private law remain different. For example, "money" in regulatory law typically encompasses both cash and "book money". In contrast, these two concepts fall into very different categories in private law: the law of property and the law of obligations. One must be wary not to confound the characterisations of regulatory law and private law. The same goes for the conflicts of regulatory law on the one hand and conflicts of private law on the other. Even though private law may serve to pursue regulatory goals, it has its own independent scope and effects. For example, a state that prohibits cryptocurrencies or other crypto-assets cannot avoid dealing with the private law issues involved, for instance if they have been acquired before a ban entered into force or are held by foreign residents. Moreover, the connecting factors

502 Alan Watson (transl.), *The Digest of Justinian*, vol. 1 (University of Pennsylvania Press 2009) Book One Title 1 (Justice and Law) para 1.

used by regulatory law differ from those of Private International Law. While the first is informed by specific one-sided goals, such as the protection of investors, for the pursuit of which a "genuine connection" is considered sufficient, the latter is inspired by the desire to find the "closest connection", i.e. the legal system with which the facts present the most significant link. For these reasons, it is necessary to study the Private International Law of the crypto economy separately from its international regulation. Inevitably, there will be connection points that need to be highlighted.

CHAPTER 3

Private International Law of the Crypto Economy

The crypto economy raises quite arduous Private International Law problems, such as: Which law governs the transfer of crypto-assets? Which law protects them against theft or other torts? Which law determines whether they can be subject to property rights? Can they be inherited? Can they be acquired in good faith?

These questions are not easy to answer. They are of paramount importance, though, for two reasons: First, the global nature of the blockchain makes it necessary to determine the applicable law beforehand, and second, national private laws provide strongly divergent solutions to those issues. Identifying the applicable private law is thus of utmost relevance. This will be the subject of Chapter 3.

This Chapter will start by analysing private law issues raised by the crypto economy (3.1). It will be shown that the law applicable to most of these issues can be determined using classic conflict-of-laws rules (3.2). All other issues, particularly the law governing proprietary rights, call for a characterisation of crypto-assets, which is difficult (3.3). In addition, finding the proper connecting factor for crypto-assets is challenging (3.4). Given these problems and the various ways in which national legal systems have responded to them, a new rule of Private International Law specifically for assets recorded on a blockchain will be developed (3.5). Next, the law applicable to certain other special phenomena will be addressed, namely, the law applicable to stablecoins (3.6), smart contracts (3.7) and DAOs (3.8). Then, the thorny procedural, enforcement and insolvency issues arising in the crypto economy will be discussed (3.9). Thereafter, it is time to explore the prospect of international uniform law regarding the crypto economy (3.10). Finally, a new approach will be proposed to create a symbiosis between law and technology, which relies on the information recorded on the blockchain and rectifies it only when necessary (3.11).

3.1 Issues of Private Law Raised by the Crypto Economy

Private International Law is the servant of substantive private law. It is premised on the existence of substantive law rules and influenced by substantive law policies. Moreover, rules of Private International Law are needed and valued most when national substantive law rules diverge. Thus, an analysis of

 | DOI:10.1163/9789004725140_005

Private International Law as applying to the crypto economy must start from the level of substantive law.

National private laws deal with various aspects of the crypto economy. Not all of these are contentious or give rise to divergences between national systems. In many cases, applying the existing rules to the blockchain presents few problems. Sometimes, however, entirely novel issues arise. These cause challenges with which national laws struggle.

The following section will discuss several substantive private law questions surrounding the crypto economy. This overview is not intended to be exhaustive. Its purpose is not so much to provide a complete picture as to structure the issues into different categories. This will pave the way for the following Private International Law analysis.

3.1.1 *Illustration of Legal Issues*

The crypto economy has created a plethora of new assets, transactions and actors, which give rise to a variety of private law questions. For present purposes, they are grouped into two different categories to illustrate the challenges caused by the technology for the law.

3.1.1.1 Endogenous Problems

Some problems arise from a transfer recorded on the blockchain itself and may therefore be called "endogenous problems".[503] They can be illustrated through three examples: (Example 1) A wants to send 1.1 BTC (Bitcoin) to its counterparty B and accidentally sends 11 BTC; (Example 2) C is induced by fraud to provide D with 30 ETH (Ether); (Example 3) E transfers 1,000 XMR (Monero) to F as a ransom to unlock a freeze of its server. In all of these cases, a private law remedy may aid the party who transferred the assets.

The fact that the blockchain is immutable does not call into question the effectiveness of such remedies. For example, they could be set in action by a court of law that may order a retransfer by the recipient, i.e., a transfer in the opposite direction.[504] This may be practical when a contractual party received more than what was due, such as in Example 1. In Examples 2 and 3, obtaining or enforcing such an order may be difficult, as the recipient will typically be unknown. Still, some cases illustrate that it is possible to go down the judicial

503 Matthias Lehmann, 'Who Owns Bitcoin? Private Law Facing the Blockchain' (2020) 21 Minnesota Journal of Law, Science & Technology 93, 103.

504 ibid 120–123.

route, for instance, by tracing the asset and seeking a court order for restitution as well as a disclosure order against the intermediary that holds them.[505]

3.1.1.2 Exogenous Problems

Exogenous problems seem more difficult. These are all changes to a legal situation or relationship that do not have any root in or effect on the blockchain itself. Nevertheless, they involve a transfer of or a change in the rights over a crypto-asset because of an external event.[506] The paradigmatic case is succession, which causes an *ex lege* transfer of the deceased's assets to the heirs or the creation of an estate. This transfer is not recorded on the blockchain but occurs under the law.

Another example is the opening of bankruptcy proceedings, which generally imposes a prohibition on the debtor from disposing of her assets and creates a right of the bankruptcy administrator to sell them for the benefit of the creditors.[507] Again, these changes under the law happen outside the blockchain and are not reflected on it. Nevertheless, the consequences of the opening of insolvency proceedings are legally binding.

3.1.1.3 Parallelism between Blockchain and Private Law

These two problems illustrate how private law and the blockchain may go separate ways. However, we should not lose sight of the fact that they go together perfectly in many, even though not in all, cases. Indeed, the vast majority of transfers on the blockchain are underpinned by a private law transaction. Still, this transaction must be valid according to the relevant private law rules. It is therefore necessary to identify which law applies to any transaction in question.

---

505 See, e.g., High Court for England and Wales (Comm), 13 December 2019, *AA v Persons Unknown & Ors,* Re Bitcoin [2019] EWHC 3556 (granting alternative service – inside or outside of the jurisdiction – for an injunction against unknown hacker(s) to which the victim of a ransom attack had transferred crypto-assets by as well as against the two companies operating a crypto exchange that held these assets as intermediaries); High Court for England and Wales (Comm), 15 July 2021, *Fetch.AI Limited et al v Persons Unknown et al,* [2021] EWHC 2254 (granting a property injunction against the unknown perpetrators of an alleged crypto fraud as well as a worldwide freezing order and ancillary information disclosure order against the crypto exchange that held the assets).

506 Lehmann (n 503) 130.

507 Philip R Wood, *Principles of International Insolvency* (Sweet & Maxwell 2007) para 1–002 (stating that two essential features of insolvency law are that individual actions by creditors against the debtor are frozen and that all assets of the debtor belong to the pool which is available to the creditors for the payment of their claims).

3.1.2 *Contractual Issues*

Crypto-assets today are frequently the object of transactions, for instance, to buy and sell or to loan. This raises the question of how these transactions should be characterised under contract law. The focus here is on traditional contracts, which are entered into and performed by human beings. "Smart contracts", a new and different phenomenon entirely, will be analysed separately below.[508]

3.1.2.1 Contracts with Crypto-Assets as Consideration

The first question is whether contracts concerning crypto-assets are valid. This may be problematic under some legal systems. For example, as is well-known, the Common law requires "consideration" as a condition for the creation of a binding contract. Crypto-assets, or the promise to deliver crypto-assets, count as "consideration" in this sense, and contracts concerning them are thus enforceable at Common law.[509] This is not surprising since anything or any detriment can be consideration as long as it is bargained for.[510]

Another question concerns identifying the precise substantive law rules that govern such contracts. Many private law systems have special rules for contracts of "sale", "purchase", or "purchase-sale", depending on the name used in each legal system.[511] Typically, counter-performance under these contracts is not described in terms of "money" or "legal tender" but merely as "payment" or "price".[512] There can thus hardly be any doubt that a contract for the delivery of goods against cryptocurrency qualifies as a sales contract.[513] This is also true for uniform law texts, particularly the Convention on the International Sale of

---

508 See *infra* 3.7.

509 Amy Held, Alisdair MacPherson, and Burcu Yüksel Ripley, 'England and Scotland' in Matthias Lehmann and Tetsuo Morishita (eds), *Cryptocurrencies in National Laws – A Global Survey* (forthcoming Brill).

510 See, e.g., New York Supreme Court, 14 April 1891, *Louisa W Hamer v. Franklin Sidway*, 11 N.Y.S. 182 (accepting the promise to refrain from smoking and swearing as proper consideration for the promise of the payment of money).

511 See US Uniform Commercial Code (UCC) (speaking of "sale"); UK Sale of Goods Act (1979) (speaking of "sale"); Art. 1582 French Civil Code (*Code civil*) (speaking of "sale" – *vente*); § 433 German Civil Code (*Bürgerliches Gesetzbuch*) (speaking of "purchase" – *Kauf*); Art. 1445 Spanish Civil Code (*Código civil*) (speaking of "purchase and sale" – *compra y venta*).

512 See, e.g., Art. 2–106(1) and 2–401 UCC (requiring a "price"); Sec. 2(1) UK Sale of Goods Act (1979) (requiring "money consideration"); Art. 1582 French Civil Code (*Code civil*) (requiring that one party obliges itself to pay – *à payer*); § 433 German Civil Code (*Bürgerliches Gesetzbuch*) (requiring the payment of a price); Art. 1445 Spanish Civil Code (*Código civil*) (requiring the payment of a certain price).

513 See Lehmann and Morishita (n 230).

Goods (CISG), which obliges the buyer only to "pay the price" without further specification.[514]

The acceptance of crypto-assets as contractual counter-performance in private law varies remarkably from the situation under regulatory law, where cryptocurrencies are generally not considered "legal tender".[515] National private laws typically distinguish quite neatly between both questions. While the status as legal tender requires an unequivocal legislative basis, the private law status as "payment" or "price" depends merely on the factual acceptance of cryptocurrencies or other crypto-assets as a means of payment. The situation is somewhat similar to anti-money laundering, where the law adopts a sociological viewpoint.[516] Nevertheless, the lack of legal tender status has some repercussions for the private law regime. In particular, unless the parties agree specifically that the buyer may fulfil her obligations by providing cryptocurrencies or other crypto-assets, such assets may be used for payment purposes only when they are recognised as legal tender under the law governing the contract (*lex contractus*).[517]

Similar considerations apply to other types of contracts where one party performs against payment by the other party. Here, too, crypto-assets may serve as counter-performance. This is true for any rental, lease, or service contract; it also true for construction, travel or medical care contracts. In most legal systems, all of these contracts can be paid for in crypto-assets, provided the parties agree.[518]

3.1.2.2 Contracts with Crypto-Assets as Main Object

Matters are more complicated when crypto-assets are provided not merely as consideration or counter-performance, but as the main object of the transaction. In this case, determining the applicable substantive law rules may require an assessment of the assets' precise legal nature.

A judgment of the Tribunal de Commerce de Nanterre of 2020 illustrates the point perfectly.[519] An English company had borrowed a considerable number of Bitcoin (BTC) from a French crypto exchange. During the term of the loan, the Bitcoin hard fork of 2017 occurred, which resulted in the rise of a new

---

514 Art. 53 United Nations Convention on Contracts for the International Sale of Goods (CISG), done in Vienna on 11 April 1980 ("The buyer must pay the price for the goods … ").

515 See *supra* 2.2.1.1.

516 ibid.

517 Proctor (n 263) 74–76 paras 2.25–2.28.

518 See Lehmann and Morishita (n 230).

519 Commercial Court (*Tribunal de commerce*) of Nanterre, *SDE Bitspread Ltd c. SAS Paymium*, 26 February 2020, n° 2018F00466.

and parallel cryptocurrency known as Bitcoin Cash (BCH).[520] Because the English company had held BTC prior to the hard fork, it received a corresponding number of BCH. These were then claimed by the French crypto exchange. The French court considered the BTC to be fungible and consumable movables; and therefore characterised the contract regarding them as a loan for consumption (*prêt de consommation*).[521] From this, the court concluded that property rights over the BTC passed from the creditor to the borrower. The English company was therefore held entitled to keep the BCH it had received due to the hard fork in 2017.

As the summary shows, the case was just as much about contracts as it was about property law. Those legal systems that recognise property rights in intangible objects, like French law and more generally those of the Romanic tradition, have little difficulty applying the traditional contract and property law rules to transactions concerning crypto-assets. As explained in more detail below, other legal systems admit only corporeal things as objects of property rights.[522] In these legal systems, the same limitations imposed in property law may also apply to the potential object of a sale or other contract.[523] Still, even these legal systems accept that certain intangible rights and phenomena like electricity (power) can be "sold". Hence, an argument can be made that contracts concerning crypto-assets can be characterised as sales contracts.

3.1.2.3 Other Types of Contracts

The reciprocal exchange of two crypto-assets is generally considered a contract of barter.[524] An exception applies where one of the two serves as the contract's main object and the other is counter-performance, that is, the payment or price. For instance, an exchange of Dai – a stablecoin issued by the MakerDAO – against Ether could be construed either as a barter of two crypto-assets or a sale of Dai purchased with Ether. The parties' intentions and the general function performed by two crypto-assets in the market determine the most appropriate characterisation.

520 See *supra* 1.1.1.5.

521 Commercial Court (*Tribunal de commerce*) of Nanterre, *SDE Bitspread Ltd c. SAS Paymium*, 26 February 2020, n° 2018F00466.

522 See *infra* 3.1.5.

523 See, e.g., for German law Jens-Hinrich Binder, 'Germany' in Matthias Lehmann and Tetsuo Morishita (eds), *Cryptocurrencies in National Laws – A Global Survey* (forthcoming Brill).

524 E.g. under the laws of Austria, Denmark, Hungary, and Taiwan; see Lehmann and Morishita (n 230).

There is also consensus across legal systems on the fact that crypto-assets can be donated.[525] Indeed, it would be difficult to defend the contrary position, as any object, interest or value can be gratuitously transferred. A difficulty may be to determine the point in time when a donation of crypto-assets becomes irrevocable. This question is important in many legal systems in which an informal agreement to make a donation will become binding only after it has been performed.[526] Under these legal systems, it is important to identify when exactly the transfer of ownership is finalised or "perfected". In the context of the blockchain, this is a problem, but it is not unsolvable. One may refer, for instance, to the time when the donee obtains the factual power to dispose of the assets as decisive. From this point, the donation can be considered performed, and the donation contract will be binding.

3.1.2.4 Capacity of the Parties and Form of the Contract

In addition to questions relating to the nature of the contract, many other legal issues arise from agreements concerning the blockchain and crypto-assets. One of these is the capacity to contract. All legal systems have provisions that protect minors from incurring certain contractual obligations. Given the policy underpinning these provisions, they must also be followed in the crypto economy; there is no reason to accept a lower standard of protection of minors in the virtual world as compared to the real world. However, applying these rules raises the problem of pseudonymity on the blockchain, which makes it difficult to determine the age of any party contracting within the blockchain. This raises the question of whether all participants in a blockchain network can be presumed to have contractual capacity.

The validity of a contract may be subject to formal requirements, such as a written document. This raises the question of whether this requirement is met when a contract is concluded on the blockchain. On closer examination, this question is misleading because contracts are rarely concluded via the blockchain but by other means, such as emails or text messages. These transactions are distinct from the transfer of the crypto-asset on the blockchain. The real question is whether these means of concluding contracts meet the formal requirements of the governing law. The considerations that apply here are no different than in other areas of the digital world.[527]

525 ibid.

526 See, e.g., § 516 German Civil Code (*Bürgerliches Gesetzbuch*); for English law Halsbury's Laws (4th edn, 2004) vol. 20(1), para 67.

527 See on the equivalence between information in writing and electronic transferable records Art. 8 UNCITRAL Model Law on Electronic Transferable Records (2018).

3.1.3 *Succession Law Issues*

Under the typical law of succession, any right, obligation or asset of the deceased forms part of the estate or passes directly to the heirs. There is no reason why assets recorded on a blockchain should be treated any differently. Thus, there is hardly any doubt that crypto-assets can be the object of inheritance and wills.[528]

It is rarely necessary to characterise the asset in any way to determine the legal effects of succession. This may, however, be required when a legal system provides different rules for succession to movables and immovables. In these cases, it may be necessary to classify crypto-assets as belonging to one or the other category. There are good reasons to prefer the characterisation as a movable, since crypto-assets can easily change their location.[529]

However, the main difficulties of succession to crypto-assets lie elsewhere. In particular, it is very hard for the estate administrator, the executor of a will or the heir to track down any crypto-asset given its virtual nature. Even where the deceased's holdings are known, for instance because she kept them with a particular intermediary or recorded them in a list or file, it may prove challenging to find or access the corresponding private keys. Yet these are practical problems, which call for a practical solution. They do not raise doubts about the legal status of crypto-assets in succession.

3.1.4 *Tort Issues*

Differences between legal systems emerge in the protection of crypto-assets in tort. These are frequently illustrated by cases of so-called crypto "theft". By contrast to the theft of physical objects, which involves dispossession, crypto theft usually entails the unlawful exercise of control over the asset and transfer to another address, e.g. after the private key has been obtained through hacking or a phishing attack. The tort category also includes situations where crypto-assets are obtained by fraud, threats or extortion.

Most Civil law countries, especially those following the Romanic tradition, feature a general tort rule that provides for liability whenever "damage" is caused by the fault of another person.[530] These legal systems have no problem in offering tort protection to crypto holders who have suffered damage.

Other legal systems, such as German law,[531] make distinctions by reference to the asset itself. Although these systems fully protect objects of property

528 See Lehmann and Morishita (n 230).

529 See also the discussion for Private International Law, *infra* 3.2.4.1.

530 See, e.g., Art. 1240 French Civil Code (*Code civil*); Art. 1902 Spanish Civil Code (*Código civil*); Art. 2032 Italian Civil Code (*Codice civile*).

531 See § 823(1) German Civil Code (*Bürgerliches Gesetzbuch*).

rights, they are less generous concerning other entitlements, such as claims, which are considered as belonging exclusively to the realm of the law of obligations. In these legal systems, it is typically required to characterise a crypto-asset one way or the other. Where property rights are limited to corporeal assets, this may affect the protection of crypto-assets in tort.[532]

Problems may also occur in Common law systems. An example is the ruling on jurisdictional issues by the High Court of Justice for England and Wales in the case *Lubin Betancourt Reyes et al. v Persons Unknown et al.*[533] The claimants alleged that the first defendant, whose identity was unknown, had programmed and installed phishing malware on the first claimant's computer, transferring Tether (USDT) to a public address. Judge Pelling ruled that this set of facts did not pass the test for a claim under the tort of conversion, drawing a comparison between crypto-assets on the one hand and debts, copyrights and other "choses in action" on the other hand. The argument was that like choses in action, crypto-assets could not be "possessed" and therefore not be converted.[534] This assessment reflects a widely held view. Yet it is not shared by other Common law courts, which accept crypto-assets as potential objects of property rights.[535]

Even where a legal system rejects a property characterisation of crypto-assets, it may still protect them via liability rules for other torts, such as fraud, intimidation or breach of confidence. In some countries, for instance, hacking or a similar interference with a computer is a criminal offence, which will trigger civil liability for the resulting damage.[536] Common law courts may achieve results similar to tort protection via the rules on unjust enrichment or constructive trust.[537]

In summary, applying national law to crypto theft, fraud or other torts may be fraught with difficulties and can lead to discussions about the legal nature of the assets. However, the problems are not unsurmountable, as other types of liability can apply to crypto-assets that do not qualify as objects of protection in tort.

532 See Binder (n 523).

533 High Court of England and Wales, 26 April 2021, *Lubin Betancourt Reyes et al. v Persons Unknown et al* [2021] EWHC 1938 (Comm).

534 ibid para 12.

535 See *infra* 3.1.5.

536 See Binder (n 523).

537 See High Court of England and Wales, 13 December 2019, *AA v Persons Unknown et al*, [2019] EWHC 3556 (Comm); 21 December 2020, *Ion Science Limited v Persons Unknown*, unreported, discussed in Amy Held, 'Does Situs Actually Matter When Ownership to Bitcoin is in Dispute?' (2021) 36 Butterworth's Journal of International Banking and Financial Law 269; 15 July 2021, *Fetch.AI Limited et al v Persons Unknown et al*, [2021] EWHC 2254 (Comm).

3.1.5 *Property Law Issues*

The problems come to a head when the crypto-assets themselves are the focus of legal analysis. This is the case when the question is whether they can be objects of property rights and other rights *in rem* or, as commonly summarised, "proprietary rights". Here, characterisation of the new phenomena can no longer be avoided. What are crypto-assets? Are they mere claims or receivables, or can they be the objects of property rights in the same way as tangible things?

The answer is highly relevant for investor protection in the event of the insolvency of crypto intermediaries, such as the collapse of Mt. Gox or the more recent case of FTX have demonstrated. However, it is also determines other questions, such as whether crypto-assets can be used as collateral for secured transactions or how and under what terms such assets can be transferred and acquired.

Those who hold crypto-assets, by virtue of their exclusive knowledge of or access to the private key, certainly think they have property rights in them. This reflects the way in which the underlying technology is presented by its inventor(s). For example, the Bitcoin white paper uses the words "owner" and "ownership", but without indicating the law under which such rights should exist.[538]

Some legal systems have little difficulty in accepting property rights in crypto-assets. A case in point is French law, which recognises property rights in intangible objects.[539] This position is shared by many other legal systems of the Civil law tradition, such as Austria, the Czech Republic, Italy, Macao, the Netherlands and Sweden.[540] This does not, however, solve all problems relating to the modern phenomena. For instance, it is still unclear which transfer rules should apply to intangible property, e.g. those on movables or those on immovables. If one opts for the rules on movables, one must replace the transfer of "possession" that is required in many legal systems[541] with another criterion, such as the transfer of "control" over the crypto-asset. If one opts for applying the rules on immovables, one must draw an analogy between the centralised land register and the decentralised blockchain ledger, which is not without pitfalls either. The Romanic legal tradition does not provide a conclusive answer to these questions, but at least it has paved the way to the recognition of intangible things as objects of property rights.

---

538 Nakamoto (n 4) 2.

539 See *supra* 3.1.2.2.

540 See Lehmann and Morishita (n 230).

541 An exception is French law, which accepts transfer by mere consensus.

Nevertheless, many systems of the Civil law tradition do not accept property rights in crypto-assets and, more generally, in virtual asset, e.g. Croatian, German or Japanese law.[542] These systems follow the theory of corporeality, according to which property rights can only exist regarding tangible assets. At its most extreme, this theory limits the objects of property rights or rights *in rem* to tangible objects of the physical world. This inevitably results in difficulties in accepting modern forms of property, which frequently have no tangible underlying object, e.g. intellectual property rights or property rights in crypto or other virtual assets. It seems that these difficulties can only be overcome by a far-reaching overhaul of the fundamental principles of these legal systems, which is needed to accommodate the modern phenomena.

In the Common law, the issue arises distinctly. Historically, the law of personal property was divided into two categories: "choses in possession" and "choses in action".[543] The first covers tangible objects over which physical power could be exerted. The second relates to claims against other persons. Crypto-assets do not fall into either of these categories because they do not relate to tangible objects and do not generally provide a cause of action against another person, except for specific cases such as a security token representing a bond or a utility token embodying a claim. Nevertheless, several courts in Common law countries have considered Bitcoin and other crypto-assets as "property".[544] This assessment is shared by the UK Jurisdiction Taskforce.[545] The problem for the Common law is therefore not whether to recognise crypto-assets as objects of property but rather how to make them fit into the existing dichotomy of choses in possession and choses in action.

In the present context, it would be inappropriate to assess or criticise any of the positions taken by national laws. Though rights in crypto-assets must be protected, including under international law,[546] the question of *how* to ensure such protection remains. Whether this protection is achieved through property law or another regime, such as the law of obligations, is left to the discretion of the national legislator. The debate should, however, be centred on policy analysis and not on the doctrinal idea according to which property can

542 Lehmann and Morishita (n 230).

543 See English Court of Appeal, *Colonial Bank v Whinney* (1885) 30 Ch D 261, 285 (Fry LJ).

544 See, e.g., High Court of Singapore, *B2C2 Ltd v Quoine Pte Ltd* [2019] SGHC(I) 03, para 142; High Court of New Zealand, *Ruscoe v Cryptopia Limited (in liquidation)* [2020] NZHC 728, para 141.

545 UK Jurisdiction Taskforce, 'Legal Statement on Cryptoassets and Smart Contracts' (2019) 16 para 57 ("We conclude that cryptoassets possess all the characteristics of property set out in the authorities").

546 See *supra* 1.4.2.6.

"only" exist in corporeal assets. Comparative law shows that this idea is misguided because many legal systems cast the net of property law much wider and capture intangible phenomena. It is also safe to assume that countries categorically limiting the notion of property to corporeal assets will increasingly encounter difficulties due to the inexorable rise of intangible objects of economic value in the digital age.

Whether crypto-assets fall within property law is, moreover, only the first of other equally difficult questions. If they do, one must decide next *which* rules of property law apply to them.

One question is, for instance, which rules apply to transfers of crypto-assets: those on movables, on immovables, or others that may still have to be developed? The answer may be decisive for the smooth functioning of the crypto economy. Suppose one opts for applying the rules on movables. In that case, the concept of "possession" must be replaced by another criterion, such as "control" over a given crypto-asset in those systems that require the transfer of possession as a condition for the transfer of ownership.[547] This condition of transferring possession does not exist in some national laws, such as French law and Italian law, where the contract alone effects the transfer of ownership. However, this leads to the problem of limping situations, due to discrepancies between the applicable law and the blockchain. As a general guideline, the formal requirements for transfer should be minimal and aligned with the particularities of the blockchain. This means that the record on the blockchain should be taken as the main reference point, supplemented by other conditions that ensure only voluntary transfers are effective.

Other problems exist, such as how security rights in crypto-assets can be created. In the modern crypto economy, there is an increasing trend of using crypto-assets as collateral. However, the requirements for creating such rights are unclear. For example, how can a subsequent disposition of the crypto-asset by the debtor be prevented? By a transfer of control? And if so, control over what? Or by registration on the blockchain? And where or how exactly?

Another question is whether and to what extent the *bona fide* acquisition rule applies. The *bona fide* rule promotes the easy circulation of assets because it frees purchasers from the need to make inquiries into the rights of their predecessors, which will, in most cases, be impossible given the pseudonymous environment of the blockchain. The rule is, therefore, essential for securing the easy transfer, negotiability and fungibility of crypto-assets, which are indispensable if crypto-assets are to fulfil their role as means of payment and objects of trade. How exactly this rule is to be applied still need to be worked

547 See already *supra* n 542 and accompanying text.

out. Questions that need to be addressed include, for example, whether negligence on the part of the acquirer excludes good faith. Is it sufficient that the purchaser was unaware of the seller's lack of title? What about crypto-assets stolen or lost by fraud?

Special rules will be required for the acquisition of crypto-assets via an intermediary. As a general rule, such an intermediary should not become the owner of assets it acquires on behalf of or for its customers' account. Instead, property should vest in the customers themselves. This is the best way to protect their interests in the event of the intermediary's insolvency. The legal techniques for achieving this result may vary from one jurisdiction to another. Where crypto-assets are transferred by a person who is not an owner, legal systems should refer to the knowledge of the customer, not that of its intermediary, to determine whether a *bona fide* purchase occurred.

3.1.6 *Conclusion*

This brief comparative overview has shown that many of the issues raised by the crypto economy can be solved using traditional rules of private law. In contract law, crypto-assets may be provided as counter-performance under a contract where the parties agree. The protection of crypto-assets under tort law is equally clear, although legal systems achieve this result differently. The most challenging issue is whether crypto-assets can be the object of property rights and what their legal regime would be. It is here that legal systems diverge the most.

3.2 Traditional Private International Law and the Crypto Economy

The search for the applicable law in the crypto economy is often presented as a complex enigma that is impossible to solve. This is because of the absence of links with the territory of a state.[548] Some think that this poses an existential challenge to Private International Law, with a need to rethink its categories.[549] Yet, often the applicable law can be determined by using traditional conflict-of-laws rules. This is so in those areas where the application of traditional

548 Mathias Audit, 'Le droit international privé confronté à la blockchain' (2021) Revue critique de droit international privé 669, 678; also sceptical Michael Ng, 'Choice of Law for Property Issues Regarding Bitcoin under English Law' (2019) 15 Journal of Private International Law 315, 336 et seq.

549 Florence Guillaume, 'Aspects of Private International Law Related to Blockchain Transactions' in Daniel Kraus and others (eds), *Blockchains, Smart Contracts, Decentralised Autonomous Organisations and the Law* (Edward Elgar 2019) 49; Koji Takahashi, 'Law applicable to proprietary issues of crypto-assets' (2022) 18 *Journal of Private International Law* 339.

substantive law also does not pose any problems, i.e. regarding contracts (3.2.1), torts (3.2.2) and succession (3.2.3). However, in other areas the existing conflicts rules do not adequately capture the reality of intangible assets recorded on a distributed ledger. This is particularly true for property law (3.2.4).

3.2.1 *The Law Applicable to Contracts Concerning Crypto-Assets*

3.2.1.1 Party Autonomy and Domicile of Seller or Service Provider

The law governing contracts concerning crypto-assets is relatively easy to determine. For instance, it is quite straightforward to identify the law applicable to contracts concerning crypto-assets, such as a sale, donation or lease. One can use the ordinary conflict-of-laws rules regarding contracts.

The Private International Law of contracts is dominated by the principle of party autonomy.[550] Hence, the parties can select the law applicable to contracts. However, this liberty is restricted in many cases, e.g. in the area of consumer contracts.[551]

In the absence of a choice, various connecting factors may be considered. Some conflict-of-laws rules refer to the law of the country with the "closest ties" or "most significant relationship" with the contract, which is to be determined by various factors.[552] This is illustrated, e.g. by the US, where many federal states use a variety of connecting factors, such as the domicile of either of the contracting parties or the place where the contract is concluded, to identify the legal system with the most significant relationship with the contract.[553] By contrast, most other legal systems opt for a more precise rule in the interest of legal certainty. These systems refer to the law in force at the place where the party providing the characteristic performance has its habitual residence,

---

550 See, e.g., Art. 41 sentence 1 Law on the Application of Law to Foreign-Related Civil Relations of the People's Republic of China; Art. 7 Inter-American Convention on the Law Applicable to International Contracts, done in Mexico, D.F. on 17 March 1994; Art. 7 Japanese Act on the General Rules on the Application of Law (Hō no Tekiyō ni Kansuru Tsūsokuhō); Art. 3 EU Rome I Regulation (Regulation (EC) No 593/2008 of the European Parliament and of the Council of 17 June 2008 on the law applicable to contractual obligations (Rome I) [2008] OJ L177/6); Art. 1210 Russian Civil Code; Art. 116 Swiss Federal Act on Private International Law; Art. 187 US Restatement (Second) on the Conflict of Laws (1971).

551 See *infra* n 557 and accompanying text.

552 Art. 9 Inter-American Convention on the Law Applicable to International Contracts ("closest ties"); Sec. 188 US Restatement (Second) on the Conflict of Laws (1971) ("most significant relationship").

553 Sec. 188(2) US Restatement (Second) on the Conflict of Laws (1971). The provision also refers to the place of performance of the contract, see *infra* 3.2.1.2.

central administration or place of business.[554] This is typically the party that provides the non-monetary performance, e.g. the seller or service provider. A special rule applies to contracts relating to immovables, which many jurisdictions submit to the law at the place where the immovable is situated.[555]

Regardless of which conflict-of-laws rule is followed, there will be little difficulty in determining the law governing contracts relating to crypto-assets. That is because applying these rules does not require determining the location of the crypto-asset. Instead, they use other factors, such as the place where the contract was concluded or the place where the provider of the characteristic performance has its habitual residence. The law applicable to a donation of crypto-assets can be determined in the same way because for the choice-of-law rule the place where the donated asset is located is unimportant. The same applies to contracts concerning immovables paid in cryptocurrency; again, there is no need to analyse the location of the cryptocurrency to determine the governing law.

The picture is different when the crypto-asset is the main object of the contract rather than the means of payment. In this case, the principle of party autonomy and the default connecting factors can be applied with ease. The only change that occurs is in those countries that refer to the habitual residence of the party providing the characteristic performance: what counts now is the place where the crypto provider has its habitual residence or place of business.[556]

Not much changes where consumers are involved. In these cases, party autonomy is either restricted or excluded altogether.[557] In the absence of a choice, the law of the consumer's state of domicile or habitual residence

554 See Art. 41 sentence 2 Law on the Application of Law to Foreign-Related Civil Relations of the People's Republic of China; Art. 8(2) Japanese Act on the General Rules on the Application of Law; Art. 1211(2) Russian Civil Code; Art. 4(1), (2) in conjunction with Art. 19(1) EU Rome I Regulation; Art. 117 Swiss Federal Act on Private International Law.

555 See Art. 8(3) Japanese Act on the General Rules on the Application of Law; Art. 1213 Russian Civil Code; Art. 4(1)(c) EU Rome I Regulation; Art. 119 Swiss Federal Act on Private International Law.

556 See on those countries *supra* n 554.

557 See Art. 42 sentence 2 Law on the Application of Law to Foreign-Related Civil Relations of the People's Republic of China; Art. 11(1) Japanese Act on the General Rules on the Application of Law; Art. 6(2) EU Rome I Regulation; Art. 120(2) Swiss Federal Act on Private International Law; Art. 1212(1) Russian Civil Code; Sec. 1–301 US Uniform Commercial Code (UCC).

applies.[558] Again, implementing these rules in a blockchain context should not create any difficulty.

3.2.1.2 Identifying the Place of Performance for Contracts Concerning Crypto-Assets

Problems may arise, however, where the place of performance plays a role in identifying the applicable law. Modern systems of Private International Law usually avoid using the place of performance as a connecting factor precisely because it is difficult to localise. However, the place of performance still features in some conflict-of-laws rules.

In the US, for instance, the place of performance is one of many factors used to determine the law governing contracts.[559] In the EU, it plays a role for the manner of performance and the steps to be taken in the event of non-performance or defective performance.[560] The place of performance may furthermore be relevant when identifying the law governing a contract for the exchange or barter of two or more crypto-assets. This is especially so in those countries that refer to the place where the party providing the characteristic performance has its habitual residence, central administration or place of business, as there is no characteristic performance in case of a contract for barter.[561] The place of performance may also be relevant when giving effect to the overriding mandatory rules of a third state, such as a prohibition on contracts relating to crypto-assets.[562]

Determining the place of performance of a contract involving crypto-assets may be simple when they are transferred using a physical medium, e.g., a USB key on which the private key is stored. But such cases are exceptional. Typically, and in line with their design, crypto-assets are transferred via the blockchain. Where does such a transfer take place? This question creates considerable difficulties.

Using the place where the node confirming the transfer is located would be unsatisfactory, as this depends on entirely unforeseeable circumstances,

558 Art. 42 sentence 1 Law on the Application of Law to Foreign-Related Civil Relations of the People's Republic of China; Art. 11(2) Japanese Act on the General Rules on the Application of Law; Art. 6(1) EU Rome I Regulation; Art. 120(1) Swiss Federal Act on Private International Law; Art. 1212(2) Russian Civil Code; Sec. 1–301 US Uniform Commercial Code (UCC).

559 Sec. 188(2) US Restatement (Second) on the Conflict of Laws (1971).

560 Art. 12(2) EU Rome I Regulation.

561 See the reference *supra* n 454.

562 See Art. 9(3) EU Rome I Regulation (allowing courts to give effect to the overriding mandatory provisions of the country where a contractual obligation has to be performed in case the contract is unlawful under these provisions).

namely, which node will solve the mathematical algorithm in the proof-of-work contest first. This cannot be determined in advance by the parties. Drawing an analogy to intellectual property rights or licenses is also not possible, as the use of crypto-assets is not limited to a particular country. Particular attention should be given to any stipulation in the contract as to the place of performance. In the absence of any such stipulations, the only viable connecting factor that remains is the place where the recipient has its habitual residence. In contrast, the Convention on the International Sale of Goods (CISG) favours the place of business of the seller over that of the buyer as the place of performance;[563] yet this rule is adapted to the context of the physical world, in which this place can be easily identified, and the CISG provision is not a conflict-of-laws rule anyway.

In sum, contracts regarding crypto-assets should be deemed to be performed at the place where the crypto-asset recipient has its habitual residence or principal place of business. Whilst this place may be unforeseeable for the seller, the potential uncertainty can be overcome at the time of contracting by the seller asking the recipient to confirm her address. Should she give a false or otherwise incorrect address, the place of performance should remain nevertheless fixed there because it has become an integral part of the agreement between the parties. This agreement should be understood and interpreted objectively, i.e. according to its terms. Any subjective reservations of the parties should be ignored.

3.2.1.3 Capacity to Contract and Form of Contract

The capacity to contract is generally governed by the law of each contracting party. This is either the law of their nationality[564] or that of their habitual residence.[565] However, applying these laws to blockchain transactions is complicated because the nationality and habitual residence of the parties are generally unknown. For international contracts, the law of the place where the contract was concluded to play some role.[566] However, this place is often also unknown because the contract is typically concluded at a distance. In

563 See Art. 31(c) United Nations Convention on Contracts for the International Sale of Goods (CISG).

564 Art. 7(1) Introductory Act to the German Civil Code (*Einführungsgesetz zum Bürgerlichen Gesetzbuch*); Art. 1195(1) and Art. 1197 Russian Civil Code; Art. 4(1) Japanese Act on the General Rules on the Application of Law.

565 Art. 12 Law on the Application of Law to Foreign-Related Civil Relations of the People's Republic of China; Art. 36 Swiss Federal Act on Private International Law.

566 See, e.g., Art. 4(2) Japanese Law on the General Rules on the Application of Law; Art. 13 EU Rome I Regulation.

the virtual space, a different connecting factor will be needed. This could be the place where the contracting parties are located at the time the contract is concluded.

As for the law governing the form of the contract, such alternative rule already exists. Many jurisdictions consider a contract concluded at a distance to be formally valid if it complies with the law of the place where one of the parties was present at the time of contracting.[567] Admittedly, this is not a perfect solution, since it is often impossible to know where a party was located when the contract was concluded. However, this is not a problem specific to the blockchain; the same difficulties are encountered with all contracts concluded over the internet. Moreover, this problem can be easily overcome in practice, as the party alleging the validity of a contract will usually be able to identify where she was when the contract was concluded.

3.2.1.4 Public Policy and Overriding Mandatory Rules

The application of foreign law is subject to the rules on public policy, also known as "internationally mandatory rules" or "overriding mandatory rules" (in French: *lois de police* or *lois d'application immédiate*).[568] Insofar as they are part of the law of the forum, they override any rule of the law that would otherwise apply. This exception is particularly significant for countries that prohibit or limit crypto-asset transactions. They will usually consider such rules of the *lex fori* as taking priority over the rules of a foreign law that the parties have selected or otherwise govern their contract.

Some jurisdictions also give effect to public policy rules of other (third) states.[569] Whether and to what extent they will do so depends on the purpose and effects of the third state's law, particularly whether its purpose is shared by the forum state or at least considered legitimate. An obstacle in this respect is the significant policy differences regarding the crypto economy. One cannot expected, for instance, a state which allows transactions in crypto-assets to give effect to a third state's law that prohibits them. As a result, there will be

567 See Art. 10(4) Japanese Law on the General Rules of Application of Law; Art. 11(2) Rome I Regulation; Art. 124(2) Swiss Federal Act on Private International Law.

568 See Art. 4 Law on the Application of Law to Foreign-Related Civil Relations of the People's Republic of China; Art. 1192 Russian Civil Code; Arts. 9(1), (2) EU Rome I Regulation; Art. 18 Swiss Federal Act on Private International Law; Sec. 187 US Restatement (Second) on the Conflict of Laws (1971).

569 See, e.g., Art. 9(3) EU Rome I Regulation; Art. 19 Swiss Federal Act on Private International Law.

a lack of cooperation in enforcing such prohibitions not only in the regulatory sphere, but also at the level of private law.

3.2.2 *The Law Applicable to Torts in the Crypto Economy*

Most legal systems identify the law applicable to a tort by the *lex loci delicti* rule. To do so, they use two different connecting factors: 1. the place where the event giving rise to the damage occurred (*lex loci delicti commissi*),[570] and 2. the place where the damage was suffered by the victim (*lex loci damni*).[571] Some legal systems combine both criteria in the sense that the *lex loci damni* is to be followed where the occurrence of damage in another country was foreseeable for the tortfeasor or where it was at least not unforeseeable; otherwise they refer to the *lex loci delicti commissi*.[572] Typically, torts involving crypto-assets are committed over the internet, which gives rise to the possibility that the *loci delicti commissi* and *loci damni* are completely different places in the world. Therefore, it is vital to determine which of these criteria is followed (1 or 2). In addition, one must also take account of "modern" approaches to the conflict of tort laws (3).

3.2.2.1 Lex loci delicti commissi

Generally, no particular issues arise when identifying the *locus delicti commissi* in a blockchain context. The tortfeasor must have acted somewhere, for instance at his domicile, at a university or at a café. It may not be easy to find this place. Still, the difficulties are no greater than in other cases involving the internet, where the tortfeasor also often acts at an unknown location and under a pseudonym. In any event, most legal systems require the defendant and his whereabouts to be known as a condition for the admissibility of an action.[573] This significantly limits the difficulties for the court because the claimant must have investigated the *locus delicti commissi* before bringing the action.

---

570 See, e.g., Art. 1219(1) sentence 1 Russian Civil Code.

571 See, e.g., Art. 4(1) EU Rome II Regulation (Regulation (EC) 864/2007 of the European Parliament and of the Council 11 July 2007 on the law applicable to non-contractual obligations (Rome II) [2007] OJ L199/40).

572 See, e.g., Art. 17 Japanese Act on the General Rules on the Application of Law (applying the law of the place of the event giving rise to the damage if the place of damage is usually unforeseeable); Art. 133(2) Swiss Federal Act on Private International Law (applying the law of the place of damage on the condition that this place is foreseeable).

573 See, e.g., § 253(2) German Code of Civil Procedure (*Zivilprozessordnung*) (requiring the identification of the party in the complaint); Art. 54 French Code of Civil Procedure (*Code de Procédure Civile*). But see *infra* 3.9.1.1. for England and Wales, where actions against "persons unknown" are possible.

3.2.2.2 Lex loci damni

The application of the *locus damni* rule creates a much greater challenge. In the virtual environment of the blockchain, assets are not physically stored in some place, but recorded on a ledger, an identical copy of which is held by a plethora of nodes distributed all over the globe. When such an asset is "stolen", e.g. by hacking the private key and using it to transfer the assets to another account, it is impossible to locate the place of damage in geographical terms.

Courts facing this problem can try to identify the location of the assets in question. In this case, they will often encounter the same difficulties as in property law matters.[574] As it is not easy to identify the place of a crypto-asset, courts in these countries may look for other ways of locating the damage. In particular, they might consider the victim's domicile as a fictitious place where the damage has materialised. When trying to localise the immaterial damage resulting from the violation of personality or privacy rights, the Court of Justice of the EU has used the "centre of interests" of the victim, which is regularly the victim's habitual residence.[575] The same reasoning can also be applied for crypto torts.[576] The tortfeasor can hardly object that the victim's domicile was not predictable. Those who commit a tort in the pseudonymous and distributed virtual world of the blockchain must know that their acts might be unlawful in many different states and may consequently lead to their liability.

3.2.2.3 Combination of lex loci delicti commissi and lex loci damni

The problem is less pronounced in those systems that apply either the *lex loci delicti commissi* or the *lex loci damni*, depending on the extent to which the place of damage was foreseeable.[577] The courts in these systems could stick with the *lex loci delicti commissi* and exclude the application of the *lex loci damni* on the basis that, in the pseudonymous and distributed environment of the blockchain, it is impossible to foresee where exactly the damage will occur. Alternatively, they could say that the tortfeasor could have foreseen damage happening somewhere abroad; in this case, they would end up with the *lex loci damni* and the same problems of localisation as the approach described

574 See *infra* 3.2.4.

575 CJEU, Joined Cases C-509/09 and C-161/10, *eDate Advertising v X and Olivier Martínez et al. v MGN Limited* [2011] ECR I-10302, paras 48–49.

576 See Matthias Lehmann and Emeric Prevost, 'La localisation du dommage dans le Web3 / Locating Damage on Web3' (2022) 6 Revue de droit des affaires internationales/International Business Law Journal 736, 753–755.

577 See on Japanese and Swiss law *supra* n 572.

above. Thus, the construction of the combined rule will decide on the applicable law.

3.2.2.4 "Modern" Approaches: Governmental Interest, Comparative Impairment and Better Law

Since the so-called "conflicts revolution" in the 1960s, some – but by far not all – US states have replaced the *lex loci delicti* rule with different methods to determine the law governing torts.[578] The most prevalent are "governmental interest analysis", the "comparative impairment test", and the "better law approach". These approaches have in common that the analysis is delocalised from the place of the tort. Despite their methodological shortcomings in other respects, this is a decisive advantage when it comes to crypto cases.

Take, for instance, governmental interest analysis. It is hard to determine the relevant state interests regarding torts committed on the blockchain. Yet surely a state whose law provides property protections to crypto-asset holders has an interest in shielding its residents from being deprived of "their" crypto-assets by a tort. On the other hand, it is hard to imagine that the state in which the tortfeasor has its residence or place of business will have a legitimate interest in applying its law in such a case. For instance, where the law of this state denies any protection to crypto holders, it would be a stretch to assume this state would have an "interest" in extending its rule to victims resident in other states. Conversely, where the tortfeasor's law provides for stricter liability than the law of the victim's state, it will be equally difficult to defend any interest of the tortfeasor's home state in applying its laws. Thus, governmental interest analysis would, in all cases, result in following the law of the victim's domicile. This coincides with the solution proposed here for the *lex loci damni* rule.[579]

The comparative impairment test yields the same outcome. The interests of the state in which the victim is domiciled would be particularly affected if its property protections were not respected, much more so, it is suggested, than the interests of the state of the tortfeasor limiting the tortfeasor's liability. In the inverse case, in which the victim's state does not provide protection against crypto torts, but the tortfeasor's state does, the latter's interests would also not be more impaired by the application of the rule of the first than by the opposite solution. In other words, the non-application of its law affects the interests

578 For an overview, see Simeon C Symeonides, 'The American Choice-of-Law Revolution in the Courts: Today and Tomorrow' (2002) 298 Collected Courses of the Hague Academy of International Law 9.

579 See *supra* 3.2.2.2.

of the victim's state more than that of the tortfeasor's state. Therefore, the law of the victim's state should be applied as a priority over the latter in all cases.

The results of the better law approach are more difficult to predict. After all, each court will naturally tend to consider its own law superior to that of other states. However, in light of the needs of crypto investors, a state whose law denies protection to the victims of crypto thefts, fraud and other torts will find it hard to justify why this rule is "better" than that of a legal system that does provide such protection. Therefore, it seems safe to assume that the better law approach will also come out in favour of the victim.

In sum, the modern approaches yield results similar to those of the countries that retain the *lex loci damni* rule if this traditional rule for torts is construed in the aforementioned manner.

3.2.2.5 Summary

There is no uniform answer to what law governs blockchain torts. Those countries that favour the application of the *lex loci delicti commissi* will, in line with their general approach, look for the place where the tortfeasor acted. This also applies to those countries that adopt a combined approach and interpret the criterion of foreseeability of damage abroad strictly. All of them will face the difficulty of determining the place where the tortfeasor acted.

Other countries will look for the place where the damage occurred. This includes the countries that follow the *lex loci damni* approach, and those that adopt the combined approach and interpret the foreseeability of damage abroad criterion more leniently. All of these countries will face the puzzle of how to determine the place where damage on a pseudonymous and distributed network occurs. A possible solution could be to refer to the place where the victim has her habitual residence, central administration or principal place of business. The various so-called "modern" approaches can yield the same result.

3.2.3 *The Law Applicable to Succession to Crypto-Assets*

As with substantive succession law, relatively few problems arise when applying the existing conflict-of-laws rules for succession to crypto-assets. The typical connecting factors, i.e. the nationality or the last domicile of the deceased,[580] do not pose any particular challenges in the crypto context. The same is true for the law applicable to wills, which is generally independent of the objects bequeathed.

---

580 Haopei Li, 'Some Recent Developments in the Conflict of Laws of Succession' (1990) 224 Collected Courses of the Hague Academy of International Law 9; Andrea Bonomi, 'Succession', in *Encyclopedia of Private International Law*, vol. 2 (2017) 1683.

A problem only arises for those countries that submit immovables to the succession law of the state in which they are situated.[581] The courts of these countries must decide 1. whether crypto-assets are immovables and 2. where they are situated. The first question is unlikely to be answered in the affirmative, so the second will rarely become relevant. Although one may consider applying the transfer rules for immovables to crypto-assets,[582] such application would only be *per analogiam*, leaving the characterisation of the assets untouched. However, the idea that crypto-assets are immovables is hard to defend, given their high global mobility.

Thus, it is unlikely that crypto-assets will give rise to particular conflict-of-laws challenges in the context of succession. It may be different for the issue of whether the deceased was the owner of certain crypto-assets in his control at the time of his death. This preliminary question must be answered under the applicable property law.[583]

Whether and how the heirs may obtain information about the deceased's crypto-assets and access to the relevant private keys are questions of a different order entirely. These issues are not purely practical, but also legal; for example, whether the heir has a right to claim information about the crypto-assets held for the deceased by an intermediary. Such questions cannot be left to the law governing property issues, as this would point to a variety of different laws. Nor can they be determined by the law of the custodian who held the assets for the deceased, as this would undermine the effectiveness of the law governing succession. Instead, the *lex successionis* should be applied.

3.2.4 *Which Law Applies to Property Rights in Crypto-Assets?*

As with substantive private law, the real trouble in Private International Law begins with the question of proprietary rights (or rights *in rem*). The difficulties are even more challenging, since none of the conventional conflict-of-laws rules for proprietary rights under any legal system are adequate for the crypto economy. This will be demonstrated by a brief analysis of the three most important rules in this area.

---

581 See, e.g., US conflicts law: Sec. 239 US Restatement (Second) on the Conflict of Laws (1971); English conflicts law: Lord Collins of Mapesbury and Jonathan Harris (gen eds), *Dicey, Morris and Collins on the Conflict of Laws*, vol. 1 (16th edn, Sweet & Maxwell 2022) 1500 paras 28R-017 et seq.

582 See *supra* 3.1.5.

583 See *infra* 3.5.

3.2.4.1 Lex rei sitae

The law governing most tangible goods is the law of the country in which they are situated (*lex rei sitae*). Virtually all jurisdictions of the world follow this rule.[584] It applies to immovables and most movable goods (for exceptions, see *infra* 3.2.4.2). However, it is difficult to apply to crypto-assets because these only exist in the virtual space. Any attempt to localise them in the real world will fail because of their intangible nature and the decentralised nature of the blockchain on which they are recorded.[585] To use the place of a hard drive, a USB key or a sheet of paper on which the private key to these crypto-assets is recorded would be equally misguided. The location of the private key is impossible to predict and may change at any time.[586] Furthermore, the private key may be copied and kept in more than one country, which would lead to the potential applicability of the laws of more than one state to the same crypto-asset.[587] Applying the conflict-of-laws rules for movables to crypto-assets would therefore be inappropriate.

3.2.4.2 Lex registri

For goods that frequently cross national borders, like aeroplanes or trains, the *lex rei sitae* rule is displaced by the law of the place of their registration.[588] This *lex registri* rule is also followed to determine entitlements in registered intellectual property rights, such as patents or trademarks.[589] Therefore, one might also try to apply it to assets recorded on a blockchain.

However, in contrast to the registers for airplanes, trains or patents, the blockchain is not run by a particular state. It is a private network that has no special connection to any state. Hence, the conditions for applying the *lex registri* are not met.

---

584 See Louis d'Avout, 'Property and proprietary rights', in *Encyclopedia of Private International Law*, vol. 2 (2017) 1428; Khalil A Sfeir, *Droit international privé comparé*, vol. 1 (Sader 2005) 674 para 544.

585 See Audit (n 548) 678; Held (n 537) 269. See also *infra* 3.4.1.

586 Audit, ibid 679; Hubert de Vauplane, 'Blockchain and Conflict of Laws' (2017) 4 Revue trimestrielle du droit financier 50, 52.

587 See *infra* 3.4.1.4.

588 See Berend Crans, 'Chapter 9: Rights in Aircraft' in Isabella H P Diederiks-Verschoor and Pablo Mendes de Leon (eds), *An Introduction to Air Law* (9th edn, Kluwer Law International 2012) 345, 349 et seq (underlining the divergences that may exist between different legal systems and the lack of harmonisation of conflicts rules at the international level).

589 Dário Moura Vicente, 'Intellectual Property, Applicable Law', *Encyclopedia of Private International Law, vol. 2* (Edward Elgar 2017) 962.

3.2.4.3 Lex conto sitae

A very different rule is followed for intermediated securities, such as shares and bonds. The law applicable to them will usually be determined by reference to the account to which they are credited and can, therefore, be called "lex conto sitae".[590] Two variations of this rule exist.[591] The first refers, in principle, to the place of establishment of the relevant intermediary making the book entries, which is why it is known as the "Place of the Relevant Intermediary Approach (PRIMA)".[592] The Hague Convention on Intermediated Securities follows this approach in principle, but allows the parties to select between several places of business of the intermediary in the intermediation agreement.[593] The second approach focuses on where the account is managed, which is why it is called the "Relevant Account Approach".[594] This position, which determines the law objectively by excluding any possibility of choice, is followed, for example, by the EU's Finality and Financial Collateral Directive.[595]

The scope of these rules is limited to "securities" and "financial instruments", such as shares or bonds. Therefore, it is clear that they do not cover cryptocurrencies, payment tokens, utility tokens and stablecoins, which do not fall under either category. Theoretically, applying these rules to crypto-assets that qualify as securities and financial instruments – particularly investment

590 See Andy Ruzik, 'Art. 9 Financial Collateral Directive (FCD)' in Matthias Lehmann and Christoph Kumpan (eds), *European Financial Services Law* (Nomos Beck Hart 2019) para 7.

591 See Jean-Pierre Deguée and Diego Devos, 'La loi applicable aux titres intermédiés: l'apport de la Convention de La Haye de décembre 2002' (2006) Revue de Droit Commercial Belge 5; Matthias Haentjens, *The Law Applicable to Indirectly Held Securities: The Plumbing of International Securities Transactions* (SDU Uitgevers 2006); Matthias Lehmann, 'Financial Instruments', *Encyclopedia of Private International Law*, vol. 2 (Edward Elgar 2017) 739.

592 On PRIMA, see, e.g., Christophe Bernasconi and Thomas Keijser, 'The Hague and Geneva Securities Conventions: a Modern and Global Legal Regime for Intermediated Securities' (2012) 17 Uniform Law Review 549; Pascale Bloch and Hubert de Vauplane, 'Loi applicable et critères de localisation des titres multi-intermédiés dans la Convention de La Haye du 13 décembre 2002' (2005) 132(1) Journal du droit international (Clunet) 3; Roy Goode, 'The Hague Convention on the Law Applicable to Indirectly Held Securities: A Market-oriented Approach to the Conflict of Laws' in Florian Faust and Gregor Thüsing (eds), *Beyond Borders: Perspectives on International and Comparative Law: Symposium in Honour of Hein Kötz* (Carl Heymanns Verlag 2006) 63.

593 Art. 4 of the Hague Convention on the Law Applicable to Certain Rights in Respect of Securities Held With an Intermediary, done on 5 July 2006.

594 See Bloch and de Vauplane, (n 592) 3, para 51.

595 Art. 9(2) Finality Directive (Directive 1998/26/EC of the European Parliament and of the Council of 19 May 1998 on settlement finality in payment and securities settlement systems [1998] OJ L166/45); Art. 9 Financial Collateral Directive (Directive 2002/47/EC of the European Parliament and of the Council of 6 June 2002 on financial collateral arrangements [2002] OJ L168/43).

tokens – would be possible. However, such an application would struggle with the fact that these rules were specifically designed for the system of intermediated holding of securities, with central depositories and often very long intermediation chains involving different financial intermediaries. Both approaches are therefore unsuited to the direct holding system made possible by blockchain networks, which function on their most basic level without accounts, depositaries or custodians.[596] Hence, the rules on intermediated securities are inappropriate and ill-suited to govern crypto-assets because of both their scope and content. This does not exclude the possibility to take inspiration from them where crypto-assets are held with a custodian.[597]

3.2.5 *Conclusion*

Most problems relating to the crypto economy can be resolved with the ordinary conflict-of-laws rules. This is because the connecting factors used by these rules do not refer to the blockchain as such, but to events or facts external to it. This makes it possible to identify the law governing contracts, torts and successions involving crypto-assets relatively easily. In this respect, there is no need to develop new, specialised conflict-of-laws rules.

The consequence of applying the existing conflict-of-laws rules to these legal relations will result in the application of different national laws, even for legal relations arising from the same blockchain. As a result, there is no such thing as a "unitary law" that applies to all transactions on the entire network. Contracts and torts relating to the Bitcoin network may be subject to English, South African or Australian law, depending on the parties involved and the facts of the case. Such legal plurality might be regretted as undermining the uniformity of the applicable law. On the other hand, it merely reflects the "closest connection" principle and the fact that the network is connected to various states.

The conventional rules of Private International Law fail, however, when determining the applicable property law. Neither the *lex rei sitae* rule, nor the *lex registri* rule, nor the *lex conto sitae* rule yield any convincing result. This is due to the virtual, anational and intermediary-free nature of these assets. As for substantive private law, these features create the biggest challenges also for Private International Law. The reason is that property law is asset-focused: it determines the rules not from the point of view of the persons involved, but from that of the asset itself. This is also true for the international aspects of property law. Since the assets – i.e. their location or registration – are the focus of the law, their localisation is inevitable.

---

596 See in detail *infra* 3.3.2.4.

597 See *infra* 3.5.5.4.

To sum up, Private International Law faces the biggest challenges in property law, i.e., in questions regarding the law applicable to property rights, such as ownership and other rights *in rem* in the crypto economy. The search for the closest connection is driven by the idea that legal relations or "things" have some geographical link to the territory of a particular state. The crypto economy not only challenges this understanding but takes it *ad absurdum*. As a result, one may be forgiven for thinking that the whole edifice of Private International Law is outdated and needs a significant overhaul.

3.3 The Confusion over the Proper Category for Crypto-Assets

As the previous two sections showed, most of the difficulties raised by the crypto economy revolve around crypto-assets and the rights over them. This section will, therefore, focus on the assets themselves. The question to be answered is: What are they, legally speaking?

3.3.1 *Methodological Questions*

3.3.1.1 Characterisation in Regulatory Law and Private Law

We have already dealt with the question of characterising crypto-assets in Chapter 2.[598] This question haunts regulators and private lawyers in a different context. In private law, the answer to this question is relevant for numerous important issues, such as how these assets are treated in insolvency, how they can be transferred, and whether they can be acquired in good faith. The proper categorisation also prefigures many other legal questions, e.g. whether and how these assets can be inherited, what the proper procedure for enforcement against them is, and how they are protected against tortious interference. The proper nature of crypto-assets may also play a role in somewhat surprising contexts, such as calculating damages for late delivery and whether they can be used to make capital contributions to a corporation.[599]

Hence, characterisation is a problem that cuts across different areas of the law. In the regulatory realm, it can be resolved by a different characterisation depending on to the context, for instance, by defining crypto-assets as

598 See *supra* 2.2.

599 See Jasper Verstappen, 'Netherlands' in Matthias Lehmann and Tetsuo Morishita (eds), *Cryptocurrencies in National Laws – A Global Survey* (forthcoming Brill); Meliha Sermin Paksoy, 'Turkey' in ibid.

"money" for the purposes of anti-money laundering rules, but as "securities" for the purposes of securities law. The different purposes of the regulatory rules in question can justify this divergent characterisation. In private law, the situation is different. Here, internal connections linking different areas of private law mean that a uniform characterisation is indispensable. To illustrate, a transfer of crypto-assets may have effects under some property laws only if there is valid agreement under the law of contract. In many countries, the protection of crypto-assets in tort depends on whether they can be objects of proprietary rights. Security rights over such assets, such as a lien or a pledge, may be created, but only where the security right provider is the owner. The list of such internal connections within legal systems continues. They express and condition the coherence of private law as a whole, which would be destroyed by characterising crypto-assets differently for different areas of private law. This explains why many courts and authors around the world seek to identify a single category for crypto-assets that is valid for all private law rules.

3.3.1.2 The Relation between Substantive Private Law and Private International Law Characterisation

Substantive private law shapes Private International Law. The latter more or less slavishly follows the categories of the former and merely adapts them to the international context. This is the position of the prevailing doctrine favouring characterisation by using the categories of the *lex fori*, which are only slightly broadened to accommodate functionally similar institutions under foreign law.[600] Any attempt at characterising a new phenomenon, like crypto-assets, in Private International Law must therefore start from the level of substantive law.

600 See, e.g., Pierre Mayer, Vincent Heuzé and Benjamin Remy, *Droit international privé* (8th edn, LGDJ 2019) 130 para 162; Matthias Audit and Louis d'Avout, *Droit international privé* (9th edn, LGDJ 2022) 253 para 275; Gerhard Kegel and Klaus Schurig, *Internationales Privatrecht* (9th edn, C.H. Beck 2004) 337–340 § 7 III 2. a); Alfonso-Luis Calvo Carravaca and Javier Carrascosa González (eds), *Tratado de Derecho Internacional Privado*, vol. 1 (Tirana lo Blanch 2020) 560–562 para 112–114; Paul Torremans and James J Fawcett (eds), *Cheshire, North & Fawcett: Private International Law* (15th edn, OUP 2017) 43; Lord Collins of Mapesbury and Jonathan Harris (gen eds), *Dicey, Morris and Collins on the Conflict of Laws*, vol. 1 (6th edn, Sweet & Maxwell 2022) 49 para 2–011 et seq.; Peter Hay, Patrick J Borchers, Symeon C Symeonides and Christopher A Whytock, *Conflict of Laws* (6th edn, West Academic Publishing 2018) 129 § 3.3; Sec. 7(2) Restatement (Second) Conflict of Laws (1971).

But the process can also work in the inverse direction, i.e. from the conflict-of-laws level to the substantive law level. In fact, Private International Law may serve as a prism through which "the true nature" of a legal concept or institution can be revealed. This is especially the case where the proper categorisation at the substantive level is unclear. In this situation, it is worth primarily looking at the conflicts level and adopting an autonomous characterisation there. Given the disputed situation on the substantive level, there is hardly any other option.

Such an autonomous Private International Law approach must, to some degree, be independent from a pure substantive law analysis. In its stead, an autonomous approach must introduce proper conflict-of-laws arguments. This will often involve a consequentialist approach, which looks at the results any particular categorisation yields in terms of determining the applicable law and choosing the most appropriate one. In other words, one must check the potential outcome of each possible conflict-of-laws category before adopting it. The literature today acknowledges such results-oriented arguments as being a necessary part of the process of characterisation.[601]

Once the proper category has been found at the level of conflict of laws, one can return to the substantive law level. Sometimes, the category identified as most appropriate for conflict-of-laws purposes may also influence the modernisation of substantive law. Since Private International Law is, by its very nature, quite harmonious worldwide, this might spur a virtuous cycle of harmonisation of national law. However, this link is not perfect: there will always remain some differences between substantive law and conflict of laws because of their differing scopes of application and purposes.[602] But when the substantive law

601 Explicitly Trevor C Hartley, 'The Modern Approach to Private International Law: International Litigation and Transactions from a Common-Law Perspective' (2006) 319 Collected Courses of the Hague Academy of International Law 9, 191; see also Mayer, Heuzé and Remy (n 600) 133 para 168 (referring to the effects [*effets*] of the conflict-of-laws rule); Audit and d'Avout (n 600) 254 para 276 (arguing that the objective (*finalité*) of the conflict-of-laws rule should be taken into account); for EU conflict of laws see, e.g., Roberto Baratta, 'The Process of Characterisation in the EC Conflict of Laws: Suggesting a Flexible Approach' (2004) 6 Yearbook of Private International Law 155, 164 et seq.

602 See the example in Audit and d'Avout (n 600) 253 para 275 (*pacte commissoire* – contractual in French domestic law, proprietary in French Private International Law); see also the example in Paul Torremans and James J Fawcett (eds), *Cheshire, North & Fawcett: Private International Law* (15th edn, OUP 2017) 49; emphasising the specific conflict-of-laws interests when creating a conflicts rule; Felix M Wilke, *A Conceptual Analysis of European Private International Law* (Intersentia 2019) 115 et seq; but cf Stefania Bariatti, 'Classification (characterization)', *Encyclopedia of Private International Law*, vol. 1 (Edward Elgar 2017) 358, 359.

characterisation strongly diverges from that of conflict-of-laws, this should be sufficient reason to rethink the former.

3.3.2 *Traditional Characterisations*

In the following section, several categories will be surveyed to inquire whether or not they may be appropriate for crypto-assets. In line with the methodological remarks just made, the categories will be analysed from a twofold perspective: 1. whether they are suitable from a substantive law point of view, and 2. the consequences of a particular characterisation from a conflict-of-laws point of view.

3.3.2.1 Money

The first conflict-of-laws category that comes to mind for the new phenomena is "money". This best fits the original purpose of Bitcoin as a means of payment. It also resonates with contract law, where cryptocurrencies and payment tokens often are provided as counter-performance for the main object of the contract.[603]

However, in private law, the term "money" does not have a single but many different meanings.[604] First, it covers "fiat money", which is issued in coins and banknotes. Though crypto-assets are not issued by a state and are not legal tender, they could be treated in an analogous way when used between private individuals. In terms of private law, coins and banknotes are tangible objects, which, in the case of banknotes, double as negotiable instruments. Coins and banknotes can be the object of property rights, and a similar characterisation of crypto-assets would support the needs of the crypto economy. In addition, crypto-assets can be transferred directly, or peer to peer, just like coins and banknotes. However, the legal rights relating to the latter, like those over any chattel, largely depend on possession.[605] While it is impossible to have physical possession of crypto-assets, it is not excluded to view control via the use of a private key as analogous to "possession".[606] Admittedly, however, such analogy is somewhat stretched insofar as the characteristics of crypto-assets are distinct from those of movables.

It is perhaps more promising to turn to the second type of money, i.e. "book money" or "scriptural money". Book money is a claim against a bank recorded

---

603 See *supra* 3.1.2.1.

604 See already in the regulatory context *supra* 2.2.1.1.

605 Proctor (n 263) 30 para 1.46 ("Both coins and notes are chattels in possession, in the sense of the rights which may be exercised over them").

606 See *supra* para 3.1.5.

in its ledger.[607] Although the blockchain was meant to overcome intermediaries such as banks and replace them with direct holdings, most crypto-assets today are held with an intermediary, such as a crypto exchange or a wallet provider. Therefore, it does not seem excluded *a priori* to use the category of "book money" or "scriptural money" for crypto-assets held with such an intermediary.

As a downside, such characterisation would deny clients any property protection. Yet it may be argued that this is precisely in line with the nature and structure of the crypto economy, where one can never be sure that the intermediary controls or has access to sufficient crypto-assets to cover its clients' holdings. Moreover, describing transfers through "recordings" in an "account" seems to reflect the reality of crypto trading more accurately than an analogy to the transfer of possession.

Categorising crypto-assets as "money" is therefore ambiguous. It hangs somewhat in the balance between banknotes and coins on the one hand, and book or scriptural money on the other. Whether one leans towards one or the other cha-racterisation depends on whether one prefers to emphasise direct (peer-to-peer) transfers, or the fact that most crypto-assets are held and transferred by intermediaries in a process resembling transfers from account to account.

Given the ambiguity of substantive law, it is worth looking at the consequences of a characterisation as "money" from the perspective of Private International Law. From this vantage point, an assimilation with fiat money might trigger the application of the *lex monetae* rule. According to this rule, the content of a monetary obligation is defined by the law of the state under whose authority the currency was issued.[608] To illustrate, a debtor who has promised to pay US$1 must pay what the United States defines as US$1 on the payment date, regardless of any inflation or deflation. This rule is acknowledged all over the world and is indeed prescribed by Public International Law.[609] Private

607 Proctor (n 263) 28 para 1.40 (asserting that scriptural money is a form of contractual claim).

608 Art. 147(1) Swiss Federal Act on Private International Law; Proctor (n 263) 366; Lord Collins of Mapesbury and Jonathan Harris (gen eds), *Dicey, Morris and Collins on the Conflict of Laws*, vol. 2 (16th edn, Sweet & Maxwell 2022) 2335 para 37R-001; Caroline Kleiner, 'Money and Currency', *Encyclopedia of Private International Law*, vol. 2 (Edward Elgar 2017) 1259..

609 See F A Mann, 'Money in Public International Law' (1949) 26 British Year Book of International Law 259, 261 (calling the rule "universally accepted" and "indubitable").

cryptocurrencies, however, do not have a state as an issuer; hence, the reference to their legal system leads to a vacuum unless one is willing to accept the existence of a *lex cryptographia*, which has been rejected as a chimera above.[610] The *lex monetae* rule is thus ill-suited for cryptocurrencies.[611] However, it will apply with all its force to digital currencies, which central banks around the globe are preparing to issue.

This does not mean that parallels between cryptocurrencies and state-issued money must be discarded entirely under Private International Law. There are also other conflicts rules concerning banknotes and coins, which relate not to their content but to the rights that may be exercised over them. One example is the rule according to which property rights in banknotes or coins are governed by the *lex rei sitae*.[612] However, this rule is incompatible with crypto-assets, which do not have a location.

What about the characterisation of book money in Private International Law? Book money is typically submitted – either by an express choice of law or by the principle of the closest connection – to the law at the place of establishment of the bank.[613] Though there are, as yet, few licensed banks active in the crypto world, other intermediaries, such as crypto exchanges and wallet providers, take on a similar role. One could therefore follow similar rules for determining the law applicable to their crypto holdings. Along these lines, it has been suggested that the transfer of cryptocurrencies be modelled on the Electronic Fund Transfers (EFTS) between licensed credit institutions (i.e. between banks).[614] Such transfers are governed by the chosen law or the law of the party that provides the characteristic performance, i.e. makes the transfer.

The problem with this approach is that, both conceptually and practically, crypto-assets are different from book money. Many of them are held "directly", with the corresponding private key stored on, e.g., a hard disk, a USB key or a

610 See *supra* 1.5.3.

611 Andrew Dickinson, 'Cryptocurrencies and the Conflict of Laws' in David Fox and Sarah Green (eds), *Cryptocurrencies in Public and Private Law* (OUP 2019) 93, 120 para 5.76 (stating that there is no equivalent to the *lex monetae* in the cryptocurrency-context).

612 Caroline Kleiner, 'Money in Private International Law: What Are the Problems? What Are the Solutions?' (2009) 11 Yearbook of Private International Law 565, 579 (submitting 'monetary chattels' to the *lex rei sitae*).

613 ibid, 580 (stating that the law applicable to the bank in charge of the account is undoubtedly better placed to govern the "immaterial money holder", i.e. book money).

614 Burcu Yüksel Ripley, 'Cryptocurrency Transfers in Distributed Ledger Technology-Based Systems and Their Characterisation in Conflict of Laws' in Justin Borg-Barthet, Katarina Trimmings, Burcu Yüksel Ripley and Patricia Zivikovic (eds), *From Theory to Practice in Private International Law* (Hart Publishing 2024) 109.

piece of paper. Therefore, they cannot be captured by reference to the place of the relevant intermediary or account. Consequently, the reference to the law of the intermediary does not always yield results.

In sum, while certain similarities between cryptocurrencies and state-issued money ("coins and banknotes") or book money (or "scriptural money") cannot be excluded, such characterisations must be rejected for the purposes of Private International Law. The reason is their inappropriate consequences in the conflict of laws. The connecting factors used for the proprietary rights in and the transfer of fiat money and book money do not work for assets that are intangible and not necessarily held with an intermediary.

3.3.2.2 Claims

Another possibility discussed in national law is to consider crypto-assets as claims.[615] This characterisation is remarkably consonant with their intangible nature. It would also allow for their transfer in a relatively easy way. Claims are transferred by way of assignment. In many legal systems, such assignment is effected by simple agreement between the assignor and the assignee.[616] Yet, in other legal systems, assignment does not become effective against the debtor until notice is given to her.[617] The creditor of a claim, however, does not have rights under property law and therefore does not enjoy any property protection in the insolvency of the debtor. Most importantly, native crypto-assets, like Bitcoin and other cryptocurrencies, lack a debtor. The claims category fits at best those digital assets that represent a claim, such as tokenised bonds and utility tokens.

It is still worth discussing whether the Private International Law rules for "claims", especially those for their assignment, could be used for crypto-assets.[618] Several reasons militate against this view.

First of all, the conflict-of-laws rules for the assignment of claims presume the existence of a debtor. For example, some aspects of the debtor-and-assignee relationship are typically submitted to the law governing the claim.[619]

---

615 See, e.g., Tomislav Jakšić, 'Croatia', and Changmin Chun, 'South Korea' in Matthias Lehmann and Tetsuo Morishita (eds), *Cryptocurrencies in National Laws – A Global Survey* (forthcoming Brill).

616 See, e.g., § 398 German Civil Code (*Bürgerliches Gesetzbuch*).

617 See, e.g., Art. 1324 French Civil Code (*Code civil*).

618 Financial Markets Law Committee (FMLC), 'Distributed Ledger Technology and Governing Law: Issues of Legal Uncertainty' (2018) 17 <http://www.fmlc.org/dlt-and-governing-law.html> accessed 15 April 2024.

619 Art. 29 United Nations Convention on the Assignment of Receivables in International Trade, done in New York on 12 December 2001.

This concerns the effectiveness of the assignment between the two parties, the conditions for invoking it against the debtor, and for the discharge of the debtor's obligations. These rules are irrelevant for most crypto-assets since they do not represent a claim against a debtor.

Second, the rules on the relationship between the assignor and the assignee and between the assignee and third parties are inadequate for the crypto economy. Typically, these refer to the law governing the underlying claim or to the domicile of the assignor.[620] They therefore do not provide for any register on which the claim is recorded. Yet this register plays a central role for crypto-assets. Were the register is governed by a specific law – either by a choice of law or by a close connection, e.g. via a central operator in case of a permissioned network – it would be sensible to apply this law also to the assets recorded on the register as well as to their transfer.

Characterising crypto-assets as claims and their transfer as an assignment is therefore not recommended. The conflicts rules for assignments are a poor fit for crypto-assets because they include rules based on the debtor, which is often lacking in the crypto context, and because they ignore the existence of a register, which plays a pivotal role in the crypto economy. Again, it is thus the consequences of the characterisation that speak against it.

3.3.2.3 Securities (Financial Instruments)

Crypto-assets, as a societal innovation, make economic value easily transferable and tradable. In this, they share similarities with "securities" or "financial instruments", such as bonds or shares. In addition, there are many other similarities between crypto-assets and securities or financial instruments. Like shares, crypto-assets may also be issued in bulk and traded on exchanges. While crypto-assets exist only digitally, this is also increasingly the case for bonds and shares: in most countries, they are no longer certificated but dematerialised. From a private law perspective, a further characteristic shared by crypto-assets and securities is that both may represent another asset. Stablecoins, in particular, can be compared to structured financial instruments, such as asset-backed securities (ABS). An additional advantage of characterisation as a security or financial instrument is that it protects the property of the holder.

However, there are also strong differences between crypto-assets and securities or financial instruments. In particular, the latter always have an issuer, while this is not necessarily true for the former. Furthermore, the category "securities" does not capture native crypto-assets, such as Bitcoin or other

620 See, e.g., Art. 30(1), (2) United Nations Convention on the Assignment of Receivables in International Trade.

cryptocurrencies, which do not represent any rights. Also, the transfer of securities is executed almost exclusively via intermediaries, while for crypto-assets, peer-to-peer transfer remains relevant as an important backup option. Such option does not exist with dematerialised securities.

Private International Law considerations reinforce these doubts. The conflict-of-laws rules regarding substantive rights and obligations differ depending on the type of the instrument. For example, rights and obligations resulting from a share are generally considered to be governed by the *lex societatis*,[621] while those arising from bonds and derivatives are governed by the law chosen by the parties or, in the absence of a choice, by the law of the market on which they are traded.[622]

For proprietary rights, two conflict-of-laws rules for "securities" or "financial instruments" must be distinguished. Insofar as these instruments are still embodied in a physical document and are directly held, the *lex rei sitae* rule applies. This rule does not work for crypto-assets, even those held directly, because they have no "location". For securities held with an intermediary, which are typically – though not always – dematerialised, the law of the place of the intermediary or from which the account is managed plays a dominant role.[623] Yet this connecting factor does not work for crypto-assets held directly. Moreover, giving the law of the intermediary or the account a dominant role in identifying the applicable law ignores the structural differences between the blockchain and the world of intermediaries. The blockchain, as a register characterised by its decentralised nature, has no equivalent in the world of intermediated securities. More specifically, entries in the books of an intermediary may not have the same legal value as those on a decentralised ledger. This does not exclude, though, recourse to the custodian as a subsidiary connecting factor for indirectly held assets where the applicable law cannot be identified otherwise.[624]

3.3.2.4 Negotiable Instruments

A better approach may be to characterise crypto-assets as "negotiable instruments". Unlike securities, such as shares and bonds, which are generally issued

621 See, e.g., Art. 25(2)(g) Italian Legge 31 maggio 1995, n. 218; Art. 155 lit. f Swiss Federal Act on Private International Law; Art. 14(1) Law on the Application of Law to Foreign-Related Civil Relations of the People's Republic of China (mentioning "rights and obligations of shareholders" as being governed by the *lex societatis*).

622 See Matthias Lehmann, 'Financial Instruments', *Encyclopedia of Private International Law*, vol. 2 (Edward Elgar 2017) 216–217.

623 See *supra* 3.3.2.3.

624 See *infra* 3.5.5.4.

in large numbers on identical terms, negotiable instruments, such as cheques or bills of exchange, are issued individually. Insofar as they can represent goods or rights to them, e.g., in the case of bills of lading, they may be compared with asset-backed tokens. Furthermore, negotiable instruments are objects of property rights and can be transferred peer to peer.

The similarities end, however, when it comes to the mode of transfer. A change of ownership in negotiable instruments typically requires an indorsement by a signature and delivery. This reflects the origins of instruments such as bills of exchange or cheques, which date back to a mercantile practice developed in the medieval period, under which obligations were made visible and tradable by incorporating them into a piece of paper.[625] True, it is increasingly recognised that the legal requirement of a written form or a signature can be met by electronic communication according to the principle of "functional equivalence".[626] Theoretically, this principle could be extended to "communications" and records on the blockchain, particularly to transferring information authorised by using the private key.[627] Nevertheless, the underpinnings of crypto transfers are quite different to those of electronic negotiable instruments. The transfer of crypto-assets is supported by distributed ledger and cryptographic technology, creating the conditions of scarcity, pseudonymity and exclusivity that are unique to the blockchain. By contrast, electronic negotiable instruments such as digital bills of lading recorded in a central register do not have the same characteristics. They are not scarce, pseudonymous or exclusive. On the contrary, they can be copied, have an identifiable author and can be controlled by different parties simultaneously (e.g. the buyer and its bank). They are, therefore, not comparable with crypto-assets; they are simply electronic documents.

There are further counterarguments from a Private International Law perspective against a parallel between crypto-assets and negotiable instruments. For identifying the law applicable, e.g., to a bill of exchange, the location of the paper document plays a pervasive role. Many rules regarding negotiable instruments refer to the place where these instruments are issued or change

625 On this, see Tim Parks, *Medici Money: Banking, Metaphysics and Art in Fifteenth-Century Florence* (Profile Books 2013).

626 See Art. 9(2) and (3) United Nations Convention on the Use of Electronic Communications in International Contracts, done in New York on 23 November 2005; Art. 8 UNCITRAL Model Law on Electronic Transferable Records, adopted on 7 December 2017.

627 See Koji Takahashi, 'Blockchain-based Negotiable Instruments: with Particular Reference to Bills of Lading and Investment Securities' in Andrea Bonomi, Matthias Lehmann and Shaheeza Lalani (eds), *Blockchain and Private International Law* (Brill 2023) 494.

hands.[628] The traditional connecting factor of the *situs* is, thus, tailored to the corporeal nature of these instruments. No analogy, however, can be made for a purely virtual system, where instruments are fully digitised and neither written nor signed. The signature cannot substitute the use of the private key, because the location of the private key is usually unknown to the other parties and also cannot be determined from the instrument itself. Hence, the reference to this place to determine the rights and obligations deriving from an instrument, or the title to it, would be wholly inadequate in the DLT context.

As a solution to this problem, it has been suggested to use the *lex creationis* as a connecting factor.[629] In this context, the *lex creationis* is taken to mean "the law under which the right represented by the negotiable instrument is created, such as the law applicable to the underlying claim".[630] The core principle of this proposal is to extend the scope of the law governing the underlying right to the digital asset which represents the claim. This solution would not only imply a reversal of the hierarchy between the representation and the object represented but also mark a significant departure from the traditional conflict-of-laws rules governing negotiable instruments. Nevertheless, it may work in the specific context of trade finance because the law governing the underlying right can easily be identified, e.g. a claim arising from a contract of carriage is governed by the law of the contract. Still, some important exceptions must be made, particularly for instruments issued on permissioned blockchains for which a governing law has been chosen, and for instruments held with an intermediary.[631] In these cases, other connecting factors would seem more important than the *lex creationis.*

It remains an open question whether the law of trade finance instruments using DLT will develop in a different direction to the rest of the law on the crypto economy. In any event, the solutions reached here must not necessarily

628 See for the Common law: Paul Torremans and James J Fawcett (eds), *Cheshire, North & Fawcett: Private International Law* (15th edn, OUP 2017) 1298; John D Falconbridge, 'Situs and Transfer of Intangibles in the Conflict of Laws' (1935) 13 Canadian Bar Review 265, 268 (underlining that "the situs of the debt is the same as that of the instrument"); for German law: Christiane Wendehorst, 'Art. 43 EGBGB' in Jan von Hein (ed), *Münchener Kommentar zum Bürgerlichen Gesetzbuch*, vol. 13 (8th edn, C.H. Beck 2021) para 203 (noting that all issues related to the acquisition and transfer of property in negotiable instruments are governed by the "*lex cartae sitae*").

629 Takahashi (n 627).

630 ibid. It bears highlighting that this notion of *lex creationis* is idiosyncratic to the author and deviates from the general understanding of the notion, see *infra* 3.4.2.2.

631 ibid.

be identical to those in the law of negotiable instruments. It is unlikely that the latter will provide a model for determining the law applicable to crypto-assets.

3.3.2.5 Intellectual Property Rights

Patents, copyrights, trademarks and other intellectual property rights share with crypto-assets the following features 1. they are property (or rather: can be objects of property rights)[632] and 2. they relate to an intangible object. These two characteristics could be invoked to argue that crypto-assets should be submitted to the same rules. Yet the similarities stop there and give way to many critical differences. In particular, intellectual property rights entail prohibitions against specific actions, such as using an invention, publicly performing a play, or manufacturing fake products, whereas crypto-assets do not. Moreover, intellectual property rights are traded at a far lesser frequency than rights in crypto-assets. For example, patent rights generally stay in the hands of the same holder for long periods of time, whereas bitcoin will change hands quite often.

Given the lower trading frequency, it is less problematic that the transfer of patents and other intellectual property rights is subject to relatively cumbersome and complex conditions. These rules, however, are a poor fit for crypto-assets, which need to be quickly transferable. This may be why characterising crypto-assets as intellectual property did not find much favour in national substantive laws.

From the perspective of Private International Law, this characterisation is also not suitable. The conflict-of-laws rules for intellectual property rights are subject to debate.[633] In this regard, the law of the country for which protection is sought (*lex loci protectionis*) or the law of the country from which they

632 The question whether intellectual property rights should really be recognised as "property" is quite disputed, see, e.g., Michael A Carrier, 'Cabining Intellectual Property Through a Property Paradigm' (2004) 54 Duke Law Journal 1, 30–31, 34 (noting dangers of exclusionary rights in property, such as the magnification of inequalities, but noting that many of them have been prevented by the incorporation of limits into property law and that intellectual property rights have generally been effective in promoting innovation); Peter S Menell, 'The Property Rights Movement's Embrace of Intellectual Property: True Love or Doomed Relationship?' (2007) 34 Ecology Law Quarterly 713, 720–721 (citing, *inter alia*, philosophical, functional and political differences between real and intellectual property).

633 See, e.g., Josef Drexl and Annette Kur, *Intellectual Property and Private International Law: Heading for the Future* (Hart Publishing 2005); James J Fawcett and Paul Torremans, *Intellectual Property and Private International Law* (OUP 2011); Toshiyuki Kono (ed), *Intellectual Property and Private International Law: Comparative Perspectives* (Hart Publishing 2012). On the different attempts at harmonisation, see Toshiyuki Kono, 'Efficiency in Private

originate (*lex originis*) play a dominant role.[634] These connecting factors fail for crypto-assets, which, by their nature, have no country of protection or origin.

In sum, the rules specific to intellectual property rights are ill-suited for crypto-assets because of their characteristics, which call for differentiated treatment.

3.3.2.6 Data

From an empirical perspective, the most accurate description of crypto-assets is arguably "data". After all, they are nothing but information digitally stored. Nevertheless, there are crucial differences between data and crypto-assets. On the one hand, data can be easily copied and replicated, which means that there is no exclusive control over it. On the other hand, data usually does not lose value when it is copied, in other words, it is a non-rivalrous good. By contrast, crypto-assets cannot be easily copied because the blockchain protocol prevents double spending, and the person in control effectively loses the value associated with the crypto-asset if another person copies the private key. In other words, crypto-assets are rivalrous goods and can be subject to exclusive control. It is precisely these characteristics that give them value and distinguish them from data.

Data can also have economic value, e.g. the data of customers. However, they are usually not valuable as a single piece of information, but only as part of a much larger aggregate ("big data"). There are rules against copying and reusing personal data, in particular the rules on data protection. However, these rules do not treat data as objects of commercial value but rather view data from the perspective of personality and privacy rights. Such rules are inadequate for information recorded on a blockchain, which is designed to be easily transferable, but, at the same time, must be protected from copying.

The Private International Law rules for data do not fare much better. These do not even exist as yet but are in need of development. This may be done by analysing existing data protection rules and extrapolating criteria that could be used for a multilateral conflict-of-laws rule. For instance, the EU legislation on personal data protection provides for its scope of application using two criteria: 1. the establishment of the data controller or processor in the EU, and 2. the presence of the data subject whose personal data is being processed

---

International Law (2014) 369 Collected Courses of the Hague Academy of International Law 359, 465–470.

634 Dário Moura Vicente, 'Intellectual Property, Applicable Law', *Encyclopedia of Private International Law, vol. 2* (Edward Elgar 2017) 962, 964–965; Toshiyuki Kono and Paulius Jurčys, 'General Report' in Toshiyuki Kono (ed), *Intellectual Property and Private International Law: Comparative Perspectives* (n 633) 1, 144.

"in the Union." The second criterion is subject to the condition that the data being processed relates to the offer of goods or services to these data subjects or to the monitoring of their conduct and behaviour in the EU.[635] However, it is unclear whether these criteria merely determine the scope of regulatory duties, or can also be used to determine the scope of any private rights of enforcement. Should they also be relevant for private rights, it may be possible to "multilateralise" either of them and produce a conflict-of-laws rule for data protection. Still, neither of these criteria seems appropriate in the crypto context, which is underpinned by a network of nodes rather than a single "controller" or "processor", and in which the identity and location of the "data subjects" are normally unknown. A specific conflicts rule for personal data protection, which is yet to be developed, is therefore unlikely to fit the crypto economy.

3.3.2.7 Summary

None of the existing private law categories satisfactorily captures the new phenomenon of crypto-assets. This is mainly due to the latters' features: intangibility, exclusivity, rivalrousness, recording on a ledger, easy transferability, and high trading frequency. No other good or asset known in private law combines these different traits. In addition, the categories underpinning the traditional conflict-of-laws rules for property do not lend themselves to being used as a legal umbrella for crypto-assets. The results they yield not are not a good fit for tradable values recorded on a decentralised ledger.

3.3.3 *New Categories on the Block*

Given that the existing Private International Law rules are ill-suited for the blockchain, it is worth considering a new private law category for crypto-assets. In light of the confusion over proper characterisation, some legal systems have introduced entirely novel categories to accommodate the new reality of crypto-assets. Several of the most notable examples are studied here.

3.3.3.1 Controllable Electronic Record

In the US, the National Conference of Commissioners on Uniform State Laws (also known as the "Uniform Law Commission" – ULC) has amended the Uniform Commercial Code (UCC) in 2022 by adding Article 12 on "controllable electronic records". This term includes assets based on DLT but is not limited

635 Art. 3(1), (2) GDPR (Regulation (EU) 2016/679 of the European Parliament and of the Council of 27 April 2016 on the protection of natural persons with regard to the processing of personal data and on the free movement of such data (General Data Protection Regulation) [2016] OJ L119/1).

to them. The ULC instead opts for a technologically neutral approach by defining its central concept as "records stored in an electronic medium that can be subjected to control".[636] Such control depends on two conditions. First, either the record, a record attached or logically associated to it, or the system must give a person the power to avail herself of substantially all the benefits of it and to transfer control to another person. Second, the record enables this person to identify itself in any way as having that power.[637] This definition is quite similar to concepts of property and possession in Roman law, which are translated to the virtual space.

The UCC sets out a few substantive rules concerning controllable electronic records. It provides for a "shelter principle" and a "take free rule" to protect *bona fide* purchasers.[638] It also allows a debtor to discharge his obligations by payment to the person who controls the registered electronic record.[639] Furthermore, it equates control over controllable electronic records with control over other tangible assets with respect to secured transactions law.[640] Most other aspects are, however, left to "other law", i.e. the non-harmonised law of federal states. This concerns, in particular, the question whether the assets are objects of a property right or not. The UCC's self-restrained approach here and in other respects has been hailed as "decentralized commercial law".[641]

3.3.3.2 Registered Right or Crypto-Asset

As a response to the challenges posed by DLT, the Swiss legislator has introduced the concept of the "registered value right" (*Registerwertrecht, droit valeur inscrit, diritto valore registrato*) into the Swiss Code of Obligations in 2020.[642] According to the statutory definition, a registered value right is a right that, pursuant to an agreement of the relevant parties, is recorded on a register and can be asserted and transferred to others solely by virtue of the register.[643] This definition shows that the new category is limited to tokens reflecting or representing legal rights, such as a claim or a membership of, say, a company.

636 See Art. 12–102(a)(1) UCC.
637 Art. 12–105(1) UCC.
638 Art. 12–104(d) and (e) UCC.
639 Art. 12–106 UCC.
640 Art. 9–107A UCC.
641 Marek Dubovec, 'Toward Decentralized Commercial Law For Digital Assets' (2022) 19 Northwestern Journal of Technology and Intellectual Property 239.
642 See Swiss Federal Act on the Adaptation of Federal Law to Developments of Distributed Ledger Technology (*Bundesgesetz zur Anpassung des Bundesrechts an Entwicklungen der Technik verteilter elektronischer Register*).
643 Art. 973d(1) Swiss Code of Obligations.

It does not cover cryptocurrencies and payment tokens because they are not property under Swiss law. Therefore, the Swiss legislator thought it unnecessary to introduce special rules regarding the transfer of rights in cryptocurrencies and payment tokens.[644] Yet excluding the most widely traded crypto-asset in this way seriously limits the scope of the new category.

In substantive law, the new "registered value right" attracts similar treatment to that afforded to negotiable instruments. The Swiss Code of Obligations provides that the record must identify the person to the benefit of whom the debtor must and is allowed to perform.[645] It opens the possibility of *bona fide* purchases made in reliance on the record[646] and sets out a special procedure to invalidate register value rights, similar to that for lost or stolen negotiable instruments.[647] This last provision is a considerable legal innovation, which may prove very useful for cases in which private keys are hacked, accidentally lost or deleted.

The major advantage afforded by the new category of "registered value rights" is how they are treated in the event of insolvency of an intermediary that holds them for a customer. Although the Swiss legislator has shied away from using the word "property", the new law affords the titleholder similar protections to those conferred on an owner. It also provides for privileges in insolvency and a special procedure for the insolvency administrator to return the assets.[648] Interestingly, the latter provisions are not limited to register value rights but cover all "crypto-based assets" (*kryptobasierte Vermögenswerte, cryptoactifs, beni crittografici*). This concept is much broader than registered value rights; notably, it comprises cryptocurrencies and payment tokens.[649]

3.3.3.3 Data and Online Virtual Assets

The Chinese Civil Code features a special rule for "data and online virtual assets" (数据、网络虚拟财产).[650] The rule is, however, very basic because it

644 Swiss Federal Council, 'Botschaft zum Bundesgesetz zur Anpassung des Bundesrechts an Entwicklungen der Technik verteilter elektronischer Register' (2020) Federal Gazette 223, 258–259.

645 ibid 242.

646 Art. 973e Swiss Code of Obligations.

647 Art. 973h Swiss Code of Obligations.

648 Art. 242a and 242b Swiss Federal Act on Debt Enforcement and Bankruptcy (*Bundesgesetz über Schuldbeitreibung und Konkurs – SchKG*).

649 Pascal Favrod-Coune, 'Les cryptoactifs dans la procédure d'exécution forcée: saisie, revendication, réalisation' (2023) Journal des Tribunaux 66, 71; Corinne Zellweger-Gutknecht and Rolf H Weber, 'Private Zahlungsmittel und Zahlungssysteme' Jusletter 11 January 2021, 8.

650 Art. 127 Chinese Civil Code.

merely states that where laws specifically provide protection for these assets, they shall be followed. The rule is thus simply a placeholder for other law. So far, the Chinese legislator has neither defined the term "data and online virtual assets" nor declared how they will be protected.

Nevertheless, the very existence of the provision is especially interesting, particularly in light of the aversion to cryptocurrencies and other privately created crypto-assets shown by the People's Republic of China in its ban against such assets.[651] The category of "data and online virtual assets" may be useful for cases concerning Chinese residents who still hold legacy assets acquired before the ban came into effect or those concerning foreign residents who hold digital assets that are, for whatever reason, governed by Chinese private law. The category could potentially also be used as a basis for a Digital Yuan (e-CNY) issued by the People's Bank of China, though this is still unclear. It must also be noted that the "data and online virtual assets" category is not limited to data or values recorded on a blockchain. It also encompasses other phenomena, such as "virtual game objects", which may be obtained in a computer game.[652]

The new category is of limited value for the Private International Law of the crypto economy. The Law on the Application of Law to Foreign-related Civil Relations of the People's Republic does not mention it, but perhaps it is just a matter of time before data and online virtual property trickle down to the level of Chinese conflict of laws.

3.3.3.4 Electronic Securities or Crypto Negotiable Instruments

A very peculiar approach has been taken by the German legislator, which has introduced a special "Act on Electronic Securities" (*Gesetz über elektronische Wertpapiere*) in 2020.[653] This Act allows the issuance of electronic securities and deals with them both from a regulatory and a private law point of view. Initially, the Act was limited to bonds and investment fund participations, but was extended to shares in 2024.[654] The possibility of putting bonds and fund participations on the blockchain is a watershed for Germany, which has hitherto relied on paper certificates in financial markets. However, the new Act still shows traces of old thinking by creating a fiction that all electronic securities are corporeal.[655]

651 See *supra* 2.1.1.1.

652 See *supra* 2.2.2.1.

653 Act on Electronic Securities (*Gesetz über elektronische Wertpapiere – eWpG*), Federal Gazette 2021, part I, 1423.

654 See Future Financing Act (*Zukunftsfinanzierungsgesetz*), Federal Gazette 2023, part I, 354.

655 § 2(3) German Act on Electronic Securities.

The category of “electronic securities” comprises two very different subtypes: 1. digitised “jumbo” certificates (*Zentralregisterwertpapiere*) and 2. crypto negotiable papers (*Kryptowertpapiere*). Jumbo certificates represent a vast number of securities – typically a whole issuance. The new Act allows physical jumbo certificates to be replaced with digital ones, which legally are treated in the same way. Of particular interest for the present analysis are crypto-negotiable papers, for which the Act provides wholly new and specialised rules for transfer, acquisition and presumption of ownership.[656] These are not modelled on the rules that apply to tangible objects but are more akin to those governing property transfers and acquisitions in a land register. In particular, transfers require both an agreement of the parties and the entry into the register.[657] Good faith acquisition is presumed, unless the transferee knew that the transferor did not have property rights.[658]

3.3.3.5 Digital Assets

Some jurisdictions use the term “digital asset” to denote cryptocurrencies and tokens. An example is Kazakhstan.[659] Interestingly, Kazakh law bans large parts of the crypto economy, but nevertheless provides private law rules for crypto-asset dealings. Kazakh law divides digital assets into two subcategories: “secured” and “unsecured” digital assets. Secured digital assets represent rights, such as property rights in commodities, and can be freely transferred. Unsecured digital assets are those received as a reward for participating in the operation and maintenance of the blockchain. In other words, they are created or “mined” during the validation process. The circulation of digital assets within Kazakh territory is prohibited, meaning they cannot be sold, gifted or inherited. In addition, there are no rules of Private International Law for these assets.

Even though the substantive provisions of the regime are somewhat discouraging, the term “digital asset” is clearly on the rise. Indeed, UNIDROIT has used this expression in the very title of the 2023 Principles on Digital Assets and Private Law, which will be discussed more thoroughly below.[660]

---

656 § 24–27 German Act on Electronic Securities.

657 § 25 German Act on Electronic Securities.

658 § 26 German Act on Electronic Securities.

659 See Farkhad Karagussov and Alexey Bondarev, ‘Kazakhstan’ in Matthias Lehmann and Tetsuo Morishita (eds), *Cryptocurrencies in National Laws – A Global Survey* (forthcoming Brill).

660 See *infra* 3.10.1.

3.3.4 *Conclusion*

Finding a proper category of private law and Private International Law for crypto-assets is fraught with difficulties. Accordingly, some legal systems have introduced new concepts specifically for virtual assets recorded in digital form. However, there remain many outstanding questions, in particular as regards the types of assets these new concepts cover, the applicable substantive rules, and how the law governing such assets will be determined.

3.4 The Confusion over the Appropriate Connecting Factor

Whilst the problems surrounding categorisation are difficult, there is an even more difficult issue to resolve. Finding the appropriate connecting factor for crypto-assets arguably creates the most difficulties for Private International Law. The discipline is founded on the premise that the law of the state with the closest or most significant link to a legal relationship should apply.[661] However, a crypto-asset is designed to have no "closest" or "most significant connection" to any state and is therefore impossible to localise. This leads to an enormous challenge for Private International Law.

3.4.1 *Nailing Jelly to the Wall: Trying to Localise the Blockchain*

Since crypto-assets are recorded on the blockchain, one might focus on the blockchain network and look for the state to which it is most closely connected.[662] The problems with this approach are however immediately apparent. The blockchain was conceived as an a-national system of transfer. It was deliberately designed not to have any significant connection with any specific state to avoid the system being taken over, seized, or otherwise interrupted by a third party. This was achieved through decentralisation: transfers of crypto-assets are simultaneously verified and recorded by computers distributed all over the planet. The blockchain seems to be linked to no country or, conversely, to all countries around the world.

Nevertheless, the network does present some links to the real world, the use of which as a connecting factor merits examination.

---

661 See already Friedrich Carl von Savigny, *A Treatise on the Conflict of Laws* (W Guthrie tr, 2nd edn, Rothman 1972) para 346, 360 (speaking about the "seat" of the legal relationship).

662 See Ng (n 548) 336 (calling this "the most principled connecting factor for property issues in BTC").

3.4.1.1 The Place of the Nodes

The entire blockchain is stored on so-called "full nodes", which also fulfil other functions, such as the validation (mining) of transfers. In a figurative sense, the blockchain can therefore be said to "exist" where the nodes are located. Nevertheless, this location can be rejected relatively quickly for Private International Law. The reason is simple: The nodes perform identical functions and are scattered all over the world. Referring to the nodes as a connecting factor would lead to the simultaneous applicability of many national laws.

On the other hand, it might be possible to identify, through technological means, which node confirmed the relevant transfer and where this node is located. Still, there is no significant connection between the transaction and this state. The reasons for this are twofold.

First, it is impossible to predict in advance which node may validate a transfer.[663] The aleatory nature of these processes makes confirmation by a particular node fortuitous.

Second, confirmation of transfer is undertaken by more than a single validating node. To be permanently recorded on the blockchain, the other nodes must also accept the new block containing the transfer. Since such confirmation requires the consensus of the majority of nodes, the law of the state where such nodes are located could also be deemed to present a significant connection.

In conclusion, the location of the validating node cannot be used as a connecting factor.

3.4.1.2 The Place of the Central Operator

For permissioned blockchains,[664] reference could be made to the operating authority – sometimes called the "central operator" – to identify the law applicable to the network.[665] Echoing the PRIMA rule for intermediated securities, this method has been termed "Place of the Relevant Operating Authority" (PROPA) approach.[666] Using this approach, it might be particularly appropriate to consider the operating authority's principal place of business or place of incorporation. The law in force there could be used to determine the validity

---

663 On these mechanisms, see Michel Rauchs and others, 'Distributed Ledger Technology Systems: A Conceptual Framework' (August 2018) 107 fn 62, 63. See also *supra* 2.3.1.2.

664 On the notion see *supra* 1.1.2.5.

665 Financial Markets Law Committee (n 618) 18 para 6.17 (describing this solution as "neat" and providing a "high level of immediate certainty", while not being without problems, e.g. regarding the identification of the relevant operator).

666 ibid para 6.16.

and effects of all transfers on the blockchain and the proprietary rights over all assets recorded on it.

Although this solution would provide high legal certainty, it is not plain sailing.[667] In particular, identifying the relevant operating authority may not always be easy. The operating authority may also move its headquarters to another country, which would cause a change in the applicable law that could possibly deprive the network participants of their rights. Nevertheless, the place of the network's operating authority provides a quite significant connection to a particular country and is therefore suitable as a relevant factor in identifying the applicable law.[668] Yet its practical application is limited because it does not work for permissionless blockchains.

3.4.1.3 Lex supervisionis operatoris registri

Some states place network operators under special supervision and extend their national private laws to the blockchains they operate. This is the approach taken by Germany in its Act on Electronic Securities. This Act contains a conflict-of-laws rule that refers, primarily, to the country that supervises the network's operator.[669] Remarkably, this is a multilateral and not merely a unilateral rule. Consequently, a German court must apply foreign private law where the network operator is supervised by a foreign country.

Applying the *lex supervisionis operatoris registri* leads to consonance between regulation and private law. Several arguments support this solution. First, private and public law issues are often closely intertwined in the crypto context. Investors' rights may be safeguarded by both private and regulatory means: some of the corresponding obligations of intermediaries, such as disclosure duties, organisation duties or duties to avoid conflicts of interest, may serve a dual regulatory and private law function. Second, the country where the blockchain operator is supervised has a close connection to the corresponding crypto-assets. One of the main aims of financial supervision is the protection of investors, who may reasonably expect that the private law rules of the supervising state will also apply. Third, a state that regulates and supervises crypto issuers typically will have special private law rules adapted

667 See also ibid para 6.17.

668 Takahashi (n 549) 355 (underlining that this place may be seen as the "centre of gravity of the network").

669 § 32(1) German Act on Electronic Securities (n 653). Where the network operator is not supervised, a subsidiary rule applies, which refers to the law of its seat; where this seat cannot be identified, the law at the place of the issuer applies (§ 32(2) German Act on Electronic Securities). See also *infra* 3.5.2.1.

to the blockchain.[670] The fact that the legislator has decided to regulate blockchain issues at all demonstrates its awareness of the specific problems that the technology raises. This state is therefore more likely than others to provide an adequate private law framework for crypto assets.

There is, however, a problem with this approach. Most blockchain networks do not even have an "operator"; and if they do, such operator is rarely supervised by the authorities of a single jurisdiction. Instead, the network will be subject to several supervisors or none. Therefore, in most cases, relying on the state of the operator's supervisory authority to identify the applicable private law rules will be unworkable.

3.4.1.4 The Place of the Private Key(s)

An intriguingly simple solution to the conflict-of-laws conundrum caused by the blockchain would be to refer to the location of the private key to determine the law governing crypto-assets.[671] Such an approach is not necessarily based on a misleading analogy to movables. A more effective argument is that the private key gives the holder the power to dispose of the digital asset.[672] It could even be said that this spending power *is* actually the asset.

However, private keys are extremely difficult to localise.[673] They may be stored in a non-custodial wallet, located in cyberspace, or kept on a laptop that can be moved from one country to another. Even where they are recorded on a physical medium, e.g. on a piece of paper, difficult problems of changing applicable law (*conflit mobile*) may occur due to the mobility of the underlying physical object. Problems also arise from the fact that one can never be entirely sure that no copy of the private key exists, which would lead to a double localisation. The place of the private key is also problematic because, for security reasons, a new private key is often created with every transfer. As a result, the applicable law might also have to change with every transfer.

670 See, e.g., the law of Germany or Liechtenstein, which combine regulatory rules and private law rules in one act, see *supra* 3.3.3.4. and *infra* 3.4.2.1.

671 See, e.g., for Austrian conflict of laws Markus Aigner, 'Das internationale Privatrecht und die Blockchain – ein unlösbarer gordischer Knoten?' (2021) Zeitschrift für Rechtsvergleichung 211, 218 (calling the wallet in which private keys are recorded the "centre of power").

672 See ibid.

673 Maisie Ooi, 'Choice of Law in the Shifting Sands of Securities Trading' in Andrew Dickinson and Edwin Peel (eds), *A Conflict of Laws companion* (Oxford University Press 2021) 199, 213 et seq; Audit (n 548) 678 (highlighting that it would be impossible to identify the applicable law in advance if the *situs* of the private key would be used).

Against this backdrop, referring to the location of the private key is not convincing.[674]

3.4.1.5 The Place of the Master Key

In some contexts, a master key creates a sequence of public and private keys. For instance, a wallet may contain several private keys derived from the same master key (called a "seed"). If the master key is known, the complete hierarchy of private keys can be easily retrieved.[675]

Because of the role it plays, the master key has been debated as a relevant factor in determining the applicable law.[676] However, this solution is fraught with the same problems as those that arise with attempts to use the private key. The master key may be difficult to localise, it may be moved, or there may be several copies of it.

A master key of a very special nature has been envisaged by the UK Financial Markets Law Committee.[677] The Committee considered the possibility of using the location of an "*encryption private master* key" to determine the law applicable to an entire blockchain. The main problem with this connecting factor is that no such key exists for any of the major blockchains we know today. This is no accident; if such a key existed, it would call into question the very concept of DLT. Furthermore, even supposing that such a key exists, the idea of using it as a link suffers from the same weaknesses as those of the *seed key*: it may be challenging to locate, it may be moved, or there may be multiple copies of it. Consequently, this connecting factor should also be rejected.

3.4.1.6 The Programmer's Usual Place of Residence

In the absence of any other closer connection, one might consider the law of the place where the person who has programmed the software on which the network is based has her habitual residence.[678] This connecting factor is very specious. It is doubtful whether the initial programmer's residence should have a lasting impact on the applicable law after the blockchain network has been created.[679] Insolvable problems also arise where the location and iden-

674 See also ibid.

675 Imran Bashir, *Mastering Blockchain: Distributed Ledger Technology, Decentralization, and Smart Contracts Explained* (2nd edn, Packt Publishing 2018) 190.

676 Financial Markets Law Committee (n 618) 18–19 para 6.18 (in the context of proprietary issues of the blockchain).

677 ibid.

678 ibid 21 para 6.28 (referring to the "primary residence of the coder").

679 ibid.

tity of the programmer are unknown, such as in the case of the first blockchain network, Bitcoin.

An alternative solution could be to take into account, at least as one relevant factor for the determination of the applicable law, the residence of the person running the internet website that provides the software required to run a node or interact with the blockchain or from which software updates can be downloaded.[680] Yet this solution is equally fraught with difficulties, as this person or her whereabouts are often unknown. In addition, one must also consider the possibility that this person might move to another country. Should this mean a change in the applicable law? At the very least, the network participants would be rather surprised by this result.

Furthermore, in a crypto ecosystem, there is rarely a single programmer. A blockchain is usually the work of a team of several programmers. They typically live and work in different countries and use the internet to communicate.[681] To which country is such a team most significantly connected? One suggestion is to look for a "lead programmer".[682] Yet if this solution were to be adopted, one would turn the search for the applicable law into an intensive fact-finding exercise, which is neither efficient nor conducive to legal certainty. There is also a risk that different courts will come to different conclusions as to who the lead programmer actually is, which means that a harmonious determination of the governing law cannot be ensured. This goes a long way in showing how inadequate the place of the programmer is as a connecting factor in the context of conflict of laws.

3.4.1.7 Place of a Connected Institution

Sometimes, there is a legal entity that is linked or associated with a blockchain, such as the Bitcoin Foundation, headquartered in Washington, D.C., or the Ethereum Foundation, based in Switzerland. One could use the country where these entities have their seat or are incorporated to determine the law applicable to the network.

However, there are several problems with this approach. First, the precise link to the network is not always easy to identify. The Bitcoin Foundation, for instance, merely focuses on coordination, marketing and lobbying in favour of the Bitcoin cryptocurrency without taking an active role in developing the

680 For the latter solution, see Ng (n 548) 338 (suggesting to apply the law of Massachusetts to the Bitcoin network, *inter alia* because the lead developer who took over from Satoshi Nakamoto lived there).
681 See already *supra* 2.4.4.
682 Ng (n 548) 338.

Bitcoin network or protocol.[683] Second, there could be more than one entity associated with a particular blockchain. MIT Media Lab's Digital Currency Initiative is, for example, another entity associated with Bitcoin. Third, the entities associated with a network may change over time, and it is unclear why this should entail a change of the law applicable to the network.

For the same or similar reasons, one must reject further attempts at establishing other types of connections to certain institutions, such as using a software license issued by a specific entity or providing funding to the developers. In a world that is essentially decentralised, such criteria seem like grasping at straws.

3.4.1.8 The Elusive Nature of Situs

The preceding list shows how hard it is to pin down the blockchain geographically. The methodology of conflict of laws, therefore, runs into a dead end. As with characterisation, no silver bullet can solve all problems simultaneously and satisfactorily.

The difficulties of determining the applicable law to the blockchain are not entirely new. The process of digitalisation, in general, and the emergence of the internet, in particular, have created considerable difficulties for Private International Law as a discipline.[684] Yet in the case of the blockchain, these challenges are even more acute because the blockchain is based on the storage of identical information on computers scattered all over the world. This is no coincidence but has been done intentionally to prevent any state from controlling or influencing the distributed ledger's content. By design, the blockchain thus has no "closest link" or "most significant connection" with any state.

3.4.2 *Slicing and Dicing: Determining the Law Applicable to Aspects of the Blockchain*

The connecting factors examined so far attempt to capture the blockchain as a whole; such as by reference to the location of the master key or the habitual residence of the programmer. All have failed. One must therefore accept that permissionless blockchains cannot be subjected to a single law. Instead, a plurality of different laws will govern transfers and assets recorded on them. This may be regretted as complicating the task of Private International Law. On the

683 See Antoon Spithoven, 'Theory and Reality of Cryptocurrency Governance' (2019) 53 Journal of Economic Issues 385, 388 (noting that the Bitcoin Foundation coordinates efforts of cryptocurrency communities such as funding of core programmers, lobbying with legislators to make cryptocurrency a success, and developing a platform).

684 See, e.g., Pedro de Miguel Asensio, *Conflict of Laws and the Internet* (Edward Elgar 2020); Tobias Lutzi, *Private International Law Online: Internet Regulation and Civil Liability in the EU* (OUP 2020).

other hand, the diversity of applicable laws reduces the power of a single jurisdiction over the blockchain, which, as must be remembered, is essentially a global phenomenon. This also prevents unpleasant surprises for investors who are not connected to a particular foreign jurisdiction and do not know its laws. Therefore, it is necessary to be less ambitious and more granular. This means to look for connecting factors only for certain parts of the blockchain.

3.4.2.1 Lex emittentis

One idea is to apply the law of the issuer of a token to questions relating to ownership rights in the token. This approach does not attempt to determine the law governing all transfers and assets on a particular blockchain. It is more segmented because it is possible for many different issuers to issue their tokens on a single blockchain. Still, this approach would lead to a class of assets being governed by a single law, in a similar way as bonds of the same issuance are subject to one law.

The Liechtenstein Act on Tokens and Trustworthy Technologies takes the *lex emittentis* approach.[685] This Act combines rules of public and private law. Its Article 3 provides that token issuers are subject to both types of rules insofar as they have their seat or domicile on the territory of the Principality of Liechtenstein.[686] The *lex emittentis* principle is another instance of consonance between private law and regulatory law.

However, the problem with this criterion is that, in practice, the issuer of a crypto-asset often cannot be identified. This is the case, for instance, for tokens issued on a decentralised exchange (DEX). Furthermore, the legal personality of the issuer may be unclear, such as in the case of a DAO. Even where an issuer is known, it may be hard to determine its place of incorporation or its principal place of business. Yet where these are known, they can be helpful as connecting factors.

3.4.2.2 Lex Creationis

A related but different proposal refers to the law under which a particular asset has been created. This so-called *lex creationis* approach has been hailed as the most theoretically sound and practical rule for resolving competing proprietary claims to intangibles.[687] It was originally conceived for dematerialised

---

685 Liechtenstein Act on Token and Trustworthy Technologies (*Token und Vertrauenswürdige Technologien Gesetz* – TVTG).

686 See Art. 3(2) lit a) TVTG.

687 See Moise Ooi, *Shares and other Securities in the Conflict of Laws* (OUP 2003) para 7.80 et seq.

securities, such as shares and bonds. Still, there is no reason why it should not extend to investment tokens, which can be shares and bonds registered on a blockchain.

The problem is that for cryptocurrencies and tokens that do not embody any rights, the *lex creationis* approach is of no use. Also, it is worth reiterating that most legal systems reject the *lex creationis* rule for intermediated securities. This is due to the enormous amount of time, energy and money necessary for an intermediary to research the applicable law and obey the idiosyncratic steps that this law imposes on transferring assets.

Still, the *lex creationis* approach may be helpful for crypto-assets that are not typically held with an intermediary but transferred peer-to-peer. Examples include trade documents, such as bills of lading or letters of credit, that are recorded on a blockchain. For these, one could think about applying the law designated in the instrument.[688]

3.4.2.3 The Incompleteness of the Segmented Approach

Any conflict-of-laws rule that does not consider the blockchain as a whole but only certain parts will inevitably be incomplete. While some crypto-assets have issuers with known locations, this is not always the case. And while some crypto-assets embody a specific right and could be connected to the law governing this right, this is rather the exception than the rule in practice. Hence, slicing and dicing the blockchain does not provide a complete solution.

3.4.3 *Summary*

This section has shown the considerable difficulties that arise when determining the location of a crypto-asset. These difficulties should come as no surprise, given that the blockchain is designed to avoid particularly close connections to any specific country. They are, further, more significant in the context of Private International Law than in the regulatory context, where any connection justifies applying a state's law. By contrast, Private International Law imposes the higher test of determining the closest connection, which is a real enigma in the case of blockchain technology.

While the solution is not easy, it is not entirely impossible either. Contrary to the views of many, the blockchain and the crypto-assets registered on it can be connected to certain countries. Blockchain technology therefore does not call for the traditional conflict-of-laws methodology to be abandoned. The preceding analysis has yielded several connecting factors that can be used in certain

688 For the somewhat different understanding by Koji Takahashi, see *supra* 3.4.2.2.

circumstances and under certain conditions. Among them were, for instance, the place where the operator of a permissioned network has its establishment or habitual residence, and the place where the issuer of a token has its the seat. These factors do not provide a complete solution; however, they may be useful as the building blocks of a complex and sophisticated conflict-of-laws rule. Such rule will be developed in the next section.

3.5 A Uniform Conflict-of-Laws Rule for Proprietary Rights in Virtual Assets

It became evident in the preceding chapters that none of the traditional rules of Private International Law can be satisfactorily used to identify the property law governing crypto-assets.[689] There are two reasons for this. The first reason is that the traditional categories of conflict of laws are not suited to the new phenomena of the crypto economy.[690] The second reason is that there is not a single factor that lends itself to designating the applicable law to blockchain assets, but several, which do not exhibit any discernible hierarchy.[691] As a result, the most promising approach seems to be to develop a novel and special conflict-of-laws rule for these new assets. Ideally, this rule should be uniformly adopted across the globe, in line with the general objective of Private International Law to create decisional harmony, i.e. courts around the world determining the applicable law in the same way.

Before such a rule can be developed, some fundamental objections against introducing new rules in Private International Law must be examined (3.5.1). This will be followed by a short overview of emerging conflict-of-laws rules in the crypto sphere (3.5.2). These will then be used as building blocks for elaborating a new conflict-of-laws rule specific to the crypto economy. We will discuss its scope (3.5.3), the role of party autonomy (3.5.4), the law applicable in the absence of choice (3.5.5), the necessary public policy exception and a new exception of technological order (3.5.6). Finally, the special case of the law applicable to CBDCs will be considered (3.5.7), before drawing some conclusions (3.5.8).

689 See *supra* 3.2.4.
690 See *supra* 3.3.2.
691 See *supra* 3.4.1.

3.5.1 *General Observation: the Introduction of Categories into the Conflict of Laws*

The structure of Private International Law is resistant to change: the main categories that are used have mostly stayed the same since the 19th century when the foundations of the discipline were laid by jurists such as Friedrich Carl von Savigny and Joseph Story. The connecting factors by which these categories are linked to a specific state and its law are a different matter: these have significantly evolved since the 19th century. A good example is the increasing use of habitual residence as a replacement for nationality.[692] The fundamental categories themselves, however, such as contracts, property or succession (inheritance), are firmly anchored in the structure of Private International Law and will perhaps remain so forever.

The relative consistency and durability of conflict-of-laws categories does not mean there is not occasionally the need to add new categories with accompanying new rules. Societal change, economic evolution or technological revolutions often lead to new categories in substantive law, which require novel conflict-of-laws rules. The development of special rules for registered partnerships and the recognition of surrogacy as a standalone problem in Private International Law are prime examples.[693]

Is there a need for a novel conflict-of-laws category for virtual assets recorded on a blockchain? There is scope for doubt. Sceptics may point to a number of national legal systems that deal with these phenomena based on the traditional rules of their national law, without introducing special notions or rules.[694] In addition, the principle of technological neutrality seems to speak against creating a separate category for assets recorded and traded digitally.[695] Although this principle has its origins in regulatory law, the underlying rationale makes sense in Private International Law too, because rules not tailored to a specific type of technology are future-proof and more open to future innovation.

On the other hand, it has been shown that none of the existing rules of Private International Law can adequately capture crypto-assets. In addition, new categories are being developed for them at the level of substantive law, which could also be used for conflict-of-laws purposes. Furthermore, the principle of

692 See Heinz-Peter Mansel, 'Nationality', *Encyclopedia of Private International Law* vol. 2 (Edward Elgar 2017) 1297–1298.

693 On these developments, see, e.g., Gérald Goldstein, 'La cohabitation hors mariage en droit international privé' (2006) 320 Collected Courses of the Hague Academy of International Law 9; Cristina González Beilfuss, 'Party Autonomy in International Family Law' (2020) 408 Collected Courses of the Hague Academy of International Law 89.

694 See *supra* 3.1.

695 See *supra* 2.1.2.

technological neutrality is not applied without exception. In particular, it has not stopped the introduction of special conflicts rules for certain market practices, e.g. for negotiable instruments embodying legal rights in paper. Paper negotiable instruments were prevalent in the past, but were largely abandoned due to technological developments leading to the dematerialisation of many of these instruments, particularly shares and bonds. This change had significant repercussions for Private International Law, where the traditional *lex cartae sitae* rule was superseded by more modern conflicts rules, such as the PRIMA or the "relevant account" approach.[696] This illustrates that rules of Private International Law are not set in stone but must adapt to changing societal, economic or technological circumstances.

However, caution is necessary. Certainly, it would be wrong to introduce a new conflicts rule for an ephemeral fad. Any new category should be based on a genuine need due to long-term change, and therefore be couched in terms that will not be outdated tomorrow.

3.5.2 *Emerging Conflict-of-Laws Rules for the Blockchain*

3.5.2.1 National Rules

Before drafting a new conflict-of-laws rule, taking stock of the situation in national laws is essential. Some countries have started to adopt special rules of Private International Law for the blockchain. These deserve close attention, as they may contain pointers for an "ideal" conflict-of-laws rule.

As mentioned, the US *Uniform Commercial Code* (UCC) has been amended with the addition of Article 12 on "controllable electronic records".[697] To identify the law governing these records, Section 12–107 UCC contains a very elaborate conflict-of-laws rule, which applies not only in interstate but also in international situations. The provision refers repeatedly to the principle of party autonomy, in complex guises and repetitious formulations. Essentially, choice of law may be made in three different ways: 1. in the controllable electronic record itself, 2. in the rules of the system in which the electronic record is recorded, or 3. in a record attached or logically associated with the controllable electronic record.[698] As these criteria are to be considered one after the

696 See *supra* 3.3.2.4.

697 See *supra* 3.3.3.1.

698 The long-winded and complex formula of Sec. 12–107 UCC is due mainly to the distinction drawn between the choice of law of the record's "jurisdiction" and its "governing law". This distinction does not have much relevance, though, since the local law of the jurisdiction also governs the applicable law unless otherwise agreed, see Sec. 12–107(2) UCC.

other in order, they are described as a "waterfall".[699] Where no law has been chosen, the UCC refers to the law of Washington, D.C.[700]

Germany is another country that has reacted to the new developments. Section 32 of the Act on Electronic Securities of 2020 contains a specific conflict-of-laws rule.[701] This rule refers, in the first place, to the law of the state whose authorities supervise the register's operator.[702] In the absence of such supervision, the seat of the register's operator is used to determine the applicable law; if this seat cannot be determined, the issuer's seat is decisive.[703] The breadth of this rule is questionable. In particular, it is not clear whether it extends to digital assets not listed in the scope provision of the Act.[704] Irrespective of this debate, the rule offers interesting ideas that may be used more generally. In particular, the seat of the register's operator or the asset's issuer might be useful.

The Principality of Liechtenstein also features an interesting rule in its "Trustworthy Technologies (TT) Act".[705] According to its Article 3(2), the Act applies where 1. the issuer of a token has its seat or domicile in the Principality or 2. the parties have expressly agreed on its application. At first sight, this provision is not a conflict-of-laws rule but only defines the territorial scope of the TT-Act. On closer inspection, however, it contains an implicit conflict-of-laws rule since the Act will not apply unless the law of Liechtenstein applies in the first place. To achieve its purpose, the Act must thus also declare that Liechtenstein law applies in all cases that fall within its scope. The particularity of this conflict-of-laws rule, apart from the fact that it is implicit, is that it is unilateral

699 Sec. 12–107 UCC, Official Comment 5.

700 Sec. 12–107(5) UCC.

701 § 32 eWpG.

702 § 32(1) eWpG.

703 § 32(2) eWpG.

704 For a broad scope, see, e.g., Michael F Müller, '§ 32 eWpG' in Michael F Müller and Christian Pieper (eds), *Gesetz über elektronische Wertpapiere (eWpG)* (C.H. Beck 2022) para 4; Oliver L Knöfel, 'Elektronische Wertpapiere im Internationalen Privatrecht' in Helmut Grothe, Peter Mankowski and Frederick Rieländer (eds), *Europäisches und internationales Privatrecht* (C.H. Beck 2022) 164; Felix Wilke, 'Das IPR der elektronischen Wertpapiere' (2021) Praxis des Internationalen Privat- und Verfahrensrechts (IPRax) 502, 505; Sophia Schwemmer, 'Das Tokensachstatut' (2022) IPRax 331, 336; for a restricted scope, see, e.g., Matthias Lehmann, 'Internationales Privat- und Zivilprozessrecht' in Sebastian Omlor and Mathias Link (eds), *Handbuch Kryptowährungen und Token* (2nd edn, Recht und Wirtschaft 2023) 244 para 169.

705 See *supra* 3.5.2.1.

in nature. It determines only the applicability of Liechtenstein law, not that of other states. The rule applies to "tokens", which are very broadly defined.[706]

In Switzerland, the legislator has adapted several provisions of the Federal Act on Private International Law in response to blockchain technology. One rule concerns the law applicable to the question of whether a claim is represented and transferred by an "instrument in paper or equivalent form",[707] with the term "equivalent form" intended as covering crypto-assets.[708] This rule submits the issues of whether a claim is represented by an instrument and its transfer to the law designated in the instrument; and, failing such designation, to the law at the seat or habitual residence of the issuer. The same rule applies to instruments purporting to represent property.[709] The pledge of "an uncertificated security, a certificated security or an equivalent instrument" – i.e. a crypto-asset – is submitted to the law of the habitual residence of the pledgor.[710] Moreover, Swiss law refers explicitly to the Hague Intermediated Securities Convention, which Switzerland has ratified, through a special provision that leaves it to the Convention to define the notion of "intermediated securities."[711] As a result, the question of whether crypto-assets fall under the scope of the Convention will be determined by the Convention itself. Strictly speaking, this is trite, given that conventions always define their scope of application. The provision thus has more pedagogical than legal value.

While these countries have adopted specific legislative rules on conflict-of-laws issues regarding the blockchain, other countries deal with these problems in the context of litigation. An example is England and Wales, where the courts, following a proposal by Andrew Dickinson,[712] have held in certain cases on jurisdiction that the "lex situs of a crypto-asset is where the

706 See Art. 2(1)(c) Liechtenstein TVTG (defining as a "token" information in a trusted technology system that represents a claim, a membership right, a right in chattel or any other absolute or relative right).

707 Art. 145a(1) Swiss Federal Act on Private International Law.

708 Swiss Federal Council, 'Botschaft zum Bundesgesetz zur Anpassung des Bundesrechts an Entwicklungen der Technik verteilter elektronischer Register' (2020) Federal Gazette 223, 298.

709 Art. 106(1) Swiss Federal Act on Private International Law. On the exception of Art.106(3) of the Act, see *infra* 3.6.2.

710 Art. 105(2) Swiss Federal Act on Private International Law.

711 Art. 108a Swiss Federal Act on Private International Law.

712 Andrew Dickinson, 'Cryptocurrencies and the Conflict of Laws' in David Fox and Sara Green (eds), *Cryptocurrencies in Public and Private Law* (OUP 2019) para 5.108.

person or company who owns it is domiciled".[713] Subsequent cases did not use *domicile*, but the place of *residence* or *business* of the owner of the assets.[714] The approach has been applied to several native assets, such as Bitcoin and Binance Coin, as well as a stablecoin (Tether).[715] However, the legal value of these rulings is not beyond doubt because they did not concern the merits, but merely the question of whether service out of the jurisdiction was appropriate or not.[716]

The High Court of Singapore also follows a similar approach to the English courts.[717] However, instead of the person who *owns* crypto-assets, this court refers to the person who *holds* such assets. Under the English approach to determining situs, extrapolated to the conflict of laws, proprietary issues would be governed by the law of the habitual residence or place of business of the owner. This creates a circularity, which the Singaporean approach avoids. The difference was especially important in the case decided, which turned on the question of ownership of assets in insolvency proceedings. Like the English cases, the ruling concerned the possibility of service out of the jurisdiction, not the applicable law, which limits its value as precedent.

This brief overview of national conflict-of-laws rules yields a fragmented picture. Not only do the rules diverge considerably concerning scope, especially in the definition of the objects to which the particular rule applies; they also use very different connecting factors: party autonomy, the place of supervision, the seat or domicile of the issuer, and the domicile, residence, or establishment of the person owning the asset. The risk of new divergences in conflict of laws looms large.

3.5.2.2 The UNIDROIT Principles on Digital Assets and Private Law

Conflict-of-laws rules that diverge between legal systems are problematic for reasons well-known to any conflicts lawyer. They open up opportunities for forum shopping, create limping legal relationships, and may lead to judicial wars. In the case of the crypto economy, it is even worse because divergence in the rules is incompatible with the nature of the blockchain as a global mechanism for the storage and transfer of value. Accordingly, the initiatives of various

---

713 High Court of England and Wales, 21 December 2020, *Ion Science v Persons Unknown* (unreported) para 13.

714 High Court of England and Wales, 15 July 2021, *Fetch.AI Limited et al v Persons Unknown et al*, [2021] EWHC 2254 (Comm) para 145.

715 Cf ibid para 3.

716 Held (n 537) 272 (arguing against a value of the rulings as binding precedent).

717 Singapore High Court, *Cheong Jun Yoong v Three Arrows Capital Ltd*, (2024) SGHC 21.

international organisations to harmonise the conflict-of-laws rules for the crypto economy are to be welcomed. These have already yielded some concrete results, most notably the "Principles on Digital Assets and Private Law", which were adopted by UNIDROIT in May 2023.[718] While the Principles primarily focus on harmonising substantive law, Principle 5 sets out a uniform conflict-of-laws rule for "proprietary rights" in digital assets.

Principle 5 adopts party autonomy as its starting point. It refers to the choice of the law expressed: 1. in the asset itself or 2. in the "system" in which the asset is recorded.[719] This has obvious parallels to the approach taken in the UCC, as discussed above.[720] Where no law has been chosen, Principle 5 refers to the law in force at the statutory seat of the issuer, provided that this seat is "readily ascertainable to the public".[721]

Where none of these conditions are met, Principle 5 provides two options. Option A refers to the specific rules of the forum, and to the extent that these do not exist, to the Principles. Option B provides that the Principles themselves apply.[722] Both options are substantive rules of Private International Law (*règle matérielle de droit international privé*) because the national law that would otherwise apply is displaced by a substantive rule of the forum or of the Principles. The latter option, according to which uniform soft law principles replace national law, is particularly novel.

Where neither the law of the forum nor the Principles address the particular issue in dispute, the Principles provide that a foreign law may apply.[723] Such foreign law is to be identified "by virtue of the rules of private international law of the forum State". No indication whatsoever is given as to what these rules of the forum state might be or should look like.

Where crypto-assets are held with a custodian, Principle 5 refers to the law expressly specified in the custody agreement.[724] This law is said to govern certain aspects of the custody relationship, such as the duties owed by the

---

718 <https://www.unidroit.org/wp-content/uploads/2023/04/C.D.-102-6-Principles-on-Digital-Assets-and-Private-Law.pdf> accessed 26 September 2024. For the sake of disclosure, it bears mentioning that the author was an observer of the UNIDROIT Working Group on Digital Assets and Private Law on behalf of the European Banking Institute (EBI).

719 Principle 5(1)(a), (b) UNIDROIT Principles on Digital Assets and Private Law (2023).

720 See *supra* 3.5.2.1.

721 Principle 5(1)(c) UNIDROIT Principles on Digital Assets and Private Law (2023).

722 Principle 5(1)(d) UNIDROIT Principles on Digital Assets and Private Law (2023).

723 Principle 5(1)(d) Option A (iii) and Option B (ii) UNIDROIT Principles on Digital Assets and Private Law (2023).

724 Principle 5(3) UNIDROIT Principles on Digital Assets and Private Law (2023).

custodian to the customer.[725] It also covers certain property law aspects, in particular those providing protection for the customer in the event of the custodian's insolvency.[726] This is more in line with the purpose and scope of the Principles, which focus on substantive private law.

3.5.2.3 The HCCH Project

The Hague Conference on Private International Law (HCCH) has been less active in addressing the conflict-of-laws issues arising from digital assets. In 2020, the Council on General Affairs and Policy (CGAP) invited the Permanent Bureau, "subject to available resources, to monitor developments with respect to the private international law implications of DLT", and asked it to present a report at the next meeting.[727] The 2021 report by the Permanent Bureau suggested the creation of an expert group "to assess the desirability, necessity (including assessing the extent to which the existing HCCH instruments can be used for digital assets) and feasibility of a new instrument on jurisdiction, law applicable, and recognition and enforcement of judgments in respect of digital assets".[728]

In 2022, when it became clear that UNIDROIT was intending to include a Principle for the conflict of laws in the Principles on Digital Assets and Private Law, the two organisations intensified their contact over this point. A proposal for a joint HCCH-UNIDROIT "Project on Law Applicable to Cross-Border Holdings and Transfers of Digital Assets and Tokens" was endorsed by the HCCH CGAP on 10 March 2023.[729] However, after the adoption of the UNIDROIT Principles on Digital Assets and Private Law in May 2023 and further meetings between the two organisations, the HCCH CGAP decided in March 2024 that "the work of the Project was concluded".[730] The Project had not moved to the stage of making concrete proposals.

725 See the reference to Principle 11 in Principle 5(3) UNIDROIT Principles on Digital Assets and Private Law (2023).

726 See the reference to Principle 13 ibid.

727 HAGUE CONFERENCE ON PRIVATE INTERNATIONAL LAW (HCCH), Council on General Affairs and Policy (CGAP), 'Conclusions et recommendations' (3–6 March 2020) para 15 <https://assets.hcch.net/docs/70458042-f771-4e94-9c56-df3257a1e5ff.pdf> accessed 15 April 2024.

728 HCCH, 'Developments with respect to PIL implications of the digital economy, including DLT' (Prel. Doc. No 4 of November 2020) para 30.

729 HCCH CGAP, 'Conclusions et recommendations' (7–10 March 2023) para 18 <https://assets.hcch.net/docs/5f9999b9-09a3-44a7-863d-1dddd4f9c6b8.pdf> accessed 15 April 2024.

730 HCCH CGAP, Conclusions & Decisions, March 2024, para 8.

In 2024, the HCCH began a separate project on "Digital Tokens".[731] In parallel, the Conference will study the conflict of jurisdictions and laws relating to Central Bank Digital Currencies (CBDC s).[732] At the time of writing, the scope and outcomes of these projects are still unclear.

3.5.2.4 Work Outstanding

Despite their far-reaching scopes, the current initiatives to harmonise the Private International Law rules in relation to the crypto economy are still incomplete. In particular, the UNIDROIT Principles on Digital Assets and Private Law leave many questions open.[733] Amongst other things, they do not deal with the law governing "linked assets", such as those represented by a stablecoin, a trade finance token or any other token with an underlying or referenced asset.[734] They also do not provide a fallback rule for identifying the national law that applies when the governing law has not been chosen, the issuer is not ascertainable, and the asset is not subject to custody.[735] By merely providing for applying the rules of Private International Law of the forum, without indicating what these rules should look like, the Principles leave considerable room for national legislators to come up with idiosyncratic solutions. This will inevitably result in continuing divergence and fragmentation in the legal treatment of blockchains.

Therefore, it is still necessary to consider what an ideal conflict-of-laws rule would look like. Principle 5 of the UNIDROIT Principles on Digital Assets and Private Law will still be important because, despite its shortcomings, it can potentially become the means through which harmonised conflict-of-laws rules in this area can be achieved. However, this Principle needs to be expanded with some complementary provisions. To this end, the connecting factors used in the national rules discussed at the start of this section may prove helpful.

3.5.3 *Scope*

3.5.3.1 Assets Covered

Formulating a new conflict-of-laws rule must start with its scope. This brings its main object into focus. How should this be defined?

731 ibid, para 12.
732 ibid, para 10.
733 See *supra* 3.5.2.2.
734 See Principle 4 UNIDROIT Principles on Digital Assets and Private Law (2023) (expressly excluding the law governing linked assets from the Principles' scope).
735 See Principle 5(1)(d) Option A (III) and Option B (II) UNIDROIT Principles on Digital Assets and Private Law (2023).

3.5.3.1.1 *Virtual Assets*

Of all the suggested terms, "virtual assets" seems to be the most suitable designation for the new category. This term is brief and easy to understand, as it emphasises the two most characteristic features of the phenomena that need to be regulated.

The first characteristic feature of the phenomena is that they exist only in the virtual world. This makes these objects special and is the reason why the existing rules for tangible assets cannot be applied. The term "virtual assets" reflects this important characteristic and is broad enough to accomodate any future technological development. It seems preferable over the term "digital assets" used by UNIDROIT because "digital" can refer to a specific technological method. The same is true for expressions which may be found in national laws, such as "crypto", "electronic", "data" or "online".[736]

The term "assets" reflects that the phenomena generate public demand and are limited in supply. Very few objects in the virtual world possess these qualities. In particular, data and other information usually do not qualify as "assets" because they can be infinitely multiplied through copying.

In essence, the notion of an "asset" is not a legal but an economic concept. Economic theory is primarily concerned with scarcity[737]: How can resources in limited supply be efficiently allocated? Any resource that is not scarce – e.g. the universe, atoms, light – does not need to be allocated and is therefore not an asset in the economic sense.[738] For the same reason, information recorded electronically is, as such, not an asset. Virtual assets are different: mechanisms such as DLT exclude their copying and multiplication, hence they are scarce.

Scarcity is the *raison d'être* of the rules protecting property.[739] It is also the reason for the new conflict-of-laws rule. The scarcity of crypto-assets is intimately connected to the double spending problem, which Bitcoin sought to resolve. Scarcity also makes virtual assets similar to existing assets, such as money, financial instruments and other objects of value. Yet it would be

736 See the new categories of private law *supra* 3.3.3.

737 N. Gregory Mankiw and Mark P Taylor, *Economics* (Cengage Learning 2017) 2 (noting that scarcity means that society has limited resources and therefore cannot produce all the goods and services people wish to have). See also Carl Menger, *Grundsätze der Volkswirtschaftslehre* (Wilhelm Braumüller 1871) 52–53 (noting that "economic goods" are those which are not available in sufficient quantity to completely satisfy demand for them).

738 The notion of scarcity depends on human capacities and needs, which can change, as illustrated by the growing disputes over water.

739 Menger (n 737) 56 (explaining that the demand for scarce goods creates the need for protecting against their violent usurpation).

a mistake to limit the new category to assets underpinned by this particular technology. Any other method of producing scarce assets that exist only in the virtual world will cause the same issues and justify applying the same conflict-of-laws rule.

3.5.3.1.2 *Relation to Value*

Virtual assets typically have value since there is demand for them and a limited supply. The Swiss legislator expresses that with the term "registered value rights".[740] Value can be determined, for example, on a market where such assets are traded and where a particular price for them can be ascertained.

One should, however, refrain from using the term "value" to define the new category. Otherwise, it may seem necessary to check whether an asset has a specific market value before applying the novel conflict-of-laws rule to it. Whilst the term "value" could also be understood more broadly to include merely emotional or sentimental value, this would stretch the word beyond its utility as a defining term. Value should be considered only as an *accidens*, not as a *definiens* of virtual assets.

3.5.3.1.3 *Relation to Control*

One feature of the new phenomenon that is often stressed is their amenability to control. For instance, the UNIDROIT Principles on Digital Assets and Private Law define a digital asset as "an electronic record capable of being subject to control".[741] This is reminiscent of the UCC, which defines the term "controllable electronic record" as "a record stored in an electronic medium that can be subjected to control […]".[742]

This criterion is nevertheless problematic. Control, or controllability, may indicate scarcity, but it is not necessarily the same thing. It is possible, for instance, to control water coming from an ocean or light coming from the sun, yet this does not necessarily make it a good or an asset because it is not scarce. Control or controllability is merely a condition for the possibility of using an asset, as well as for exercising rights over it and excluding others from it. But it is not the essential characteristic that turns an object into an asset.

If control or controllability is not a sufficient condition for the existence of a digital asset, is it at least a necessary condition? This is also doubtful. For instance, it is difficult to say that intellectual property rights can be "controlled"; nevertheless, they are certainly "assets". This does not seem to follow

740 See *supra* 3.3.3.2.

741 Principle 2(2) UNIDROIT Principles on Digital Assets and Private Law (2023).

742 Sec. 12–102(a)(1) UCC.

from amenability to "control" but from the monopoly right over a specific invention or work of art, which makes them scarce.

The emphasis on control apparently originates from a parallel with possession over tangible things.[743] However, such possession is not always a condition for the existence of property rights. For instance, it is impossible to have possession over inventions or works of art, yet they are still subject to intellectual property rights. Even with important objects in the physical world, such as real estate, the possibility of possession is more of a legal construct than a factual reality.

Introducing the concept of control was thought necessary to draw a distinction between a crypto-asset and a credit to a bank account. The credit standing to a bank account is also information recorded electronically, but it is not an "asset" owned by the customer. It is merely a contractual debt owed by the bank to the customer. This becomes clear in insolvency, where the customer cannot exercise a property right but needs to register a claim. Crypto-assets are different because it seems the customer is entitled to them, even when they are in custody.

The difference, however, is not because crypto-assets can be brought under the customer's control. Indeed, when they are held via a custodian, the position viewed from the outside is little different from that of money credited to a bank account. The crucial difference is that crypto-assets are recorded on a distributed ledger and not only in a bank account; they exist independent of the relationship between the crypto custodian and the client.[744] By contrast, scriptural money does not exist outside the intermediary relationship, but is merely the customer's claim against the bank. Critically, this claim does not need to be backed by central bank money. There is therefore no natural "scarcity" of scriptural money: it can be created at will by banks, subject only to regulatory constraints such as own funds requirements.

Therefore, what is important is not actually "control" but the fact that the asset is recorded *independently* from the intermediary. This demonstrates that the asset exists on its own outside of the relationship with the intermediary, which is what makes virtual assets different from scriptural money. This is also what makes them scarce.

---

743 See UNIDROIT Principles on Digital Assets and Private Law (2023), Comment 2 (describing control as a functional equivalent of possession while warning that they are not identical).

744 Incidentally, this is also the reason why one uses the term "custody" for virtual assets, in an apparent analogy to the custody of intermediated securities.

In sum, virtual assets may often have value and be subject to control, but these are ancillary features and not their essential characteristics. What makes them an asset is their scarcity. Since they are scarce, they become the object of competition between potential owners, creditors, purchasers and other persons. In other words, they are rivalrous goods. This creates the need to attribute rights over them that are valid against everyone, or *erga omnes*, which in turn leads to the necessity of identifying the law governing such rights. We have thus identified the quintessential characteristic that distinguishes virtual assets from other objects, which explains the need for this new category and determines its scope.

3.5.3.1.4 *Particular Applications*

It follows from the preceding analysis that the new conflict-of-laws rule should cover all assets that are 1. virtual and 2. scarce. The essential condition for the latter attribute is that they cannot be spent twice, excluding intellectual property rights that are governed by special rules already. The technological means by which this is achieved does not matter.

The new rule thus covers not only all assets created using DLT, such as native assets or tokens, but also other virtual and scarce objects that may be created via alternative technologies. A good illustration is CBDCs, for which a gamut of technological solutions other than DLT has been considered.[745] Any of these technologies would have the same effect of achieving and securing scarcity, and any digital currencies based on them would thus qualify as virtual assets.

However, the concept of a "virtual asset" does not begin nor stop with cryptocurrencies and tokens. Some of the oldest examples of objects falling within this definition of virtual assets are quite different: items existing and used in computer games, such as digital avatars, skins, armour, weapons or clothes. They are equally scarce in supply and generate demand amongst the community of gamers.[746] These "in-game items" are context-dependent as they can only be used in certain circumstances and are not easily transferable to another

745 One option discussed is WingCash, which uses a unique webpage with an immutable URL including both a currency code and a unique identifier similar to a serial number. Another option is BitMint, which relies on quantum-grade randomness. See Benjamin Geva, Seraina Neva Grünewald and Corinne Zellweger-Gutknecht, 'The e-Banknote as a "Banknote": A Monetary Law Interpreted' (2021) 41 Oxford Journal of Legal Studies 1119.

746 To illustrate, the Dutch Supreme Court had to decide already in 2012 about the theft of a virtual amulet and mask, see Hoge Raad, 31 January 2012, Nederlands Jurisprudentie 2012, 536 (ruling that in-game items can be goods within the meaning of Art. 310 Dutch Criminal Code).

gaming environment. Still, they must be considered virtual assets, so long as their scarcity is secured by some technological means. The same applies to digital money that can only be earned and spent in certain games.[747] Though they may also use crypto-graphy, they are typically stored on a server and part of a "centralised" network. Nevertheless, there can be hardly any doubt that they need to be legally treated in a similar way as cryptocurrencies and tokens based on DLT.

3.5.3.2 Questions Covered

3.5.3.2.1 *Property Protection*

The essential function of the national law identified as applicable by the new conflict-of-laws rule is to resolve rival claims to virtual assets. This law is the functional equivalent of property law rules governing tangible assets on the one hand and of rules governing the ownership of intangible assets, such as claims or other intangible property, on the other. These rules typically decide the following issues: 1. what powers are associated with entitlement, particularly vis-à-vis third parties; 2. how the entitlement is protected, such as through the right to reclaim possession or control from third parties; 3. how the entitlement is acquired and lost, e.g. through transfer, and 4. how limited rights in the asset, e.g. a security right, are created.[748]

The rather broad reach of any new rule is reflected in Principle 5 of the UNIDROIT Principles, which states that it covers all "proprietary issues". The commentary clarifies that this is much broader than the general scope of the Principles; Principle 5 applies to numerous issues that are excluded from the substantive scope under Principle 3(3).[749] The commentary considers that the broader scope of Principle 5 is justified by the necessary coherence between the law governing proprietary issues.[750] The need for harmonised conflict-of-laws rules goes further than the need for harmonised substantive law: it is precisely when the substantive rules differ that uniform conflict-of-laws rules make most sense.

The law identified under the new conflict-of-laws rule would cover all issues traditionally resolved by property law. It would decide, amongst other things,

747 See Yongwei Chen and Hua Cheng, 'The Economics of the Metaverse: A Comparison with the Real Economy' (2022) 3 Metaverse 19 (explaining how Linden Dollars and Robux can be earned and used).

748 On the functions of property law from a comparative and economic perspective, see Ugo Mattei, *Basic Principles of Property Law: A Comparative Legal and Economic Introduction* (Greenwood Press 2000).

749 UNIDROIT Principles on Digital Assets and Private Law (2023), Comment 5.2.

750 ibid.

whether virtual assets are to be treated as though they were tangible assets, or claims, or an entirely different category. It would also identify the rules applicable to transfers, e.g. whether it is the rules for movable goods, or those for the assignment of claims, or special rules. Finally, this law would resolve issues as to whether entitlements to virtual assets can be acquired in good faith and whether virtual assets can be the subject of security interests.

Conflict of laws generally is agnostic with regard to the content of the applicable law and the question which substantive rules of a legal system cover a particular issue. In particular, it does not decide whether the law of property or other rules protect the persons who control these assets. As has been shown, some national laws provide very little or no protection for holders of crypto-assets. In contrast, others do consider these assets as objects of property rights and protect their holders accordingly.[751] Conflict of laws does not change this diversity in national laws, but merely manages it by determining which national law applies to which assets.

3.5.3.2.2 *Relation to Insolvency Law*

Drawing the boundary between the law governing virtual assets and insolvency law is challenging. Let us imagine that A transfers to B a crypto-asset that was at the time governed by the law of state X. B then entrusts the crypto-asset to the custody of wallet provider C in state Y. Now imagine that C becomes insolvent and insolvency proceedings are opened in state Y. Which law governs the rights of B?

First, the particular right B has in the insolvency of C must be determined under the law of the forum of the bankruptcy proceedings, the *lex fori concursus*. This principle is widely accepted today, irrespective of which theory of international insolvency law is applied.[752] It is clear, for instance, that the *lex fori concursus* determines the priority of creditors.[753] The UNIDROIT Principles acknowledge this by carving out from the scope of the law identified in Principle 5 any substantive or procedural rule relating to "the ranking of categories of claims" in insolvency proceedings.[754]

751 See *supra* 3.1.5.

752 See, e.g., Toshiyuki Kono, 'Efficiency in Private International Law' (2014) 369 Collected Courses of the Hague Academy of International Law 359, 485–491 (discussing the theories of territorialism, universalism and contractualism).

753 Hannah L Buxbaum, 'Rethinking International Insolvency: The Neglected Role of Choice-of-Law Rules and Theory' (2000) 36 Stanford Journal of International Law 23, 54 (tracing this principle back to the times of Friedrich Carl von Savigny and Joseph Story).

754 Principle 5(7)(a) UNIDROIT Principles on Digital Assets and Private Law (2023).

The *lex fori concursus* also covers the characterisation of the right in question, e.g. whether it is a property right, a security right or a mere claim. This is a central issue of any insolvency proceeding, which has fundamental implications for the distribution of the debtor's assets. It would be fanciful to assume that the legislator in the state of insolvency would leave such a central issue to the law of other states. Consequently, it is the law applicable to the insolvency procedure that decides whether the holder of a particular virtual asset is to be regarded as its owner, as a collateral taker, or merely as a creditor. Furthermore, the *lex fori concursus* also governs other typical insolvency issues, such as the possibility of avoiding transactions or the procedure for the realisation and distribution of assets.[755]

On the other hand, whether B has acquired ownership or any similar title to a specific virtual asset cannot be left to the *lex fori concursus*. Because this acquisition happened before the bankruptcy proceedings were opened and when the asset was governed by the law of state X, only the law of X can apply to this issue.[756] Assuming that the law of state X considers virtual assets objects of property rights or similar rights, B may have acquired title to the asset. What this means in the bankruptcy of C is for state Y to decide. The UNIDROIT Principles try to convey this by stating that "the law applicable in accordance with this Principle governs all proprietary issues in respect of digital assets with regard to any event that has occurred before the opening of that insolvency-related proceeding".[757] While the intention behind this rule is undoubtedly correct, it places too much emphasis on the moment the insolvency proceedings are opened: the application of the law governing the asset or the *lex fori concursus* is not so much a question of timing than the fact that the asset is acquired *outside* of the insolvency proceedings.

In sum, for insolvency issues, there is a clear dividing line to be drawn: the law applicable to the asset determines which person is entitled to the asset. At the same time, the *lex fori concursus* decides the effects of this entitlement in the context of insolvency proceedings.

755 See in this regard Principle 5(7)(b) and (c) UNIDROIT Principles on Digital Assets and Private Law (2023).

756 Håkan Nial, 'Selected Problems of Private International Law' (1960) 101 Collected Courses of the Hague Academy of International Law 259, 304 (noting that the question whether, e.g., a pledgee has obtained a valid title to the goods is decided by the law of the country where the goods were at the time when the title is alleged to have passed).

757 Principle 7(6) UNIDROIT Principles on Digital Assets and Private Law (2023).

3.5.3.3 Condition of Internationality?

The UNIDROIT Principles on Digital Assets and Private Law, including Principle 5, do not contain any condition of internationality. However, the applicability of many texts of Private International Law presupposes a connection to at least two different systems or a foreign legal system.[758] French doctrine speaks of a "foreign element" (*élément d'extranéité*) as a precondition for the application of any conflict-of-laws rule.[759] Such a condition could also be imposed on the rule governing virtual assets.

Yet it must be remembered that the blockchain, by its very nature, touches upon more than one legal system. Hence, it is reasonable to assume that use of the blockchain in itself suffices to bring a transaction into the international sphere.[760] This is particularly important for the choice of the applicable law.[761]

This assumption may only be rebutted in particular situations. An example is a permissioned blockchain whose participants are all from a single state: a blockchain could be set up by financial institutions based in a single country, who want to cooperate on a distributed network. However, such cases are and will likely remain a rare exception.

3.5.4 *Party Autonomy*

Having determined the scope of the new conflicts rule, it is time to consider its possible content. Identifying the state with the strongest link to the blockchain is notoriously difficult. Where a situation presents equally strong connections to several legal systems, one solution is to allow the parties to choose the applicable law. The principle of party autonomy is most strongly associated with the law applicable to contractual obligations. Still, it is increasingly recognised in other areas too, such as the law applicable to torts and other non-contractual obligations (e.g. claims in unjust enrichment), in family law and succession law.[762] The principle of party autonomy could also be the appropriate solution for identifying the applicable law to assets recorded on a blockchain.[763] This

758 See, e.g., Art. 1(1) and (2) Inter-American Convention on the Law Applicable to International Contracts; Art. 1(1) EU Rome I Regulation; Art. 1(1) EU Rome II Regulation.

759 See, e.g., Mayer, Heuzé and Remy (n 600) 77–93.

760 Audit (n 548) 671; Florence Guillaume, 'Blockchain: le pont du droit international privé entre l'espace numérique et l'espace physique' in Ilaria Pretelli (ed), *Conflict of Laws in the Maze of Digital Platforms* (Schulthess 2018) 164, 174.

761 See *infra* 3.5.4.

762 See, e.g., Art. 14 EU Rome II Regulation; Art. 5 EU Rome III Regulation; Art. 22 EU Succession Regulation (Regulation (EU) No 650/2012 of the European Parliament and of the Council of 4 July 2012 on jurisdiction, applicable law, recognition and enforcement of decisions and acceptance and enforcement of authentic instruments in matters of succession and on the creation of a European Certificate of Succession [2012] OJ L201/107).

763 In favour of the possibility to choose the applicable law also Takahashi (n 549) 349–354.

is the view of UNIDROIT and the US Uniform Law Commission, which have both placed party autonomy at the top of the criteria for their conflict-of-laws rules.[764] Similarly, the Principality of Liechtenstein allows parties to choose its law.[765] Other states are, however, more reluctant to accept party autonomy for the law applicable to proprietary rights.[766]

3.5.4.1 General Objections

Extending the principle of party autonomy to property law is likely to encounter fundamental criticism. In particular, it might be argued that the law applicable to proprietary rights cannot be left to the choice of the parties because property rights have *erga omnes* effect, i.e., they affect the rights and obligations of third parties.[767] From this perspective, party autonomy in international property law is incompatible with the fundamental principle that contracts can only bind those that have agreed to them (i.e., the *res inter alios acta* principle) because third parties did not agree to the law applicable to the digital asset.

This objection has force in the real world, where the applicable property law can be easily identified by reference to the location of the relevant asset. Yet it carries less weight in the virtual world, where assets are not accessible and "visible" to third parties only through the electronic system in which they are registered. It does not seem a stretch to treat the participants in such a system as having acquiesced to the rules governing the electronic system's operation by logging in. Having said that, persons who do not participate in the network may also have an interest in the assets circulating on it. Creditors of the holder of crypto-assets may, for example, be interested in seizing them without themselves becoming a node. Still, given that the assets only exist on the blockchain, it seems fair to hold that even third parties are bound by its rules. Anyone who wants to enter the virtual world of a blockchain network must abide by its legal framework. There are, therefore, no compelling objections in principle to the free choice of law for virtual assets.[768]

---

764 See Principle 5(1)(a) and (b) UNIDROIT Principles on Digital Assets and Private Law (2023); Sec. 12–107(c) UCC.

765 See Art. 3(2)(b) Liechtenstein Act on Token and Trustworthy Technology, *supra* 3.5.2.1.

766 See, e.g., German law *supra* 3.5.2.1.

767 See, e.g., Roel Westrik and Jeroen van der Weide, 'Introduction' in Roel Westrik and Jeroen van der Weide (eds), *Party Autonomy in International Property Law* (Sellier 2011) 1, 2; Eva-Maria Kieninger, 'Die Zukunft des deutschen und europäischen Mobiliarkreditsicherungsrechts' (2008) 208 Archiv für die civilistische Praxis 182, 192; Alex Mills, *Party Autonomy in Private International Law* (Cambridge University Press 2018) 1–27.

768 Takahashi (n 549) 350–351 (who furthermore rejects the objection of the principle of *numerus clausus*).

3.5.4.2 The Choice of Law Inscribed in the Individual Assets

If party autonomy is accepted in principle, the details need to be chiselled out. This concerns the question of when and how the applicable law can be chosen, and by whom. Here, it is essential to ensure that there is a real and effective agreement between the parties. Moreover, the interests of third parties are paramount. The choice must be visible to them due to its impact on them.

The UNIDROIT Principles and the UCC both allow a choice of law for each individual virtual asset.[769] Nevertheless, there remain many questions surrounding this possibility.

From a technological perspective, implementing a choice of law in the asset itself is problematic. One possible solution would be to include information in the transfer. On the Bitcoin network, for example, a certain amount of non-transfer-related data can be added to the block header, which will be recorded on the blockchain.[770] A choice-of-law clause could easily be included. This clause could be established by the party transferring a unit of Bitcoin. For tokens, the issuer could do the same, depending on the particularities of the protocol he uses.

From a legal perspective, the clause must be accessible to all interested parties and recorded in a natural language that is understandable to them. The UNIDROIT Principles and the UCC refer to the records attached to or associated with the virtual asset. The UNIDROIT Principles provide that the records must be "readily available for review by persons dealing with the relevant digital asset".[771] This is indeed indispensable given the *erga omnes* effect of property rights, which requires that the persons concerned must be able to foresee the applicable law.

Even if such foreseeability could be ensured, other problems persist. The "choice" is not truly made by agreement between the parties. Rather, one party includes the clause in the asset or records attached to or associated with the asset, and the other passively receives the asset under the chosen law. Such unilateral choice might be justified because, technically, every transfer creates a new *Unspent Transaction Output* (UTXO), which can be considered as a new

769 Principle 5(1)(a) UNIDROIT Principles on Digital Assets and Private Law (2023); Sec. 12–107(c)(1) UCC.

770 Jake Frankenfield, 'Block Header (Cryptocurrency): Definition and How It Works' (22 September 2021) <https://www.investopedia.com/terms/b/block-header-cryptocurrency.asp> accessed 15 April 2024 (explaining how a blockchain header works); see also Antonopoulos (n 3) 216 (mentioning that RETURN operator allows to add 80 bytes of non-payment data to a transaction output).

771 Principle 5(2)(b) UNIDROIT Principles on Digital Assets and Private Law (2023); Sec. 12–107(c)(1) UCC.

asset. Nevertheless, allowing one party alone to determine the law governing the new asset may create problems, for example, where this law imposes duties on the recipient. In such cases, the choice can only be considered valid where the recipient has been given an opportunity to reject the asset.

According to one view, however, a choice of law for a crypto-asset should be permitted only where the choice is made uniformly for the entire blockchain in question.[772] This condition precludes any individual choice being made for a particular asset. Several arguments are made for this position. First, the condition is designed to avoid conflicting choices of law in several transactions over the same asset.[773] Such conflicting choices of law may create priority conflicts, e.g. in the case of the transfer of movable property or the assignment of claims. However, for transfers of a crypto-asset, such concerns are unfounded. After all, the blockchain contains a reliable mechanism for determining which transfer occurred first and therefore takes priority. Second, there is a concern that the parties might collude and act fraudulently by choosing a law that extinguishes any security rights.[774] However, this problem could be easily solved by invalidating a choice of law where it prejudices third-party rights.[775] Although the UNIDROIT Principles do not address this issue directly, they preclude modifications to the choice of law that would affect existing proprietary rights.[776] This could be read broadly as precluding any choice of law that extinguishes a security or other right of a third party.

In sum, there is no reason to impose a condition requiring a uniform choice for the whole blockchain and to preclude choices for individual assets. Diverging choices for individual assets are acceptable as long as they are readily apparent to other participants and do not undermine the rights of third parties.

Nevertheless, some uniformity in the choice of applicable law may be necessary to ensure that virtual assets remain interchangeable or "fungible". Fungibility facilitates the exchange of goods in markets because it reduces transaction costs. Fungibility requires that all assets of the same issuance or kind are subject to the same law. Indeed, fungibility and, by implication, trade might be seriously hampered if some assets are transferred under a different law than others.

In this context, a provision in the UNIDROIT Principles on Digital Assets and Private Law is essential, according to which the law specified in Principle 5(1)

772 Takahashi (n 549) 351.
773 ibid 350–352.
774 ibid 350 (calling this a "negative externality" of the choice).
775 See, e.g., Art. 3(2) phrase 2 EU Rome I Regulation.
776 Principle 5(2)(e) UNIDROIT Principles on Digital Assets and Private Law (2023).

"applies to all digital assets of the same description".[777] However, this provision does not clarify which law should prevail if conflicting choices for different assets of the same description are made. One possible interpretation is that the *issuer* of a particular token may preclude from the outset any other choice of law being made in one of the assets. Another possibility is to assume that the *law* that governs the system in which the assets are recorded can preclude the choice of a different law in the individual assets. We will revert to this point.[778]

3.5.4.3 Choice in the System

The UNIDROIT Principles and the UCC allow a choice to be made in the "system".[779] The UNIDROIT Principles clarify that this notion is to be understood widely, covering protocols, platforms and applications.[780] Each of these can contain a choice of law, which may lead to conflicting choices being made due to the layered structure of the network.

According to the UNIDROIT Principles and the UCC, conflicts between a choice in the digital asset and the system are to be resolved by reference to the "waterfall." This means that one is supposed to start at the top of the waterfall; and if the first provision cannot be applied, one proceeds to the next provision in the waterfall.[781] This structure means that if there has been a choice made in the digital asset, this will prevail without exception over the choice made in the system, because it is higher in the hierarchy. However, where a choice of law has been made for the whole system, it may not be evident to third parties that this may be circumvented by an individual choice of law for the asset itself. Moreover, the protocol programmers may wish to preclude such a choice to maintain the assets' easy transferability and fungibility, and secure legal certainty. Therefore, one should leave it to the system as to whether it precludes an individual choice. On the other hand, it does not play any role if the governing law excludes an individual choice of law. A choice of law must usually be understood as referring to the substantive rules of a particular law, excluding its provisions on the conflict of laws.[782]

But what about differing choices in the network protocol on the one hand and in that of a specific platform or application on the other? To solve this type of conflict, UNIDROIT suggests that states should adopt a specific rule, without

777 Principle 5(2)(d) UNIDROIT Principles on Digital Assets and Private Law (2023).
778 See *infra* 3.5.4.3.at the end.
779 Principle 5(2)(d) UNIDROIT Principles on Digital Assets and Private Law (2023).
780 ibid, Comment 5.6.
781 See UNIDROIT Principles on Digital Assets and Private Law (2023), Comment 5.5.
782 See, e.g., Art. 8 Hague Principles on Choice of Law in International Commercial Contracts (2015).

however giving any indication as to the content of such a rule.[783] Before we address this question, let us look into the workings of the choice for the system.

A choice in the protocol code of the system – i.e. in the software on which the network operates – is not straight-forward. To ensure human beings can read it, the choice-of-law clause must be programmed into the source code, not in the binary code, which is only machine-readable. But even if this condition were met, one cannot be certain that users will be aware of the clause because not everybody reads the source code. A choice through code should therefore not be recognised.

Yet there are other technological solutions. UNIDROIT stresses that in determining whether a specific law has been chosen, consideration should be given to the records attached to or associated with the system.[784] The UCC explicitly allows the choice of law in such records.[785] These "records" mean any kind of electronically or otherwise recorded information.[786] They are not to be confused with information recorded on the blockchain itself, which is the essence of the virtual asset. One could, for instance, imagine a window that opens on the user's screen every time a particular blockchain protocol is downloaded from the internet, containing information on the specific law governing the network. The process is not dissimilar to terms and conditions popping up in a window on the internet when a consumer orders goods. It is true that the information communicated this way will not reach every investor who acquires on-chain assets. Neither would it reach third parties, such as creditors, who do not participate in the network. However, this does not pose a major obstacle for the biggest networks, for which the choice of law will certainly be known. For other networks, investors and creditors can be expected to inform themselves on the rules governing a particular network, platform or application before they acquire or seize assets recorded on it.

Let us now come back to the question of which choice should prevail in layered networks: the choice made for the network as a whole, on the one hand, or the choice made for the particular platform or application, on the other? The answer results from what has been said before. It is only a choice brought to the user's attention and that she can ascertain is valid. Therefore, the question must be resolved from the perspective of the user. She will be bound only by the choice that was communicated to her. If two conflicting choices were made, e.g. for the network protocol and the platform, then the oneon

783 ibid.

784 Principle 5(2)(b) UNIDROIT Principles on Digital Assets and Private Law (2023).

785 Sec. 12–107(c)(3) UCC.

786 UNIDROIT Principles on Digital Assets and Private Law (2023), Comment 5.16.

the higher level – i.e. that for the platform – should prevail because it is more specific. However, this only applies on the condition that the rules at the lower level – i.e. the network level – allow for a different choice of law. Where they preclude any other choice of law to preserve the fungibility and tradability of the assets, a choice at a higher level has no effect.

3.5.4.4 Rarity of Choice in Practice

If the possibility of choosing the applicable property law is accepted, another significant problem remains: choice of law is rarely used in the crypto economy. As of yet, none of the existing major blockchain networks has been subjected, explicitly or implicitly, to a national law. This absence of a choice of law is not the result of any oversight on the part of blockchain enthusiasts. Rather, it is more likely a deliberate omission in line with their political vision. Choosing a state law to govern their dealings would hardly be compatible with their anti-governmental ideology, which spurred the development of the technology in the first place. It would be completely contradictory for them to submit their supposedly a-national and alegal network to a national legal system.

The situation is different for "permissioned" networks, which cannot be joined without the authorisation by the central operator.[787] This operator is often a bank or other regulated and supervised entity. Therefore, it is not uncommon for these networks to be expressly submitted to the law of some specific jurisdiction.[788] Such a choice must be respected.

For permission*less* networks, the rarity of choice of law in practice explains why the principle of party autonomy – at least today – does not yield a satisfying ans-wer for identifying the governing law. This is unlikely to change in the short term, given the anti-government attitude of the blockchain community. That does not exclude that the principle of party autonomy will be helpful in the future, when choice of law might become more frequent. UNIDROIT and

787 Michel Rauchs and others, 'Distributed Ledger Technology Systems: A Conceptual Framework' (Cambridge Centre for Alternative Finance (CCAF), August 2018) 61. The terminology is not uniform. Often, notions like "private" or "closed" blockchains are used. These may however also be understood as relating to the *participation* in the network, and not to the function of *validation*. Where the latter is restricted, it is appropriate to use the term "permissioned".

788 See, e.g., the Corda blockchain network developed by the consortium R3, which is composed of banks and other regulated institutions, see INTERNATIONAL SWAPS AND DERIVATIVES ASSOCIATION (ISDA), 'Private International Law Aspects of Smart Derivatives Contracts Utilizing Distributed Ledger Technology' 22 <https://www.isda.org/a/4RJTE/Private-International-Law-Aspects-of-Smart-Derivatives-Contracts-Utilizing-DLT.pdf> accessed 15 April 2024.

the ULC believe this to be the case. Both trust that explicitly offering the possibility to make such a choice will incentivise the blockchain community to make one. Even if blockchain practices may eventually change in this way, there remains an urgent need for additional conflict-of-laws rules for cases in which no national law has been chosen.

3.5.4.5 Summary

Party autonomy is the best solution for determining the property law governing blockchain networks, protocols and assets. Whether the blockchain participants will accept and use the possibility of choice remains to be seen. Where such a choice is made and is visible to third parties, it should be respected.

3.5.5 *Law Applicable in the Absence of a Choice*

3.5.5.1 The Need for Rules Using Objective Connecting Factors

Where the applicable law has not been chosen – as in almost all cases today – one must look for factors that connect the situation to a particular state. These default rules, or "objective connecting factors", are part of the foundation of Private International Law and can be found in conflict-of-laws rules and codifications worldwide.[789] They are also used in many conventions that harmonise Private International Law.[790]

The UNIDROIT Principles use an alternative solution. Where the applicable law has not been chosen, the UNIDROIT Principles suggest the state should refer to the *lex fori* or the Principles themselves,[791] unless there is an issuer with a clearly ascertainable statutory seat.[792] Foreign law should be applied only where neither the *lex fori* nor the Principles provide any solution.[793]

This approach to conflict of laws is unique. It places the Principles – despite their *soft law* character – above national law. This could be justified on the basis that the Principles only apply to the extent that states adopt them. It is, therefore, the *forum state*, and not UNIDROIT, that decides that the substantive rule of Private International Law applies. It could be further argued that

---

789 See, e.g., Simeon C Symeonides, *Codifying Choice of Law Around the World: An International Comparative Analysis* (Oxford University Press 2014) 178–184 (on the use of the closest connection in conflicts rules regarding contracts and torts).

790 See, e.g., Art. 4 and 5 Hague Convention on the Law Applicable to Traffic Accidents, done on 4 May 1971; Art. 4, 5 and 6 Hague Convention on the Law Applicable to Products Liability, done on 2 October 1973.

791 Principle 5(1)(d) UNIDROIT Principles on Digital Assets and Private Law (2023).

792 On this exception *infra* 3.5.5.3.

793 Principle 5(1)(d) Option A (III) and Option B (II) UNIDROIT Principles on Digital Assets and Private Law (2023).

this solution is a necessary response to two particularities of the blockchain: First, the fact that objective connections are notoriously difficult to find; and second, the fact that blockchain developers resist making a choice of the applicable law.

In practical terms, however, the approach chosen by UNIDROIT has serious downsides. Recourse to the *lex fori* fuels legal fragmentation as the rules concerning proprietary rights in digital assets vary widely from country to country. The reference to the UNIDROIT Principles only partially mitigates this problem, as they contain many gaps that national laws will fill in differently. Moreover, the Principles do not indicate how the rules of Private International Law of the forum should be designed, which opens the door for even more divergence between legal systems.

The UCC uses an even more radical approach: In the absence of a choice of law, it simply refers to the law of the District of Columbia (Washington D.C.).[794] This takes the well-known homeward trend to new and unknown extremes. While it provides a degree of legal certainty, this comes with complete arbitrariness. There is no reason why the law of a particular federal jurisdiction (Washington, D.C.) should govern all blockchain-related issues in the absence of an express choice of law.

Given these shortcomings, a logical default rule of Private International Law on which all states can agree must be devised. This is no small challenge. As stressed repeatedly, the blockchain does not have ties to any state that could satisfy the "most significant relationship" test of the US approach to the conflict of laws or the *principe de proximité* found in continental systems. However, this does not mean there are no other links that connect the blockchain to a particular jurisdiction. Some of these will now be discussed.

3.5.5.2 Central Operator

Closed or permissioned blockchains are heavily centralised. Where no choice of law has been made, one could refer to the "central operator" of closed or permissioned blockchains.[795] Given the paramount importance of its role, it seems justified to use this operator as the default connecting factor for identifying the governing property law.[796] One could refer to, e.g., the operator's statutory seat, which provides a stable and foreseeable connection. This law should govern all assets recorded on the permissioned blockchain. It also should cover the conditions for and effects of transfer, and the creation of limited rights *in rem*.

794 Sec. 12–107(5) UCC. On this rule, see *supra* 3.5.2.1.

795 On the notion of the "central operator", see *supra* 1.1.2.5.

796 See also Financial Markets Law Committee (n 618).

A similar solution has been chosen by German Private International Law, which refers primarily to the country in which the blockchain registrar is supervised, and, if the registrar is not supervised, to the country of the registrar's seat.[797] The country of supervision is, however, usually where the registrar has its seat. Should there be any divergence between the two countries, the registrar will potentially be subject to supervision in two countries: its seat and its registration. German law does not provide a solution to this problem. It seems that operators should be subject to one set of private law only, and the seat provides such a unitary connection. Therefore, it is better to refer at the outset to the law of the country where the central operator has its seat.

For the avoidance of doubt, it should be stressed that the connecting factor suggested here only relates to private law, and not to regulation, which is determined by regulatory law itself. The suggested rule is also limited to situations with a central operator, i.e., in case of permissioned or private blockchains. Further, it should be remembered that such blockchains are most likely to have a choice-of-law clause in their protocol. This must be respected unless the blockchain participants are exclusively established in a single country.[798]

3.5.5.3 The Issuer

Many crypto-assets are issued by a specific person, whether natural or legal. This is particularly so with tokens that are issued as part of an ICO. If the issuer has indicated a law that applies to the assets that are issued, one should uphold that choice based on the principle of party autonomy.[799] Where the issuer has failed to choose the applicable law, either in the asset itself or in the records attached or relating to it, one could use the issuer as the default connecting factor. This secures certainty for the participants in the network and for third parties alike. Moreover, it has the advantage of ensuring that a single law governs all assets of the same issuance, which ensures their fungibility and tradability.

From the connecting factores related to the issuer, one could use either the issuer's country of incorporation or the country of establishment. Of the two, the first is to be preferred, given its foreseeability, stability and growing acceptance in Private International Law.

The UNIDROIT Principles recognise the significance of the issuer's country of incorporation by expressly referring to the issuer's statutory seat.[800] This

797 See *supra* 3.5.2.1.

798 See on this exception *supra* 3.5.3.3.

799 See on the possibility of choice in the digital asset Sec. 12–107(c)(1), (3) UCC; Principle 5(1)(a) UNIDROIT Principles on Digital Assets and Private Law (2023) and *supra* 3.5.4.2.

800 Principle 5(1)(c) UNIDROIT Principles on Digital Assets and Private Law (2023).

seat is usually in the country of incorporation. The Principles impose the condition that third parties must be able to ascertain this seat.[801] That must be welcomed: proprietary relations can be governed only by a law that third parties can foresee.

The scope of the rule is further limited by the Principles' understanding of the term "issuer".[802] The issuer is defined as the person who puts the digital asset "into the stream of commerce for value". Moreover, the issuer is only that person which 1. identifies itself to the public "as a named person", 2. identifies its statutory seat, and 3. identifies itself as the person who has put the digital assets, or digital assets of the same description, into the stream of commerce for value.

The justification for these additional limitations is unclear. The first limitation, i.e., that the issuer must have put the digital asset into the stream of commerce for value, excludes gratuitous issuances, for instance, via airdrop, from the scope of the rule. However, there is no demonstrated need for this additional limitation. Protecting proprietary rights is generally independent of the mode of acquisition and the consideration paid for the asset. A uniform determination of the law governing proprietary rights in assets received for free is as necessary as in other cases in which assets are acquired "for value".

The second limitation, which requires a triple self-identification by the issuer, is equally doubtful. To safeguard the interests of third parties, the issuer's statutory seat only needs to be ascertainable. But this is already provided for in Principle 5(1)(c). The additional condition that the issuer must identify itself, its statutory seat and the fact that it has put the asset into the stream of commerce for value allows the issuer to circumvent the application of this rule, simply by omitting to provide the requisite information. There is no reason why the issuer should have the possibility to determine the applicable law by not making statements about its identity or location. If it wants a say over the applicable law, it should make a clear choice of law in the digital asset instead.

National lawmakers should therefore reject both limitations. The issuer's statutory seat is a much more meaningful connecting factor without them. There are good reasons for it to play a significant role in determining the law governing virtual assets.

801 ibid.

802 Principle 5(2)(f) UNIDROIT Principles on Digital Assets and Private Law (2023).

3.5.5.4 The Custodian and the Law Governing the Custody Contract

Most tokens and coins are held with an intermediary that takes care of their clients' assets, such as a crypto exchange or a wallet provider. This custodian could provide a useful connecting factor for determining proprietary rights in the assets under custody. Its role is also recognised, at least for specific issues, by the UNIDROIT Principles.[803]

From the outset, one must clearly distinguish between two types of wallets: custodial and non-custodial wallets.[804] In the case of non-custodial wallets, the crypto-assets are held directly by the customer, who retains exclusive access to the private key. That is why some also speak of "self-custodial wallets".[805]

Non-custodial wallets operate only to serve a type of backup function, similar to a file secured by a password. Consequently, they should not influence the law applicable to crypto-assets.

The situation is different for custodial wallets. In their case, an intermediary exercises control over the crypto-assets. This may influence the applicable law.

The custodian's general terms and conditions often contain a choice-of-law clause. Upholding such a clause facilitates the function of the intermediary, as it can manage all assets following a single law.[806] This is also reasonable from the perspective of the customer, who has accepted the terms of the custody agreement, including the choice-of-law clause. Applying the chosen law may seem more problematic for third parties, such as the customer's creditors or insolvency administrator, who are not privy to the custody agreement. Yet it should be remembered that these parties can access or seize the assets only via the intermediary. In this context, they can foresee or take cognisance of the applicable law. The situation here resembles that of intermediated securities, where the law agreed between the parties to the custody agreement equally impacts third parties who have not consented to the choice of law.[807]

The UNIDROIT Principles also recognise the role of the law governing the custody agreement.[808] Yet they only address the situation in which the governing law is expressly stipulated in the custody agreement. By contrast, they do

803 Principle 5(3) UNIDROIT Principles on Digital Assets and Private Law (2023).

804 See also UNIDROIT Principles on Digital Assets and Private Law (2023), Comment 10.11 and 10.13-10.15.

805 Nik Yeo, 'Crypto Exchanges: the Basics' (2023) 38 Butterworth's Journal of International Banking and Financial Law 459.

806 This was the reason for allowing a restricted choice of law in the Hague Intermediated Securities Convention, see *supra* 3.3.2.3.

807 See *supra* 3.3.2.3.

808 Principle 5(6) UNIDROIT Principles on Digital Assets and Private Law (2023).

not deal with situations in which the agreement lacks a choice-of-law clause. In such a case, it makes sense to use the statutory seat of the intermediary as the connecting factor. The client and third parties typically know or can easily obtain information about this place. They should consider all assets in the custody of an intermediary as being under the umbrella of the latter's law. This enhances legal certainty and makes the management of such assets much easier.

The UNIDROIT Principles limit, on the other hand, the role of the law chosen in the custody agreement to the contractual relationship and extend it only to specific proprietary issues, in particular the protection of the customer in the case of insolvency.[809] Yet once a virtual asset is held in custody, *all* proprietary questions relating to the asset should be subject to the law governing the custody relationship. This law should regulate, *inter alia*, whether the custodian or the customer is to be considered the owner, as well as the conditions for the creation and validity of *in rem* rights by the custodian or third parties. Even the proprietary effects, if any, of a transfer between two clients of the same custodian that is recorded only in the books of the custodian, but not on the blockchain, would be appropriately determined under this law.

Notwithstanding the foregoing, the law governing the custody agreement can only cover proprietary questions during the time the asset is held in custody and which arise as a result of or in relation to the custody relationship. The acquisition of a virtual asset from and transfer to third parties not privy to the custody agreement remain outside its scope. These issues are subject to the other conflict-of-laws rules that apply to virtual assets, i.e. the principle of party autonomy and the objective connecting factors that apply in the absence of a choice of law.

3.5.5.5 The Relationship between these Connecting Factors

Situations may arise where several of the connecting factors discussed above are present. For instance, an asset recorded on a permissioned blockchain or a token issued by a particular person might also be held in custody. In such cases, the question arises as to which connecting factor takes precedence.

This problem is far from easy to solve, as it involves evaluating the relative weight to be accorded to the different connecting factors. For assets issued or recorded on permissioned and private networks, the statutory seat of the central operator should take priority. It would be rare in such cases to have different issuers, and the assets themselves would rarely be held with a custodian.

809 See the reference to Principle 13 in Principle 5(3) UNIDROIT Principles on Digital Assets and Private Law (2023).

Hence, the statutory seat of the central operator should trump the other connecting factors.

Clarification is further required for situations where a choice must be made between the law of the issuer and the law governing the custody relationship. This is a particularly thorny issue, as both connecting factors seem to be of equal or at least similar weight. From an outcomes-oriented perspective, it could be argued that the issuer ought to be able to determine the law applicable to all proprietary rights in the assets it issues to ensure uniformity across the issuance as a whole. Yet such uniformity is illusory because it could be overridden by a choice made in relation to a specific asset. Moreover, if the law of the issuer were given primacy over the law governing the custody agreement, the cost of holding assets in custody would likely become prohibitive. It seems therefore preferable for the law of the custody relationship to prevail over the law of the issuer. The issuer nevertheless still is able to make an express choice of law and thereby exclude the law of custody.

3.5.5.6 The Person with the Power of Control and Disposal

Some assets remain that are not recorded on a closed or permissioned blockchain and do neither have a custodian or an issuer. These cases are admittedly rare, given that most crypto-assets today are held with an intermediary, but they nevertheless do occur. The prime example is the cryptocurrency of a permissionless network that is held directly, such as bitcoin holdings where the private keys are stored on a USB key. These situations are particularly problematic, given that none of the connecting factors mentioned above are present: there is no central operator, issuer, or custodian to which they can be linked. These assets constitute, therefore, the Ground Zero of Private International Law.

In such cases, the only remaining solution is to apply the law of the person presently in control of the asset to determine her ownership or the rights of any other person. One could refer, for instance, to the habitual residence of natural persons or the principal place of business or place of incorporation of legal persons. The justification for using this law to determine property issues is that no other point of contact can be unequivocally identified.

A similar solution has been used by the English courts, which have referred to the habitual residence or place of business of the person who "owns" the crypto-asset to determine the location of crypto-assets, with possible implications for the applicable law.[810] This formulation suffers from a *petitio principii,*

---

810 See *supra* 3.5.2.1.

though, because the person *owning* the asset can only be identified after the law governing proprietary issues regarding the asset has been determined.[811] But it can also be understood as giving preference to the person who *controls* the asset at the *relevant time*. This is actually how it was applied by the English courts and how the High Court of Singapore later expressed it.[812] The *relevant time* is when a legally relevant fact occurs, such as a theft, and not when an action is brought before the courts.

Still, strong objections can be made. One possible counterargument is that the person in control will often be unknown, given the pseudonymity of the blockchain. Yet this argument ignores that the question of the applicable law will mainly arise in litigation. In this context, the person in control at the relevant time will usually be known or identify himself voluntarily. It may, for instance, be the victim whose assets have been stolen and who now brings a claim against the hacker and his custodian. As the English cases demonstrate, there will be no difficulty in identifying the person in control over the crypto-asset and their location at the time of the theft.

Another objection is that the person in control may change their residence.[813] This issue is, however, not limited to the particular rule in question but also arises in other contexts, e.g. consumer cases where the consumer has changed his domicile. Private International Law deals with the resulting *conflit mobile* problem by retaining the habitual residence, principal place of business or place of incorporation at the time of the transaction, the tort or any other event that is central to the dispute. This is precisely why it is so important to ascertain control "at the relevant time."

One could still object that the rule will not work in case of joint transferors.[814] This is true, but such situations are scarce in practice, especially for assets held directly. Should they occur, it will often be possible to find a common connecting factor as between the transferors, for instance, the place where they have known each other or where they regularly meet.

It has also been asserted that the connecting factor would not work in the case of chain "assignments" (i.e. transfers).[815] This is, however, misconceived;

---

811 See Held (n 537) 270 (" ... such proposition presumes what is required to be proved: who is the 'owner' of the relevant cryptoasset?").

812 High Court of Singapore, *Cheong Jun Yoong v Three Arrows Capital Ltd* [2024] SGHC 21.

813 Financial Markets Law Committee (n 618) para 6.22 <http://www.fmlc.org/dlt-and-governing-law.html> accessed 15 April 2024 (criticising that a major disadvantage of the rule is that it will often not give a clear answer to questions of entitlement in circumstances of a change of habitual residence by the transferor).

814 ibid para 6.22 (criticising that the rule will not give a clear answer in case of joint transfers).

815 ibid (drawing a parallel to the assignment of claims).

one can apply the law of the person in control at the time of each transfer. This admittedly leads to another objection: such approach would "artificially split up the ledger".[816] However, such a "split" in the ledger simply reflects the nature of the blockchain as distributed worldwide. Because the blockchain was consciously designed to avoid any significant connection to a state, there is hardly any other choice but to subject the ledger to different laws. Rather than being "artificial", such a split seems to be the solution most aligned with the true nature of a fully distributed blockchain. With no governing law having been chosen and no other objective connecting factors being present, one has to use the only connecting factor available, namely the person who has control over the crypto-asset in question.

It cannot be denied that the criterion suggested here is far from ideal. It is a solution *faute de mieux*. But its defects are mitigated because it will only apply in a very subsidiary way. In addition, it is subject to an important exception where the party presently in control of the crypto-asset has obtained it through violence, threat or fraud. In these cases, one should instead refer to the law at the place of habitual residence or establishment of the person who previously exercised control.

3.5.6 *Public Policy Exception*

Almost every conflict-of-laws rule is subject to the public policy exception. This exception, which comes into play at the end of the conflict-of-laws process that identifies the applicable law, may oust the application of the law so identified if it would, in the individual case, produce results contrary to the fundamental values of the *forum*. The rules for determining the law applicable to virtual assets would be equally subject to this exception.

3.5.6.1 State Public Policy

National courts will reject the application of a foreign law where the result would be incompatible with the *forum*'s most fundamental notions of justice. However, recourse to the public policy exception in property law is rare. This is likely to be true even in a context as disputed as the rules governing the crypto economy.

Many countries prohibit their citizens and companies from acquiring and transferring Bitcoin and other crypto-assets.[817] They may well consider a foreign law validating acquisitions of such assets as amounting to a violation of their public policy (*ordre public international*). Nevertheless, their courts must

---

816 ibid.

817 See *supra* 2.1.1.1.

examine carefully in each individual case whether invalidating such transactions or transfers is in the national interest.

Countries that are more tolerant of the crypto economy may also reject the application of foreign law. This might be the case, for example, where this law allows transfers of virtual assets for money laundering, arms and drug trafficking or similar criminal purposes. The public policy exception may also be triggered when the network participants choose a national law that upholds transfers tainted by violence, threats or fraud. These situations would certainly be at odds with the fundamental principles of most other legal systems, so rejecting the application of such a law would be easily justifiable.

3.5.6.2 Technological Public Policy

States might adopt laws, either through legislation or the courts, that are incompatible with the basic technical operation of the blockchain. One could imagine that a state's law completely departs from control as a condition for the validity of a transfer and allows transfers of ownership over a virtual asset merely by agreement or by a record in the books of an intermediary. How should a court respond if such a law has been chosen or were to apply as a result of using an objective connecting factor?

It is hard to say that such a situation would contravene the most basic notions of justice or fundamental principles of law, as these have yet to be formed in relation to blockchain networks. However, such a national law would be at odds with the fundamentals of the technology itself. The blockchain is underpinned by the idea that any transfer requires using two keys, one public and one private. Any blockchain transfer that is done, or deemed to be done, in a different manner is contrary to the most basic notions of how the blockchain works and would therefore compromises its proper functioning.

A law that allows a transfer without a change of control could be seen as violating technological public policy or *ordre technologique*. This concept seems necessary to fill a gap in the current setup of Private International Law. It ensures the minimal conditions required for the functioning of the crypto economy.

The consequences following from a violation of technological public policy would be the same as they are for a violation of a state's public policy: the foreign law will not be applied. Instead, the court must choose a solution that takes account of the blockchain's content and respects its basic operating principles.

It is too early to foresee whether this new idea of a technological public policy will gain traction. Yet for the technology to work, its fundamental underpinnings must be respected. For the avoidance of doubt, it is important to stress that the proposition advanced here differs from placing the rule of code over the rule of law. States that permit the use of virtual assets have an interest in ensuring that the technology works. They therefore must help ensure that technological public policy is upheld.

3.5.7 *The Law Governing* CBDCs

Digital currencies issued by central banks are a special case. They are not part of the crypto economy because they are backed by a state, rather than being of private origin. In addition, many CBDCs are not underpinned by DLT but by some other technology.[818] Nevertheless, they are virtual assets that raise questions of Private International Law. The answer to these questions will likely depend on the how a particular CBDC is structured.

At this early stage of development, various models are being proposed. These can be divided into two categories: 1. models based on the issuance of tokens ("*token-based models*") and 2. models based on accounts ("*account-based models*").[819] In the case of account-based models, the account may be held directly with the central bank or indirectly with a commercial bank.[820] Many other parameters have yet to be decided and may vary between CBDCs.

Whatever model is chosen, it seems that the conflict-of-laws rules outlined for crypto-assets will not apply to CBDCs. This is due to the particularities of their origin and operation. The registration of CBDC units and their transfer will result from a set of technical processes and legal rules that emanate from a particular state. Without these processes and rules, CBDC units would not exist and cease to function. For this reason, it seems out of the question for the rules of another state to supersede those of the issuing state. It would be hard to imagine, for example, that the holder of an e-CNY or a digital Pound Sterling could be determined according to techniques and rules other than those of the People's Republic of China or the UK, respectively. As a result, these states must also answer how these assets can be acquired and to whom they belong.

Thus, the *lex monetae* principle, which holds that a state determines the private law issues arising from its currency, will apply even more broadly here than in the case of classic, tangible fiat money. The law of the issuing state not only will determine the structure of CBDCs, including their composition and divisions, but also govern issues of property law, such as the rules governing the asset transfer. This remains at the time of writing, of course, only a

818 On CBDCs see *supra* 1.2.1.6.

819 Bossu and others (n 261) 9; *Steven L Schwarcz, 'Regulating Digital Currencies: Towards an Analytical Framework'* (*2021*) *102 Boston University Law Review* 1037, 1046.

820 Bossu and others, ibid 10; *Schwarcz, ibid* 1051.

prediction, which stands to be proved or disproved by future developments. However, it seems likely that many problems will arise with the administration of CBDCs by intermediaries. In this respect, the interoperability of the various CBDC protocols will be vital for the smooth operation of world trade.

3.5.8 *Conclusion*

Despite the distributed nature of blockchain networks, it is possible to formulate a conflict-of-laws rule that reflects their particular characteristics. Several connecting factors can link a virtual asset to a specific legal system. The fears that the blockchain creates an existential challenge for Private International Law are therefore grossly exaggerated. Nevertheless, the connecting factors for the crypto economy are quite specific and must be elaborated with great attention to detail. The UNIDROIT Principles on Digital Assets and Private Law provide a crucial first basis for a possible conflict-of-laws rule but remain insufficient. This chapter has outlined what further work is required to complement and deepen this initial first step.

3.6 The Law Governing Stablecoins

Determining the applicable law to stablecoins presents particular challenges, as such tokens are related to another asset in some way. It is, therefore, necessary to distinguish between three different questions: 1. the law governing the stablecoin itself (3.6.1), 2. the law governing the assets that back up the stablecoin (3.6.2), and 3. the law that governs the relationship between the stablecoin and its underlying asset (3.6.3).[821]

3.6.1 *The Law Governing the Stablecoin Itself*

Stablecoins are recorded and transferred on a blockchain. Therefore, proprietary issues in their regard must therefore be solved by using the same conflict-of-laws analysis as for other virtual assets. Nothing special applies in this regard.

An exception may be considered where the underlying asset represented by the stablecoin has a very close relationship with a particular jurisdiction. To illustrate, let us imagine that a stablecoin is backed by real estate located in

---

821 See Matthias Lehmann and Hannes Meyle, 'The Law Applicable to Stablecoins' in Andrea Bonomi, Matthias Lehmann and Shaheeza Lalani (eds), *Blockchain and Private International Law* (Brill 2023) 372.

state A. The law governing the stablecoin has not been chosen. In this case, the blockchain and the token are arguably so strongly connected with state A that they could be deemed to have their "closest connection" with the law of that state. In other words, in this particular setting the location of the underlying asset could be used determine the law applicable to the stablecoin. However, the assumption of the "closest" connection could be overridden by the choice of a different law. Moreover, tokens that evidence such a tight link to a particular state are rare.

3.6.2 *The Law Governing the Underlying Assets*

The assets underlying stablecoins are diverse: shares, bonds, money, real estate, mortgages or commodities. In their respect, the conventional conflict-of-laws rules must be applied. This means that for non-intermediated shares, the *lex societatis* is to be followed; for intermediated securities, the PRIMA approach or a similar rule will apply; money held with a bank will be governed by the law of the bank; for tangible objects – whether movable or immovable – the *lex rei sitae* must be followed; and for virtual assets, the applicable law should be determined by the conflict-of-laws rules elaborated above.

As a result, in relation to the underlying assets, the ownership issue will ultimately be decided by conventional conflict-of-laws rules. The fact that these assets are used in a stablecoin arrangement cannot remove them from their governing law.

3.6.3 *The Law Governing the Relation between the Stablecoin and the Underlying Assets*

The third and most challenging part of the analysis concerns the link between the crypto-asset and the underlying asset. This link determines whether a stablecoin represents an asset; it is of utmost importance because it guarantees the value and stability of the stablecoin. What law governs it?

In many cases, the law governing the underlying asset must also decide whether the latter can be represented on a blockchain.[822] For tangible assets, this means that the *lex rei sitae* will govern the question of whether they can be tokenised. This is necessary for two reasons: First, creditors, insolvency administrators, and other parties have legitimate expectations that this law will determine whether the underlying assets can be part of a stablecoin portfolio. Such parties cannot know whether these underlying assets have become

822 In this sense ibid 397.

part of a stablecoin portfolio under some other law, e.g. the law chosen for the stablecoin. Second, the law where the underlying assets are situated should determine whether they are represented by a stablecoin because this country exerts enforcement power over these assets.

The same approach should be used for any underlying assets with a strong relationship to a particular law. An example is shares in a company. The question of whether they can be tokenised belongs to the *lex socieatis*.

However, underlying assets that have a tenuous relation with one state, such as claims, might be treated differently. For such assets, the link and the underlying asset could be subject to a different law. The Swiss Federal Act on Private International Law adopts this position and submits the link between the underlying asset and the token to the law chosen in the token or, failing such choice, the law of the country where the token issuer has its seat.[823] This approach is advantageous in that it facilitates the tokenisation of claims governed by different laws. The approach could possibly be extended to other intangible assets, such as virtual assets.

Under the Swiss Federal Act on Private International Law, the same rule also applies to the question of whether goods are represented by a document of title (in paper or any equivalent form).[824] However, with regard to these tangible objects, the rule is subject to a specific limit. In the event of a priority dispute over goods, the Swiss Federal Act on Private International Law states that the law of the place where the goods are located is decisive.[825] This reveals the gravitational pull of the *lex rei sitae* for tangible property, which is difficult to resist.

3.6.4 *Summary*

When analysing stablecoins and, more generally, any token backed by or refencing some other underlying assets, three different legal relationships must be distinguished, which may be governed by different laws: 1. the law governing the stablecoin itself is to be determined by the conflict-of-laws rules for virtual assets. 2. the law governing the underlying asset that backs or is referenced by the stablecoin must be determined by the ordinary conflict-of-laws rules, e.g. the *lex societatis*, the *lex rei sitae* or the specific rules for virtual assets. 3. the law governing the relationship between the stablecoin and the underlying or referenced asset is usually determined by the same law as that under 2., except

823 Art. 145a(1) Swiss Federal Act on Private International Law, see *supra* 3.5.2.1.
824 Art. 106(1) Swiss Federal Act on Private International Law.
825 Art. 106(3) Swiss Federal Act on Private International Law.

for intangible assets, such as claims or virtual assets. For the latter, a different law may apply, such as the law chosen by the token issuer.

3.7 The Law Governing Smart Contracts

Particular issues arise with smart contracts and other "DApps" that run on the blockchain. These may be used for various purposes, such as securing contractual performance, and play very different roles and fulfil very different functions depending on the specific application in question. Several different types of smart contracts must therefore be distinguished to determine the law governing them. In the following analysis, smart contracts with four different functions will be examined: 1. those that facilitate contractual enforcement (3.7.1), 2. those that facilitate the conclusion of contracts (3.7.2), 3. those that facilitate the virtual transfer of assets or their encumbrance with collateral rights (3.7.3), and 4. those that allow the exercise of voting rights, for instance in a DAO (3.7.4). For each of them, the governing law will be identified.

3.7.1 *Mechanism for Contractual Enforcement*

Most often, smart contracts facilitate the automated execution of an existing contractual obligation. In these cases, they are a means of performing the contract and do not fall under a separate category. Rather, they fall under the law governing the contract (*lex contractus*).[826] Hence, the same Private International Law rules as those governing contractual obligations apply, i.e. the chosen law or, failing that, the law of the country with the closest connection.[827]

However, the place of contractual performance in itself may play a role in the conflict of laws. In some jurisdictions, it is used as a connecting factor to determine the required form of the contract.[828] The performance itself may also be subject to a special conflict-of-laws rule. Some jurisdictions provide that, for issues relating to the method of performance (i.e. how the contractual obligation is to be performed), the law at the place of performance is to be taken into account.[829]

826 See, e.g., Art. 14(c), (d) Inter-American Convention on the Law Applicable to International Contracts; Art. 12(1)(c) EU Rome I Regulation; Art. 1215(3) Russian Civil Code.

827 See *supra* 3.2.1.

828 Art. 13 Inter-American Convention on the Law Applicable to International Contracts.

829 See Art. 125 Swiss Federal Act on Private International Law; Art. 12(2) EU Rome I Regulation.

In these cases, the place where the smart contract is "performed" becomes important. The problem is, however, that smart contracts do not exist in the real world but are called into execution within the distributed ledger environment, e.g. by the transfer of a certain amount of crypto-assets to the smart contract's public address. Finding the place where a smart contract is performed is therefore as impossible as locating the blockchain itself.

One could go for secondary connecting factors, such as the habitual residence or domicile of the programmer. However, this would run into the same difficulties that have already been discussed: the domicile or habitual residence may be unknown or may change, and are impossible to be located in the case of a transnational group of programmers.[830] Using the location of some or one of the programmers would be unacceptable for Private International Law, because this would amount to an arbitrary selection.

The only conclusion that one can draw is that a place of performance for a smart contract does not exist. This is not disastrous though. It merely means that the special rules regarding the place of performance of contracts do not apply. Regarding formal requirements for the conclusion of a contract, other connecting factors or laws may take their place, in particular, the *lex contractus*. Where the place of performance is important for the method of performance, it will also be superseded by the *lex contractus*. In the case of performance in the virtual world, the latter will apply alone, without any other law being taken into account.

3.7.2 *Mechanism for Concluding Contracts*

Although it is not common today, smart contracts may in the future facilitate the creation of new contractual obligations. The legal literature envisages circumstances in which the smart contract acts as an "artificial agent" and facilitates the forming of a contract between parties.[831] One must avoid falling into the trap, however, of considering that the smart contract might have some type of legal personality. The smart contract is merely software and, as such, can neither have rights or obligations nor be subject to claims.

Nevertheless, a smart contract might be used to bring about a contract between natural or legal persons or any other parties endowed with legal personality. This is the contract in the legal sense and must not be confused with the bytes and bits constituting the smart contract. The smart contract

830 See *supra* 2.4.3. and 2.4.4.

831 Mateja Djurovic and André Janssen, 'The Formation of Blockchain-Based Smart Contracts in the Light of Contract Law' (2018) 26 European Review of Private Law 761 (leaving open whether the algorithm can be considered as an independent electronic agent).

concerns merely the formalities surrounding the conclusion of a contract and may therefore be subject to the conflict-of-laws rules governing the formal validity of contracts.[832]

These rules often refer to the law of the place where the contract has been concluded (*lex loci solutionis*), at least as an alternative connecting factor.[833] Given that smart contracts exist in the virtual world only and have no physical location, it is impossible to determine where they are concluded. One could however use subsidiary criteria, such as the place of location or residence of the parties or their agents to the contract at the time the contract is entered into.[834] If this fails, one must simply disregard the place of conclusion and validate the contract using another law, in particular the *lex contractus*.[835]

3.7.3 *Mechanism for the Transfer of Crypto-Assets or the Creation of Collateral Rights*

Smart contracts may also be used in transactions in which crypto-assets are transferred, or the holder of a crypto-asset is, in other ways, temporarily or permanently deprived of its control over the asset. Such transactions include staking, yield farming, crypto lending and liquidity mining.[836]

The consequences that arise from these transactions cannot be discussed in general terms; all depends on their purpose. In line with the latter, the legal characterisation may oscillate between secured transactions, loans, companies and trusts.[837] The applicable law will have to be determined by reference to the legal category to which the transaction belongs. The appropriate category must be selected in accordance with the Private International Law rules of the forum, taking into account, as far as possible, the international nature of the operation.[838]

832 Luís de Lima Pinheiro, 'Laws Applicable to International Smart Contracts and Decentralized Autonomous Organizations (DAOS)' (2 June 2023) 7 <https://papers.ssrn.com/abstract=4467408> accessed 15 April 2024 (underscoring the importance that choice-of-law rules on formal validity can assume for smart contracts).

833 See Art. 13 Inter-American Convention on the Law Applicable to International Contracts; Sec. 199(2) Restatement (Second) on the Conflict of Laws (1971); Art. 11(1) EU Rome I Regulation.

834 See Art. 11(2) EU Rome I Regulation.

835 See, for example, Art. 11(1) EU Rome I Regulation.

836 See on them *supra* 1.2.4.2.

837 Matthias Lehmann and others (n 91), 67–87.

838 See ibid, 89–102.

A virtual asset may also be "sent" to a smart contract as collateral to secure the performance of some contractual obligation. In this type of situation, the transfer of control to the smart contract may fulfil any necessary conditions for creating a security right in the asset. To determine the applicable law, the conflicts rules for secured transactions must be used.

Many countries do not (yet) have special rules for secured transactions over intangible assets. Switzerland submits the pledge of crypto-assets to the law at the habitual residence of the pledgor.[839] This conflict-of-laws rule should be used more generally, as it has many advantages. In particular, it allows the governing law to be easily identified in the absence of other connecting factors.

However, where the parties to the secured transaction have chosen an applicable law, such a choice should be heeded. The reasons are the same as for crypto-assets; in particular, the choice ensures legal certainty.[840] The law chosen should not only govern the contractual aspects of the secured transaction (i.e. the *inter partes* aspects), but also the proprietary aspects (i.e. the *erga omnes* aspects). However, an exception must be made where a law has been chosen for the whole blockchain from which no deviations in single transactions are permitted.[841] In this case, the law governing the blockchain as a whole must be taken as also governing each transaction over the blockchain assets, including secured transactions.

3.7.4 *Mechanism for the Exercise of Voting Rights*

Smart contracts are used extensively by DAOs for various purposes. One of these purposes is voting. DAOs may require participants to use a specific type of token – often called 'membership token' – to vote for or against a particular project.[842] Those tokens may be temporarily locked or held in escrow by a smart contract to ensure they cannot be used twice or transferred until the voting process is completed. Once the voting period is over and the outcome is determined, the smart contract may restore the tokens to the participants' accounts.

---

839 Art. 105(2) Swiss Federal Act on Private International Law.

840 See *supra* 3.5.4.1.

841 Matthias Haentjens and Matthias Lehmann, 'The Law Governing Secured Transactions in Digital Assets' in Andrea Bonomi, Matthias Lehmann and Shaheeza Lalani (eds), *Blockchain and Private International Law* (Brill 2023) 456, 471.

842 Chris Brummer and Rodrigo Seira, 'Legal Wrappers and DAOs' (30 May 2022) 21 <https://papers.ssrn.com/abstract=4123737> accessed 15 April 2024 (mentioning the example of a social DAO in which a membership token that allows holders to access a token-gated Discord server, as well as participate in snapshot votes about potential group activities).

This voting process should be subject to the law governing the DAO, as set out in the following section.[843]

3.7.5 *Summary*

The law governing smart contracts cannot be determined in the abstract. Instead, it depends on the smart contract's purpose and effects. These must be examined in each individual case to find the appropriate conflict-of-laws rule for the smart contract in question.

3.8 The Law Governing DAOs

DAOs are decentralised organisations designed to solve governance problems through technology.[844] The relationships between members can nevertheless give rise to disputes. For example, the decisions surrounding the projects that are submitted to the participants for voting or the way in which the minority is protected against abuse by the majority can be contested. Such governance problems should, in principle, be resolved by the code. However, a default rule must be used when the code fails to address the issue. As things currently stand, this can only be the law of a particular state. Thus, the need to determine the national law governing the DAO arises.

Moreover, the relations of DAOs with third parties may also cause questions. For example, a contract might be concluded between the DAO and a third party to implement specific projects or maintain the organisation's website. The contract itself will be subject to the ordinary conflict-of-laws rules, such as the principle of party autonomy. Nevertheless, it may be necessary to establish the law governing the DAO to determine, for example, whether it has legal personality and the legal capacity to enter into a contract. Here again, a special problem of Private International Law for the crypto economy arises.

3.8.1 *Choosing a Legal Form*

DAOs can make use of traditional legal structures that are available under the law of a particular state. Examples are the corporation, the partnership, or a non-profit organisation, such as the foundation. These structures are known as *legal wrappers*.[845] They allow the DAO to obtain a legal identity, which is required to enter into transactions with the outside world. A legal wrapper can

843 See *infra* 3.8.

844 See *supra* 1.2.3.2.

845 Brummer and Seira (n 842).

also limit the risks of members by protecting them from personal liability for the DAO's activities.

The problem with these traditional legal structures, however, is that they often do not correspond to the revolutionary conception of the DAO. Most traditional legal structures require centralised management, such as a board of directors. This is incompatible with the idea of decentralised governance.

As a response to this problem, some countries have enacted specific legislation with private law rules that better reflect the nature of a DAO. Such legislation has been adopted by several US states[846] and by the Marshall Islands.[847] They reflect genuine competition between national legislators, who seek to provide the most attractive package for incentivising DAOs to obtain legal identities in their country. The special legislation contains rules of corporate law, e.g., concerning "automated" governance or the limited liability of members. They also provide for special designations that build upon existing corporate forms, such as "DAO LLC" (Decentralized Autonomous Organization Limited Liability Corporation)[848] or "BBLLC" (Blockchain-Based Limited Liability Company).[849]

Where a DAO uses a corporate form provided for in national law, whether a traditional or a special one, the Private International Law rules for international company law apply. In this respect, many states follow the incorporation theory.[850] Applying this theory to the crypto economy presents no issues: Where a DAO has been incorporated in a particular state, the law of that state applies. The main alternative to the incorporation theory is the seat theory, also followed by many states.[851] This theory encounters more problems when

---

846 Vermont, An act relating to blockchain business development, No. 205 (S.269); Wyoming, An act relating to corporations; providing for the formation and management of decentralized autonomous organizations; providing definitions; and providing for an effective date, No. 73 (SF0038); Tennessee, Tenn. Code Ann 48–250-101 et seq.

847 Republic of the Marshall Islands, Decentralized Autonomous Organizations Act (An Act to provide for the formation and management of decentralized autonomous organizations as domestic limited liability companies pursuant to the Limited Liability Company Act 1996, Chapter 4 of Title 52), 2022.

848 Art. 17-31-104 (d) Wyoming Act No. 73.

849 11 V.S.A. § 4173.

850 Stephan Rammeloo, *Corporations in Private International Law* (Oxford University Press 2006) 95–96; Peter Hay, Patrick J Borchers, Symeon C Symeonides and Christopher A Whytock, *Conflict of Laws* (6th edn, West Academic Publishing 2018) 1339–1344; Marc-Philippe Weller and Chris Thomale, 'Companies', *Encyclopedia of Private International Law* (2017) 405–406.

851 See Rammeloo, ibid 95–96; Hay, Borchers, Symeonides and Whytock ibid 1340; Weller and Thomale, ibid 406.

applied to DAOs. By definition, DAOs do not have a central administration or seat where they can be located. The seat theory thus does not yield any result regarding the law applicable to a DAO.

If it is not clad in a legal wrapper, connecting the DAO to a particular state will be even more difficult. In these cases, the entity is not incorporated, so the incorporation theory is of no help. Other connecting factors to a specific state may be tenuous or ambiguous. For example, the members of a DAO are usually spread all over the globe, and the programmer may be anonymous, or their place of residence may be unknown.

3.8.2 *Stateless DAOs?*

To solve this conflict-of-laws problem, a very ingenious solution has been proposed. It is suggested to recognise the DAO in question as a foreign corporation, even though it is not governed by any state's law.[852] The argument is that such a DAO would not necessarily lack organisational rules – these rules would just not be found in the law of a state but rather in the code underpinning the organisation. Formally, this theory is based on the principle of functional equivalence between paper and electronic records.[853] This principle, which derives from technological neutrality, is a mainstay of modern international law. According to it, a legal instrument in electronic form must be treated equivalent to its paper form.[854] From this, the theory extrapolates that the functional equivalent of a state law for a DAO would be its digital code. A DAO so organised would thus be a "foreign" DAO from the viewpoint of the Private International Law of all states in the world and would have to be recognised as such by their courts.

Couching the theory in terms of functional equivalence belies the paradigmatic shift it entails. Indeed, the theory goes well beyond a mere functional equivalence between paper and electronic records; to the contrary, it confers an enormous privilege on entities created digitally. If this theory were accepted, DAOs would enjoy legal personality and their members limited liability, notwithstanding the lack of incorporation under the law of any state. Piercing through the way the proposal has been framed, one can see that it is ultimately nothing other than the idea that "code is law".[855] This raises the

852 Sven Riva, 'Decentralized Autonomous Organizations (DAO s) in the Swiss Legal Order' (2019/2020) 21 Yearbook of Private International Law 601, 636 (for Art. 145 Swiss Federal Act on Private International Law).

853 ibid 635.

854 See, e.g., UNCITRAL Model Law on Electronic Transferable Records (2018), Article-by-article commentary, para 18.

855 On this slogan, see *supra* 1.5.2.

question of why digital organisations should be treated more favourably than those created in other ways. If DAOs can be incorporated without a state law, why should not entities founded *ad hoc* in the real world also be given the same privilege?

A further concern is that the code will be insufficient as a governance mechanism. Expecting it to cover all disputes among the DAO members would be unrealistic. Practical considerations therefore call for a default system of corporate rules. National legal systems usually provide a vast array of such rules for all types of possible company disputes. Which system should be used in the case of a stateless DAO?

As a response to this issue, a group of academics and practitioners known as COALA (*Coalition of Automated Legal Applications*) has created a "Model Law for DAOs".[856] Besides functional equivalence with traditional corporations, the "model law" also seeks "regulatory equivalence", which is defined as "the establishment of equivalence between the function of a legal rule and the function of a technology".[857] The text describes the purposes and activities a DAO might pursue, defines governance principles, limits the potential grounds of joint and several liability of the members, provides for tax-transparent treatment, and contains solutions for DAO-specific problems, such as contentious forks, modifications, upgrades or migrations. The whole text is designed as a legislative model that purports to take priority over the general corporate or business law of the adopting state.

The "Model Law for DAOs" is an interesting attempt at bridging the gap between the supposedly alegal nature of these organisations and the law-bound reality of the physical world. Some of its rules are very progressive and useful, such as those that address the legal consequences of hard forks.[858] On other crucial issues, the text remains quite rudimentary and merely refers to the by-laws of the DAO. An example is the protection of minority rights.[859] Another remarkable feature is the absence of any mandatory capital requirements. Taken as a whole, one gets the impression that the Model law's primary purpose is to avoid applying specific state rules rather than to set rules of its own.

From an international perspective, the most striking aspect of the "Model Law" is that it does not require incorporation. It recommends that states set up

856 COALA, 'Model Law for Decentralized Autonomous Organisations (DAOs' <https://coala.global/wp-content/uploads/2021/06/DAO-Model-Law.pdf> accessed 15 April 2024.
857 ibid 8.
858 Art. 16 Model Law for Decentralized Autonomous Organisations.
859 Art. 10 Model Law for Decentralized Autonomous Organisations.

an "accreditation authority" to ensure Model law compliance. Still, it does not call for DAOs to be incorporated or registered in any country. Again, it must be asked why such privilege should be extended to digital autonomous organisations but not to non-digital organisations. The "Model Law" imposes no prerequisites for the DAOs' legal personality and their members' limited liability, and provides few guarantees for the interests of the general public. Moreover, the lack of any requirement to register in a particular state and the residual application of the *lex fori* in the final instance may lead to severe conflicts of laws on the international plane, for which the "Model Law" provides no solution.

3.8.3 *The Default Rule*

Even if a DAO is not formally incorporated in a particular jurisdiction, this does not necessarily mean that it would not fall within the scope of some national law. The main question, however, is how to identify this law. One suggestion is using the rules for contracts directly or by analogy.[860] It is true that on the basis of every DAO is ultimately a contract. However, this is also true for all other corporations, which are often considered as a "nexus of contracts".[861] This contractual basis does not justify applying the conflict-of-laws rules for contracts. To determine whether or not the DAO as an entity has legal personality, the appropriate conflict-of-laws rules for the entity must be applied. But which one?

Most legal systems provide for a default type of company when several persons join together for a particular aim. This can be, for instance, a "partnership" in the Common law tradition, a "*société civile*" in the Romanic tradition, a "*Gesellschaft bürgerlichen Rechts*" in the Germanic tradition, or some other, similar form. Many of these types of companies are endowed with legal personality, so they can be sued and incur obligations. In addition, under most legal systems, the members are liable for any debts incurred by the entity. Already, suits against DAOs and their members have been brought on this basis.[862]

To determine which law governs such disputes, the conflict-of-laws rules for default unregistered entities must be used. In this, most countries will use

860 de Lima Pinheiro (n 832) 25–26 (suggesting to apply Art. 3 and 4 EU Rome I Regulation).

861 See Michael C Jensen and William H Meckling, 'Theory of the Firm: Managerial Behavior, Agency Costs and Ownership Structure' (1976) 3 Journal of Financial Economics 305, 310 (describing most organisations as legal fictions "which serve as a nexus for a set of contracting relationships among idividuals"). For a critique of this view, see William W Bratton, 'Nexus of Contracts Corporation: A Critical Appraisal' (1988) 74 Cornell Law Review 407.

862 See *Sarcuni et al v. bZx* DAO *et al.* (S. D. Cal., May 2, 2022) (suit brought against several DAO s that allegedly are general partnerships).

the same conflict-of-laws rules as for corporations, with the consequence that either the law of incorporation or the law of the seat will apply.[863] But another option is also available. Given the proximity between these entities and general contract law, as well as the fact that they are neither registered nor necessarily have a seat, it is possible to extend the principle of party autonomy from international contract law to cross-border partnerships.[864] Consequently, it would be possible for the founders of a DAO to choose the national law of a country as the applicable law without having to register or establish a seat there.

Where a choice of law is lacking, regard must be had to all the circumstances of the case. It is possible to refer, for instance, to the domicile or the habitual residence of the "core team" that has set up the DAO and/or runs its website, or that of the "project team" that develops new projects or selects those to be submitted to the members for voting. Yet the members of these teams are often of different nationalities and will have their domiciles or habitual residences in various countries, as DAO teams are typically transnational and collaborate over the internet.[865] In these cases, it is necessary to look for other connecting factors, such as the place where these persons meet, regularly or irregularly, or the place from which a project website is maintained, or updates are uploaded. Admittedly, these subsidiary connecting factors are weak, subject to change, and do not necessarily point to a single location.

The case of *"The DAO"* illustrates the problems, but also possible solutions. Two programmers developed the project in 2016, one of which was a German national and resident, the chief technology officer (CTO) of a company incorporated in Germany.[866] In addition, several "Curators" had the discretion in deciding whether or not to submit a proposal to a vote by the participants.[867] All relations with persons external to the DAO were entrusted to a company called *"DAO.Link"*, incorporated under Swiss law.[868] Thus, factors

863 See, e.g., Lord Collins of Mapesbury and Jonathan Harris (gen eds), *Dicey, Morris and Collins on the Conflict of Laws*, vol. 2 (16th edn, Sweet & Maxwell 2022) 1605–1606 para 30–010-30-011; Michel Menjuq, *Droit international des sociétés* (6th edn, LGDJ 2021) 101–106.

864 Wulf-Henning Roth, 'Internationalprivatrechtliche Aspekte der Personengesellschaften' (2014) 43 Zeitschrift für Unternehmens- und Gesellschaftsrecht 168, 196 (referring to the will of the founders to create the partnership under a specific law, which may manifest itself to the outside world by the way in which the partnership appears in commerce).

865 See *supra* 2.4.2, 2.4.3 and 2.4.4.

866 SEC (n 89).

867 ibid 7–8.

868 Laurent Leloup, *Blockchain: La révolution de la confiance* (Éditions Eyrolles 2017) 86.

connected *"The DAO"* to both Germany and Switzerland. Which of these two countries had the closest connection was to be decided in the particular case.

There is always the objection that the closest connection in such cases is subject to different interpretations by different courts. But the alternative solution, namely, that every court will apply its own law, is even worse. It is preferable to have a transnational discussion about the state to which a particular DAO is linked, as only such a discussion may lead to convergence in the rules for determining the applicable law to a DAO around the globe.

3.8.4 *Summary*

Identifying the law applicable to a DAO is critical because it provides the legal basis for its functioning, i.e. the rules that apply to its internal governance and its legal personality, which is necessary to interact with the rest of the world. In most cases, it will be possible to determine a national law governing a DAO, either because a particular jurisdiction has been chosen to provide a "legal wrapper", or because there will be a certain link to a specific state that is more significant than that to other states. The difficulties in finding such a link will potentially be enormous. Very often, there will be no single jurisdiction to which the DAO is clearly connected. It should nevertheless be emphasised that the metho-dology of Private International Law does not require finding a particularly close link with a legal system. It suffices to identify the *closest* connection, i.e. the state that is more closely connected than any of the others, in order to be able to resolve private disputes under a specific national law. Finding such a comparatively closer connection should be possible in almost all cases.

3.9 Procedural, Enforcement and Insolvency Problems

Virtual assets are of considerable value today. For this reason, it is understandable that creditors will target virtual assets to enforce their claims, and that those who have been deprived of their virtual assets will seek restitution. However, any attempts to do so face several legal obstacles, which are becoming increasingly prevalent in practice. First, the claimant must overcome several procedural hurdles to obtain a judgment or other enforceable title (3.9.1). Once this is done, the second problem becomes how and where to enforce the judgment or title (3.9.2). Finally, the treatment of virtual assets in insolvency proceedings also raises many questions (3.9.3).

3.9.1 *Obtaining an Enforceable Title*

3.9.1.1 The Information Problem

Two situations must be distinguished at the outset. In the first, a creditor seeks to attach the assets of her debtor to satisfy her money claim. In this situation, the debtor is known and any asset will do. The difficulty is rather knowing whether the debtor has any crypto-assets at all.[869]

In the second situation, a person seeks to recover a specific crypto-asset. This may be an asset that the person has lost, e.g. due to a hack, and which it wants to recover *in specie*. In this case, it is necessary to identify and find the current holder of the asset.

In both circumstances, the creditor has to confront the pseudonymity of the blockchain. While it is not easy to trace a crypto-asset, it is by no means impossible. It must be remembered that the blockchain is a permanent, transparent and tamper-proof record of all transfers of crypto-assets. Of course, there are exceptions for so-called "dark net coins", such as Dash, Monero or Zcash, which are designed in a way that conceals transaction histories.[870] On an ordinary blockchain, however, there is a good chance of discovering the address to which a virtual asset is currently attributed.

Determining the holder's "real world" identity may prove more difficult, but this problem is not unsurmountable. The fact that most virtual assets today are held in custody is particularly helpful. Custodians mark stark points of centralisation in the otherwise decentralised crypto economy. They often use well-known public addresses to store their virtual assets, which can facilitate tracing and locating the lost asset. In the alternative or in addition, the victim of a crypto hack may seek assistance from the courts and law enforcement authorities. For instance, they may ask for information from several custodians to determine whether they currently hold the asset.

Still, these steps might not necessarily be effective to identify the current holder, i.e. the customer of the intermediary. Some jurisdictions have long-established procedural mechanisms that may help overcome these issues. In England and Wales, for example, actions may be brought against "persons unknown". The court may combine them with disclosure orders, known as *Norwich Pharmacal* and *Bankers Trust* orders,[871] against third parties to the litigation, aiming at identifying the defendant to the action. These disclosure

869 More on this *infra* 3.9.2.2.

870 See on dark net coins *supra* 1.2.1.3.

871 These procedural orders were named after the cases in which they were first granted: *Norwich Pharmacal v Commissioners of Customs & Excise*, [1974] UKHL 6; *Bankers Trust Company v Shapira*, [1980] 1 WLR 1274.

orders can be served on parties worldwide. In the crypto-asset cases, such disclosure orders were obtained and served to third-party custodians outside of the UK.[872]

3.9.1.2 Jurisdiction to Adjudicate

Once the defendant has been identified, the claim can be brought to court. First, the tribunal must establish its jurisdiction over the dispute. In this regard, the general rules of jurisdiction apply.

Courts in Common law systems generally consider jurisdiction in terms of service on the defendant. This usually requires the defendant's physical presence in the court's district at the time of service of the claim. There are, however, exceptions. In the US, several states have adopted 'doing business statutes' that extend the courts' jurisdiction to anyone doing business in the territory of the state.[873] In England and Wales, the courts may give permission to serve the claim outside of the state's territory if there is a significant connection between the claim and the territory.[874] This includes, in principle, jurisdiction *in rem* if the claim concerns property within the jurisdiction. This will be, however, difficult for virtual assets, given their intangible nature. The Common law courts have found a workaround by identifying the location of virtual assets with the domicile, habitual residence or place of business of the current owner or holder.[875]

In Civil law countries, general jurisdiction hinges on the defendant's domicile.[876] In addition, special heads of jurisdiction can be established, e.g. at the place of performance of a contract or at the place where a tort or delict

---

872 See, e.g., High Court of Justice for England and Wales, 13 December 2019, *AA v Persons Unknown & Ors*, Re Bitcoin [2019] EWHC 3556 (Comm); 21 December 2020, *Ion Science v Persons Unknown* (unreported), discussed by Held (n 537); 26 April 2021, *Lubin Betancourt Reyes et al. v Persons Unknown et al* [2021] EWHC 1938 (Comm); 15 July 2021, *Fetch.AI Limited et al v Persons Unknown et al* [2021] EWHC 2254 (Comm).

873 These statutes can be found in the law of most federal states of the US. Their use has been limited on Constitutional grounds, see US Supreme Court, 3 December 1945, International Shoe v. State of Washington, 326 U.S. 310. See, however, also US Supreme Court, 27 June 2023, *Mallory v. Norfolk Southern Railway Co.*, 600 U.S. 122 (allowing the application of doing business statutes where the defendant has submitted, voluntarily or otherwise, to the jurisdiction of the courts of the State in question).

874 See British Ministry of Justice, 'Practice Direction 6B – Service Out of Jurisdiction' (updated 8 June 2023) <https://www.justice.gov.uk/courts/procedure-rules/civil/rules/part06/ pd_part06b> accessed 8 April 2024.

875 See *supra* 3.5.5.6.

876 See, e.g., Art. 4 EU Brussels Ibis Regulation (Regulation (EU) No 1215/2012 of 12 December 2012 on jurisdiction and the recognition and enforcement of judgments in civil and commercial matters (recast) [2012] OJ L351/1).

has occured.[877] A court cannot exercise *in rem* jurisdiction over movables. However, some Civil law countries accept jurisdiction where the defendant owns movable and immovable assets in their territory (so-called asset-based jurisdiction).[878] The courts of these countries will face the same difficulties as Common law courts in determining the location of a given virtual asset.

3.9.1.3 Provisional Measures

Obtaining an enforceable title may be a lengthy process, giving the defendant considerable time to dispose of the asset by transferring it to another address or person. The rights that the claimant seeks to establish may, therefore, be undermined. To prevent this, the claimant may apply to the courts for a provisional or interlocutory measure prohibiting the holder from transferring the asset.

Again, the English courts are very generous to the claimant. They regularly issue interim proprietary and/or freezing orders against the current holder.[879] Although these orders are directed against the defendant, who is typically a "person unknown", they also can have effects against third parties on notice of the order, such as a crypto custodian. These third parties may find themselves in contempt of court if they knowingly participate in a breach of these orders. The orders also purport to bind crypto custodians established outside England and Wales. An English court can conveniently combine them with a disclosure order requiring the intermediary to identify the customer. Similar remedies are available in other Common law jurisdictions. For instance, US courts have also issued asset-freezing orders in relation to crypto-assets.[880]

Another method of controlling a defendant's assets available in Common law countries is "receivership".[881] This is an equitable remedy that can be granted at the interlocutory stage. The court will prohibit the enjoined respondent from receiving any property belonging to him. Instead, it will

877 Art. 7(1) and (2) EU Brussels Ibis Regulation.

878 See, e.g., § 23 German Code of Civil Procedure (*Zivilprozessordnung*).

879 See, e.g., High Court for England and Wales, 13 December 2019, *AA v Persons Unknown & Ors, Re Bitcoin* [2019] EWHC 3556 (Comm); 26 April 2021, *Lubin Betancourt Reyes et al v Persons Unknown et al* [2021] EWHC 1938 (Comm); 15 July 2021, *Fetch.AI Limited et al v Persons Unknown et al* [2021] EWHC 2254 (Comm).

880 See, e.g., Federal District Court for the Eastern District of Texas, 23 July 2013, *SEC v. Shavers*, No. 4:13-CV-416, Order Freezing Assets and Granting Other Ancillary Relief, at 3.

881 Andrew W Balthazor, 'The Challenges of Cryptocurrency Asset Recovery Symposium: The Role and Contributions of the International Law Commission to the Development of International Law: Comments' (2018) 13 FIU Law Review 1207, 1224.

appoint a receiver, who will temporarily hold the assets until the end of the legal proceedings.

Many other legal systems are yet to develop sufficient provisional measures for to virtual assets. This is particularly true in Civil law countries.

The International Union of Judicial Officers (*Union Internationale des Huissiers de Justice* – UIHJ) has published a "Global Code of Digital Enforcement"[882] that sets out proposals for domestic law reform. It suggests, *inter alia*, that judges should have the power to adopt provisional or interlocutory measures regarding digital assets, such as ordering the transfer of the private key, suspending access to the assets, or creating an escrow account.[883] Such powers would certainly be welcome as an improvement to the current situation. More problematic is the suggestion of allowing judicial officers or enforcement agents to adopt provisional or interlocutory measures without requiring any authorisation from a judge.[884] This would not accord with the usual distribution of powers between the courts and the enforcement agents, which are delimited by the time a judgment is rendered.

3.9.2 *Enforcement Issues*

Once a court decision has been rendered, the question then becomes how it can be enforced. In this, three problems arise: first, the territorial jurisdiction to enforce; second, gathering information about the assets of the judgment debtor; and third, the proper procedure for seizing virtual assets.

3.9.2.1 Power to Enforce

It goes without saying that national enforcement proceedings are limited to the territorial confines of each state. This follows from the general prohibition under general Public International Law against states using force outside their national territory.[885] The Global Code of Digital Enforcement is therefore correct to stress the "importance for the international principles of sovereignty and territoriality of enforceability".[886]

The territorial limitation on enforcement creates few problems for corporeal assets, but it is highly problematic for crypto-assets: where are they situated? By now, it should be clear that it is impossible to locate virtual assets. The

882 Marc Schmitz (ed), *Code mondial de l'exécution digitale/Global Code of Digital Enforcement* (Bruylant 2021).

883 Art. 41(1) and (2) Global Code of Digital Enforcement.

884 Art. 41(3) Global Code of Digital Enforcement.

885 See *supra* 2.3.1.1.

886 Art.11(1) Global Code of Digital Enforcement.

connecting factors proposed above for determining the governing property law[887] reflect the most significant relationship or closest link to a particular system in the sense of Private International Law but not a *location* in the strict sense of the principle of territoriality under Public International Law. They are therefore of no use in the enforcement context.

One conclusion that could be drawn is that enforcement powers would be unlimited in the virtual world. All states could seize all virtual assets. However, this rule must be qualified as applying only to virtual assets that are unidentified, or which cannot be controlled by anyone.[888] For all other assets, a borderless, unlimited enforcement power would lead to a race among creditors, a fight for virtual assets between judicial officers of different states, and therefore chaos at the global level. Another solution must be found to determine the territorial limits of enforcement powers in the crypto economy.

The territorial limits of enforcement are mainly a practical matter. States with an interest in the (limited) assets of the debtor try to seize as many of the debtor's assets as possible; and nothing prevents them from doing so, as long as they act within their own territory. The Global Code of Digital Enforcement reflects this idea by stating that "[i]dentified and accessible assets, wherever they are, should be seized according to the enforcement law of their location, respecting the international principles of sovereignty and territoriality of enforceability".[889] However, the reference to "location" is problematic, as virtual assets do not have such a location. The important point is being able to identify and access virtual assets from within the territory of the enforcing state. Thus, it is confirmed elsewhere in the Code that "[t]he competence of judicial officers or enforcement agents to seize and sell a digital asset should be governed by the place where it is identified and accessed".[890]

It remains to be determined how virtual assets are to be identified and accessed from a legal point of view. The Global Code of Digital Enforcement suggests using the law of the debtor's domicile.[891] This certainly is an ingenious proposal. If adopted, a single law would determine where the debtor's virtual assets can be identified and accessed worldwide. If the debtor's domicile would allow access, then the courts of any state could seize the debtor's virtual assets; if the debtor's domicile would however consider the assets as

887 *Supra* 3.5.

888 See Art. 11(2) Global Code of Digital Enforcement (applying the law of the state of enforcement to unidentified and/or inaccessible digital assets).

889 Art. 11(1) Global Code of Digital Enforcement.

890 Art. 12(2) Global Code of Digital Enforcement.

891 Art. 12(1) Global Code of Digital Enforcement.

inaccessible, then no court in the world would be able to seize them. Such a rule would introduce a degree of harmonisation into enforcement law and prevent a global competition for the debtor's virtual assets amongst states.

Nevertheless, one should not be overly optimistic about the chances of this solution being adopted. It is unlikely that other states would apply the law of the debtor's domicile to decide which of the debtor's assets they can seize. Generally, each state applies its law when it comes to enforcing civil judgments and other titles. States are, furthermore, entitled to do so under the rules of Public International Law, which do not subject the scope of enforcement procedures to foreign law, let alone to the law of the debtor's domicile. Moreover, a conflict-of-laws rule pointing to the debtor's domicile could incentivise some states to enact protective rules for its residents' virtual assets, with the goal to becoming "safe harbours from enforcement". Digital nomads could flock there to establish their domicile, and then travel freely around the world, shielded from foreign enforcement measures through their domicile's law. This situation would hardly be acceptable for other states. In the inverse situation, in which the state of the debtor's domicile is more permissive than the law of the state of enforcement when it comes to seizing virtual assets, it is equally hard to justify why the state of enforcement should not follow its own law when determining whether a particular asset can be seized. In short, the problems of identifying and accessing digital assets do not seem to be a legal problem, but instead, a practical problem to be resolved by reference to the facts. Consequently, there is little reason to refer to a foreign legal system to resolve this issue.

As a result, states are most likely to follow their laws and principles when determining whether and how a virtual asset can be identified and seized. This will inevitably lead to competition amongst different states over the same asset. For instance, a debtor travelling outside of the country where he is domiciled may find that his virtual assets are subjected to enforcement measures. The private keys he carries with him could be seized or, if travelling to the countries that use imprisonment as a coercive measure, he himself could be imprisoned until he transfers specific virtual assets. This may seem harsh, but the situation is no different for any movable assets that the debtor carries with him or for specific acts that he is obliged to perform.

A different rule would apply for assets held in custody: These assets can only be accessed in the country of the custodian. A creditor wishing to seize virtual assets held with a foreign custodian must bring enforcement proceedings in the country of the custodian. In this case, the debtor's domicile or the presence on their territory is irrelevant. In particular, the debtor cannot be forced to instruct the custodian to transfer the assets if the assets can be seized directly from the custodian. This follows from the principle of proportionality, a guiding principle of enforcement.[892] All in all, enforcement over virtual assets held in custody is similar to enforcement over a bank account.

3.9.2.2 Information about Virtual Assets of the Debtor

Another question is how a judgment or other title should be enforced against virtual assets. Two issues must be distinguished: 1. the enforcement of money judgments against virtual assets and 2. the enforcement of judgments concerning a specific virtual asset.

In the first case, the creditor will need to know whether and where the debtor holds any virtual assets. In the second case, the creditor already knows the debtor has the assets, but she may need to learn where and by what method the assets are currently held.[893]

Most national legal systems confer on the creditor the right to obtain information about the debtor's assets. As proposed by the Global Code on Digital Enforcement, this should extend to virtual assets.[894] Yet in many cases, the debtor will resist giving information about her virtual assets and even try to hide them.

It seems more promising to seek information from custodians, such as crypto exchanges or wallet providers. To obtain information from them, the creditor could apply to a court for a procedural order. Many legal systems provide a legal basis for requiring third parties to disclose relevant information.[895] However, these rules are typically limited to money held with banks and do not cover virtual assets held with crypto custodians.

Legal reform is urgently needed to remedy this shortcoming. The Global Code of Digital Enforcement suggests that national law should establish a database or register of virtual assets with a reporting obligation on the part of the person concerned.[896] However, it is doubtful that this solution would work, given the high volume of trading in virtual assets and the fact that traders will resist disclosing their virtual asset holdings.

---

892 See Art. 5 European Convention on Human Rights, as interpreted by the ECtHR, 21 October 2013, *Del Río Prada v Spain*, App no 42750/09. See also Art. 4 Global Code of Digital Enforcement.

893 See *supra* A 1.

894 Art. 49 phrase 1 Global Code of Digital Enforcement.

895 See, e.g., in the EU Art. 14 European Account Preservation Order Regulation (Regulation (EU) 655/2014 of the European Parliament and the Council establishing a European Account Preservation Order procedure to facilitate cross-border debt recovery in civil and commercial matters [2014] OJ L189/59).

896 Art. 48 Global Code of Digital Enforcement.

An alternative is to oblige virtual asset custodians to comply with information requests by courts and enforcement agents.[897] Given the global nature of blockchain networks, such obligations to comply should not be limited to requests made to domestic custodians within the jurisdiction of the requesting court or enforcement agent but should also extend to foreign custodians. Indeed, English courts are already issuing such requests worldwide with their disclosure orders.[898]

This may potentially lead to crypto custodians being inundated with information requests from various countries. However, they will have the information that is requested, given their regulatory obligations, such as the know-your-customer rules. The central role played by custodians as lynchpins of the crypto economy comes with special responsibilities in enforcement.

3.9.2.3 Seizing Virtual Assets

Seizing virtual assets equally is a source of problems. Given their intangible nature, how can they be seized, i.e. taken into control? In this respect, it is necessary to distinguish between the different ways in which virtual assets are held.

3.9.2.3.1 *Assets Held Directly*

The first type of enforcement concerns assets held directly by the debtor. The Global Code of Digital Enforcement suggests that judicial officers or enforcement agents should be able to access crypto-assets on all "computer media and other media" wherever they may be located, as long as the debtor holds them.[899] Underpinning this is the idea that the power to seize such an asset must be independent of where it is stored. This is correct: Any virtual asset *controlled* by the debtor falls under the enforcement jurisdiction of the authorities who have power over the debtor, such as those at the place of his domicile or at the place where he is present.

Nevertheless, it must be emphasised that it is the virtual asset that is being seized, and not the private keys or the medium on which it is recorded. Seizing a computer on which the debtor's crypto-assets are stored but which is located abroad, on the grounds that the debtor is domiciled in the state of enforcement, would violate the principle of territoriality of enforcement measures.

---

897 See also Art. 49 phrase 2 Global Code of Digital Enforcement, which provides a disclosure obligation of everyone who "manages digital assets". Although the wording is unclear, this may be a reference to custodians.

898 See *supra* 3.9.1.1.

899 Art. 54 Global Code of Digital Enforcement.

However, this does not exclude the possibility of seizing the physical carrier on which the private keys are stored under the condition that this medium is located within the territory of the enforcing state.[900] This is permitted for all other physical objects found within the territory of the enforcing state, and there is no reason why it should be different for the medium on which virtual assets are stored. However, there is always the possibility that the debtor may have stored other copies on other physical media, allowing him to dispose of the assets. It is therefore advisable to prohibit the debtor from any such disposals when seizing the carrier. Thus, the Global Code of Digital Enforcement suggests serving or notifying the debtor in parallel with a document of seizure.[901] This document contains a summons and notice that the debtor can no longer dispose of the crypto-assets and that he will incur criminal sanctions if he fails to comply with the prohibition.[902]

3.9.2.3.2 *Assets Held in Custody*

Enforcement is executed differently for virtual assets held with a custodian. The document of seizure must be addressed to the custodian, e.g. a crypto exchange or wallet provider, who holds the assets for the client-debtor. As stressed above, such measures are available only in the country of the custodian.[903]

According to the Global Code of Digital Enforcement, enforcement proceedings over digital assets in the hands of a third party cannot be commenced before the third party has been served with or notified of the seizure document.[904] The third party must be given a reasonable period of time to declare whether it holds the crypto-assets for the debtor.[905] Seizure is only permitted if the third party confirms that it holds assets for the debtor.[906]

Such procedure risks delaying enforcement and offers opportunities for non-compliance. In particular, the custodian could transfer the asset legally to another party during the "reasonable period" allowed. It could also prevent seizure by denying that it holds assets for the debtor.

Therefore, it is preferable to treat the asset as seized from the moment the document is served on the custodian. Should it turn out that the latter does not hold assets for the debtor, the seizure would have no effect. The information

900 Art. 55(2) Global Code of Digital Enforcement.
901 ibid.
902 Art. 56 Global Code of Digital Enforcement.
903 See *supra* 3.9.2.3.2.
904 Art. 50 Global Code of Digital Enforcement.
905 Art. 51 Global Code of Digital Enforcement.
906 Art. 51 Global Code of Digital Enforcement.

request should be treated separately. It can be issued before the seizure as a provisional measure.

3.9.3 *Insolvency Issues*

Virtual assets also raise many questions in the event of insolvency. Insolvency may affect either an individual who holds such virtual assets or a custodian who manages them for its customers. The main problems are the same: they concern 1. the opening of the insolvency proceedings, 2. the law governing the proceedings, 3. the scope of the proceedings, and 4. the treatment of virtual assets in such proceedings.

3.9.3.1 Opening of Insolvency Proceedings

To determine whether insolvency proceedings can be opened, the usual connecting factors apply, such as the debtor's domicile, her place of business, or the centre of her main interests (COMI).[907] Applying these factors to the crypto economy does not pose any major obstacles, as it will rarely be necessary to refer to the blockchain in order to identify these places. Instead, other criteria will be decisive, such as the place of incorporation or place of business of the debtor or the domicile of its clients.

Difficulties arise if a business is exclusively run on the blockchain. For example, one could think of a DeFi platform, e.g., a DEX or a DAO. Where such entities use a legal wrapper, they are given legal personality under national law, which allows them to be the subject of insolvency proceedings. These proceedings can be opened in the state where the entity is registered. For other entities, it will be more difficult, as the focus will turn to identifying their principal place of business or centre of main interests. In these cases, other factors may need to be used, such as the place of the majority of their members.

Insolvency proceedings may also be opened in the place where the assets or "property" is located.[908] This may be problematic for virtual assets, which are, by nature, difficult to locate. Where the assets are recorded on a permissioned blockchain and all its participants are established in a particular country, the virtual assets could be deemed to be located in that country. For all other cases,

907 See Sec. 109(a) US Bankruptcy Code (11 U.S. Code § 109); Art. 3(1) EU Insolvency Regulation (Recast) (Regulation (EU) 2015/848 of 20 May 2015 on insolvency proceedings [2015] OJ L141/19).

908 See Sec. 109(a) US Bankruptcy Code (11 U.S. Code § 109); Art. 34 EU Insolvency Regulation (Recast).

the domicile or the main habitual residence of the person exercising control over the virtual asset should be considered the place where the asset is located.[909] Since the domicile or principal habitual residence in the district of the insolvency court are in themselves heads of jurisdiction over insolvency proceedings, the place where the assets are located has no real importance on its own.

3.9.3.2 Law Governing Insolvency Proceedings

Insolvency proceedings are governed by the law of the state where the insolvency proceedings are opened (*lex fori concursus*). This law governs, *inter alia*, the effects of the insolvency proceedings, the priority amongst the creditors, and avoidance and claw-back measures. The preliminary question of third-party rights *in rem* in assets falling within the insolvency estate is to be determined in accordance with the conflict-of-laws rules regarding proprietary rights.[910]

3.9.3.3 Scope of the Insolvency Proceedings

A further question is whether virtual assets are part of the insolvency estate at all. The answer to this depends on the theory of insolvency that is adopted.[911]

In countries where the principle of universality is followed, the answer is easy: all debtor assets, wherever located, belong to the estate. This encompasses virtual assets, making it unnecessary to determine their exact location.

In countries where the principle of territoriality is followed, the proceedings cover only assets located in the jurisdiction of the court or authority opening the insolvency proceedings. Given that virtual assets cannot be located, it is suggested here that the domicile or habitual residence of the person controlling the assets should be used in these cases.[912] Accordingly, the scope of the insolvency proceedings would be limited to virtual assets controlled by persons domiciled in the territory of the state opening the proceedings.

3.9.3.4 Insolvency Treatment of Virtual Assets

Another question that arises is how virtual assets will be treated in insolvency proceedings. This is particularly important where a custodian, such as a crypto exchange or wallet provider which manages such assets for its customers, has

909 See *supra* 3.5.5.6.

910 See *supra* 3.5.

911 See, e.g., Kono (n 752) 489–491 (discussing the theories of territorialism and universalism).

912 See *supra* B 1.

become insolvent. In these situations, the most relevant question is the nature of the rights that the custodian's customers have, in particular whether and how they can recover virtual assets held for them by the custodian.

All states treat creditors and owners differently in insolvency: Creditors must register their claim and participate in the insolvency proceedings, which comes with the risk that they will not recover the full value of their claim. On the other hand, the owner of an asset can request the insolvency administrator to remove the asset from the insolvency estate.

Which of these two treatments is to be followed will be decided by the *lex fori concursus*. It will determine whether virtual assets are part of the estate or whether the customer can separate them from the proceedings.

Even where virtual assets are treated as property, there will still be outstanding questions. In particular, there is uncertainty across most legal systems as to how owners can obtain their virtual assets. Because of the latters' intangible nature, the insolvency practitioner cannot simply hand them over. The rules for the return of tangible movables, based on possession, cannot be applied to the restitution of virtual assets; neither directly nor by analogy. At the same time, the rules applicable to other intangible assets, such as claims, do not work either.

The Swiss legislator has found an original solution to this problem. It has introduced special provisions in its Debt Enforcement and Bankruptcy Act, which require the insolvency administrator of a bankrupt intermediary to transfer the assets to another provider.[913] The crypto-asset must, however, either been held individually for the customer, or collectively for several customers with each customer's share being ascertainable. This alternative is equivalent to the distinction between individually segregated accounts and omnibus accounts in the law of intermediated securities.[914] The customer's rights are thus guaranteed, even if his crypto-assets have not been registered under a separate blockchain address. He will have to bear, however, the costs associated with the transfer to another provider.[915]

913 Art. 242a Swiss Federal Act on Debt Enforcement and Bankruptcy (*Bundesgesetz über Schuldbeitreibung und Konkurs*).

914 See Paola Lucantoni, 'Art. 39 EMIR' in Matthias Lehmann and Christoph Kumpan (eds), *European Financial Services Law* (Nomos Beck Hart 2019) para 10–13 (explaining omnibus client segregation and individual client segregation).

915 Art. 242a(4) Swiss Federal Act on Debt Enforcement and Bankruptcy.

3.9.4 *Summary*

The crypto economy is a source of significant issues in terms of civil procedure, enforcement and insolvency. Many of these are problems that arise from the pseudonymity characteristic of the blockchain; they can be solved by recourse to custodians and other intermediaries. Other difficulties are caused by the intangible nature of the assets. Still others concern the extent of the powers of the state to adjudicate or enforce. Others, finally, relate to the treatment of virtual assets in the event of insolvency, for which special rules must be crafted. These problems are not unsolvable, but they all require either the existing legal framework to be interpreted in a specific way, or the addition of new, special rules.

3.10 Global Private Law for a Global Phenomenon

By its very nature, the crypto economy is not bound to any particular country but transcends state borders. Though not impossible, identifying an applicable law is fraught with difficulties. Moreover, severe fragmentation is likely to occur because each state adopts its own national rules of private law for certain crypto-assets, transactions, services or service providers. The applicability of different laws to different parts of the same network deals a serious blow to the efficiency and usefulness of blockchain technology, which induces welfare losses. We not only forego the possibility of worldwide investments and payment transfers without costly national intermediary infrastructures but also miss the opportunity for financial inclusion by providing access to sophisticated financial services to the unbanked population in emerging countries.

As with in the regulatory area, the question therefore arises as to whether uniform rules are more appropriate to the crypto economy than applying different national rules. This question is even more urgent in private law, given that private relationships transcend state borders. Subjecting them to diverging rules has harmful consequences, such as forum shopping, limping legal relationships, and judicial wars.

In the following section, the prospects for substantive law harmonisation will be analysed by reference to the UNIDROIT Principles on Digital Assets and Private Law, the primary text in the area (3.10.1). However, such harmonisation will always remain incomplete. It needs to be complemented by conflict-of-laws harmonisation (3.10.2).

3.10.1 *Substantive Law Harmonisation: the UNIDROIT Principles on Digital Assets and Private Law*

3.10.1.1 Ambition and Purpose of the Principles

As a response to the emerging crypto economy, UNIDROIT adopted in 2023 the "Principles on Digital Assets and Private Law".[916] The purpose of the Principles is to facilitate transactions in digital assets.[917] They seek to guide parties as well as courts, lawyers and others who will "consider the effects of such transactions".[918] The primary addressees are states, though, who are advised to enact legislation consistent with the Principles.[919] The Principles are a soft law instrument: they are not a binding treaty or convention, but are merely non-binding recommendations. Furthermore, they do not contain detailed rules but only high-level guidelines. They do not seek to harmonise the entire law relating to crypto-assets or crypto transactions but only specific aspects essential for guaranteeing transnational trade security.

3.10.1.2 Scope of Application

3.10.1.2.1 *Digital Assets*

The UNIDROIT Principles cover "digital assets". This term was examined above and rejected in favour of the term "virtual assets".[920]

A digital asset in the sense of the Principles is "an electronic record which is capable of being subject to control".[921] This generic formulation does not refer to DLT or the blockchain. It has been chosen to comply with the principle of technological neutrality. The notion of control will be analysed in more detail below.[922] It is necessary to note already at this point that using "control" as a cornerstone in the definition of digital assets results in the Principles having a scope of application that is very broad – even overly broad. This can be illustrated by using the example of password-protected data files, e.g. Word or Excel files. As such files are subject to the control of the person with the password, they would classify as a digital asset under the UNIDROIT Principles. The Commentary hastens to add that the Principles will not have any material utility

916 <https://www.unidroit.org/wp-content/uploads/2023/04/C.D.-102-6-Principles-on-Digital-Assets-and-Private-Law.pdf> accessed 26 September 2024.

917 UNIDROIT Principles on Digital Assets and Private Law (2023), Comment 0.1.

918 ibid Comment 0.3.

919 ibid Comment 0.4.

920 See *supra* 3.5.3.1.1.

921 Principle 2(2) UNIDROIT Principles on Digital Assets and Private Law (2023).

922 See *infra* 3.10.1.6.

or impact on such a file.[923] The drafters struggled with the example because it is counter-intuitive to think Word or Excel files are "assets." The simple reason is that the file can be copied infinitely by the person controlling it, and is therefore not scarce.[924] Consequently, it is not the file that has value, but the artistic or other work it represents, or the information contained in it. These aspects are already covered by intellectual property law and data protection. Thus, additional protection as a "digital asset" is unnecessary.

At the same time, the scope of the Principles may also be too narrow because it excludes certain virtual assets. Identity and other "social, community and reputation tokens" are a case in point. These are a new type of virtual assets, which aim to represent a person's characteristics, features, traits, and achievements on the blockchain.[925] In line with their purpose of identifying their holder, these tokens typically cannot be transferred to another person. For this reason, it can hardly be said that such tokens are under the holder's "control". Yet this does not mean that they are unworthy of protection.

Nevertheless, the UNIDROIT Principles cover most of the assets that are relevant to the crypto economy. They even address stablecoins, if only the digital tokens themselves and not the underlying assets.[926] Whatever its shortcomings, the broad scope of the Principles has the advantage of being quite comprehensive, capturing the most relevant virtual assets.

3.10.1.2.2 *Proprietary Rights*

Property law issues – or "proprietary rights" in digital assets, as the Principles say – lie at the core of the Principles. They cover, in particular, good faith acquisition, secured transactions and clients' rights in the event of a crypto custodian's insolvency. Such emphasis is fitting, as property law is where the thorniest legal issues arise.[927] Many other legal areas, such as contract and tort, are not addressed; here, the ordinary rules of the state implementing the Principles will apply.

However, numerous property law issues are also left out by the Principles. These include, for instance, the question of whether a person has a proprietary right in a digital asset, whether such a right has been validly transferred, or

923 UNIDROIT Principles on Digital Assets and Private Law (2023), Comment 2.17.

924 On scarcity as the prime reason for the need to recognise rights in virtual assets, see already *supra* 3.5.3.1.2.

925 Akash Takyar, 'What Are Soulbound Tokens, and How Do They Work?' (LeewayHertz – Software Development Company, 14 December 2022) <https://www.leewayhertz.com/soulbound-tokens/> accessed 15 April 2024.

926 See Principle 4 UNIDROIT Principles on Digital Assets and Private Law (2023).

927 See *supra* 3.2.4.

whether a security right in a digital asset has been validly created. These and many other property issues are explicitly excluded from the Principles' scope and are to be governed by "other law" of the adopting state, meaning law not harmonised by the Principles.[928]

Throughout the Principles, there are further specific exclusions for issues that are left to be governed by "other law". These include, for instance, assets linked to a digital assets (Principle 4); the legal effect and the perfection of security rights in digital assets or in assets linked to them (Principle 14(2) and (3)); the enforcement of security rights in digital assets (Principle 17(1)); procedural matters, including enforcement, regarding digital assets (Principle 18); and the ranking of categories of claims, transaction avoidance and enforcement issues in insolvency (Principle 19(2)). Functionally, these Principles are merely "scoping provisions", i.e. they delineate the scope of the Principles by excluding certain matters. Nevertheless, they up take significant space in the text as a whole.

3.10.1.3 Property Rights in Digital Assets and Their Protection in the Event of Insolvency

The core provision is Principle 3(1), which reads as follows: "A digital asset can be the subject of proprietary rights." This is a bit of an understatement. What it actually means is "digital assets *should* be the subject of proprietary rights," as the commentary to Principle 3 makes clear.[929] The commentary also advises states to specify the category to which digital assets belong if their law distinguishes different categories of assets and submits them to diverging legal consequences.[930]

Naturally, the Principles cannot harmonise the entirety of property law. Therefore, the treatment and protection of digital assets largely depend on the particularities of the applicable national law. The Principles provide only limited guidance in this respect. This concerns, for instance, the possibility of innocent acquisition,[931] which is discussed in more detail below.[932]

The most crucial protection relates to the treatment of digital assets in the event of insolvency. According to Principle 19(1), a proprietary right that has

---

928 For a full list of excluded matters, see Principle 3(3) UNIDROIT Principles on Digital Assets and Private Law (2023).

929 UNIDROIT Principles on Digital Assets and Private Law (2023), Comment 3.1 ("Principle 3(1) therefore provides, as a matter of principle, that Principles law (as defined under Principle 2(3)) should provide that digital assets can be the subject of proprietary rights.").

930 UNIDROIT Principles on Digital Assets and Private Law (2023), Comment 3.2.

931 Principle 8 and 9 UNIDROIT Principles on Digital Assets and Private Law (2023).

932 See *infra* 3.10.1.4.

become effective against third parties is also effective against the insolvency representative, creditors and other third parties in insolvency proceedings. This provision may seem tautological, but it makes the crucial point that holders of digital assets must be protected as owners in the event of insolvency. The precise consequences of this characterisation are left to national law. At any rate, holders of digital assets must receive the same treatment as owners of other assets.

3.10.1.4 Innocent Acquisition

Another core provision is Principle 8. This Principle secures the protection of the innocent or "good faith" acquirer. It lays down two conditions for such acquisition: 1. the transferee obtains control over the asset, and 2. the transferee complies with requirements "equivalent to those found in the relevant good faith acquisition and take-free rules as specified by the relevant State".

The last condition reflects the idea of equal treatment. A *bona fide* acquirer of a digital asset should not be treated any better or worse than an acquirer of other assets. Still, much depends on the property category in which digital assets are placed by a national legislator, because the rules on good faith acquisition differ as between asset types. They distinguish, e.g., according to whether the object of acquisition is movable, immovable or intangible, such as a claim.

For this reason, the Principles themselves set out the standards of good faith for specific cases. For instance, good faith is excluded where the acquirer "actually knows or ought to know that another person has an interest in the digital asset and that the acquisition violates the rights of that other person in relation to its interest" (Principle 8(5)(a)). The Principles furthermore make clear that the acquirer is under no duty to inquire into the existence of such interests of another person (Principle 8(5)(b)). There is also a rule of attribution for organisations: an organisation is deemed to have the knowledge of the individual who is responsible for making the transaction (Principle 8(5)(c)). No provision is made, however, for the knowledge of an agent to be attributed to the principal. The Principles further protect the good faith of clients whose digital assets are maintained by a custodian, by providing that the knowledge of the custodian cannot be attributed to the client (Principle 12(1)).

The Principles allow for an innocent acquisition even when the transferee obtains control from a transferor who is acting wrongfully (Principle 8(4)). The parallel with corporeal movables would be the innocent acquisition of stolen goods, which is not universally recognised across legal systems.[933] However,

933 See, e.g., § 935(1) German Civil Code (*Bürgerliches Gesetzbuch*); Art. 2276(2) French Civil Code (*Code civil*); Art. 464(1) Spanish Civil Code (*Código civil*).

systems that exclude the *bona fide* acquisition of stolen goods typically make an exception for money and negotiable instruments.[934] Arguably, digital assets are functionally close to money and negotiable instruments because they are transferred frequently.

Under the "take free rule" in Principle 9(2), the innocent acquirer obtains the digital asset free of any competing rights. According to the "shelter rule" in Principle 9(3), no proprietary rights can be asserted against her. Innocent acquisition is excluded in the case of gratuitous transfers such as gifts, with the exception of secured transactions (Principle 8(5)(d)).

All in all, the rules on innocent acquisition are quite remarkable. They are modelled on a similar provision in the Geneva Convention on Intermediated Securities,[935] but the level of protection given to the innocent acquirer is much higher. Particularly significant is the explicit exclusion of any duty of inquiry or investigation imposed on an acquirer about the property situation of the asset (Principle 8(5)(b)(ii)). This secures the easy transferability and tradability of digital assets. If national legal systems implement these Principles on innocent acquisition, they will become an essential building block for the viable and efficient operation of a global crypto economy.

3.10.1.5 "Regular" Acquisition

Protecting only innocent acquirers is, however, insufficient. It is important also to provide for regular acquisitions from a lawful holder. In this respect, the Principles contain a significant gap. They merely state that a transferor may not transfer more rights than he possesses – according to the old maxim *nemo dat quod non habet* or *nemo plus iuris transferre potest quam ipse habet* – and provide that the transferee of a digital asset will receive all of the proprietary rights that the transferor had in his power and wanted to transfer.[936] Otherwise, the Principles are silent and do not address important issues, such as the conditions of transfer, the time at which it is perfected, and finality. This silence could come back to haunt the Principles because innocent acquisition builds on the rules governing the regular acquisition of assets. Without clear provisions on how digital assets are acquired under normal circumstances, the protection of the innocent acquirer will be insufficient.

934 See, e.g., § 935(2) German Civil Code (*Bürgerliches Gesetzbuch*); Art. L.211-16 French Monetary and Financial Code (*Code monétaire et financier*) (regarding financial securities); Art. 464(4) Spanish Civil Code (*Código civil*) with reference to the Spanish Commercial code (*Código de comercio*), Art. 545.

935 See Art. 18 UNIDROIT Convention on Substantive Rules for Intermediated Securities, done in Geneva on 9 October 2009.

936 Principle 9 UNIDROIT Principles on Digital Assets and Private Law (2023).

What is more, the Principles could even create disturbances in the smooth running of the crypto economy. Indeed, it seems that under the Principles, an innocent acquirer who has obtained control of an asset for the first time is to be considered the owner of that asset, without considering any subsequent confirmations.[937] In practice, however, a wait-and-see period is conventional for any transfer on the Bitcoin network.[938] This is done because subsequent block confirmations can still correct any "soft forks" on the chain.

Since property protection under the Principles seems to kick in earlier, a divergence between the law and the blockchain could arise. That would be unfortunate, as the law should not be used to correct the normal running of a technological process. Moreover, one may wonder about the practical implications of such divergences between law and technology: Will the beneficiaries of once-confirmed but later rejected transactions be able to sue the final recipient of the digital asset? Will the court order a correction of the blockchain in such a case or force the final recipient to make a reverse transfer? To avoid such situations, it would have been advisable to properly define the moment the title passes and the transferee obtains the digital asset concerning the particularities of the technology.

3.10.1.6 The Notion of "Control"

The term "control" plays a fundamental role in the Principles, not only for defining their scope but also as a condition of innocent acquisition and creating security interests. It therefore merits closer attention. The definition in Principle 6 requires that the person exercising control has particular abilities and can be identified as having these abilities by virtue of the asset, protocol or system. The abilities mentioned are modelled on the control over tangible assets but are not limited to a mere parallel to possession. They also comprise other aspects, in particular: 1. the power to avail oneself of substantially all the benefit from the asset; 2. the power to exclude others from availing themselves of this benefit; and 3. the exclusive power to transfer the asset.[939] A very similar definition of control has been adopted by the UCC.[940]

937 See the conditions of innocent acquisition in Principle 8(1) UNIDROIT Principles on Digital Assets and Private Law (2023), according to which the recipient must have obtained "control" of the digital asset, in addition to complying with the requirements equivalent to innocent acquisition and take-free rules under national law.

938 Jordan Tuwiner, 'Bitcoin Confirmations' (Buy Bitcoin Worldwide, updated 1 June 2023) <https://buybitcoinworldwide.com/confirmations> accessed 15 April 2024.

939 See Principle 6(1)(a) UNIDROIT Principles on Digital Assets and Private Law (2023).

940 Sec. 12–105 UCC (defining control regarding controllable electronic records as the power to (A) avail oneself of substantially all the benefit from the electronic record plus (B)

The various aspects of "control" seem to have been included to ensure that the holder indeed derives benefits from the asset comparable to those that may be derived from tangible assets. The drafters may have felt that such a definition was necessary to delineate digital assets from credits to bank accounts, which are also electronically recorded.[941]

While the concern of the drafters of the UNIDROIT Principles (and the UCC) is understandable, the way they have chosen to address this concern gives rise to some doubt. The elements they use to define control – i.e. the ability to avail oneself of substantially all the benefit, the power to exclude others, and the exclusive power to transfer – are equivalent to *usus, abusus* and *fructus* in the sense of Roman law.[942] These are attributes of property rights, not of possession. The ability to exclude others – mentioned in Principle 6(1)(a) – is a *consequence*, rather than a condition, of property.[943] By turning this ability into a condition of control and thus of property protection, the Principles blur the distinction between possession and ownership, which is a mainstay of legal traditions worldwide. Moreover, they also enter on a collision course with other texts. For instance, the UNCITRAL Model Law on Electronic Transferable Records (2018) describes control as a "functional equivalent to possession".[944] The definition of control in the UNIDROIT Principles, on the other hand, is much closer to the notion of ownership.

The Principles furthermore require that the ability to exclude others is "exclusive" (Principle 6(1)(a)(i)). They use the same condition for the ability to transfer (Principle 6(1)(a)(iii)). However, this "exclusiveness" is not taken as seriously as it may appear at first sight. It is clarified subsequently that exclusivity is not questioned by limits of use or programmed changes inherent in the digital asset itself, the relevant protocol or system; nor by the voluntary sharing

the exclusive power to (1) prevent others from availing themselves of substantially all the benefit from the electronic record, (2) to transfer control of the electronic record to another person or cause another person to obtain control of another controllable electronic record as a result of the transfer of the electronic record, while enabling the person readily to identify itself in any way as having these powers).

941 See already *supra* 3.3.2.1. on the comparison to holders of bank accounts.

942 Max Radin, 'Fundamental Concepts of the Roman Law' (1925) 13 California Law Review 207, 210 (calling the *ius utendi fruendi abutendi* an "analysis of the idea of ownership" but drawing the attention to its practical limits).

943 See, e.g., US Supreme Court, 4 December 1979, *Kaiser Aetna v. United States*, 444 U.S. 164, 176 (calling the right to exclude others "one of the most essential sticks in the bundle of rights that are commonly characterized as property").

944 UNCITRAL Model Law on Electronic Transferable Records (2018), Article-by-article commentary, para 107.

of control with other persons.[945] These qualifications were necessary because without them, control would be denied where an asset is subject to restrictions imposed by the code or where it is held jointly by several persons. They nevertheless give rise to considerable doubts about the role and relevance of the exclusive ability to exclude others and transfer them as conditions for control.

Exclusivity is further difficult in relation to the requirement that the abilities associated with control be demonstrable, as set out in Principle 6(1)(b). If this requirement were taken literally, a person asserting a right in a digital asset would have to prove that no other person has such control. Since it is impossible to prove a negative, this cannot be made a requirement, as the maxim goes: *negativa non sunt probanda*. Accordingly, the Principles provide that exclusivity will be presumed where a party can show the ability to exclude others and transfer the asset.[946] Again, this raises the question as to the utility of exclusivity as a criterion for control.

3.10.1.7 Custody of Digital Assets

Most crypto-assets today are held by an intermediary, in particular, a wallet provider or a crypto exchange. The true battlefield of the crypto economy is therefore the rights and duties arising from such custody.

Principle 10 defines the term "custody" by the condition that the custodian must be obliged to maintain the digital asset for the client.[947] This also covers any sub-custody relationship. The Principles require that the client must not have the exclusive ability to effect a change in control over the digital asset.[948] This requirement operates to exclude non-custodial wallets, which are managed by the customers with direct access to their private keys, from the definition of "custody". Moreover, the Principles limit the term "custodian" to professional service providers.[949] Any holdings of digital assets by non-professionals, e.g. friends or family members, will thus fall outside the scope of the rules on custody.

A more dubious restriction of the custody notion is the exclusion of any agreement, where "it is clear from the agreement that, if the service provider enters into insolvency-related proceedings, the digital asset would be part of the service provider's assets available for distribution to its creditors".[950] The

945 Principle 6(3) UNIDROIT Principles on Digital Assets and Private Law (2023).
946 Principle 7(1)(b) UNIDROIT Principles on Digital Assets and Private Law (2023).
947 Principle 10(3)(b) UNIDROIT Principles on Digital Assets and Private Law (2023).
948 Principle 10(3)(c) UNIDROIT Principles on Digital Assets and Private Law (2023).
949 Principle 10(3)(a) UNIDROIT Principles on Digital Assets and Private Law (2023).
950 Principle 10(4) UNIDROIT Principles on Digital Assets and Private Law (2023).

commentary explains that this rule is "designed to act as an incentive to service providers to make the nature of the agreement clear on its face".[951] However, such provision may also be abused. For instance, a service provider could state in its general terms and conditions that the assets held for clients will be part of its insolvency estate. In addition to relieving the custodian from its duties towards the client and improving the position of its creditors, such a term would seriously undermine the client's position in the event of the custodian's insolvency. It might be argued that this is the client's fault; after all, he has agreed to the custodian's general terms and conditions. However, this ignores the reality that clients often accept general terms and conditions without reading them since they lack the ability to influence their content. The rules of unfair terms control in contracts would suitably address this problem, but these are not elaborated to the same degree in legal systems worldwide; in addition, they are rarely used in relation to property law issues.

Principle 11 sets out the duty to safeguard the assets and to comply with the client's instructions as the custodian's primary duties and provides further for several optional duties.[952] It specifically permits sub-custody and the maintenance of the assets of all clients in an "undivided pool",[953] such as an omnibus address on a blockchain. Principle 11 also provides for the creation of security interests in client assets in favour of the custodian.[954] This panoply of rules contains the nucleus of a transnational regime for custody. Although it goes beyond pure property law and ventures into contract law and even regulatory law, this regime may prove very useful in the future as a template for regulating custody relations in the crypto economy.

Protecting clients in the event of the intermediary's insolvency is of utmost importance, as has been demonstrated by several spectacular failures of intermediaries.[955] Such protection is afforded by Principle 13, another of the core Principles. This provides that the client's digital assets do not form part of the custodian's insolvency estate (Principle 13(1)). Moreover, it obliges the insolvency administrator to take reasonable steps to transfer control from the custodian to the client or an alternative custodian of the client's choice (Principle 13(4)). The Principles also contain rules on any shortfalls suffered in client accounts. The suggestion that any shortfall should be met first by any asset of the same description maintained by the custodian (Principle 13(6)) has its

951 UNIDROIT Principles on Digital Assets and Private Law (2023), Comment 10.7.

952 Principle 11(1) and (3) UNIDROIT Principles on Digital Assets and Private Law (2023).

953 Principle 11(2) UNIDROIT Principles on Digital Assets and Private Law (2023).

954 Principle 11(5) UNIDROIT Principles on Digital Assets and Private Law (2023).

955 See *supra* 1.4.2.5.

roots in the US practice of intermediated securities, and is quite controversial. It is a huge boon for the clients, and a drag on the custodian's other creditors. It would effectively reserve all the relevant assets that belong to the custodian as a kind of backup for the clients, thereby diminishing the general insolvency estate and to the detriment of other creditors. Since many countries may have difficulties with this provision, it has been put in square brackets. The following provision, which provides for a *pro rata* division of the shortfall among all clients (Principle 13(7)), is likely to be more readily accepted since it is consonant with the principle of equity.

3.10.1.8 Secured Transactions in Digital Assets

The Principles recommend that states introduce provisions to facilitate the use of digital assets as collateral. Principle 15 clarifies that a security right over a digital asset can be obtained in two ways: by controlling the asset; or by maintaining the asset in custody. It is to be understood, though, that these are minimum and not sufficient conditions. They must be supplemented, in particular, by an agreement between the asset holder and the creditor in whose interest the asset will be given as collateral.

The Principles also address priority as between competing security interests. A security interest obtained through control will enjoy priority over others (Principle 16). This makes sense because, in the crypto economy, control is the primary method of identifying interests in a digital asset. The rule diverges considerably from the rules that apply to intermediated securities.[956] Yet this can be rationalised by the fact that digital assets are not necessarily always held in custody with an intermediary, but can also be held directly.

3.10.1.9 Assessment

As seen from this overview, the UNIDROIT Principles on Digital Assets and Private Law are far from providing a complete set of uniform rules for digital assets. Instead, they merely provide guidelines for a few selected issues that have been identified as the most important. These include innocent acquisition, custody of digital assets, and secured transactions. Many other issues have been left out, including many relating to property law, such as the conditions

956 The UNIDROIT Convention on Substantive Rules for Intermediated Securities gives security rights created under the rules of the Convention priority over those that are created under non-Convention law, see its Art. 19(1). Furthermore, it ranks the security rights created under the rules of the Convention according to the time they have been created (Art. 19(2)).

and timing of the acquisition of a digital asset or the effects of vitiated consent on the ownership of an asset.

The approach chosen by UNIDROIT can be described as "eclectic harmonisation". It is open to criticism. Legal certainty will not be greatly enhanced if it is left to the discretion of individual states to define when property rights have been acquired. Investors also need protection against delicts, e.g. hacking or similar tortuous interferences with their assets. Those who invest in stablecoins need certainty regarding their rights in the underlying assets. None of these issues are addressed by the Principles, at least not directly.

Still, these shortcomings must be assessed against the background of political realities. A treaty or convention in an area as controversial as the blockchain was always going to be unrealistic. Moreover, it would have been impossible to reach consensus on uniform rules of property law, which is deeply rooted in legal traditions that vary considerably from state to state. With this in mind, the text deserves to be hailed as a significant achievement. UNIDROIT has rapidly elaborated new principles for an entirely novel phenomenon. This was critical to avoid further legal fragmentation. Many states are yet to reform their laws to accommodate digital assets. It is hoped that when they do, they will take the Principles as a blueprint or at least as a source of inspiration.

3.10.2 *Conflicts-of-Laws Harmonisation as the Indispensable Corollary of Substantive Law Harmonisation*

It might be thought that harmonising the substantive law would make Private International Law superfluous. However, this is not the case: harmonised private law always needs Private International Law as a complement. There are two reasons for this: first, as it is unlikely that all states of the world will implement the proposed rules, there will always remain the need to clarify the relationship between the legal systems that have implemented the harmonised rules, and those that have not. Second, by contrast to uniform rules, harmonisation leaves legislators room to deviate from the international standards and adapt these for their national legal systems.[957] Conflicts may therefore arise even between those national laws that embrace harmonised standards.

Conscious of these problems, UNIDROIT included in its Principles on Digital Assets and Private Law a special principle on the conflict-of-laws, which has

957 Katharina Boele-Woelki, 'Unifying and Harmonizing Substantive Law and the Role of Conflict of Laws' (2010) 340 Collected Courses of the Hague Academy of International Law 271, 298–299 (emphasising the need to distinguish between harmonisation and unification).

been analysed above.[958] In addition, the Hague Conference on Private International Law (HCCH) is currently working on a project on "Digital Tokens". It is hoped that this initiative will be successful and that the law applicable to assets registered on a blockchain will be determined in the same way across the globe through common conflict-of-laws rules. In this way, the consequences of the gaps still present in the harmonised body of substantive law could be mitigated.

3.11 Towards a New Balance between Law and Technology

Despite the undeniable progress made by international institutions, the prospects for a fully uniform law in the near future are rather slim. Even if states were to universally follow the UNIDROIT Principles on Digital Assets and Private Law – which is at this point far from being sure –, this would not result in uniform rules, because the Principles merely suggest harmonising certain aspects of property law.[959] Many issues remain outside their scope and would continue to be governed by national rules that diverge. On the level of Private International Law, the situation is hardly any better. The national rules that have emerged do not provide any hope for clear-cut convergence.[960]

This leads to the question of whether one could deal with private law issues raised by the crypto economy in a completely different manner.

3.11.1 *Determining Property Rights without Determining the Law Applicable to the Property*

In an article published in 2019, I suggested a radical solution for determining proprietary rights regarding crypto-assets. My proposal was 1. to presume the blockchain to be an accurate reflection of the distribution of proprietary rights and 2. to correct this distribution of rights through legal remedies only where necessary.[961] If this suggestion were followed, the title to virtual assets would generally be determined by the information recorded on the blockchain, and the law would deviate from this register only in exceptional situations. Such a situation could arise, for instance, where the transfer of crypto-assets has been induced by mistake or tainted by fraud, or where the private key has been

958 See *supra* 3.5.
959 See *supra* 3.10.1.1.
960 See *supra* 3.5.2.1.
961 Lehmann (n 503).

hacked.[962] Another situation that calls for rectification is where transfers of crypto-assets have been made in contravention of a state's laws, such as prohibitions in criminal law, tax law, embargos or economic sanctions. Apart from these exceptional cases, blockchain records should be considered the final and definitive reflection of legal rights to crypto-assets.

The advantages of such an approach would be threefold: first, the complex question of determining the governing property law – using rules of Private International Law – would no longer be necessary. This would not only save time and effort, but also eliminate divergence as between national courts in determining the applicable law. Second, it would be unnecessary to apply the substantive rules of a specific national private law to identify the owner of a particular crypto-asset. Instead, one could simply presume that the information recorded on the blockchain is correct. This would again be very economical in terms of time and energy. Third, and most importantly, any conflicting determinations of ownership by national legal systems would be excluded. Since all states and their courts would accept the blockchain as being in principle accurate, and since the blockchain provides the same information for everyone, all states would agree about the identity of the holder of a proprietary right in each crypto-asset. In other words, the law would be uniform worldwide in the blink of an eye, without the need to elaborate and agree on international conventions, principles or model laws.

It would be different, of course, in those cases in which the property distribution as recorded on the blockchain will need to be rectified. These situations would require the application of rules of national law, e.g. rules on mistakes, fraud or theft. Fortunately, there is greater similarity across jurisdictions in these areas of law than there is for proprietary rights in blockchain assets. In addition, the law governing these issues can be identified with relative ease and certainty. This is due to the fact that the traditional rules of Private International Law for contract or tort law do not use the blockchain or crypto-assets as connecting factors but refer to external actors or events. For example, it is much easier to identify the law governing a contract over the sale of bitcoins than the law governing the proprietary rights in such bitcoins.[963] As a result, there is a much broader consensus here than there is on the question of ownership.

If adopted, this proposal would result in a truly harmonious symbiosis between law and technology. On the one hand, the blockchain will preserve its value as a register of values and entitlements, in line with its original purpose. On the other hand, the law will intervene where the technology's results are

962 These are the "endogenous" problems, see *supra* 3.1.1.1.

963 See *supra* 3.1.

contrary to the principles of fairness and justice. This approach allows deploying the full benefits of the technology while maintaining the requirements of justice protected by the rule of law.

In this vein, a new balance between technology and law would be created, which are combined in an entirely new way. The blockchain could finally play the role for which it was designed in the first place: that of an authoritative record of ownership. Identifying the "real" owner by means of a parallel legal construction under national property law would no longer be necessary. In this way, fortuitous and contradictory results due to different determinations of the governing law and their diverging application would be avoided. The complex and time-consuming legal second-guessing of the blockchain would be a thing of the past.

Remarkably, this new balance will be achieved without resorting to the slogan "code is law" or the chimera of a *lex cryptographia*. On the contrary, it is the result of giving each area its proper domain: to the blockchain the determination of entitlement, and to the law the correction of injustices and illegalities. Both can cohabit peacefully and harmoniously as long as neither overreaches into the sphere of the other.

3.11.2 *Objections*

The proposal may however be criticised. First, it may be pointed out that a claim for the retransfer of crypto-assets will not always be sufficient to preserve the rights of legitimate former holders. For example, having a claim for retransfer under the law of restitution or unjust enrichment is not the same as being regarded as the rightful owner of a crypto-asset. The difference becomes painfully visible in insolvency proceedings, where only the owner can recover a crypto-asset, whereas the creditor will have to register his claim and risks receiving only a reduced share of the asset's value.

However, such difference already exists today. It is currently impossible to demand a rectification of the blockchain. People who have lost their assets due to a mistake may not recover "the asset" itself but can only demand a reverse transaction of the same or a similar asset. The situation is different in cases of fraud or hacking, which do not change the property situation but may cause a transfer on the blockchain. A tortfeasor, such as a fraudster or hacker, must not be considered the owner of the assets lost by the victim. Therefore, an exception for hacked or otherwise illegally obtained crypto-assets is necessary.[964] This should also cover blackmail and similar situations. However, the

---

964 Lehmann (n 503) 128–130.

exception must be limited and should not include other cases, e.g. transfers based on mistake or an invalid contract. Otherwise, it would lead to a legal second-guessing of the titles recorded on the blockchain, which would seriously limit the latter's usefulness to the point that it may be deprived of its sense.

Another possible criticism is that a property analysis is indispensable for complex transactions over crypto-assets, particularly those on second-generation blockchains. For instance, to create a limited right *in rem*, it needs to be clear who the actual owner is.[965] For this reason, the creation of collateral rights through secured transactions is usually preceded by an analysis of the current property distribution.

However, there are means to circumvent this problem. One could, for example, create security rights by a purely factual method in which the security provider gives up control over the asset on the blockchain for the creditor's benefit. This would still lead to questions regarding the validity of the security right, e.g. in case of a lack of consent. Yet these questions could be resolved by referring to a particular national law, e.g. that of the security provider.[966] While this would entail a partial application of national law, it would be far less complex than a complete analysis from a property law perspective.

For sure, these objections are significant. The tentative answers that were given reduce the benefits of the suggested "entitlement without property law" approach. Still, one must weigh these downsides against the upsides. The upsides of dispensing with the need to determine the applicable property law and form a parallel legal construction of the blockchain may well be worth the downsides.

3.11.3 *Conditions*

For this approach to work, several conditions must be met. The first condition is that the blockchain indeed accurately reflects the legal situation regarding proprietary rights in the recorded assets in the vast majority of cases. This may be true for some blockchains but not necessarily for all. For this reason, one would have to work out criteria to determine and ensure the reliability of such systems. In this regard, regulatory tools could play a decisive role.

The second condition for the proposal's success is that all national legal systems worldwide recognise the blockchain's accuracy. This is a very far-reaching condition that should not be taken for granted. Indeed, the suggested approach would require different parts of society to accept some hard truths.

965 On this topic, see, e.g., Haentjens and Lehmann (n 841).

966 See the suggestion ibid.

First, lawyers must accept that property rights can exist without property law; news that will be challenging to digest. They must acknowledge the inherent incompatibility between a global mechanism for the transfer and storage of value, and the application of a national law to proprietary rights in assets recorded on them. In addition, they must accept that no national law is called upon to identify the owner but that the blockchain itself fulfils this function. This requires innovative thinking and a readiness to part with deeply entrenched beliefs.

On the other side of the spectrum, the technologically inclined circles must also accept some hard truths. They tend towards the opposite extreme to lawyers by rejecting *any* legal correction of the situation recorded on the blockchain. To accept the approach suggested here, they would have to admit the inherent limits of the blockchain. In particular, they need to realise the ledger's reductionist reflection of the real world, in which additional problems may occur that the code does not take into account. They will also have to come to terms with the fact that law and justice are complex matters, which require more sophisticated answers than a distributed database with cryptographically coded information can deliver.

Against this background, one may be sceptical about whether the suggested solution will ever be accepted or remain the dream of a professor in the ivory tower. Perhaps today's society is not (yet) ripe for a radically new balance between law and technology. As for now, the debate takes place separately in different quarters. Technophiles or "techies" are full of enthusiasm for their new invention and deeply sceptical about any need for the law, while the discussion among lawyers is dominated by conventional legal ideas, such as determining the governing law by rules of Private International Law. In order to accept the proposal made here, it will be necessary that both camps increase their understanding of the other's fields and start an informed discussion. Only then will it be possible to make the most out of the blockchain while preventing injustices.

Conclusion

Now this book has come full circle. It has shown the crypto economy's tremendous promises but also the equally tremendous challenges it poses for international law.

The good news is this: For the first time in history, a global mechanism for the secure storage and transfer of information and value has been created. This mechanism has led to a new type of economy that is global by design. So far, globalised markets grew from a particular country and then spread to others while remaining firmly rooted in one or more of them. The crypto economy is different: it has no anchor in a particular country but operates directly on a worldwide level. True, there are centralised crypto service providers that are established in particular countries. However, a blockchain is not dependent on such intermediaries, but on the contrary exists independently of them. The transnational nature of blockchain networks is written into their DNA.

The crypto economy built on blockchains may thus usher in a new age of globalisation, one which is truly global and does not rely on any particular country or a few dominant countries. This makes it much more resistant to national influences and national interests. An ecosystem of this kind guarantees a free space in which people from all over the world can transact with each other without hindrances by particular states and without having to rely on tangled and complex relationships between national intermediaries. The crypto economy also levels the playing field between actors from different countries and removes discrimination because, in the virtual space, origin no longer matters.

Yet at the same time, the proper function of the crypto economy requires a secure legal framework, both from a regulatory and a private law perspective. Regulation is necessary because the crypto economy harbours dangers for the general interest, such as the potential for abuse by criminals or the obstacles it creates for the efficiency of monetary policy, as well as dangers for private interests, such as the risk of fraud, hacking, or insolvency of a crypto intermediary. Rules of private law are indispensable for preventing and resolving disputes that may arise within the crypto economy, e.g. in case of transfers made by mistake or by incapacitated persons. Since the code provides insufficient answers to these questions, the crypto economy cannot rely on technology alone. It also needs a legal framework.

 | DOI:10.1163/9789004725140_006

Here lies the crux, though. As the world is divided into different states, the legal framework can – at least for the time being – only be provided by national law. It is therefore necessary to identify the applicable national legal system. Hence the conundrum of pressing an innately global phenomenon into a Procrustean bed of different national legal systems.

The task of coordinating these different legal systems falls on international law. It provides criteria to limit their application or identify directly the applicable law. Many of these criteria are based on geography or nationality. Yet in this regard, the blockchain resembles a legal spectre: it is everywhere and nowhere at the same time (in other words, it is "omnipresent"), and its participants act under the veil of pseudonymity. This makes it difficult to identify the applicable rules to facts and acts on the blockchain.

Even if this hurdle is overcome, other problems loom on the horizon. Enforcing any national law is problematic because states compete to impose their law on the crypto economy, which leads to legislative competition and arbitrage. This creates inefficiencies in the application of national law. While these problems are known from other products and services, they are compounded in the case of the blockchain. No state can enforce its rules unilaterally on a mechanism that is truly global.

The application of different national rules not only hurts states and private individuals, but also has negative repercussions on the crypto economy. In particular, it leads to the fragmentation of the blockchain. Legally, a single network is divided and fragmented by different laws. This runs directly against the blockchain's supposed global and alegal functioning. Crypto issuers and service providers are put in an even worse position than issuers and providers of traditional financial products and services. While the latter normally have to comply only with a limited number of legal systems, a crypto provider must deal with the full panoply of national legal systems worldwide.

The remedy for these ailments is straightforward: more uniform solutions and more cooperation between states are needed. Since a global law does not yet exist and a *lex cryptographia* is nothing more than a mere chimera, the states need to propel the uniformisation of their laws. This requires more than mere harmonisation. What is needed is a truly uniform law that reflects the global functioning of the blockchain. Without a global regulator, states must also cooperate by extending each other a helping hand to enforce such rules.

This coordination and cooperation exercise must span regulatory and private law alike. No doubt the political obstacles are high. Hardly any other issue divides states as much as the blockchain. Their reactions are wildly divergent and range from outright prohibition to regulatory promotion. Although there are some promising signs of global coordination and cooperation, for instance in the area of anti-money laundering, we will likely see continuing frictions over the issue.

However, the states must realise that they can hardly prevent an innovation from breaking through. Blockchains will not disappear from the face of the earth because of a regulatory decision or the refusal to provide private law protection. The crypto economy can benefit all states, if its worst excesses are contained, by taking globalisation to the next higher level and making it independent of any particular nation. This should incentivise the states to work more closely on a uniform legal framework and secure its efficient application in every country. There is hardly any alternative to such coordination and cooperation if the world is to avoid the blockchain's dangers and stand to benefit from its potential.

Coordination and cooperation may require a reform of the current international architecture. It may require joint projects across several international organisations, encompassing those tasked with regulatory and those tasked with private law harmonisation. It may demand the creation of new bodies with direct decision-making and enforcement powers. The reality of blockchain assets may even call for a new balance between technology and law, one in which the records on the blockchain are given the benefit of the doubt and are only questioned where injustice or illegality can be proven. In this sense, the global reality of the blockchain may also be a driver for the evolution of a more global law. This may not be a bad thing.

Bibliography

Books

Antonopoulos A M, *Mastering Bitcoin* (2nd edn, O'Reilly 2017).

Antonopoulos A M and Wood G, *Mastering Ethereum* (O'Reilly 2018).

Armour J and others (eds), *Principles of Financial Law* (Oxford University Press 2016).

Audit M and d'Avout L, *Droit international privé* (9th edn, LGDJ 2022).

Bashir I, *Mastering Blockchain: Distributed Ledger Technology, Decentralization, and Smart Contracts Explained* (2nd edn, Packt Publishing 2018).

Blockchain France, *La Blockchain décryptée: les clefs d'une revolution* (Netexplo 2016).

Brunton F, *Digital Cash: The Unknown History of the Anarchists, Utopians, and Technologists Who Created Cryptocurrency* (Princeton University Press 2019).

Calvo Carravaca A-L and Carrascosa González J (eds), *Tratado de Derecho Internacional Privado*, vol. 1 (Tirant lo Blanch 2020).

Caroll L, *Through the Looking Glass* (Henry Altemus Company 1897).

Chowdhury N, *Inside Blockchain, Bitcoin, and Cryptocurrencies* (CRC Press 2019).

Collins L A and Harris J (gen eds), *Dicey, Morris & Collins on the Conflict of Laws* (16th edn, Sweet & Maxwell 2022).

Crawford J and Brownlie I, *Brownlie's Principles of Public International Law* (8th edn, Oxford University Press 2012).

Custers B and Fosch-Villaronga E (eds), *Law and Artificial Intelligence: Regulating AI and Applying AI in Legal Practice* (Springer 2022).

Drexl J and Kur A (eds), *Intellectual Property and Private International Law: Heading for the Future* (Hart Publishing 2005).

Dupuy P-M and Kerbrat Y, *Droit international public* (16th edn, Dalloz 2020).

Fawcett J J and Torremans P, *Intellectual Property and Private International Law* (2nd edn, Oxford University Press 2011).

De Filippi P and Wright A, *Blockchain and the Law: The Rule of Code* (Harvard University Press 2018).

Gupta P and Tham T M, *Fintech: The New DNA of Financial Services* (De Gruyter 2018).

Haentjens M, *The Law Applicable to Indirectly Held Securities: the Plumbing of International Securities Transactions* (SDU Uitgevers 2006).

Hafner K and Markoff J, *Cyberpunk: Outlaws and Hackers on the Computer Frontier* (Simon & Schuster 1991).

Hay P and others, *Conflict of Laws* (6th edn, West Academic Publishing 2018).

Hayek F A, *Denationalisation of Money: The Argument Refined* (3rd edn, The Institute of Economic Affairs 1990.

Higgins R, *Problems and Process: International Law and How We Use It* (Oxford University Press 1994).

Hörnle J, *Internet Jurisdiction, Law and Practice* (Oxford University Press 2020).

Hudson A, *The Law on Financial Derivatives* (6th edn, Sweet & Maxwell 2018).

Johnstone S, *Rethinking the Regulation of Cryptoassets* (Edward Elgar Publishing 2021).

Karimzadi S, *Money and Its Origins* (Routledge 2013).

Kegel G and Schurig K, *Internationales Privatrecht* (9th edn, C.H. Beck 2004).

Kerrigan C, *Artificial Intelligence: Law and Regulation* (Edward Elgar Publishing 2022).

Keynes J M, *The Collected Writings of John Maynard Keynes: Activities, 1940–44: Shaping the Post-war World: The Clearing Union*, vol. 25 (Palgrave Macmillan 1980).

Kono T (ed), *Intellectual Property and Private International Law: Comparative Perspectives* (Hart Publishing 2012).

Lannoye V, *The History of Money for Understanding Economics* (revised in June 2023, 2nd edn, Vincent Lannoye 2015).

Lehmann M and Morishita T (eds), *Cryptocurrencies in National Laws – A Global Survey* (forthcoming Brill).

- Binder J-H, 'Germany'
- Chun C, 'South Korea'
- Held A and Yüksel Ripley B, 'England and Scotland'
- Jakšić T, 'Croatia'
- Karagussov F and Bondarev A, 'Kazakhstan'
- Lehmann M and Morishita T, 'General Report'
- Paksoy M S, 'Turkey'
- Verstappen J, 'Netherlands'.

Leloup L, *Blockchain: La révolution de la confiance* (Éditions Eyrolles 2017).

Lessig L, *Code and Other Laws of Cyberspace, Version 2.0.* (2nd edn, Basic Books 2006).

Lewis M K, *Understanding Ponzi Schemes: Can Better Financial Regulation Prevent Investors from Being Defrauded?* (Edward Elgar Publishing 2015).

Lutzi T, *Private International Law Online: Internet Regulation and Civil Liability in the EU* (Oxford University Press 2020).

Magnuson W, *Blockchain Democracy: Technology, Law and the Rule of the Crowd* (Cambridge University Press 2020).

Mankiw N G and Taylor M P, *Economics* (4th edn, Cengage Learning 2017).

Marx K, *Das Kapital*, vol. 1 (42nd edn, Dietz Verlag 2021).

Mattei U, *Basic Principles of Property Law: A Comparative Legal and Economic Introduction* (Greenwood Press 2000).

Mayer P, Heuzé V and Remy B, *Droit international privé* (12th edn, LGDJ 2019).

McCann H, *Offshore Finance* (Cambridge University Press 2006).

Menger C, *Grundsätze der Volkswirtschaftslehre* (Wilhelm Braumüller 1871).

de Miguel Asensio P, *Conflict of Laws and the Internet* (Edward Elgar Publishing 2020).

Menjuq M, *Droit international des sociétés* (6th edn, LGDJ 2021).
Mills A, *Party Autonomy in Private International Law* (Cambridge University Press 2018).
von Mises L, *The Theory of Money and Credit* (2nd edn, Yale University Press 1953).
Narayanan A and others, *Bitcoin and Cryptocurrency Technologies* (Princeton University Press 2016).
Nozick R, *Anarchy, State, and Utopia* (2nd edn, Basic Books 2013).
Ooi M, *Shares and other Securities in the Conflict of Laws* (Oxford University Press 2003).
Parks T, *Medici Money: Banking, Metaphysics and Art in Fifteenth-Century Florence* (Profile Books 2013).
Proctor C, *Mann on The Legal Aspect of Money* (7th edn, Oxford University Press 2012).
Raj K, *Foundations of Blockchain: The Pathway to Cryptocurrencies and Decentralized Blockchain Applications* (Packt Publishing 2019).
Rammeloo S, *Corporations in Private International Law* (Oxford University Press 2006).
Raval S, *Decentralized Applications: Harnessing Bitcoin's Blockchain Technology* (O'Reilly 2016).
Ryngaert C, *Jurisdiction in International Law* (2nd edn, Oxford University Press 2015).
von Savigny F C, *Private International Law and the Retrospective Operation of Statutes. A Treatise on the Conflict of Laws and the Limits of Their Operation in Respect of Place and Time* (W Guthrie tr, 2nd edn, Rothman 1972).
Sfeir K A, *Droit international privé comparé*, vol. 1 (Éditions juridiques Sader 2005).
Sheridan I, *Financial Regulation and Technology: A Legal and Compliance Guide* (Edward Elgar Publishing 2022).
Shetty S, Kamhoua C and Njilla L (eds), *Blockchain for Distributed Systems Security* (Wiley 2019).
Shin L, *The Cryptopians: Idealism, Greed, Lies, and the Making of the First Big Cryptocurrency Craze* (PublicAffairs 2022).
Schmitz M (ed), *Code mondial de l'exécution digitale/Global Code of Digital Enforcement* (Bruylant 2021).
Schürger J, *Equivalence and Substituted Compliance in International Financial Markets Law* (Oxford University Press 2023).
Symeonides S C, *Codifying Choice of Law Around the World: An International Comparative Analysis* (Oxford University Press 2014).
Tanwar S, *Blockchain Technology, From Theory to Practice* (Springer 2023).
Torremans P and Fawcett J J (eds), *Cheshire, North & Fawcett: Private International Law* (15th edn, Oxford University Press 2017).
Quiniou M, *Blockchain: The Advent of Disintermediation* (Wiley 2019).
Valdez S, *An Introduction to Western Financial Markets* (2nd edn, Palgrave Macmillan 2015).
Watson A (transl.), *The Digest of Justinian*, vol. 1 (University of Pennsylvania Press 2009)
Welfare A, *Commercializing Blockchain* (Wiley 2019).

Westrik R and van der Weide J (eds), *Party Autonomy in International Property Law* (Sellier 2011).

Wilke F M, *A Conceptual Analysis of European Private International Law* (Intersentia 2019)

Wischmeyer T and Rademacher T (eds), *Regulating Artificial Intelligence* (Springer 2019).

Wood P R, *The Law and Practice of International Finance Series: Principles of International Insolvency* (2nd edn, Sweet & Maxwell 2007).

Articles

Aigner M, 'Das internationale Privatrecht und die Blockchain – ein unlösbarer gordischer Knoten?' (2020) 61 Zeitschrift für Rechtsvergleichung 211.

Alexander K, 'International Organization of Securities Commissions' in C Tietje et A Brouder (eds), *Handbook of Transnational Economic Governance Regimes* (Martinus Nijhoff 2009) 439.

Ankenbrand T and others, 'Proposal for a Comprehensive (Crypto) Asset Taxonomy' (2020) 2020 Crypto Valley Conference on Blockchain Technology (CVCBT) 16–26 <http://arxiv.org/abs/2007.11877> accessed 22 February 2023.

Aramonte S, Huang W and Schrimpf A, 'DeFi Risks and the Decentralisation Illusion' (December 2021) BIS Quarterly Review 21 <https://www.bis.org/publ/qtrpdf/r_qt2112b.pdf> accessed 15 April 2024.

Arner D W, Barberis J N and Buckley R P, 'FinTech, RegTech, and the Reconceptualization of Financial Regulation' (2017) 37 *Northwestern Journal of International Law & Business* 371.

Atik J and Gerro G, 'Hard Forks on the Bitcoin Blockchain: Reversible Exit, Continuing Voice' (2018) 1 Stanford Journal of Blockchain Law & Policy 24.

Audit M, 'Le droit international privé confronté à la blockchain' (2021) 4 Revue critique de droit international privé 669.

Auer R and Boehme R, 'The Technology of Retail Central Bank Digital Currency' <https://www.bis.org/publ/qtrpdf/r_qt2003j.htm> accessed 15 April 2024.

Auer R and others, 'The Technology of Decentralized Finance (DeFi)' (2023) BIS Working Papers No 1066.

d'Avout L, 'Property and proprietary rights', *Encyclopedia of Private International Law*, (2017) vol. 1, 1428.

Back A, 'Hashcash – A Denial of Service Counter-Measure' (2022) <http://www.hashcash.org/papers/hashcash.pdf> accessed 15 April 2024.

Bacon J and others, 'Blockchain Demystified: A Technical and Legal Introduction to Distributed and Centralised Ledgers' (2018) 25 Richmond Journal of Law and Technology 1.

Balthazor A W, 'The Challenges of Cryptocurrency Asset Recovery' (2018) 13 FIU Law Review 1207.

Baratta R, 'The Process of Characterisation in the EC Conflict of Laws: Suggesting a Flexible Approach' (2004) 6 Yearbook of Private International Law 155.

Bariatti S, 'Classification (characterization)', *Encyclopedia of Private International Law*, (2017) vol. 1, 358.

Barsan I, 'Legal Challenges of Initial Coin Offerings (ICO)' (2017) 3 Revue trimestrielle de droit financier 54.

Beltramini E, 'Against Technocratic Authoritarianism. A Short Intellectual History of the Cypherpunk Movement' (2021) 5 Internet Histories 101.

von Bogdandy A and Rau M, 'Lotus, The', *Max Planck Encyclopedia of Public International Law* (June 2006).

Berentsen A and Schär F, 'Stablecoins: The quest for a low-volatility cryptocurrency' in A Fatás (ed), *The Economics of FinTech and Digital Currencies* (CEPR Press 2019) 65.

Bernasconi C and Keijser T, 'The Hague and Geneva Securities Conventions: a Modern and Global Legal Regime for Intermediated Securities' (2012) 17 Uniform Law Review 549.

Bloch P and de Vauplane H, 'Loi applicable et critères de localisation des titres multi-intermédiés dans la Convention de La Haye du 13 décembre 2002' (2005) 132(1) Journal du droit international (Clunet) 3.

Boele-Woelki K, 'Unifying and Harmonizing Substantive Law and the Role of Conflict of Laws' (2010) 340 Collected Courses of the Hague Academy of International Law 271.

Bonneau J, 'Hostile Blockchain Takeovers (Short Paper)' in A Zohar and others (eds), *Financial Cryptography and Data Security* (Springer 2019) 92.

Bonomi A, 'Succession', *Encyclopedia of Private International Law* (2017) vol. 2, 1683.

Born G B, 'A Reappraisal of the Extraterritorial Reach of U.S. Law' (1992) 24 Law and Policy in International Business 61.

Bossu W and others, 'Legal Aspects of Central Bank Digital Currency: Central Bank and Monetary Law Considerations' (2020) WP/20/254 IMF Working Papers No 20/254 <https://www.imf.org/en/Publications/WP/Issues/2020/11/20/Legal-Aspects-of-Central-Bank-Digital-Currency-Central-Bank-and-Monetary-Law-Considerations-49827> accessed 15 April 2024.

Bower J L and Christensen C M, 'Disruptive Technologies: Catching the Wave' (1995) 73 Harvard Business Review 43.

Bratton W W, 'Nexus of Contracts Corporation: A Critical Appraisal' (1988) 74 Cornell Law Review 407.

Briola A and others, 'Anatomy of a Stablecoin's Failure: The Terra-Luna Case' (2023) 51 Finance Research Letters No 103358.

Brummer C, 'Disruptive Technology and Securities Regulation' (2015) 84 Fordham Law Review 977.

Brummer C and Seira R, 'Legal Wrappers and DAO s' (30 May 2022) <https://papers.ssrn.com/abstract=4123737> accessed 15 April 2024.

Buterin V, 'Ethereum – A Next Generation Smart Contract & Decentralized Application Platform' (Blockchain research network, 2014) <https://ethereum.org/content/whitepaper/whitepaper-pdf/Ethereum_Whitepaper_-_Buterin_2014.pdf> accessed 15 April 2024.

Buxbaum H L, 'Rethinking International Insolvency: The Neglected Role of Choice-of-Law Rules and Theory' (2000) 36 Stanford Journal of International Law 23.

Buxbaum H L, 'Morrison v. National Australia Bank: Defining the Domestic Interest in International Securities Litigation' (2011) 105 American Society of International Law Proceedings 402.

Buxbaum H L, 'Public Regulation and Private Enforcement in a Global Economy: Strategies for Managing Conflict' (2019) 399 Collected Courses of the Hague Academy of International 269.

Campbell-Verduyn M and Goguen M, 'The Mutual Constitution of Technology and Global Governance: Bitcoin, Blockchains, and the International Anti-Money-Laundering Regime' in M Campbell-Verduyn (ed), *Bitcoin and Beyond: Cryptocurrencies, Blockchains, and Global Governance* (Routledge 2018) 69.

Canelis D, 'China has the power to destroy Bitcoin … and it's already manipulating the network'(2018)<https://thenextweb.com/hardfork/2018/10/08/china-means-intent-destroy-bitcoin/> accessed 15 April 2024.

Carney M, 'The Growing Challenges for Monetary Policy in the Current International Monetary and Financial System' (2019) Jackson Hole Symposium 1 <https://www.bankofengland.co.uk/-/media/boe/files/speech/2019/the-growing-challenges-for-monetary-policy-speech-by-mark-carney.pdf> accessed 15 April 2024.

Carrier M A, 'Cabining Intellectual Property Through a Property Paradigm' (2004) 54 Duke Law Journal 1.

Carriero V, 'Smart Contracts in the Blockchain Context: What Happens?' (2019) 1 European Journal of Privacy Law & Technologies 60.

ChangeHero, 'Ethereum Classic: Code Is Law' (Medium, 7 February 2020) <https://medium.com/coinmonks/ethereum-classic-code-is-law-f07f183d5f42> accessed 15 April 2024.

Chason E D, 'How Bitcoin Functions as Property Law' (2018) 49 Seton Hall Law Review 129.

Chason E D, 'Cryptocurrency Hard Forks and Revenue Ruling 2019–24' (2019) 39 Virginia Tax Review 279.

Chaum D, 'Security Without Identification: Transaction Systems to Make Big Brother Obsolete' (1985) 28 Communications of the Association for Computer Machinery (ACM) 1030.

Chaum D, Fiat A and Naor M, 'Untraceable Electronic Cash' in S Goldwasser (ed), *Advances in Cryptology – CRYPTO'88* (Springer 1990) 319.

Cheng J, 'China Rolls Out Pilot Test of Digital Currency' (Wall Street Journal, 20 April 2020) <https://www.wsj.com/articles/china-rolls-out-pilot-test-of-digital-currency-11587385339> accessed 5 April 2024.

Chohan U W, 'Oversight and Regulation of Cryptocurrencies: BitLicense' in S Goutte, K Gesmi and S Saadi (eds), *Cryptofinance, A New Currency for a New Economy* (World Scientific Publishing Co Pte Ltd 2021) 105.

Chohan U W, 'Non-Fungible Tokens: Blockchains, Scarcity, and Value' (2021) Critical Blockchain Research Initiative (CBRI) Discussion Papers Series: Notes on the 21st Century <https://papers.ssrn.com/abstract=3822743> accessed 15 April 2024.

Church S and Randles J, 'FTX Creditors Will Get Paid In Full. They Just Want Crypto Back.' (Bloomberg.com, 15 May 2024) <https://www.bloomberg.com/news/articles/2024-05-15/ftx-bankruptcy-will-pay-customers-over-100-but-they-missed-crypto-rally> accessed 12 June 2024.

Coghlan J., 'New York Mayor Urges State to Abandon "Stifling" BitLicense Scheme' (Cointelegraph, 28 April 2022) <https://cointelegraph.com/news/new-york-mayor-urges-state-to-abandon-stifling-bitlicense-scheme> accessed 17 May 2023.

Crans B, 'Chapter 9: Rights in Aircraft' in I H P Diederiks-Verschoor and P Mendes de Leon (eds), *An Introduction to Air Law* (9th edn, Kluwer Law International 2012) 345–389.

Cross R, 'Modem Grrrl' (WIRED, 1995) <https://www.wired.com/1995/02/st-jude/> accessed 15 April 2024.

CryptoIQ, 'Coding for Better Regulatory Outcomes in The Internet Age of Bitcoin and Blockchains' (Medium, 2016) <https://medium.com/@CryptoIQ.ca/coding-for-better-regulatory-outcomes-in-the-internet-age-of-bitcoin-and-blockchains-2ddad303fbd1> accessed 15 April 2024.

Dai W, 'B-money' (1998) <http://www.weidai.com/bmoney.txt> accessed 15 April 2024.

Danneels E, 'Disruptive Technology Reconsidered: A Critique and Research Agenda' (2004) 21 Journal of Product Innovation Management 246.

Deguée J-P and Devos D, 'La loi applicable aux titres intermédiés: l'apport de la Convention de La Haye de décembre 2002' (2006) 1 Revue de droit commercial belge 5.

Dewan N and Naik R A, 'Let's Trade Crypto: Indian Supreme Court Quashes Prohibition' (Oxford Business Law Blog, 2020) <https://www.law.ox.ac.uk/business-law-blog/blog/2020/03/lets-trade-crypto-indian-supreme-court-quashes-prohibition> accessed 15 April 2024.

Dickinson A, 'Cryptocurrencies and the Conflict of Laws' in D Fox and S Green (eds), *Cryptocurrencies in Public and Private Law* (Oxford University Press 2019) 93.

Diffie W and Hellman M E, 'Exhaustive Cryptanalysis of the NBS Data Encryption Standard' (1977) 10(6) *Computer* 74.

Djurovic M and Janssen A, 'The Formation of Blockchain-Based Smart Contracts in the Light of Contract Law' (2018) 26 European Review of Private Law 753.

Dodge W S, 'The Presumption Against Extraterritoriality after Morrison' (2011) 105 Proceedings of the ASIL Annual Meeting 396.

Dubovec M, 'Toward Decentralized Commercial Law for Digital Assets' (2022) 19 Northwestern Journal of Technology and Intellectual Property 239.

Elman W, 'New Coins on the Block: How Should Cryptocurrency Hard Forks Be Taxed' (2021) 74 Federal Communications Law Journal 55.

ElminMedia, 'Bitcoin's "Halving" Sparks Migration of US Mining Computers Overseas' (TokenPost) <https://tokenpost.com/Bitcoins-Halving-Sparks-Migration-of-US-Mining-Computers-Overseas-11456> accessed 30 April 2024.

Falconbridge J D, 'Situs and Transfer of Intangibles in the Conflict of Laws' (1935) 13 Canadian Bar Review 265.

Fauzi P and others, 'Quisquis: A New Design for Anonymous Cryptocurrencies' <https://eprint.iacr.org/2018/990> accessed 15 April 2024.

Favrod-Coune P, 'Les cryptoactifs dans la procédure d'exécution forcée: saisie, revendication, réalisation' (2023) Journal des Tribunaux 66.

Fernández-Villaverde J, 'Cryptocurrencies: A Crash Course in Digital Monetary Economics' (2018) 51 Australian Economic Review 514.

De Filippi P, 'Bitcoin: A Regulatory Nightmare to a Libertarian Dream' (2014) 3(2) Internet Policy Review 1.

De Filippi P and Loveluck B, 'The Invisible Politics of Bitcoin: Governance Crisis of a Decentralised Infrastructure' (2016) 5(3) Internet Policy Review 1.

Finnley H, 'Reusable Proofs of Work' (2004) <https://nakamotoinstitute.org/finney / rpow/index.html> accessed 15 April 2024.

Frankenfield J, 'Block Header (Cryptocurrency): Definition and How It Works' (investopedia, 22 September 2021) <https://www.investopedia.com/terms/b/block-header-cryptocurrency.asp> accessed 15 April 2024.

Friedman G, 'Opinion: Why It Matters If Bitcoin Is a Currency or a Commodity' (Market Watch, 2017) <https://www.marketwatch.com/story/why-it-matters-if-bitcoin-is-a-currency-or-a-commodity-2017-12-13> accessed 15 April 2024.

Geva B, Grünewald S and Zellweger-Gutknecht C, 'The e-Banknote as a "Banknote": A Monetary Law Interpreted' (2021) 41 *Oxford Journal of Legal Studies* 1119.

Ghodoosi F, 'Contracting in the Age of Smart Contracts' (2021) 96 Washington Law Review 51.

Goforth C R, 'The Case for Preempting State Money Transmission Laws for Crypto-Based Businesses' (2020) 73 Arkansas Law Review 301.

Goldstein G, 'La cohabitation hors mariage en droit international privé' (2006) 320 Collected Courses of the Hague Academy of International Law 9.

González Beilfuss C, 'Party Autonomy in International Family Law' (2020) 408 Collected Courses of the Hague Academy of International Law 89.

Goode R, 'The Hague Convention on the Law Applicable to Indirectly Held Securities: A Market-oriented Approach to the Conflict of Laws' in F Faust and G Thüsing (eds), *Beyond Borders: Perspectives on International and Comparative Law: Symposium in Honour of Hein Kötz* (Carl Heymanns Verlag 2006) 63.

Greenberg A, 'Rethinking Technology Neutrality' (2015) 100 Minnesota Law Review 1495.

Grimmelmann J, 'All Smart Contracts Are Ambiguous' (2019) 2 Journal of Law & Innovation 1.

Guillaume F, 'Blockchain: le pont du droit international privé entre l'espace numérique et l'espace physique' in I Pretelli (ed), *Conflict of Laws in the Maze of Digital Platforms* (Schulthess 2018) 163.

Guillaume F, 'Aspects of Private International Law Related to Blockchain Transactions' in D Kraus and others (eds), *Blockchains, Smart Contracts, Decentralised Autonomous Organisations and the Law* (Edward Elgar Publishing 2019) 49.

Hacker P and Thomale C, 'Crypto-Securities Regulation: ICO s, Token Sales and Cryptocurrencies under EU Financial Law' (2018) 15 European Company and Financial Law Review 645.

Haentjens M and Lehmann M, 'The Law Governing Secured Transactions in Digital Assets' in A Bonomi, M Lehmann and S Lalani (eds), *Blockchain and Private International Law* (Brill 2023) 456.

Hartley T C, 'The Modern Approach to Private International Law: International Litigation and Transactions from a Common-Law Perspective' (2006) 319 Collected Courses of the Hague Academy of International Law 9.

Held A, 'Does Situs Actually Matter When Ownership to Bitcoin Is in Dispute?' (2021) 36 Butterworth's Journal of International Banking and Financial Law 269.

Hess B, *'The Private-Public Law Divide in International Dispute Resolution'* (2018) 388 *Collected Courses of the Hague Academy of International Law* 49.

Howson P, 'Tackling Climate Change with Blockchain' (2019) 9 Nature Climate Change 644.

Hinman W, 'Digital Asset Transactions: When Howey Met Gary (Plastic)' (2018) <https://www.sec.gov/news/speech/speech-hinman-061418> accessed 15 April 2024.

Hughes E, 'A Cypherpunk's Manifesto' (1993) <https://www.activism.net/cypherpunk/manifesto.html> accessed 15 April 2024.

Jackson H E, 'Substituted Compliance: The Emergence, Challenges, and Evolution of a New Regulatory Paradigm' (2015) 1 Journal of Financial Regulation 169.

Jackson J K, 'The Financial Action Task Force: An Overview' (2017) <https://crsreports.congress.gov/product/details?prodcode=RS21904> accessed 15 April 2024.

Jarvis C, 'Cypherpunk Ideology: Objectives, Profiles, and Influences (1992–1998)' (2021) 6 Internet Histories 315.

Jensen M C and Meckling W H, 'Theory of the Firm: Managerial Behavior, Agency Costs and Ownership Structure' (1976) 3 Journal of Financial Economics 305.

John A, Shen S and Wilson T, 'China's Top Regulators Ban Crypto Trading and Mining, Sending Bitcoin Tumbling' (Reuters, 24 September 2021) <https://www

.reuters.com/world/china/china-central-bank-vows-crackdown-cryptocurrency-trading-2021-09-24> accessed 15 April 2024.

Kaaru S, '13 Years Ago, Satoshi Nakamoto Sent Hal Finney 10 Bitcoins in Bitcoin's First Transaction Ever' (CoinGeek, 2022) <https://coingeek.com/13-years-ago-satoshi-nakamoto-sent-hal-finney-10-bitcoins-in-bitcoins-first-transaction-ever> accessed 15 April 2024.

Kaplanov N M, 'Nerdy Money: Bitcoin, the Private Digital Currency, and the Case Against its Regulation' (2012) 25 Loyola Consumer Law Review 111.

Kerkemeyer A, 'Blockchain-Transaktionen im Internationalen Recht' (2020) 184 Zeitschrift für das gesamte Handels- und Wirtschaftsrecht 793.

Kerkemeyer A, 'Herausforderungen des Blockchain-Netzwerks für das Gesellschaftsrecht' (2020) *Zeitschrift für Unternehmens- und Gesellschaftsrecht* 654.

Kieninger E-M, 'Die Zukunft des deutschen und europäischen Mobiliarkreditsicherungsrechts' (2008) 208 Archiv für die civilistische Praxis 182.

Kleiner C, 'Money in Private International Law: What Are the Problems? What Are the Solutions?' (2009) 11 Yearbook of Private International Law 565.

Kleiner C, 'Money and Currency', *Encyclopedia of Private International Law* (2017) vol. 2, 1256–1262.

Kono T, 'Efficiency in Private International Law' (2014) 369 Collected Courses of the Hague Academy of International Law 359.

Knight W, 'China's Central Bank Has Begun Cautiously Testing a Digital Currency' (2017) 120(5) MIT Technology Review 22.

Knöfel O L, 'Elektronische Wertpapiere im Internationalen Privatrecht' in H Grothe, P Mankowski and F Rieländer (eds) *Europäisches und internationales Privatrecht* (C.H. Beck 2022) 157.

Krispis E, 'Money in Private International Law' (1967) 120 Collected Courses of the Hague Academy of International Law 191.

Lehmann M, 'Financial Instruments', *Encyclopedia of Private International Law* (2017) vol. 1, 739–747.

Lehmann M, 'Legal Fragmentation, Extraterritoriality and Uncertainty in Global Financial Regulation' (2017) 37 Oxford Journal of Legal Studies 406.

Lehmann M, 'New Challenges of Extraterritoriality: Superposing Laws' in F Ferrari and D P Fernández Arroyo (eds), *Private International Law – Contemporary Challenges and Continuing Relevance* (Edward Elgar Publishing 2019) 258.

Lehmann M, 'Who Owns Bitcoin? Private Law Facing the Blockchain' (2020) 21 Minnesota Journal of Law, Science & Technology 93.

Lehmann M, 'Global Rules for a Global Market Place? – The Regulation and Supervision of Fintech Providers' (2020) 38 Boston University International Law Journal 118.

Lehmann M, 'Extraterritoriality in Financial Law' in A Parrish and C Ryngaert (eds), *Cambridge Handbook on Extraterritoriality in International Law* (Cambridge University Press 2023) 412.

Lehmann M, 'Internationales Privat- und Zivilprozessrecht' in S Omlor and M Link (eds), *Handbuch Kryptowährungen und Token* (2nd edn, Recht und Wirtschaft 2023) 181.

Lehmann M and others, 'Staking Your Crypto: What are the Stakes?' (2023) 19 Journal of Business & Technology Law 53.

Lehmann M and Meyle H, 'The Law Applicable to Stablecoins' in A Bonomi, M Lehmann and S Lalani (eds), *Blockchain and Private International Law* (Brill 2023) 372.

Lehmann M and Prévost E, 'La localisation du dommage dans le Web3/Locating Damage on Web3' (2022) 6 Revue de droit des affaires internationales/International Business Law Journal 736.

Lehmann M and Schürger J, 'Multilateralizing Deference – A Proposal for Reforming Global Financial Law' (2023) 56 *International Lawyer* 191.

Levy S, 'Solving the Problems of Electronic Cash' in M D Ermann, M B Williams and M S Shauf (eds), *Computers, Ethics, and Society* (2nd edn, Oxford University Press 1997) 99.

Li H, 'Some Recent Developments in the Conflict of Laws of Succession' (1990) 224 Collected Courses of the Hague Academy of International Law 9.

de Lima Pinheiro L, 'Laws Applicable to International Smart Contracts and Decentralized Autonomous Organizations (DAOS)' (2 June 2023) <https://papers.ssrn.com/abstract=4467408> accessed 15 April 2024.

Low K F K and Ying-Chieh W, 'The Characterisation of Cryptocurrencies in East Asia' in D Fox and S Green (eds), *Cryptocurrencies in Public and Private Law* (Oxford University Press 2019) 199.

Mann F A, 'Money in Public International Law' (1949) 26 British Yearbook of International Law 259.

Mann F A, 'The Doctrine of Jurisdiction in International Law' (1964) 111 Collected Courses of the Hague Academy of International Law 1.

Marin-Dagannaud G, 'Le fonctionnement de la blockchain' (2017) 8(3) Réalités industrielles 42.

May T C, 'The Crypto Anarchist Manifesto' (1988) <http://groups.csail.mit.edu/mac/classes/6.805/articles/crypto/cypherpunks/may-crypto-manifesto.html> accessed 15 April 2024.

May T C, 'The Cyphernomicon' (1994) <https://nakamotoinstitute.org/static/docs/cyphernomicon.txt> accessed 15 April 2024.

McGinnis J O and Roche K, 'Bitcoin: Order without Law in the Digital Age' (2019) 94 Indiana Law Journal 1496.

Meessen K M, 'Antitrust Jurisdiction Under Customary International Law' (1984) 78 American Journal of International Law 783.

Melinek J, 'Terra Halts Its Blockchain to Prevent Hacks Amid UST Crash' (TechCrunch, 2022) <https://web.archive.org/web/20220512175406/https://techcrunch

.com/2022/ 05/12/terra-halts-its-blockchain-to-prevent-hacks-ust/amp> accessed 15 April 2024.

Menell P S, 'The Property Rights Movement's Embrace of Intellectual Property: True Love or Doomed Relationship' (2007) 34 Ecology Law Quarterly 713.

Menger C, 'On the Origin of Money' (1892) 2 The Economic Journal 239.

Metjahic L, 'Deconstructing the DAO: The Need for Legal Recognition and the Application of Securities Laws to Decentralized Organizations' (2017) 39 Cardozo Law Review 1533.

Micheler E, 'Custody Chains and Asset Values: Why Crypto-Securities Are Worth Contemplating' (2015) 74 The Cambridge Law Journal 505.

Miller A, 'Permissioned and Permissionless Blockchains' in S Shetty, C Kamhoua and L Njilla (eds), *Blockchain for Distributed Systems Security* (Wiley 2020) 193.

Moloney N, 'Capital Markets Union, Third Countries, and Equivalence' in D Busch, E Avgouleas and G Ferrarini (eds), *Capital Markets Union in Europe* (Oxford University Press 2018) 97.

Moloney N, 'Reflections on the EU Third Country Regime for Capital Markets in the Shadow of Brexit' (2020) 17 European Company and Financial Law Review 35.

Moura Vicente D, 'Intellectual Property, Applicable Law', *Encyclopedia of Private International Law* (2017) vol. 2, 962.

Müller M F, 'Anwendungsbereich' in M F Müller and C Pieper (eds), *Gesetz über elektronische Wertpapiere (eWpG)* (C.H. Beck 2022) 17.

Nakamoto S 'Bitcoin: A Peer-to-Peer Electronic Cash System' (2008) <https://bitcoin.org/ bitcoin.pdf> accessed 15 April 2024.

Nakamoto S, 'Bitcoin Open Source Implementation of P2P Currency' (Satoshi Nakamoto Institute, 2009) <https://satoshi.nakamotoinstitute.org/posts/p2pfoundation/threads/ 1> accessed 15 April 2024.

Nemazie S, 'Is Bitcoin Legal Tender In Japan?' (Seeking Alpha, 2017) <https://seekingalpha.com/article/4133681-is-bitcoin-legal-tender-in-japan> accessed 15 April 2024.

Ng M, 'Choice of Law for Property Issues Regarding Bitcoin under English Law' (2019) 15 Journal of Private International Law 315.

Nial H, 'Selected Problems of Private International Law' (1960) 101 Collected Courses of the Hague Academy of International Law 259.

Ogus A, 'Competition Between National Legal Systems: A Contribution of Economic Analysis to Comparative Law' (1999) 48 International and Comparative Law Quarterly 405.

Ooi M, 'Choice of Law in the Shifting Sands of Securities Trading' in A Dickinson and E Peel (eds), *A Conflict of Laws Companion* (Oxford University Press 2021) 199.

Ostroff C and Malsin J, 'Turks Pile Into Bitcoin and Tether to Escape Plunging Lira' (Wall Street Journal, 12 January 2022) <https://www.wsj.com/articles/turks-pile-into-bitcoin-and-tether-to-escape-plunging-lira-11641982077> accessed 15 April 2024.

Paech P, 'The Governance of Blockchain Financial Networks' (2017) 80 Modern Law Review 1073.

Painter R W, Dunham D and Quackenbos E, 'When Courts and Congress Don't Say What They Mean: Initial Reactions to Morrison v. National Australia Bank and to the Extraterritorial Jurisdiction Provisions of the Dodd-Frank Act' (2011) 20 *Minnesota Journal of International Law* 1.

Panetta V F, 'Preparing for the Euro's Digital Future' (14 July 2021) <https://www.ecb.europa.eu/press/blog/date/2021/html/ecb.blog210714~6bfc156386.en.html> accessed 15 April 2024.

Parrish A, 'Morrison, The Effects Test, and the Presumption Against Extraterritoriality: A Reply to Professor Dodge' (2011) 105 Proceedings of the ASIL Annual Meeting 399.

Parkin J, 'The Senatorial Governance of Bitcoin: Making (De)centralized Money' (2019) 48 Economy and Society 473.

Patel D and Ganne E, 'Blockchain & DLT in Trade: Where Do We Stand?' (Trade Finance Global and World Trade Organisation, 2020) <https://www.wto.org/english/ res_e/booksp_e/blockchainanddlt_e.pdf> accessed 15 April 2024.

Paul K, 'Some Americans Already Pay Their Taxes in Bitcoin' (MarketWatch, 2019) <https://www.marketwatch.com/story/believe-it-or-not-some-americans-already-pay-their-bitcoin-in-taxes-2019-01-07> accessed 15 April 2024.

Porter T, 'Financial Stability Board' in C Tietje and A Brouder (eds), *Handbook of Transnational Economic Governance Regimes* (Martinus Nijhoff 2009) 345.

Radin M, 'Fundamental Concepts of the Roman Law' (1925) 13 California Law Review 207.

Rauchs M and others, 'Distributed Ledger Technology Systems: A Conceptual Framework' (Cambridge Centre for Alternative Finance (CCAF), August 2018) <https://www.jbs.cam.ac.uk/wp-content/uploads/2020/08/2018-10-26-conceptualising-dlt-systems.pdf> accessed 15 April 2024.

Ribstein L E and Kobayashi B H, 'An Economic Analysis of Uniform State Laws' (1996) 25 *Journal of Legal Studies* 131.

Riley J, 'The Current Status of Cryptocurrency Regulation in China and Its Effect Around the World' (2021) 7 China and WTO Review 135.

Ringe W-G, 'Regulatory Competition in Global Financial Markets' (2016) 1 *Annals of Corporate Law* 175.

Riva S, 'Decentralized Autonomous Organizations (DAO s) in the Swiss Legal Order' (2019/2020) 21 Yearbook of Private International Law 601.

Rodima-Taylor D and Grimes W W, 'Cryptocurrencies and Digital Payment Rails in Networked Global Governance' in M Campbell-Verduyn (ed), *Bitcoin and Beyond: Cryptocurrencies, Blockchains, and Global Governance* (Routledge 2018) 109.

Rodrigues U R, 'Law and the Blockchain' (2018) 104 Iowa Law Review 679.

Romano R, 'The Need for Competition in International Securities Regulation' (2001) 2 Theoretical Inquiries into the Law 387.

Romano R, 'For Diversity in the International Regulation of Financial Institutions: Critiquing and Recalibrating the Basel Architecture' (2014) 31 Yale Journal on Regulation 1.

de Rosnay M D, 'Peer-to-Peer as a Design Principle for Law: Distribute the Law' (2015) 1(4) Journal of Peer Production 1.

Roth W-H, 'Internationalprivatrechtliche Aspekte der Personengesellschaften' (2014) 43 Zeitschrift für Unternehmens- und Gesellschaftsrecht 168.

Rueckert C, 'Cryptocurrencies and Fundamental Rights' (2019) 5 Journal of Cybersecurity 1.

Ruzik A, 'Art. 9 Financial Collateral Directive (FCD)' in M Lehmann and C Kumpan (eds), *European Financial Services Law: Article-by-Article Commentary* (Nomos Beck Hart Publishing 2019) 1739.

Schwarcz S L, 'Regulating Digital Currencies: Towards an Analytical Framework' (2021) 102 Boston University Law Review 1037.

Schwarz N and others, 'Virtual Assets and Anti-Money Laundering and Combating of Financing of Terrorism (1): Some Legal and Practical Considerations' <https://www.imf.org/en/Publications/fintech-notes/Issues/2021/10/14/Virtual-Assets-and-Anti-Money-Laundering-and-Combating-the-Financing-of-Terrorism-1-463654> accessed 15 April 2024.

Schwemmer S, 'Das Tokensachstatut' (2022) 42 Praxis des Internationalen Privat- und Verfahrensrechts (IPRax) 331–338.

Sigalos M and Mangan D, 'FTX Founder Sam Bankman-Fried Sentenced to 25 Years for Crypto Fraud, to Pay $11 Billion in Forfeiture' (CNBC, 28 March 2024) <https://www.cnbc.com/2024/03/28/live-updates-ftx-founder-sam-bankman-fried-sentencing.html> accessed 12 June 2024.

Singh T and Brummer C, 'Does Today's World Need a Global Financial Regulator' (2014) 33 *International Financial Law Review* 18.

Solat S, Calvez P and Nait-Abdesselam F, 'Permissioned vs. Permissionless Blockchain: How and Why There Is Only One Right Choice' (2021) 16 Journal of Software 95.

Spithoven A, 'Theory and Reality of Cryptocurrency Governance' (2019) 53 Journal of Economic Issues 385.

Stalmans C, 'More than Just Games: Virtual Property Rights in Massively Multiplayer Online Games' (2012) 12 Asper Rev. Int'l Bus. & Trade L. 203

Symeonides S C, 'The American Choice-of-Law Revolution in the Courts: Today and Tomorrow' (2002) 298 Collected Courses of the Hague Academy of International Law 9.

Swartz L, 'What Was Bitcoin, What Will It Be? The Techno-Economic Imaginaries of a New Money Technology' (2018) 32 Cultural Studies 623.

Sweet K and Neumeister L, 'Fallen cryto mogul Sam Bankman-Fried sentenced to 25 years in prison' (Associated Press News, 29 March 2024) <https://apnews.com/article/sam-bankman-fried-ftx-cryptocurrency-sentencing-sbf-d7bb1a5e94b4c22039d74dfeab1a2ff1> accessed 15 April 2024.

Szabo N, 'Shelling Out: The Origins of Money' (2002) <https://nakamotoinstitute.org/shelling-out> accessed 15 April 2024.

Tafara E and Peterson R J, 'A Blueprint for Cross-Border Access to U.S. Investors: A New International Framework' (2007) 48 Harvard International Law Journal 31.

Takahashi K, 'Law Applicable to Proprietary Issues of Crypto-assets' (2022) 18 *Journal of Private International Law* 339.

Takahashi K, 'Blockchain-based Negotiable Instruments with Particular Reference to Bills of Lading and Investment Securities' in A Bonomi, M Lehmann et S Lalani (eds), *Blockchain and Private International Law* (Brill 2023) 494.

Takyar A, 'What Are Soulbound Tokens, and How Do They Work?' (LeewayHertz, 14 December 2022) <https://www.leewayhertz.com/soulbound-tokens> accessed 15 April 2024.

Thevenoz L, 'Intermediated Securities, Legal Risk, and the International Harmonization of Commercial Law' (2007) 13 Stanford Journal of Law, Business & Finance 384.

Tietje C and Lehmann M, 'The Role and Prospects of International Law in Financial Regulation and Supervision' (2010) 13 Journal of International Economic Law 663.

Trautman L, 'Virtual Currencies: Bitcoin & What Now After Liberty Reserve, Silk Road, and Mt. Gox' (2013) 20(4) Richmond Journal of Law & Technology 1.

Turing A M, 'On Computable Numbers, With an Application to the Entscheidungsproblem' *(1936) s2–42 Proceedings of the London Mathematical Society* 230.

Tuwiner J, 'Bitcoin Confirmations' (Buy Bitcoin Worldwide, updated 1 June 2023) <https://buybitcoinworldwide.com/confirmations> accessed 15 April 2024.

de Vauplane H, 'Blockchain and Conflict of Laws' (2017) 4 Revue trimestrielle du droit financier 50.

Verdier P H, 'Mutual Recognition in International Finance' (2011) 52 Harvard International Law Journal 55.

Vigna P, 'Fund Based on Digital Currency Ethereum to Wind Down After Alleged Hack' (Wall Street Journal, updated 17 June 2016) <https://www.wsj.com/articles/investment-fund-based-on-digital-currency-to-wind-down-after-alleged-hack-1466175033#> last accessed 15 April 2024.

van Wegberg R, Oerlemans J J and van Deventer O, 'Bitcoin Money Laundering: Mixed Results? An Explorative Study on Money Laundering of Cybercrime Proceeds Using Bitcoin' (2018) 25 Journal of Financial Crime 419.

Weller M-P and Thomale C, 'Companies', *Encyclopedia of Private International Law* (2017) 405.

Wendehorst C, 'Art. 43 EGBGB' in J von Hein (ed), *Münchener Kommentar zum Bürgerlichen Gesetzbuch*, vol. 13 (8th edn, C.H. Beck 2021).

Wilke F, 'Das IPR der elektronischen Wertpapiere' (2021) 41 Praxis des Internationalen Privat- und Verfahrensrechts (IPRax) 502.

Wright A and De Filippi P, 'Decentralized Blockchain Technology and the Rise of Lex Cryptographia' <https://papers.ssrn.com/sol3/papers.cfm?abstract_id=2580664> accessed 20 November 2023.

World Bank Group, 'Distributed Ledger Technology (DLT) and Blockchain' (2017) FinTech Note No 1.

Wymeersch E, 'Third-Country Equivalence and Access to the EU Financial Markets Including in Case of Brexit' (2018) 4 *Journal of Financial Regulation* 209.

Yaffe-Bellany D, 'How Sam Bankman-Fried's Crypto Empire Collapsed' (New York Times, 14 November 2022) <https://www.nytimes.com/2022/11/14/technology/ftx-sam-bankman-fried-crypto-bankruptcy.html> accessed 15 April 2024.

Yeo N, 'Crypto Exchanges: the Basics' (2023) 38 Butterworth's Journal of International Banking and Financial Law 459.

Yüksel Ripley B, 'Cryptocurrency Transfers in Distributed Ledger Technology-Based Systems and Their Characterisation in Conflict of Laws' in J Borg-Barthet and others (eds), *From Theory to Practice in Private International Law* (Hart Publishing 2024) 109.

Zellweger-Gutknecht C and Weber R H, 'Private Zahlungsmittel und Zahlungssysteme' Jusletter 11 January 2021, 1.

Zetzsche D A, 'Competitiveness of Financial Centers in Light of Financial and Tax Law Equivalence Requirements' in R Buckley, E Avgouleas and D W Arner (eds), *Reconceptualising Global Finance and Its Regulation* (Cambridge University Press 2016) 390.

Zetzsche D A and others, 'Regulating a Revolution: From Regulatory Sandboxes to Smart Regulation' (2017) 23 Fordham Journal of Corporate & Financial Law 31.

Zetzsche D A and others, 'The ICO Gold Rush: It's a Scam, It's a Bubble, It's a Super Challenge for Regulators' (2019) 63 Harvard International Law Journal 267.

Zetzsche D A and others, 'DLT-Based Enhancement of Cross-Border Payment Efficiency – a Legal and Regulatory Perspective' (2022) BIS Working Paper Series No 1015.

Zetzsche D A, Arner D W and Buckley R P, 'Decentralized Finance' (2020) 6 *Journal of Financial Regulation* 172.

Zetzsche D A, Buckley R P and Arner D W, 'The Distributed Liability of Distributed Ledgers: Legal Risks of Blockchain' (2018) 4 University of Illinois Law Review 1361.

Zhao F F, 'Initial Coin Offerings and Extraterritorial Application of U.S. Securities Laws' (2022) 39 Banking Law Journal 174.

Case Law

I. *European Court of Human Rights*

ECtHR, 18 September 2007, *Paeffgen GmbH v Germany*, App no 25379/04, 21688/05, 21722/05 and 21770/05.

ECtHR, 21 October 2013, *Del Río Prada v Spain*, App no 42750/09.

II. *Court of Justice of the European Union*

CJEU, Joined Cases C-509/09 and C-161/10 *eDate Advertising v X and Olivier Martínez et al. v MGN Limited* [2011] ECLI:EU:C:2011:685.

CJEU, Case C-264/14 *Skatteverket v David Hedqvist* [2015] ECLI:EU:C:2015:718.

CJEU, Case C-434/15 *Asociación Profesional Elite Taxi v Uber Systems Spain SL* [2017] ECLI:EU:C:2017:981.

CJEU, Case C-390/18 *Airbnb Ireland UC, Association pour un hébergement et un tourisme professionnels (AHTOP) et al.* [2019] ECLI:EU:C:2019:1112.

III. *International Court of Justice*

ICJ, 6 April 1955, *Nottebohm* case (second phase), I.C.J. Reports 1955, 4.

IV. *Permanent Court of International Justice*

PCIJ, *SS Lotus (France v Turkey)*, judgment of 7 September 1927, Series A, no 10.

V. *United States of America*

New York Supreme Court, 14 April 1891, *L W Hamer v. Franklin Sidway*, 1890, 11 N.Y.S. 182.

US District Court for the Eastern District of Texas, 23 July 2013, *SEC v. Shavers*, No 4:13-CV-416, 'Order Freezing Assets and Granting Other Ancillary Relief'.

US District Court for the Southern District of New York, 21 September 2017, *CFTC v. Gelfman Blueprint, Inc*, No 17–7181.

US District Court for the Eastern District of New York, 6 March 2018, *CFTC v. McDonell*, 287 F. Supp. 3d 213, review refused, 16 July 2018, 321 F. Supp. 3d 366.

US District Court for the District of Massachusetts, 26 September 2018, *CFTC v. My Big Coin Pay, Inc*, 334 F. Supp. 3d 492.

US District Court for the Southern District of New York, 24 March 2020, *SEC v. Telegram Group Inc and TON Issuer Inc*, 448 F. Supp. 3d 352.

US District Court for the Southern District of New York, 2 March 2021, *CFTC v. Reynolds*, Comm. Fut. L. Rep. P 34,935.

US District Court for the Northern District of California, 30 March 2022, *In re Tezos Securities Litigation*, No 17-cv-06779, 2018 WL 4293341:

- 'Order Granting Motion for Distribution of Net Settlement Fund', 30 March 2022;
- 'Order on the Defendant's Motion to Dismiss', 7 August 2018.

US District Court for the Southern District of California, 2 May 2022, *Sarcuni et al v. bZx DAO et al*, No 3:22-cv-00618.

US District Court for the Northern District of California, *CFTC v. Ooki DAO*

- 'Order Granting Plaintiff's Motion for Alternative Service', 3 October 2022;
- 'Amicus Curiae brief of LexPunk Regarding Plaintiff's Motion For Alternative Service', 17 October 2022;
- 'Plaintiff's Consolidated Opposition to Amicus Curiae Motions for Reconsideration of Order Granting Plaintiff's Motion for Alternative Service', 14 November 2022;
- 'Reply Amicus Curiae Brief of Andreessen Horowitz Regarding Plaintiff's Motion for Alternative Service', 7 December 2022;
- 'Reply Brief of Amicus Curiae DeFi Education Fund Regarding Plaintiff's Motion for Alternative Service', 7 December 2022.</ENL>

US District Court for the Southern District of New York, 1 March 2022, *SEC v. Terraform Labs PTE Ltd*, No 21-MC-810 (JPO).

US District Court for the Southern District of New York, 13 July 2023, *SEC v. Ripple Labs Inc et al*, 682 F.Supp. 3d 308.

US Court of Appeals 2nd Circuit, 29 May 1968, *Schoenbaum v. Firstbrook*, 405 F. 2d 200.

US Court of Appeals 2nd Circuit, 28 April 1975, *Bersch v. Drexel Firestone, Inc*, 519 F. 2d 974.

US Court of Appeals 2nd Circuit, 28 April 1975, *IIT v. Vencap Ltd*, 519 F. 2d 1001.

US Court of Appeals 10th Circuit, 24 January 2019, *SEC v. Scoville*, 913 F. 3d 1204, certiorari refused, 140 S. Ct. 483.

US Supreme Court, 3 December 1945, *International Shoe v. State of Washington*, 326 U.S. 310.

US Supreme Court, 27 May 1946, *SEC v. WJ Howey Co*, 328 U.S. 293.

US Supreme Court, 4 December 1979, *Kaiser Aetna v. United States*, 444 U.S. 164.

US Supreme Court, 26 March 1991, *EEOC v. Arabian American Oil Co*, 499 U.S. 244.

US Supreme Court, 24 June 2010, *Morrison et al v. National Australia Bank Ltd et al*, 561 U.S. 247.

US Supreme Court, 27 June 2023, *Mallory v. Norfolk Southern Railway Co*, 600 U.S. 122.

VI. *France*

Tribunal de commerce de Nanterre, 26 February 2020, *SDE Bitspread Ltd v SAS Paymium*, No 2018F00466.

Cour d'appel de Paris, Pôle 4, Chambre 4, 30 January 2023, No 20/08067.

VII. *Japan*

Tokyo District Court, Civil Division, 5 August 2015, *MtGox*, No (Wa)33320, Heisei 26 (2014); english translation: L Gullifer and others <https://www.law.ox.ac.uk/sites/files/oxlaw/mtgox_judgment_final.pdf> accessed 15 April 2024.

VIII. *India*

Indian Supreme Court, 4 March 2020, *Internet and Mobile Association of India v Reserve Bank of India*, Written Petition (Civil) No 373 (2018).

IX. *Italy*

Corte di Cassazione, 17 September 2020, No 26807.

X. *New Zealand*

High Court of New Zealand, 8 April 2020, *Ruscoe v Cryptopia Limited (in liquidation)* [2020] NZHC 728.

XI. *Netherlands*

Hoge Raad, Judgment of 31 January 2012, Nederlandse Jurisprudentie 2012, 536.

XII. *Singapore*

High Court of Singapore, 14 March 2019, *B2C2 Ltd v Quoine Pte Ltd* [2019] SGHC(I) 03.

High Court of Singapore, 26 January 2024, *Cheong Jun Yoong v Three Arrows Capital Ltd* [2024] SGHC 21.

XIII. *United Kingdom*

High Court of Justice of England and Wales, 13 December 2019, *AA v Persons Unknown et al* [2019] EWHC 3556 (Comm).

High Court of Justice of England and Wales, 21 December 2020, *Ion Science v Persons Unknown*, not published.

High Court of Justice of England and Wales, 26 April 2021, *Lubin Betancourt Reyes et al v Persons Unknown et al* [2021] EWHC 1938 (Comm).

High Court of Justice of England and Wales, 15 July 2021, *Fetch.AI Limited et al v Persons Unknown et al* [2021] EWHC 2254 (Comm).

High Court of Justice of England and Wales, 22 March 2022, *Tulip Trading Ltd v Wladimir van der Laan et al* [2022] EWHC 667 (Ch).

Court of Appeal of England and Wales, 4 June 1980, *Bankers Trust Co v Shapira* [1980] 1 WLR 1274.

Court of Appeal of England and Wales, 22 July 1985, *Colonial Bank v Whinney* [1885] 30 Ch D 285 (CA), 285.

Court of Appeal of England and Wales, 19 December 2018, *Uber BV et al v Aslam et al* [2018] EWCA Civ 2748.

Court of Appeal of England and Wales, 3 February 2023, *Tulip Trading Ltd v Wladimir van der Laan and others* [2023] EWCA Civ 83.

UK House of Lords, 26 June 1973, *Norwich Pharmacal v Commissioners of Customs & Excise* [1973] UKHL 6.

UK Supreme Court, 19 February 2021, *Uber BV et al v Aslam et al* [2021] UKSC 5.

Legal Instruments

I. *Central African Republic*

Loi n° 22.004 du 22 avril 2022 régissant la cryptomonnaie en République Centrafricaine.

II. *China*

Chinese Civil Code, 'Art. 127'.
Chinese Law on the Application of Law for Foreign-Related Civil Relations of the People's Republic of China, 'Art. 4', 'Art. 12', 'Art. 41', 'Art. 42'.

III. *Germany*

German Civil Code (*Bürgerliches Gesetzbuch* – BGB), '§ 398', '§ 433', '§ 516', '§ 823', '§ 935'.
German Code of Civil Procedure (*Zivilprozessordnung* – ZPO), '§ 23', '§ 253'.
Introductory Act to the Civil Code (*Einführungsgesetz zum Bürgerlichen Gesetzbuch* – EGBGB), 'Art. 7(1)'.
Act on electronic securities (*Gesetz über elektronische Wertpapiere* – eWpG), '§ 3(3)', '§§ 24–27', '§ 32'.

IV. *El Salvador*

Decreto n° 57 *Ley Bitcoin* 9 June 2021 (D.O. 110 vol. 431), 'I-V', 'Art. 6–12'.

V. *European Union*

a. Directives

Directive 1998/26/EC of the European Parliament and of the Council of 19 May 1998 on settlement finality in payment and securities settlement systems [1998] OJ L166/45 (Finality Directive), 'Art. 9(2)'.
Directive 2002/47/EC of the European Parliament and of the Council of 6 June 2002 on financial collateral arrangements [2002] OJ L168/43 (Collateral Directive), 'Art. 9'.
Directive 2009/110/EC of the European Parliament and of the Council of 16 September 2009 on the taking up, pursuit and prudential supervision of the business of electronic money institutions (e-Money Directive).
Directive 2014/57/EU of the European Parliament and of the Council of 16 April 2014 on criminal sanctions for market abuse [2014] OJ L173/179 (Market Abuse Directive).
Directive 2014/65/EU of the European Parliament and of the Council of 15 May 2014 on markets in financial instruments (recast) [2014] OJ L173/349 (MiFID II Directive).
Directive (EU) 2015/849 of the European Parliament and of the Council of 20 May 2015 on the prevention of the use of the financial system for the purposes of money laundering or terrorist financing [2015] OJ 2015 L141/73, 'Art. 3(18)'.
Directive (EU) 2018/843 of the European Parliament and of the Council of 30 May 2018 amending Directive (EU) 2015/849 on the prevention of the use of the financial

system for the purposes of money laundering or terrorist financing [2018] OJ L156/43, 'Art. 1(2)(d)'.

b. Regulations

Regulation (EC) 864/2007 of the European Parliament and of the Council 11 July 2007 on the law applicable to non-contractual obligations (Rome II) [2007] OJ L199/40, 'Art. 1(1)', 'Art. 4(1)', 'Art. 5'.

Regulation (EC) No 593/2008 of the European Parliament and of the Council of 17 June 2008 on the law applicable to contractual obligations (Rome I) [2008] OJ L177/6, 'Art. 1', 'Art. 3', 'Art. 4', 'Art. 6', 'Art. 7', 'Art. 9', 'Art. 11–14'.

Regulation (EU) No 650/2012 of the European Parliament and of the Council of 4 July 2012 on jurisdiction, applicable law, recognition and enforcement of decisions and acceptance and enforcement of authentic instruments in matters of succession and on the creation of a European Certificate of Succession [2012] OJ L201/107 (Succession Regulation), 'Art. 22'.

Regulation (EU) No 1215/2012 of 12 December 2012 on jurisdiction and the recognition and enforcement of judgments in civil and commercial matters (recast) [2012] OJ L351/1 (Brussels Ibis Regulation), 'Art. 4', 'Art. 7'.

Regulation (EU) No 596/2014 of the European Parliament and of the Council of 16 April 2014 on market abuse [2014] OJ L173/1 (Market Abuse Regulation).

Regulation (EU) 655/2014 of the European Parliament and the Council establishing a European Account Preservation Order procedure to facilitate cross-border debt recovery in civil and commercial matters [2014] OJ L189/59 (European Account Preservation Order Regulation), 'Art. 14'.

Regulation (EU) 2015/848 of 20 May 2015 on insolvency proceedings [2015] OJ L141/19 (EU Insolvency Regulation (Recast)), 'Art. 3(1)', 'Art. 34'.

Regulation (EU) 2016/679 of the European Parliament and of the Council of 27 April 2016 on the protection of natural persons with regard to the processing of personal data and on the free movement of such data (General Data Protection Regulation) [2016] OJ L119/1, 'Art. 3'.

Regulation (EU) No 2023/1113 of the European Parliament and of the Council of 31 May 2023 on information accompanying transfers of funds and certain crypto-assets (recast) [2023] OJ L150/1, 'Art. 4(1) and (2)'.

Regulation (EU) 2023/1114 of the European Parliament and of the Council of 31 May 2023 on markets in crypto-assets [2023] OJ L150/40 (MiCAR), 'Art. 2–3', 'Art. 5–6', 'Art. 16–19', 'Art. 23', 'Art. 29–32', 'Art. 35–39', 'Art. 41–43', 'Art. 45', 'Art. 48', 'Art. 51', 'Art. 59 et seq.', 'Art. 67', 'Art. 86–92', 'Annex IV'.

c. Others

European Commission, 'Consultation Document on a EU-Framework for Crypto-Assets' <https://ec.europa.eu/info/law/better-regulation/have-your-say/initiatives

/12089-Directive-regulation-establishing-a-European-framework-for-markets-in-crypto-assets/public-consultation_en> accessed 9 June 2023.

VI. *France*

French Civil Code (*Code civil*), 'Art. 932', 'Art. 1240', 'Art. 1324', 'Art. 2276(2)'.

French Code of Civil Procedure (*Code de procédure civile*), 'Art. 54'.

French Monetary and Financial Code (*Code monétaire et financier*), 'Art. L54-10-1', 'Art. L54-10-2', 'Art. L54-10-3', 'Art. L54-10-5', 'Art. L552-1 to L552-7', 'Art. L552-2', 'Art. L552-4', 'Art. L552-5'.

VII. *Italy*

Italian Civil Code (*Codice civile*), 'Art. 2032'.

Italian Legge 31 maggio 1995, n. 218, 'Art. 25(2)(g)'.

VIII. *Japan*

Japanese Act on the General Rules on the Application of Law (*Hō no Tekiyō ni Kansuru Tsūsokuhō*), 'Art. 4(1)', 'Art. 4(2)', 'Art. 7', 'Art. 8(3)', 'Art. 10(4)', 'Art. 11(1)', 'Art. 11(2)', 'Art. 17'.

IX. *Liechtenstein*

Liechtenstein Act on Token and Trustworthy Technologies (*Token und Vertrauenswürdige Technologien Gesetz* – TVTG), 'Art. 2–3'.

X. *Marshall Islands*

Decentralized Autonomous Organizations Act 2022.

Limited Liability Company Act 1996, 'Chapter 4, Title 52'.

XI. *Russia*

Russian Civil Code, 'Art. 1192', 'Art. 1197', 'Art. 1210', 'Art. 1212', 'Art. 1213', 'Art. 1219(1)', 'Art. 1215(3)'.

XII. *Spain*

Spanish Civil Code (*Código civil*), 'Art. 464', 'Art. 1902', 'Art. 1445'.

XIII. *Switzerland*

Swiss Code of Obligations, 'Art. 973', 'Art. 973e', 'Art. 973h'.

Swiss Federal Act on Debt Enforcement and Bankruptcy (*Bundesgesetz über Schuldbetreibung und Konkurs – SchKG*), 'Art. 242a', 'Art. 242b'.

Swiss Federal Act on the Adaptation of Federal Law to Developments of Distributed Ledger Technology (*Bundesgesetz zur Anpassung des Bundesrechts an Entwicklungen der Technik verteilter elektronischer Register*).

Swiss Federal Act on Private International Law, 'Art. 18', 'Art. 19', 'Art. 36', 'Art. 105', 'Art. 106', 'Art. 108a', 'Art. 115', 'Art. 116', 'Art. 119', 'Art. 120', 'Art. 124(2)', 'Art. 125', 'Art. 133(2)', 'Art. 145a', 'Art. 147(1)', 'Art. 155'.

Swiss Federal Act on Banks and Savings Banks (*Bundesgesetz über die Banken und Sparkassen*), 'Art. 1b'.

Swiss Banking Ordinance (*Bankenverordnung*), 'Art. 1b', 'Art. 6(2)'.

XIV. *United Kingdom*

Halsbury's Laws (4th edn, 2004) vol. 20(1), para 67.

UK Sale of Goods Act (1979), 'Sec. 2(1)'.

XV. *United States of America*

N.Y. Codes Rules and Regulations, 2019, '§ 200', '§ 200.2(p)', '§ 200.2(q)', '§§ 200.8–9, 15–16'.

Tennessee Code, '§ 48–250-101'.

Vermont, An Act Relating to Blockchain Business Development, n° 205, codified in 11 Vermont Statutes Annotated (V.S.A) 9 § 4173.

Wyoming, An Act Relating to Corporations; Providing for the Formation and Management of Decentralized Autonomous Organizations; Providing Definitions; and Providing for an Effective Date, n° 73 (SF0038), 'Art. 10', 'Art. 16', 'Art. 17'.

Commodity Exchange Act (CEA), 'Sec. 1a(9)'.

Code of Federal Regulations (CFR), 'Title 31, subtitle B, chap. X, part 1010.100'.

Dodd-Frank Wall Street Reform and Consumer Protection Act, Pub. L. 111–203, 124 Stat. 1376–2223 (2010), 'Sec. 929P'.

Securities and Exchange Act, 'section 10b'.

US Bankruptcy Code, 'Sec. 109(a) (11 U.S. Code § 109)'.

US Uniform Commercial Code (UCC), '§ 1–301', '§ 2–106', '§ 2–401', '§ 9–107A', '§ 12–102', '§§ 12–104 to 12–107'.

XVI. *International Conventions*

Hague Convention on the Law Applicable to Traffic Accidents, done on 4 May 1971, 'Art. 4–5'.

Hague Convention on the Law Applicable to Products Liability, done on 2 October 1973, 'Art. 4–6'.

Hague Convention on the Law Applicable to Certain Rights in Respect of Securities held with an Intermediary, done 5 July 2006, 'Art. 4'.

Inter-American Convention on the Law Applicable to International Contracts, done in Mexico, D.F. on 17 March 1994, 'Art. 1', 'Art. 7', 'Art. 9', 'Art. 13–14'.

UNCITRAL Model Law on Electronic Transferable Records, adopted on 7 December 2017.

UNCITRAL Model Law on Electronic Transferable Records (2018), 'Article-by-article commentary, para 18', 'Article-by-article commentary, para 107'.

UNIDROIT Convention on Substantive Rules for Intermediated Securities, done in Geneva on 9 October 2009, 'Art. 18', 'Art. 19'.

UNIDROIT Principles on Digital Assets and Private Law (2023), 'Comment 0.1', 'Comment 0.3', 'Comment 0.4', Comment 2', 'Comment 2.17', 'Comment 3.2', 'Comment 5.2', 'Comment 5.5', 'Comment 5.6.', 'Comment 5.16', 'Comment 10.11', 'Comment 10.13–10.15', 'Comment 10.7', 'Principle 2(2)', 'Principle 3(1)', 'Principle 3(3)', 'Principle 4', 'Principle 5(1)', 'Principle 5(2)', 'Principle 5(3)', 'Principle 5(6)', 'Principle 5(7)', 'Principle 6(1)', 'Principle 6(3)', 'Principle 7(1)', 'Principle 7(6)', 'Principle 8', 'Principle 9', 'Principle 10(3)', 'Principle 10(4)', 'Principle 11(1)', 'Principle 11(2)', 'Principle 11(3)', 'Principle 11(5)', <https://www.unidroit.org/wp-content/uploads/2023/04/C.D.-102-6-Principles-on-Digital-Assets-and-Private-Law.pdf> accessed 26 September 2024.

United Nations Convention on the High Seas, done in Geneva on 29 April 1958, 'Art. 5'.

United Nations Convention on Contracts for the International Sale of Goods (CISG), done in Vienna on 11 April 1980, 'Art. 31', 'Art. 53'.

United Nations Convention on the Law of the Sea, done in Montego Bay on 10 December 1982, 'Art. 91'.

United Nations Convention on the Assignment of Receivables in International Trade, done in New York on 12 December 2001, 'Art. 29', 'Art. 30'.

United Nations Convention on the Use of Electronic Communications in International Contracts, done in New York on 23 November 2005, 'Art. 9'.

XVII. *Others*

American Law Institute, Restatement of the Law Fourth, The Foreign Relations Law of the United States (American Law Institute Publishers 2018) '§ 401'.

American Law Institute, Restatement of the Law (Second) on Contracts (American Law Institute Publishers 1981) '§ 71'.

American Law Institute, Restatement of the Law (Second) on the Conflict of Laws, (American Law Institute Publishers 1971) '§ 7', '§ 187', '§ 188', '§ 199', '§ 239'.

European Law Institute (ELI), 'Principles on Blockchain Technology, Smart Contracts and Consumer Protection', <https://www.europeanlawinstitute.eu/fileadmin/user_upload/p_eli/Publications/ELI_Principles_on_Blockchain_Technology__Smart_Contracts_and_Consumer_Protection.pdf> accessed 15 April 2024.

Miscellaneous

I. *Reports and Studies*

European Central Bank, 'Stablecoins: Implications for Monetary Policy, Financial Stability, Market Infrastructure and Payments, and Banking Supervision in the Euro

Area' (ECB Occasional Paper Series No 247, 2020) <https://www.ecb.europa.eu/pub/pdf/scpops/ecb.op247~fe3df92991.en.pdf> accessed 15 April 2024.

Bank for International Settlements (BIS), 'Central Bank Digital Currencies' <https://www.bis.org/cpmi/publ/d174.htm> accessed 15 April 2024.

Bank for International Settlements (BIS), 'Annual Economic Report June 2021' <https://www.bis.org/publ/arpdf/ar2021e.pdf> accessed 15 April 2024.

Bank for International Settlements (BIS), Committee on Payments and Market Infrastructures (CPMI), 'Options for Access to and Interoperability of CBDCs for Cross-border Payments – Joint Report to the G20' <https://www.bis.org/publ/othp52.pdf> accessed 15 April 2024.

EU Blockchain Observatory and Forum, 'Decentralised Finance (DeFi)' (2022) <https://digital-strategy.ec.europa.eu/en/library/eu-blockchain-observatory-and-forum-published-report-decentralized-finance-defi> accessed 15 April 2024.

Financial Markets Law Committee (FMLC), 'Distributed Ledger Technology and Governing Law: Issues of Legal Uncertainty' (2018) <http://fmlc.org/wp-content/uploads/2018/05/dlt_paper.pdf> accessed 15 April 2024.

Financial Stability Board (FSB), 'Assessment of Risks to Financial Stability from Crypto-Assets' (2022) <https://www.fsb.org/2022/02/assessment-of-risks-to-financial-stability-from-crypto-assets> accessed 15 April 2024.

Financial Stability Board (FSB), 'Crypto-Assets: Report to the G20 on the Work of the FSB and Standard-Setting Bodies' (2018) <https://www.fsb.org/2018/07/crypto-assets-report-to-the-g20-on-the-work-of-the-fsb-and-standard-setting-bodies> accessed 15 April 2024.

Financial Stability Board (FSB), 'Recommendations to Achieve Greater Convergence in Cyber Incident Reporting: Final Report' <https://www.fsb.org/2023/04/ recommendations-to-achieve-greater-convergence-in-cyber-incident-reporting-final-report> (2023) accessed 15 April 2024.

Financial Stability Board (FSB), 'Summary Report on Financial Sector Cybersecurity Regulations, Guidance and Supervisory Practices' <https://www.fsb.org/2017/10/summary-report-on-financial-sector-cybersecurity-regulations-guidance-and-supervisory-practices> accessed 15 April 2024.

Hague Conference on Private International Law (HCCH), 'Developments with Respect to PIL Implications of the Digital Economy, Including DLT' (Prel. Doc. No 4 of November 2020) <https://assets.hcch.net/docs/8bdc7071-c324-4660-96bc-86efba6214f2.pdf> accessed 28 July 2023.

Hague Conference on Private International Law (HCCH), 'Proposal for Joint Work: HCCH-UNIDROIT Project on Law Applicable to Cross-Border Holdings and Transfers of Digital Assets and Tokens' (Prel. Doc. No 3C January 2023) <https://assets.hcch.net/ docs/a91fd233-acf7-4c42-9aad-a426c4565068.pdf> accesssed 15 April 2024.

International Swaps and Derivatives Association (ISDA), 'Private International Law Aspects of Smart Derivatives Contracts Utilizing Distributed Ledger Technology'

<https://www.isda.org/a/4RJTE/Private-International-Law-Aspects-of-Smart-Derivatives-Contracts-Utilizing-DLT.pdf> accessed 15 April 2024.

Organisation for Economic Co-operation and Development (OECD), 'Crypto-Asset Reporting Framework and Amendments to the Common Reporting Standard' (2022) <https://www.oecd.org/tax/exchange-of-tax-information/crypto-asset-reporting-framework-and-amendments-to-the-common-reporting-standard.htm> accessed 15 April 2024.

President's Working Group on Financial Markets, the Federal Deposit Insurance Cooperation, and the Office of the Comptroller of the Currency, 'Report on Stablecoins' (2021) <https://home.treasury.gov/system/files/136/StableCoinReport_Nov1_508.pdf> accessed 15 April 2024.

II. *Seminars and Conferences*

Euromoney Seminars, 'Derivatives Body ISDA Part of "Smart Contract" Blockchain Group' <https://news.fow.com/articles/3570160/derivatives-body-isda-part-of-smart-contract-blockchain-group> accessed 15 April 2024.

III. *Recommendations, Positions and Opinions*

Autorité de Contrôle Prudentiel et de Résolution (ACPR), 'Position de l'ACPR relative aux opérations sur Bitcoins en France' (Position 2014–P-01, 2014) <https://acpr.banque-france.fr/contenu-de-tableau/position-de-lacpr-relative-aux-operations-sur-bitcoins-en-france> accessed 9 June 2023.

Coalition for Automated Legal Applications (COALA), 'Model Law for Decentralized Autonomous Organisations (DAO s)' <https://coala.global/wp-content/uploads/2021/06/DAO-Model-Law.pdf> accessed 15 April 2024.

European Securities and Markets Authority (ESMA), 'Advice on Initial Coin Offerings and Crypto-Assets' (ESMA50-157-1391, 2019) <https://www.esma.europa.eu/sites/default/files/library/esma50-157-1391_crypto_advice.pdf> accessed 15 April 2024.

Financial Action Task Force (FATF), 'Virtual Currencies – Key Definitions and Potential AML/CFT Risks' (2014) <http://www.fatf-gafi.org/media/fatf/documents/reports/Virtual-currency-key-definitions-and-potential-aml-cft-risks.pdf> accessed 15 April 2024.

Financial Action Task Force (FATF), 'Guidance for a Risk-Based Approach to Virtual Currencies' (2015) <https://www.fatf-gafi.org/en/publications/Fatfgeneral/Guidance-rba-virtual-currencies.html> accessed 15 April 2024.

Financial Action Task Force (FATF), 'Guidance for a Risk-Based Approach to Virtual Assets and Virtual Asset Service Providers' (2019) <https://www.fatf-gafi.org/en/publications/Fatfrecommendations/Guidance-rba-virtual-assets.html> accessed 15 April 2024.

Financial Action Task Force (FATF), 'Money Laundering and Terrorist Financing Red Flag Indicators Associated with Virtual Assets' (2020) <https://www.fatf-gafi.org

/en/publications/Methodsandtrends/Virtual-assets-red-flag-indicators.html> accessed 15 April 2024.

Financial Action Task Force (FATF), '12 Month Review of Revised FATF Standards – Virtual Assets and VASPs' (2020) <https://www.fatf-gafi.org/en/publications/Virtualassets/Virtual-assets.html> accessed 15 April 2024.

Financial Action Task Force (FATF), 'Opportunities and Challenges of New Technologies for AML/CFT' (last updated 2021) <https://www.fatf-gafi.org/en/publications/Digitaltransformation/Opportunities-challenges-new-technologies-for-aml-cft.html> accessed 15 April 2024.

Financial Action Task Force (FATF), 'Updated Guidance for a Risk-Based Approach to Virtual Assets and Virtual Asset Service Providers' (2021) <https://www.fatf-gafi.org/publications/fatfrecommendations/documents/guidance-rba-virtual-assets-2021.html> accessed 15 April 2024.

Financial Action Task Force (FATF), 'Second 12-month Review of Revised FATF Standards – Virtual Assets and VASPs' (2021) <https://www.fatf-gafi.org/en/publications/Fatfrecommendations/Second-12-month-review-virtual-assets-vasps.html> accessed 15 April 2024.

Financial Action Task Force (FATF), 'Targeted Update on Implementation of the FATF's Standards on Virtual Assets/VASPs' (2022) <https://www.fatf-gafi.org/en/publications/Fatfrecommendations/Targeted-update-virtual-assets-vasps.html> accessed 15 April 2024.

Financial Action Task Force (FATF), 'International Standards on Combating Money Laundering and the Financing of Terrorism & Proliferation' (2012–2023) <https://www.fatf-gafi.org/en/publications/Fatfrecommendations/Fatf-recommendations.html> accessed 15 April 2024.

International Securities Services Association (ISSA), 'Infrastructure for Crypto-Assets: A Review by Infrastructure Providers' (October 2018) <https://issanet.org/content/uploads/2016/02/2018-10_ISSA_report_Infrastructure_for_Crypto-Assets.pdf> accessed 15 April 2024.

Swiss Federal Council, 'Botschaft zum Bundesgesetz zur Anpassung des Bundesrechts an Entwicklungen der Technik verteilter elektronischer Register' (2020) Federal Gazette 223-318.

IV. *Others*

British Financial Conduct Authority (FCA), 'Financial Conduct Authority's Regulatory Sandbox Opens to Applications' (2016) <https://www.fca.org.uk/news/press-releases/financial-conduct-authority%E2%80%99s-regulatory-sandbox-opens-applications> accessed 15 April 2024.

Cambridge Centre for Alternative Finance, 'Cambridge Bitcoin Electricity Consumption Index (CBECI)' <https://ccaf.io/cbeci/index> accessed 15 April 2024.

Committee on Payments and Market Infrastructures (CPMI) and Board of the International Organization of Securities Commissions, 'Application of the Principles for Financial Market Infrastructures to Stablecoin Arrangements' (2021) <https://www.bis.org/cpmi/publ/d198.pdf> accessed 15 April 2024.

Commodity Futures Trading Commission (CFTC), 'In re Coinflip, Inc., d/b/a Derivabit, and Francisco Riordan' (CFTC Docket No. 15–29).

Commodity Futures Trading Commission (CFTC), 'A CFTC Primer on Virtual Currencies' (LabCFTC, 2017) <https://www.cftc.gov/sites/default/files/idc/groups/public/documents/file/labcftc_primercurrencies100417.pdf> accessed 15 April 2024.

Commodity Futures Trading Commission (CFTC), 'Plaintiff's Consolidated Opposition to Amicus Curiae Motions for Reconsideration of Order Granting Plaintiff's Motion for Alternative Service' (14 November 2022).

FinCEN, 'Application of FinCEN's Regulations to Persons Administering, Exchanging, or Using Virtual Currencies' (FIN-2013-G001, 18 March 2013).

FinCEN, 'Application of FinCEN's Regulations to Certain Business Models Involving Convertible Virtual Currencies' (FIN-2019-G001, 9 May 2019).

G7, 'Fundamental Elements for Effective Assessment of Cybersecurity in the Financial Sector' <https://www.gov.uk/government/publications/g7-fundamental-elements-for-effective-assessment-of-cybersecurity-in-the-financial-sector> accessed 15 April 2024.

Hague Conference on Private International Law (HCCH), Council on General Affairs and Policy (CGAP), 'Conclusions et recommendations' (3–6 March 2020) <https://assets.hcch.net/docs/70458042-f771-4e94-9c56-df3257a1e5ff.pdf> accessed 15 April 2024.

Hague Conference on Private International Law (HCCH), Council on General Affairs and Policy (CGAP), 'Conclusions et recommendations' (7–10 March 2023) <https://assets.hcch.net/docs/5f9999b9-09a3-44a7-863d-1dddd4f9c6b8.pdf> accessed 15 April 2024.

International Monetary Fund (IMF), 'El Salvador: 2021 Article IV Consultation-Press Release; Staff Report; and Statement by the Executive Director for El Salvador' (2022) <https://www.imf.org/en/Publications/CR/Issues/2022/01/26/El-Salvador-2021-Article-IV-Consultation-Press-Release-Staff-Report-and-Statement-by-the-512245> accessed 15 April 2024.

International Monetary Fund (IMF), EL Salvador country team and IMF Western Hemisphere Department, 'El Salvador's Comeback Constrained by Increased Risks' (2022) <https://www.imf.org/en/News/Articles/2022/02/15/cf-el-salvadors-comeback-constrained-by-increased-risks> accessed 15 April 2024.

People's Bank of China and others, 'Five Ministries Issue Circular on Preventing Risks of Bitcoin', circular dated 3 December 2013 (人民银行等五部委发布关于防范 比特币风险的通知) <http://www.gov.cn/gzdt/2013-12/05/content_2542751.htm> accessed 15 April 2024.

People's Bank of China and others, 'Public Notice on Preventing Risks of Fundraising through Coin Offering' (人民银行等七部门关于防范代币发行融资风险的公), 4 September 2017 <http://www.gov.cn/xinwen/2017-09/04/content_5222657.htm> accessed 15 April 2024.

People's Bank of China and others, 'Notice on Further Preventing and Resolving the Risks of Virtual Currency Trading and Speculation' (关于进一步防范和处置虚拟货币交易炒作风险的通知), 15 September 2021 <http://www.pbc.gov.cn/en/3688253/3689012/4353814/index.html> accessed 15 April 2024.

Securities and Exchange Commission (SEC), 'Report of Investigation Pursuant to Section 21(a) of the Securities Exchange Act of 1934: The DAO' (Release No 81207, 25 July 2017) <https://www.sec.gov/litigation/investreport/34-81207.pdf> accessed 15 April 2024.

Securities and Exchange Commission (SEC), 'In re Munchee Inc, Securities Act of 1933' (Release No 10445, 11 December 2017) <https://www.sec.gov/litigation/admin / 2017/33-10445.pdf> accessed 15 April 2024.

Securities and Exchange Commission (SEC), 'SEC Charges Ripple and Two Executives with Conducting $1.3 Billion Unregistered Securities Offering' (2020–338, 22 December 2020) <https://www.sec.gov/news/press-release/2020-338> accessed 15 April 2024.

Securities and Exchange Commission (SEC), *'SEC v. Rivetz Corp., Rivetz International SEZC, and Steven K Sprague'* (Litigation Release No 25198, Proc File No 3:21-cv-30092, D. Mass. filed Sept. 8, 2021) <https://www.sec.gov/litigation/litreleases/lr-25198> accessed 15 April 2024.

Securities and Exchange Commission (SEC), 'SEC Files Subpoena Enforcement Action Against Terraform Labs and Its CEO' (Litigation Release No 25262, 12 November 2021) <https://www.sec.gov/litigation/litreleases/lr-25262> accessed 15 April 2024.

Securities and Exchange Commission (SEC), 'BlockFi Agrees to Pay $100 Million in Penalties and Pursue Registration of its Crypto Lending Product' (2022–26, 14 February 2022) <https://www.sec.gov/news/press-release/2022-26> accessed 15 April 2024.

Securities and Exchange Commission (SEC), *'SEC v Poloniex, LLC'* (Proc File No 3–20455, 9 August 2021) <https://www.sec.gov/news/press-release/2021-147> accessed 15 April 2024.

Swiss Financial Market Supervisory Authority (FINMA), 'Supplement to the guidelines for enquiries regarding the regulatory framework for initial coin offerings (ICO s)' (11 September 2019) <https://www.finma.ch/en/~/media/finma/dokumente/dokumentencenter/myfinma/1bewilligung/fintech/wegleitung-stable-coins.pdf?sc_lang=en&hash=68854A0D6DAFC3F8F1D4F1C9AF56BA4D> accessed 15 April 2024.

UK Jurisdiction Taskforce, 'Legal Statement on Cryptoassets and Smart Contracts' (2019).

www.ingramcontent.com/pod-product-compliance
Lightning Source LLC
LaVergne TN
LVHW020004031026
849161LV00023B/932